FROM PURITAN TO YANKEE

CHARACTER AND THE SOCIAL ORDER IN CONNECTICUT, 1690 – 1765

RICHARD L. BUSHMAN

HARVARD UNIVERSITY PRESS
CAMBRIDGE, MASSACHUSETTS
LONDON, ENGLAND

FOR MY FATHER AND MOTHER

TED AND DOROTHY BUSHMAN

OF

SALT LAKE CITY

974.602

Library of Congress Catalog Card Number: 79-92680
ISBN 0-674-32551-6

Foreword

No attempt to trace the history of liberty can deal with the detached individual in isolation. Freedom is a condition not of the single man alone but of man in relationship to a community. The group protects him against the misuse of the power of others and provides the setting within which he can advantageously exercise his own powers. Therefore, changes in the nature of the community, which necessarily either increase or restrain the capacity of the individual to act, affect his liberty.

Colonial Connecticut provides a particularly fruitful example of the processes that shaped American society and the character of its people. The circumstances of settlement established and kept intact through much of the seventeenth century a tightly organized, homogeneous community—in this volume designated Puritan—which ascribed to the individual a limited role marked out by forceful religious and secular sanctions. Yet by the eve of the Revolution the community and the people who lived in it had changed radically. The old prescriptions lost their compelling power, the role of the individual was redefined, and the community itself took on a new character—here referred to as Yankee. The interplay of the complex political, religious, and economic forces responsible for that transition are the subjects of this thoughtful book.

Particularly significant in the analysis of the process by which the Puritans of Connecticut became Yankees is the light it throws on the relationship between society and individual personality. The description of the forces in the community that gave birth to the wish to be free, among men brought up in a closed order, illuminates an important, and neglected, facet of the history of liberty in the United States.

OSCAR HANDLIN

Preface

Sometime between 1690 and 1765 Connecticut Puritans became Yankees. The transition had begun earlier and was far advanced in Boston by 1690, but in Connecticut the institutions inspired by the founders' piety persisted to the end of the seventeenth century. Then after 1690 the close-knit, tightly controlled, homogeneous community of the earlier period steadily became more open and heterogeneous. By the eve of the Revolution Connecticut was moving toward a new social order, toward the republican pluralism of the nineteenth century. With the death of old institutions had come the birth of new freedom.

This book describes the growth of liberty in pre-Revolutionary Connecticut and assesses the impact of freedom on human character. Its overarching themes are the answers to three questions: What were the changes that relaxed the restraints on men's feelings and actions? How did they respond as they felt the authority that had structured their lives slowly crumble? How did the thoughtful among them propose to keep order as traditional social cohesion dissolved?

The account of how freedom grew, which occupies most of the book, focuses on the details of life on farms and in meetinghouses, because there men felt the worth of liberty concretely. The normal pursuit of everyday ambitions engendered the expansive impulses that opened up society, and restraints relaxed because of accumulated frustrations. The organization and balance of my approach follow from this conception.

My thesis is that law and authority embodied in governing institutions gave way under the impact first of economic ambitions and later of the religious impulses of the Great Awakening. Restraint of ambition was a vulnerable spot among the interlocking institutions and beliefs that contained men through most of the seventeenth century, for Puritan preachers could not clearly distinguish laudable industry from reprehensible worldliness. As, in the expanding economy of the eighteenth century, merchants and farmers felt free to pursue wealth with an avidity dangerously close to avarice, the energies released exerted irresistible pressure against traditional bounds. When the Great Awakening added its measure of opposition, the old institutions began to crumble. By 1765, while the structure still stood, the most perceptive leaders were looking for new methods of ordering society in an age when human loyalties would be forthcoming voluntarily or not at all.

Connecticut is well suited to a study of ordinary people and local conditions, for the colony was probably less involved in imperial affairs than any other. No royal governors and few British officials were present to complicate politics and social life. Hence, when seeking the significance of a given document, it is rarely necessary to calculate the effect of relations with Britain; the contents of nearly every page reflect the situation of the common people or the maneuverings of the colonial aristocracy. Though Connecticut was closely linked to Massachusetts by the migration of people and ideas, its relative autonomy made the evolution here described more visible than in the other Puritan colony.

Connecticut invites research because the colonial records are so full and accessible. A large portion of my work was done at the Connecticut State Library, where Miss Frances Davenport and Mr. G. Wesley Dennen were unusually accommodating guides to the library's resources. The Yale University Library kindly gave permission to quote from the Lane Memorial Collection. Congregational House in Hartford gave access to the life of Samuel Nott and various county association and consociation records.

I am grateful to be working at a time when foundations and universities are generous with scholars. While preparing this book, I received aid from the Samuel S. Fels Foundation, the Frederick Sheldon Fund of Harvard University, and Brigham Young University faculty research funds.

Professors Bernard Bailyn and Oscar Handlin produce the kinds of scholarship I most admire. Both have usefully criticized the manuscript. Professor Handlin gave it an especially close reading, exercising vigorously his uncommon editorial skill. He has also been a wise friend and counselor. I am pleased that the book is part of the distinguished series coming from the Center for the Study of the History of Liberty in America.

After innumerable readings of the manuscript, my wife's well of stylistic criticisms had not run dry. More than critic, however, she has been a steady and true companion.

For the convenience of the reader in finding the full citation for each reference, all writings are listed in alphabetical order at the end of the book, and the short form of citation is used from the beginning in the footnotes. The only abbreviations that might mystify are *Conn. Recs.* for Connecticut, Colony of, *The Public Records of the Colony of Connecticut,* and Conn. Arch. for Connecticut Archives. In quoting manuscripts, directions for the expanded method suggested in Oscar Handlin, *et al., Harvard Guide to American History* (Cambridge, Mass., 1954), pages 98-99, are followed. In all but a very few instances, the spellings used in contemporary printed materials are left intact. Dates are in Old Style. Years are stated as if January 1 were New Year's Day.

RICHARD L. BUSHMAN

Provo, Utah
Spring 1966

Contents

Illustrations

PART ONE

Society in 1690

I

Law and Authority

✒§ IN THE LAST QUARTER of the seventeenth century the Puritan rulers of Connecticut valued order above all other social virtues. Disorder and sin were equivalents in their minds. Turmoil in the towns or conflict in the General Assembly interrupted the harmonious flow of divine power into the extremities of creation, while a well-ordered society evidenced God's dominion among men. Submission to His will brought tranquility to a people.

Jonathan Edwards up the Connecticut River was later to define order and cogently express the pleasure it afforded:

There is a beauty of order in society, as when the different members of society have all their appointed offices, place and station, according to their several capacities and talents, and everyone keeps his place, and continues in his proper business.[1]

The traditional image of society as an organism portrayed the harmony and control the rulers sought when they hedged men about with law and authority, bound people to their stations, and stopped trespasses on the rights of others. Europeans had elaborated the same theme for centuries, but the rulers of Connecticut, while drawing on a medieval legacy, appropriated the idea of order as their own because it so well suited their situation and temperament.

Social harmony as an end in itself was less important to the first settlers of New England than to their immediate descendants. Religious belief had been preeminent in 1630, when, painful as the departure was, the migrating founders had broken with the existing social pattern. The distortions of Christian worship in England and the yearning to establish Zion had warranted resistance to

[1] *Works*, II, 275. The material in this chapter is covered in a somewhat different fashion for Massachusetts in Haskins, *Law and Authority in Early Massachusetts*.

authority. The body politic existed for the glory of God, and when the two clashed, good order in the state was sacrificed.

Once in America, the early Puritans had struggled to reestablish coherence. While still in passage, John Winthrop told the company that they must be "knitt together in this worke as one man." [2] The town covenants, even in recalcitrant Rhode Island, symbolized the ideal of community life which the first settlers wished to recover in founding governments in "love, union and order," for the blessing of all and to the glory of God.[3]

Ostensibly, religion remained preeminent in the hierarchy of value, but community order occupied most of the rulers' field of vision. By the end of the century they were no longer critical of the ends of uniformity as their predecessors had been. Righteousness had become another name for conformity.

Failures only intensified the compulsion to control. Puritan leaders at the end of the century knew that they were more distant from their goal than their fathers had been; disruptive forces had been mounting for decades. Yet the Winthrops and the Saltonstalls were not prepared to accommodate the enemies of order. At stake were not only their power and prestige, but the very meaning of their own and their fathers' lives.

The opposition to order came as no surprise. Puritan theology plainly taught that rebellion was the natural state of men deprived by the fall of the capacity to control their passions. "Pride, Contradiction, and Rebellion," ministers reminded rulers, had possessed the hearts of men "since our Corruption by the first unhappy Apostasy." The devil ruled the human will, and "unlimitted, and unsatiable lusts" possessed people when they were under no restraint and there were none "to stop their wicked career." [4] From these innate evil impulses, "all the Disorder and Confusion in the World" took their rise.[5] Thus accounted for, troublemakers met stony faces when called before Puritan magistrates.

Rulers conceived their function to be the containment of the

[2] Quoted in Winslow, *Meetinghouse Hill*, 27.
[3] Quoted in I. Backus, *History*, I, 167.
[4] Woodward, *Civil Rulers*, 9, 4.
[5] Bulkley, *Necessity of Religion*, 40.

wicked passions unleashed at the fall. To govern was to control the corrupt human will. At the height of Connecticut's troubles with insurgents in the 1690's, Gurdon Saltonstall, minister from New London and future Governor, reminded the freemen that "Divine Wisdom" provided civil government "to give check to those wretched Principles, of Pride and Contradiction, Disorder and Confusion, which the first Rebellion hath unhappily brought into the hearts of men." The alternative to strong government was chaos. Consider, he enjoined, "what Irreligion and Profaneness, Unrighteousness, and Oppression, Disorder, and Confusion, do use to invade a People, when the Rod of Dominion is broken, the Bands of Authority dissolved, and every man is his own King." [6] Another sermon described the terrifying consequences of anarchy: "Were it not for Government, the World would soon run into all manner of disorders and confusions: mens Lives and Estates and Liberties would soon be prey to the Covetous and the Cruel"; each would be "as a wolf" to the other.[7] Government, the ministers repeated annually on election days, was "a great Blessing to this Sinful and Miserable World," for to a degree it compensated for depravity and imposed peace on society.[8] The controlling axiom of all social and political thought was the proposition that civil and ecclesiastical authorities must strictly rule every detail of human life.

The first requisite of good government was law. Deficient in both reason and will, men required rules "to guide them and to bind them to their good Behaviour." [9] The law defined evil and prescribed appropriate punishment for it. "Since Vice, Immorality and Profaneness are ever-more the common Enemies of our Comfort, and all good Order," magistrates were obliged to suppress them.[10] The multitude of ordinances regulating personal behavior was an outgrowth of the divine commission bestowed upon the civil authority to keep the peace. Tippling, sabbath-breaking, gaming, singing and dancing in public houses, lax family discipline,

[6] Sermon, 4, 6-7.
[7] Estabrook, *Sermon*, 18.
[8] W. Burnham, *God's Providence*, 2.
[9] Buckingham, *Moses and Aaron*, 43.
[10] Woodward, 37.

failure to attend worship, and sexual offences, all received punishments ranging from a small fine to death. Each was a detail in
the total pattern of order.

Always conscious of its responsibility to govern, the Connecticut
General Assembly periodically revived the sumptuary laws and
encouraged more rigorous enforcement. In 1676 the legislature
expanded statutory regulations of the standard vices. In 1684 and
1686 the Assembly urged closer attention to the laws. Two decades
later the clergy were asked to investigate moral conditions and
suggest reasons for the obvious decline. In response to their report,
the Assembly recapitulated the laws on education, profanity, the
Sabbath, and drunkenness, ordering that they be distributed
through the Colony and read publicly before each election of town
officers.[11] The almost instinctive response to disorder was to devise
more laws. Bound by their understanding of character and their
place in the divine economy, rulers could conceive of no satisfactory alternative. "When Sin and Iniquity Prevails over the Laws
already made," the preacher of the election sermon said in 1717,
"the Nature of such Times call for the Addition of further, to
Force it to Hide its Head." [12]

Sumptuary and criminal legislation forbade evil actions, but
law also included liberties or privileges, the carefully circumscribed
areas where men could rightfully expend their energies. Towns
were given liberty to build churches or to distribute land. Individuals had liberty to own and control property and to worship
God. Frequent reference to the colony statutes as the "laws and
Liberties" expressed this positive, prescriptive as well as purely
repressive aspect of law.[13]

Such liberty was far from license, the freedom to act as one
wished. The privilege of electing rulers, for example, did not
permit selection of candidates who favored a private interest, but
only the right to choose those qualified to rule for the common
good.[14] Religious liberty implied freedom to worship not as one
wanted but only as the Bible interpreted by the Puritan ministry

[11] *Conn. Recs.*, II, 281-283; III, 147-148, 202-203; V, 529-531.
[12] Cutler, *Firm Union*, 16.
[13] *Conn. Recs.*, II, 567.
[14] Fiske, *The Good Subject's Wish*, 8; Woodward, 31-32.

dictated. John Winthrop had explained how natural liberty gave men free rein, while civil liberty only allowed them to be good, just, and honest. Private will had to be moral; it would have contradicted the purpose of government to give liberty to do evil as well as good.[15]

One part of the work of government was to assure men the free exercise of their just privileges. Without law to define the boundaries of human action and government to protect peoples' rights, "Lives and Estates and Liberties would soon be a prey to the Covetous and the Cruel." [16] By seventeenth-century definitions, order and liberty were opposites of the same coin.

The hedge of laws thus both contained and protected each individual. Sumptuary legislation suppressed impulses men themselves could not discipline, while liberties marked out the channels of approved activity along which human energy might flow. Within these bounds, a man was safe so long as government functioned properly, securing to him the peaceful possession of his person and property and allowing him to worship God as commanded, protecting the observant and punishing trespassers. The image of social order in 1690 was of limited and foreseen activity within these legal forms.

However beneficial and divine the rule of law, not all yielded to it for the sake of conscience or of self-interest. Reprobate natures required strong measures, and even the elect occasionally needed discipline. Election sermons reiterated the maxim that "The Constitution of Good Laws" and a "due Execution of them" had

[15] The use of the word 'liberty' was apt in this context because it was conceivable in the seventeenth century that civil authority might forbid men to do good. To the Puritans lately escaped from Laud's oppression, the liberty to worship in the biblical pattern was considered a privilege, for all liberties were privileges wrested from an authority that had at times repressed even righteous actions. By the seventeenth century a large number of rights had been won from rulers; in many areas men were free to follow their own interests without special permission. But the struggles of the eighteenth century are unintelligible unless it is understood that people believed government might rescind their liberties if they were not vigilantly guarded. Rights had to be asserted: to assume they were secured was to risk their loss. The possibility of civil authority completely dominating its subjects, though strenuously resisted, remained lively and ominous for some time.

[16] Estabrook, 18.

to be improved for the good of the people.[17] Through law and authority, "Right is secured; Injuries are suppressed; Offenders are punished; the Obedient are Rewarded; The Good Order and Peace designed is preserved." [18]

The magistrates who administered the law included the governor and deputy governor along with the assistants and commissioners.[19] The assistants, twelve in number, were elected members of what in essence was the upper house of the legislature, though they then sat with the lower house composed of deputies or representatives from the towns.[20] The commissioners were appointed in each town by the General Court for the sole purpose of enforcing the law. These officials manned a variety of agencies of surveillance, judgment, and punishment.

By 1690 the apparatus had enlarged until it operated on four levels. In each town a constable, elected annually, was responsible for apprehending offenders.[21] Causes of up to 40s. were heard locally by two assistants or two commissioners, or by one of these and the selectmen.[22] Appeal from the court of small causes was to the county court, composed of an assistant and two commissioners or of three assistants, which also heard presentments from constables and from grand jurors appointed in each town by the Assembly to expose "breaches of any laws or orders or any misdemeanors they shal know of in their respective Countys." [23] On the colony level, a semiannual court composed of at least seven assistants heard appeals from the county courts and also tried capital crimes. The General Assembly was the ultimate court of appeal.[24]

[17] Buckingham, 43.

[18] Saltonstall, *Sermon*, 17-18.

[19] For the commissioners' role as magistrates see Farrell, "Administration of Justice," 7-8.

[20] In 1698 the two Houses were divided, but even before this time the agreement of the assistants was required for the passage of any act (*Conn. Recs.*, I, 119; IV, 267). The towns elected two deputies annually to the General Court. In both elections only the freemen voted. The qualifications for freemanship were £10 estate and the recommendation of the selectmen (*Conn. Recs.*, II, 141, 253).

[21] Connecticut Colony, *Book of General Laws, 1673,* 14-15.

[22] *Conn. Recs.,* II, 108.

[23] *Conn. Recs.,* II, 35, 61.

[24] *Conn. Recs.,* II, 28-29.

Election of these officials, even the highest, did not diminish their authority or make them responsible to the people. Democracy, in the Puritan view, was nongovernment or anarchy, and rulers had to constrain not to obey a corrupt popular will. Election was a device for implementing divine intentions rather than for transmitting power from the people to their rulers.

In Elective States, where persons are Advanc'd by the Suffrage of others to Places of Rule, and Vested with Civil Power, the Persons Chusing give not the Power, but GOD. They are but the Instruments of Conveyance.[25]

Rulers were obligated to God not to the people.

Magistrates, it is true, were admonished earnestly to seek the public good. Whether "Supream or Subordinate," one sermon said, they "are to be the Ministers of GOD, for the good of a people." [26] Though civil government was ordained for the very purpose of benefiting mankind,[27] the public good was not to be interpreted by the people, for it consisted of "The Promoting and Florishing of Civil and Sacred Order" by the "exercise of Government" through true laws so that "Subjects may lead a peaceable and quiet Life in all Godliness and Honesty." [28] A ruler was to seek the "wealth" of his people by promoting religion, turning men from vice, administering justice, protecting liberty, and preserving the peace. He was not to solicit instructions from his constituency or to enact their wishes into law. On the contrary, he was warned that action in the public interest would earn him mainly "Ill-will and reproach." [29] Men would bridle when restrained from "doing that which is right in their own sight, tho' it be never so wrong." [30] The ideal magistrate was firm in pursuing justice in the face of popular disapproval. Devotion to the public good disposed him to disregard the desires of the people in the interest of social order.

The conviction that rulers held their commissions directly from

[25] Bulkley, *Necessity of Religion*, 14.
[26] S. Woodbridge, *Obedience to the Divine Law*, 10-11.
[27] Fiske, 9-10.
[28] Woodward, 33-34; S. Woodbridge, 10-11.
[29] W. Burnham, 27-32, 23-24.
[30] Woodward, 4.

God strengthened the authority to govern strictly. The scriptural declaration, "There is no Power but of God, the Powers that be are ordained of God," stood on the first page of every law book.[31] Magistrates knew that divine authority operated through them. They were God's "Vice-royes," elevated to their stations by His will to keep order among reprobate men. As "Representatives of the Eternal King," they were rightly styled earthly "gods." [32] Their awesome responsibility to serve the public good steeled them to face unflinchingly the cajolings and wrath of the lesser men they ruled.

Potent forces supported the political ideals of which the ministers spoke. Acting externally through institutions or internally through individual convictions, law regulated Connecticut society with amazing thoroughness. Though men protested in specific cases, they never doubted the necessity for order, never questioned the system as a whole, without paying dearly. Encompassed by a view of the world in which magistrates were "accounted as sent by God himself," lawbreakers suffered not only the specified punishment but in their imaginations the wrath of God.[33] The calloused and the indifferent, and such there must have been, feared only the stocks or the lash, but for the larger portion of society the law of the land was the law of God. Disobedience was, as the Apostles had said, "resistance of the Ordinance of God." Laws bound the conscience, "Not simply as Humane, but as made by that Authority which is Divine in its Original, and to which Obedience is Commanded in the Divine Law." [34] For the majority, to resist authority was to fight their own consciences. The magistrates' chief support was the response to legal sanctions deep within each man.

Social forces reinforced civil rule. All assumed that the eminent men gifted with the qualities that commanded respect and that fitted them to rule would be elected to political office. The election sermon's inevitable list of a good ruler's qualities—wisdom, piety, courage, industry—was an admonition to choose the naturally

---

[31] *Conn. Recs.,* II, 567.
[32] Woodward, 26, 33-34; S. Woodbridge, 10-11.
[33] Woodward, 11-12.
[34] Woodward, 8, 26; Bulkley, *Necessity of Religion,* 14.

superior persons whom God had stationed at the top of the social hierarchy. Following these injunctions, the people selected the assistants, deputy governor, and governor with rare exceptions from the old families notable for piety, public service, wealth, and familiarity with power.[35] The weight of their endowments and prestige were thus added to the authority of the government.

These ruling families were not a small fixed group dominating a large mass from whom they were separated by an unbridged gap. The Connecticut social hierarchy was a gradually ascending slope with clear demarcations only at the very bottom, where bonded servants and apprentices occupied a distinct status. Elsewhere class distinctions blurred, and the ruling families at the top merged imperceptibly with the people in posts of lesser dignity directly below. Measured by wealth or social privileges, the results are the same. A graph of personal estates drawn from virtually any tax list shows a thick cluster of people with smaller estates and a gradual thinning out as the properties grow larger.[36] When seating the meetinghouse by rank, the settlers invariably squabbled over the order of precedence, for the lines that distinguished one man from another were indistinct. As Timothy Dwight was much later to say of Connecticut's class divisions, "one extended class embraces all, all mingling, as the rainbow's beauty blends." [37]

Within the town each grade of officialdom emanated from an appropriate social level, so that eminence and political power corresponded. Between 1691 and 1700, for example, all the Windsor selectmen were sons or grandsons of distinguished early settlers.[38] In Kent all but three of the twenty-five top leaders were among the wealthiest men in the town. Just below them were a group of lesser officeholders whose property was smaller but who were distinctly wealthier than the inhabitants who never held office.[39] Even surveyors of highways and grand jurors brought an appropriate degree of prominence to their positions. Everyone

[35] *Wolcott Papers*, xxv; Welling, "Connecticut Federalism," 307-308.

[36] For example, "Norwich Town Rate."

[37] *Greenfield Hill*, 36.

[38] Windsor selectmen are to be found in "Windsor Town Records," I; genealogical information is in H. R. Stiles, *Windsor*, I, II.

[39] C. S. Grant, *Democracy in the Connecticut Frontier Town of Kent*, 148-149, 151.

sensed the ascending order of social power enhancing the ascending order of civil authority.

From the Puritan point of view, some were created superior to the very end that they might govern. God placed men in their particular stations and conditions to prevent "those Querulous and Discontented Behaviours, that Roile and Disturb all things." [40] If not distributed into "various Ranks and degrees," an election sermon maintained, men would lack "some Motives and Encouragements to Vertue and Restraint from Vice, that now they have; and there could be no such thing as Government." [41] The presence of superiors, a group of Durham men felt, obligated inferiors to "Honour, Submit to, and obey those whom God hath set over us; whether in family, Church or Common-wealth." [42]

The natural authority attached to the upper stations in society qualified the persons God placed there to rule. The nomination of Wait Winthrop in 1680 typified the prevailing belief: a friend urged that he was well suited for the magistracy because he was "a very sober discreet gentleman, much advantaged by his parentage, as well as his abillitys and fulness of estate, for publique trust." [43] Failure to place individuals of this sort in the magistracy flagrantly disregarded the will of God and neglected an obvious source of power for the civil authority.

By the same principle, lesser men were expected to stay out of government. Men of wealth and important family connections might rise through town and militia offices to the upper house or the governorship, but those of small means and insignificant background could not expect to become even selectmen. "Levelism" was detested because it jeopardized authority. "The making of rulers of the lower sort of the people," one gentlemen declared simply, "will issue in contempt, let their opinion be what it will." [44] A magistrate chosen from among the lower orders, lacking the dignity and assurance that went with social prominence, would not be obeyed. Government by common men, one sermon said,

[40] Cutler, 41.
[41] W. Burnham, 11, 1-2.
[42] Quoted in Fowler, *Durham,* 44.
[43] Samuel Willis to John Allyn, 1680, *Winthrop Papers,* pt. VI, xiv.
[44] *Winthrop Papers,* pt. VI, xiv.

"directly tends at once to destroy both the Rectitude and Success of Government . . . and to enervate the Force of all their Administrations." [45] If persons "risen out of obscurity" should come to control, government must "sinke into the mire of popular confusion." One of the gentlemen suggested that the King declare "that persons of mean and low degree be not improved in the chiefest place of civill and military affairs . . . but that persons of good parintage, education, abilitye, and integrity be settled in such offices." [46]

Distinguished men, even if not in office, were expected to share the burden of government. In a sense all who occupied the upper ranks of society—the clergy, the rich, and the educated—were rulers. The position in which God placed them invested them with authority, and they were expected to give a good account of themselves. Honorable men, Solomon Stoddard up the valley in Northampton explained, "bear much sway among the people: In many cases their judgment is a law, they can easily crush evil motions, and put a stop to corrupt and factious designs; they can perswade and draw people to that which is for their good." Their lives should be a guide to everyone below them: "Many will follow the examples of principal men and out of a respect to them, comply with their wayes, and so get good habits." [47] A neglect of responsibility could be disastrous. "A Great man if he is a good man, will by his Example do a great deal of good; as on the other hand if he is a vicious man, his example will be pernicious to many." [48] Wickedness in high places released the resentments lesser people harbored silently in fear of authority. The peace of society depended not only on the preservation of the social hierarchy, but on union and good will in the upper ranks. [49]

The term "government" did not refer to the civil authority alone, but applied to the family and the church and to all the authoritative external restraints on human will. These institutions, like the social hierarchy, indoctrinated and enforced the values of

[45] Bulkley, *Necessity of Religion,* 16.
[46] Samuel Willis to Fitz-John Winthrop, December 25, 1697, and September 1693, *Winthrop Papers,* pt. V, 31-32, 17.
[47] *Gods Frown,* 13, 11-12.
[48] I. Mather, *Excellency of a Publick Spirit,* 16.
[49] Saltonstall, 29, 72; Estabrook, 16.

the social order. Indeed, coercion by the civil power was intended primarily for those whom more immediate agencies failed to contain, and the magistrates' success in governing depended on all these supporting institutions.

To strengthen control at the primary level, the General Assembly ordered that every young person submit himself to family government. Even "borders or sojourners" were to "carefully attend the worship of God in those famalys where they so board or sojourn, and be subject to the domesticall government of the said famaly." Heads of families bore the responsibility of leading in daily prayer, catechizing their children and servants, and teaching those under their care to read so that they might study the Bible and learn "the good lawes of the Colony." Grand jurors were told to watch the families in their towns and present delinquent parents to the county court to be fined or bound over to good behavior. When the clergy reported in 1715 that one source of declension was the "great deficiency in domestical or family government," the Assembly took note and called for better "execution of those good laws already enacted amongst us, for the prevention of such decays." [50] Weakness in the family endangered the entire social order, for the Puritans knew that the pattern of submission set in the home fixed the attitude toward authority throughout life and that strong family government prevented disorder in the state. The father was the model for all authority—magistrates were called the fathers of their people—and the biblical commandment to honor parents was expanded to include all rulers.

The church was also a partner in the control of society. Both secular and ecclesiastical government, Saltonstall told the Assembly in 1697, were to mobilize their forces to suppress sin:

God hath designed the Civil Government of his People, to concenter with Ecclesiastical Administrations: and (though by different Mediums) they are both levelled at the same end; the maintaining of Piety and promoting of a Covenant walk with him.[51]

The term "church discipline" as a designation for the form of ecclesiastical government reflected the cardinal purpose of judging

[50] *Conn. Recs.*, II, 281; IV, 30; V, 5, 30.
[51] *Sermon*, 53-54.

and punishing moral offenders. One minister declared that "Good order and government is the Glory and safety" of the ecclesiastical as well as the civil state; just as God ordains civil rulers "for the preservation of order and prevention of that confusion in the world, which an Anarchy leads unto, So our Lord Jesus Christ who is . . . Head of the Church, hath ordained under officers, for the preservation of order, government and discipline in it." [52]

The church covenants contained clauses pledging members to the mutual obligations of discipline. Communicants promised to subject themselves "to the government of Christ in his church" and not to "suffer sin to rest upon our Brother, but deal faithfully according to Christ's Order." Besides "Exhorting and admonishing one another in love," the fraternity laid before the church moral offenses.[53] The pastor, who also had the right to bring charges, presided in the court composed of all church members. The guilty defendant who showed contrition merely stood before the congregation to receive a rebuke from the minister, while an unrepentant sinner was suspended from communion or excommunicated, which penalty entailed ostracization as well as spiritual punishments.[54]

Church government encompassed only those who voluntarily submitted to it (those who did not own the covenant did not come under the church's "watch and care" [55]), but its moral influence dominated the entire community and was an essential part of the governing apparatus. The theology taught from the pulpit reminded the people of the miseries awaiting the rebellious, and fear of eternal punishment constrained even the unregenerate. John Bulkley thought that the impending judgment foretold in Christian doctrine was a necessary deterrent to evildoers. "Where the Powerful influences and restraints of Religion are wanting," he said, "there is little reason to hope that either Rulers or Ruled, will adorn their Places by a due discharge of the Duty's of either

[52] N. Eells, *Evangelical Bishop,* 1.

[53] Fairfield, "Greenfield Hill Church, Records," I, 6; Gilman, *Historical Discourse,* 94-96; cf. Lisbon, "Newent Congregational Church, Records," I, 6.

[54] Minister of Connecticut to the People of Connecticut, *Wyllys Papers,* 237.

[55] B. Trumbull, *Connecticut,* II, 1.

of them." Without religion, the "wisest Constitution," the best laws, "are ineffectual to bridle mens Lusts, and hold them within due Limits." Religion was "a Main Pillar by which the Common-Wealth is Supported"; its fall would "bring an Amazing Destruction upon all our Civil Interests." [56]

Firmly convinced of these propositions, Connecticut magistrates saw good reason to employ civil authority in religion. Although the worth of worship according to the New England way was in itself sufficient cause to promote church attendance, its power to restrain doubled the incentive for establishing the Congregational churches on a firm foundation. The rulers, believing it imperative to compel attendance at worship where all would hear sound preaching, punished failure to attend by fine.[57] Similarly, everyone was required to pay taxes in the minister's rate and to help build meetinghouses. The civil authority also supported doctrinal purity and defended the colony against "invasions of Atheism, Heræsy and Profaneness." [58] In 1690 none but Congregationalists worshipped legally in the colony. Though pressure from England forced the Assembly in 1708 to allow separate worship for sober dissenters, the privilege was rarely granted.[59] The rulers resisted any attempt to weaken the legal bulwarks protecting the churches.

The combined force of so many institutions invested law and authority with immense power. In nearly every dimension of life—family, church, the social hierarchy, and religion—a Connecticut subject encountered unanimous reinforcement of governing authority. The total impact was immense, because each institution was an integral part of a monolithic whole. In each community the agencies of law and authority merged so that the individual felt himself confined within a unified governing structure. The preacher's exhortation to submit to domestic government reinforced the father's dominion in his family. Church discipline carried added terrors because censures were delivered before the

[56] Bulkley, *Necessity of Religion*, 4, 9, 44, 34ff, 22, 16, 51.

[57] *Conn. Recs.*, II, 568, 88, 102.

[58] Bulkley, *Necessity of Religion*, 33.

[59] All the ecclesiastical laws are in Connecticut Colony, *Book of General Laws, 1673*, 21-22, 28, 52. On dissenters, see *Conn. Recs.*, V, 50; Greene, *Development of Religious Liberty*, 153-190.

neighbors and the town's most prominent families, and the assignment of pews in the meetinghouse according to social rank reminded everyone of the distinctions among individuals and of the deference due superiors. The total environment enjoined obedience: the stately figure of minister or commissioner as he rode through the town, the leading inhabitants' imposing two-storied houses standing near the meetinghouse at its center, the austere graves of the dead in its shadow. As interpreted by the minister's sermons, even the natural world—the storms, the wolves in the wilderness, and catastrophes at sea—spoke of the war of good and evil and of God's mighty government. Social institutions, conscience, and the forces of nature meshed in the communal experience to restrain rebellious dispositions.

The town was recognized as the proper matrix within which government could function to control each individual. When it was suggested to a man in controversy with the church that he transfer membership to the parish in the next town, he declined on the grounds that "it is safest for me to be here under the watch of this church where my brethren are about me to observe my behaviour and direct me." [60] Much later, toward the middle of the eighteenth century, Jared Eliot still defended the New England scheme of settlement against a counterproposal for large scattered estates: only in towns, where children could attend schools, where "social Worship" was readily available, and where "wild and savage Behaviour" was "put out of Countenance," was there opportunity for the exercise of "social Virtues." Since there were no contradictions in true policy, economic expediency and social order could not conflict. "Virtue, and Order" were the "true Basis of every valuable, and lasting Establishment, of a political Nature." [61]

Thus the rule of law and the agencies of civil, ecclesiastical, and social authority came to fulfillment in the creation of order in the town. As conceived and organized by Connecticut men, a well-regulated community achieved the ends of government. The constable, the grand jurymen, and the magistrates enforced the

[60] Wolcott, "Narrative," 47.
[61] *Essays*, 138.

law, restrained men from vice, and protected their liberties. Family
life was fostered, participation in public worship encouraged, and
the social hierarchy sustained.

This ideal of community life did not die easily, though it was
fated to become more a romantic idyll than a practical goal. Well
after the Revolution, Timothy Dwight described it in "Greenfield
Hill."

> In every village, smil'd
> The heav'n-inviting church, and every town
> A world within itself, with order, peace,
> And harmony, adjusted all its weal. (p. 15)

The town was a "world within itself," controlling its weal by
moral values that assured "order, peace, and harmony."

This society, based on law and authority and fully coordinated
to achieve its ends, molded the character of its members, establishing for each the rudiments of an identity. Social leaders provided
models of moral rectitude, and the law and the minister defined
good and evil. The town shaped each life to fit the pattern. As
officials, as brothers in the church, or simply as neighbors, the
people rebuked or punished any departures from the code of
behavior. All agreed on the specifications of the good life and
the reasons for seeking it.

Such a society produced personalities marked by rigorous moral
standards, but even more by a prepossession with authority. Many
prominent traits of the Connecticut Puritans were responses to
the virtually inescapable authority that dominated his life from
childhood until death. Outright rebellion was nearly impossible.
A few exceptional individuals might play the King off against
the magistracy, but this alternative was inaccessible to most. The
people as a whole accepted the legitimacy, even the sanctity, of
civil and ecclesiastical government and aligned their consciences
with the external forces pressing them to conform. Resistance
entailed alienation from both man and God.

The key to the Puritan character can be found in the responses
of individuals to the series of stern fathers who stood over them
in the homes of their childhood, in the church, in society, and
in the state. That Connecticut Puritans were, in one dimension
at least, submissive is shown by their great deference for their

rulers, both ministers and government officials. Communications to the General Assembly were phrased in a characteristic rhetoric of humility. A typical petition for parish privileges began with the humble request "that this honored Court would be pleased so far to favor us and the interests of Christ among us as to grant us liberty to embody into church estate." And it closed by asking that "your Honors would look friendly upon us and help us with your consent, counsel and prayers, that we [may abide] under the shadow of your wings. In so doing, you shall firmly oblige us to be wishing and seeking your welfare and prosperity according to the littleness of the ability of your honors' humble servants." It did not seem in poor taste to say, "we, with deepest humility as on our bended knees, lay before you our miserable, deplorable, undone condition; unless God or our King or your compassionate selves will relieve us." The petitioners constantly used diminutives to describe themselves. Besides the ubiquitous "humble" and "poor," they spoke of "but thirty-five little families" or the "weak and feeble." [62]

The petitioners always stood in relation to the Assembly as children to their fathers, a relationship frequently made explicit. Admitting their faults, their poor understanding of complex things, and the superior wisdom of the deputies and assistants, the petitioners appealed to the generosity and pity of the rulers. The posture was one of prayer, every line of which conceded the right of the superiors to rule and the need of the inferiors to be ruled.

This language was not a mere pose. Rulers expected this degree of deference, and the eminence of their position evoked a suitable humility in subjects, who liked to lower themselves before their superiors. A confession of weakness was cleansing and strengthening. Far from being disingenuous, Puritans found satisfaction in self-abasement at the feet of rulers.

Another side of the Puritan character, however, was anything but meek. The dominion of stern fathers also injected strength into all who lived under their sway. The firm hand of authority, structuring all of life, framed steady and resolute personalities, sure of the world in which they lived and as stern in exercising

[62] Larned, *Windham*, I, 81-82, 136, 98, 111.

authority as their fathers. Puritans quickly moved from the role
of child to that of father, playing both with equal conviction.
Even the magistrates adopted the rhetoric of submissiveness when
addressing the Crown, with no sense of contradicting their normal
imperiousness.[63] If at times deferential to an extreme, the Puritan
character was not flabby, not even tractable. It was sturdily struc-
trued and as capable of domineering as of submitting.

Puritans were not content to let abject submission totally define
their relationship to authority. Even more than persons living in
a permissive atmosphere, they felt the need to raise defenses
against the fathers who constantly threatened judgment and rebuke.
This inward impulse was expressed in Puritan political philosophy
as the doctrine of rights and the rule of law. Even conservatives
asserted that "God has not Subjected the Lives and Liberty's of
the Ruled, to the Arbitrary Will and Pleasure of Rulers." He
gave "Laws to their Authority," so that they were not "at Liberty
to Pursue and Accomplish their own Desires." The law defined
the line beyond which rulers became tyrants and resistance became
a duty.[64]

The spirited opposition to English and colonial authority when
subjects thought their rights violated was a defense of the self.
Property rights, for example, represented more than physical comfort or social prestige, for property was an extension of the person.
Hence the legal safeguards against government invasion of these
rights protected the individual as well. When action in England
threatened their titles, Connecticut men complained that if "we
may not secure the liberty of the law for the security of our free-
holds . . . we shall then be the most miserable of any Christian
people." [65] The Stonington men who objected to a tax imposed
by the Assembly, out of fear that their "estates, liberties and
persons [would be] subject unto servitude" [66] were not being melo-
dramatic when they blew up one dubious tax into a threat against
their lives. Without the bulwark of law they would be in their

[63] B. Trumbull, *Connecticut*, I, 438-439, 456-458, 463-465.

[64] Bulkley, *Necessity of Religion*, 27, 23-24, 29; cf. Woodward, 8;
Baldwin, *New England Clergy*, Chap. IV.

[65] Governor and Council of Connecticut to Ashurst, Aug. 29, 1705,
Winthrop Papers, pt. V, 305.

[66] *Conn. Recs.*, II, 578.

own minds defenseless against the crushing force of authority. They were "very tender" of their lawful liberties which protected the self against total domination by the fathers of society.

In the seventeenth century the occasions for justifiable resistance to colonial authority in Connecticut were few, but the sensitive concern for lawful liberties showed up every day in the courts. Connecticut men were extraordinarily quick to drag their neighbors to law at the least offense and to battle ferociously for justice.[67] A trespass by a fellow subject was resented because the neighbor seemed to be exercising authority falsely. Angered by the slightest hint of oppression, Puritans jealously defended their rights against attacks from any source.

Thus his awe of the rulers did not reduce the Puritan to slavish servitude, for the general respect for power led to stress on the limits of government. The law both restrained and strengthened the individual in his testy relations with authority.

Under the right circumstances Puritan society was well adapted to its dominant character type: the opposing tendencies to submit and to domineer were compatible with the ideal of government; each man deferred to his superiors and ruled his inferiors. But this society was not prepared to adjust to disturbances. Puritans remained at peace with one another so long as the rights of ruler and subject were well defined and observed by all. When new forces moved men to overstep their bounds, serious conflicts were inevitable. Among men so hypersensitive to encroachments on their rights, the innate fear of oppression magnified the controversies brought by social change and added to the pressure on established institutions.

In the seventeenth century the social order in Connecticut was stable because it was relatively static. Society in 1690 was still clearly fashioned on the pattern the first settlers envisioned. During the eighteenth century rapid expansion was to place greater strains on society than the agencies of government could bear. By 1765, after a series of disruptions, a new social order would be in the making.

[67] For example, E. Stiles, *Literary Diary*, 144.

II

The Town and the Economy

◅§ THE PURITAN EFFORT to regulate forbidden passions was more than a social order could hope to sustain for long. The assumption of so much responsibility for human behavior placed immense strains on the system. Energies, restrained and denied at many points, pressed for release wherever a flaw occurred.

The most troublesome weak spot was the regulation of economic ambition. The saints were urged to be industrious in their callings and to seek wealth but not to love riches, a difficult distinction to make. The preachers labored at a definition of acceptable ambition without ever discovering a rule so clear that a man could say with certainty, "Here I sin," or, "Here I am justified." To the ministers' dismay, an excessive desire for wealth could easily be disguised under the honorable appearance of diligence.[1]

New England pastors, following Calvin, urged every Christian to find a personal calling in the world in addition to the general calling to holiness. Through the pursuit of some useful work, a man served his fellows and God. "God hath placed us, as in a common Hive," Cotton Mather explained. "Let there be no Drone in the Hive: Every man is to take some fair way, that the whole Hive may be the better for him." In all piety, Mather advised his audiences to keep their accounts straight, to buy and sell with care, and to watch the successes and failures of others so as to discover the way to prosper.[2]

---

[1] The problem of constraining ambition is discussed in E. A. J. Johnson, *American Economic Thought*, 83-102, and Dorfman, *The Economic Mind in American Civilization*, I, 42-43. The religious sources of that ambition are discussed in Weber, *Protestant Ethic*.

[2] *Christian at his Calling*, 42-43, 52-55.

Work was an outlet for all the psychic energies denied expression elsewhere by the Puritan moral code, and diligence was a productive diversion that prevented a relapse into sin. "A *Calling* is not only our *Duty*," Mather said, "but also our *Safety*. Men will ordinarily fall into horrible *Snares*, and infinite *Sins*, if they have not a *Calling* to be their preservative." The curse laid upon Adam to eat his bread by the sweat of his brow was a blessing in disguise because "the Temptations of the *Devil*, are best Resisted, by those that are least at Liesure to Receive them." In reality, "an Occupation is an ordinance of God for our safeguards against the *Temptations* of the Devil." Mather declared that "the Sin of Sodom was, Abundance of Idleness. All the Sins of Sodom will abound, where Idleness is countenanced." [3] The Puritan was driven to work: fear of his own passions held him at his job, and warnings from the pulpit never let that fear die.

Many New Englanders welcomed admonitions to work hard and took satisfaction in ardently following their vocations. They agreed heartily with Mather when he said, "Away to your *Business:* Lay out your *Strength* in it, put forth your *Skill* for it; Avoid all impertinent Avocations. Laudable *Recreations* may be used now and then: But, I beseech you, Let those Recreations be used for *Sauce*, but not for *Meat*." The pleasures of watching an estate grow, of building a more imposing house, of adding acre to acre on a farm were ample compensation for the hours missed in the alehouse. If they rose above their fellows, had not the preacher said that "a man by *Diligence* in his Business, What may he not come to? A *Diligent* man is very rarely an *Indigent* man. Would a man *Rise* by his Business? I say, then let him Rise to his Business." [4] And was not their wealth a sign of divine favor? "Tis neither Skil nor Chance, that brings our Estates into our Hand, but it is of God, of whom we are told, That He is the Maker both of the Rich and of the Poor." [5]

Mather worried over those who made his pleas for industry an invitation to avarice, declaring that the "Sin of Covetousness

[3] *Christian at his Calling*, 41-43.
[4] *Christian at his Calling*, 49, 48.
[5] C. Mather, *Durable Riches*, II, 2.

is a Viler Sin, a Blacker Sin, a Sin of more dangerous importance than the Covetous do imagine it." He did not want to discourage industry: "to Desire Wealth, to Pursue Wealth, to be Thankful for Wealth, will not fix upon us the Brand of Covetousness." But there was a point where ambition reached excess: "When Wealth is more unto us, than the Creator of all our Wealth; Here, Here is the Criminal Covetousness." Then money became God, and ambition a form of idolatry. "There is not a Covetous man, but what makes a God of his Wealth." Apart from this affront, greed carried men onto hazardous ground. Mather cautioned the saints that "the *Cursed Hunger of Riches,* will make men *break through* all the Laws of God." [6]

Impassioned as were the indictments of covetousness, the ministers were unable to define satisfactorily the difference between praiseworthy industry and the *"Cursed Hunger of Riches."* The doctrine of weaned affections held that a saint might work vigorously at his business as the illustrious mintmaster John Hull did and yet live "above the world," somehow keeping "his heart disentangled and his mind in Heaven." [7] But no one could explain that way of life to those who did not comprehend it already. Most often it was presented as a matter of degree: covetousness showed itself in "an immoderate Solicitude of Mind about getting and keeping, in an inordinate fear of losing what we have gotten," and, above all, "in an Excessive Esteem of Worldly Riches." [8] But exactly where moderation stopped and excess began the preacher could not say.

A somewhat more helpful guide was the insistence that property serve the public good. Since God gave all, men should esteem themselves "but Stewards of those Things, whereof our Neighbors call us the Owners" and submit to "the Direction of the Eternal God, as to what we do with our Estates." [9] Wealth was to be liberally offered for support of the minister and as aid to the poor, and the rich were to be careful also not to charge unduly high prices, extort excessive interest, or pay unfair wages. Amid

[6] C. Mather. *A Very Needful Caution,* 26, 9, 10, 27, 14.
[7] Willard, *The High Esteeme,* 17.
[8] Sewall, *Caveat against Covetousness,* 3.
[9] C. Mather, *Durable Riches,* II, 3.

the earliest legislation in New England were laws fixing just prices to prevent avaricious trespasses upon the public good, but the eventual disappearance of such measures was another sign of the Puritan failure to discover the boundary between good and bad business.

Cotton Mather considered covetousness the sin that most threatened New England. The "men that are most Ensnared, are least sensible of their Snares." "Many an one, keeps clear of *Scandalous Enormities:* All that can be said of him, is, *He is a Civil, Moral, Honest man;* and, *He is a man that minds his Business.*" But "God knows, the man is all this while, a Covetous Idolator." [10] As another pastor complained, how often did greed "lie hid under the Specious names of *Frugality,* and good Husbandry? How often are Men guilty of it under a fair pretence of a due concern about their Temporal Affairs?" [11] So pernicious was worldly pride that even the regenerate were susceptible: "There is an inclination to this Idolatry, a Covetous Inclination to this Earth, remaining in the hearts of all the Sanctified, while they remain upon Earth. And this Evil Root, may sprout and bud forth into many actual Miscarriages." [12] This declaration was almost an admission of defeat. How could the hunger for riches be constrained when the sin was so insidious and its nature so uncertain that even the elect were deceived?

The ultimate effects of this ambiguity were discovered only when eighteenth-century economic possibilities released ambition. Mather was most familiar with the commercial aspirations of Boston merchants and was usually referring to them when he berated covetousness. But wealth was as dangerously alluring in the country as in the city. In Connecticut the most common economic ambition was the desire to produce an agricultural surplus for market. Connecticut Puritans were subsistence farmers to the degree that they could grow or make many of the things the family needed, but they were not content with this lot. They wanted to produce for the market in order to improve their living conditions and raise their standing in the community.

[10] C. Mather, *A Very Needful Caution,* 51, 34.
[11] Sewall, 5.
[12] C. Mather, *A Very Needful Caution,* 49.

Actually, living conditions compelled them to sell part of their
harvest, for no farmer, however ingenious and energetic, could
make for himself all he required. A family had to buy a musket,
a pot, and salt. Even the hardiest frontiersmen needed something
to barter, and few were content with mere subsistence. Moreover,
virtually everyone yearned for luxuries beyond the bare essen-
tials. John Winthrop explained to an Englishman in 1668 that
common laborers expected pay in "the commodities of England,
or such as will presently procure them." [13] Linen or pewter on the
table, a suit of clothes made of English fabric, or lace for a
dress were marks of prestige. The law forbidding men of lower
rank to overdress revealed the existence among common people
of an urge to display fineries obtainable only through trade.

The first settlers arrived with the expectation of marketing the
fruits of the new country in line with the development of commercial agriculture in England in the sixteenth and early seventeenth centuries. [14] In the first decade the Connecticut General
Court established a weekly market in Hartford "for all manner
of comodityes that shall be brought in, and for cattell, or any
merchandise whatsoever." [15] Edward Johnson, in 1654, said that
it was "common practise of those that had any store of Cattel,
to sell every year a Cow or two, which cloath'd their backs,
fil'd their bellies with more varieties than the Country of itself
afforded, and put gold and silver in their purses besides." He
boasted that merchants from all corners of the Atlantic came to
New England to purchase the country's staple commodities,
grains, meats, and timber. [16]

In 1655 the Massachusetts General Court sought to revive
commerce to prevent the husbandman from waxing "weary in his
imployment." [17] When the imposition of a tariff threatened trade
in Northampton in 1668, men "of all sorts" signed a protest
arguing that freedom of trade "is the advance of a people," for
without trade "we cannot subsist." [18] In the eighteenth century
it was a truism that a poor market "tends to enervate and abate

[13] To Henry Oldenburg, Nov. 12, 1668, *Winthrop Papers*, pt. IV, 135.

[14] Campbell, *English Yeoman*, 64-104.

[15] *Conn. Recs.*, I, 91.

[16] *Wonder-Working Providence*, 209ff, 247.

[17] Quoted in Bailyn, *New England Merchants*, 105.

[18] Quoted in Judd, *Hadley*, 75, 76.

the Vigour and Zeal of the Farmer, renders him Indolent, takes off the Edge of Industry." [19] A thriving trade, John Wise declared in 1721, "animates the Farmer; keeps him to his Plough; Brightens and inlivens all his Rurall Schemes; Reconciles him to all his hard Labour, and makes him look Fat and Chearful." Wise insisted that farmers, besides supporting themselves, "ought to make a clear Gain, as being most agreeable with the Law of God and Nature." [20] "Good Marketts," a Connecticut man stated confidently a few years later, are "Universally Allowed to be the Greatest Encouragements to Husbandry and Agriculture." [21]

Farming was no bonanza in seventeenth-century Connecticut, but a modest prosperity visited most men who raised a surplus. The chief components of commercial agriculture were present: a market for produce and a feasible way to reach it. Connecticut products were shipped from Boston to Newfoundland, the West Indies, and Europe, and they also stocked the New England fishing fleet.[22]

A marketable crop was ready for immediate harvest in the New England forests, the products of which were in demand all around the Atlantic. From the trees came planks and shingles and tar and turpentine for ship's stores. Timber was also worked into pipestaves used in the construction of barrels. After a farmer cleared his land by burning the woods, he converted the ashes into potash sold as an ingredient for soap.[23]

So profitable was the trade in wood products that men invaded the commons to make their harvests. The towns and the colony repeatedly forbade the cutting of communal timber for export. The inhabitants were at liberty to collect firewood and prepare lumber for their own families, but commercial exploitation jeopardized the resources of subsistence.[24]

[19] Eliot, *Essays*, 187.
[20] *Colonial Currency Reprints*, II, 186, 196.
[21] Conn. Arch., Trade and Maritime, I, 106.
[22] Bailyn, *New England Merchants*, 128-129; Bidwell and Falconer, *History of Agriculture*, 31.
[23] *Memorial History of Hartford County*, II, 341; Judd, 292-293; *Conn. Recs.*, I, 558; Windsor, "Proprietor Records," 63.
[24] *Conn. Recs.*, I, 558; III, 245-246; IV, 316; *Town Records of Derby*, 101; Judd, 99, 292; Steiner, *Guilford*, 181; Fairfield, "Town Records," B, 2, 257; Larned, *Windham*, I, 72; Walcott, "Husbandry," 224; for inter-

Although prices were sometimes low, corn and cattle also had a market. One merchant alone sent 2,000 bushels of wheat and peas to Boston in one year. After the middle of the seventeenth century beef and pork were barreled in the Connecticut Valley and shipped east for the fishing fleet or for foreign markets.[25] Some hogs and neat cattle were shipped live. In a bad year the Winthrops still made close to £3 on each head of beef.[26]

The acceptability of produce for taxes proves it had a market. The Assembly allowed people to pay rates in "good and merchantable" grain, pork, or beef, and one town accepted "good Marchantable pipe staves."[27] In 1689 military preparations were financed by provisions paid in lieu of cash at a rate determined by the price "Currant at Hartford to make it as money."[28] When collecting for a new meetinghouse in 1698, Waterbury specified that the commodities be equivalent in money to the assessment, the total payment "bareing its own charge to the merkit for to bye nayls and glass for the ministers hous."[29] A minister in Durham received his salary in produce and regularly sent it to Boston to trade for imported goods or cash.[30] When the colony needed funds, the treasurer shipped provisions collected for taxes to Boston "to be tirned into money."[31]

Transportation was as important to farmers as the existence of the market. One man hesitated to take up land in Simsbury, some miles west of the Connecticut River, because it lacked good roads. Fortunately for most, all but a few towns in the

colony poaching on timber, C. Stanley to Fitz-John Winthrop, Aug. 17, 1703, *Winthrop Papers*, pt. V, 143; J. Dudley to the Governor and Council of Connecticut, April 1, 1703, *ibid.*, pt. V, 127; for a colony law against cutting timber on another man's land, *Conn. Recs.*, VI, 60.

[25] Judd, 95; cf. pp. 367-370; Bidwell and Falconer, 108-109.

[26] Wait Winthrop to Fitz-John Winthrop, Nov. 19, 1686, *Winthrop Papers*, pt. IV, 468. Earlier the price was much higher (Edward Johnson, *Wonder-Working Providence*, 209).

[27] *Conn. Recs.*, IV, 224, 225; C. Davis, *Wallingford*, 94.

[28] Connecticut Commissioners' Engagement, September 1689, *Wyllys Papers*, 311.

[29] Bronson, *Waterbury*, 213.

[30] Fowler, *Durham*, 36-37.

[31] Caleb Stanley to Fitz-John Winthrop, Nov. 23, 1700, *Winthrop Papers*, pt. V, 60.

seventeenth century were on a navigable river or on the sea. Every little village along the Sound sent its boats to Boston or to one of the Connecticut trading centers. In 1702 the Assembly established eight lawful ports, and four more were added to the list three years later. The colony stoutly resisted attempts of the home government to force all vessels to clear from a single port because such a move might hamper trade.[32]

The expense of land transportation did not deter inland towns from carrying their produce to market. Even though Northampton people, many miles above the head of navigation on the Connecticut River, warned prospective settlers of "the charge and trouble in transporting by land near 50 miles," [33] Northampton and the neighboring towns kept open a road to the Connecticut line. Elsewhere inland towns displayed the same zeal: one of the first acts of the Woodstock settlers was to assume the burden of making a road to Providence, and Waterbury opened a highway to Farmington before building any in its center.[34] The Assembly freed Danbury from taxes for a year while the town laid out a cartway "for transportation of what they raise to the sea." [35]

Sometimes land travel directly to Boston was cheaper than the shortest route to the sea. During the 1690's Woodstock merchants carted furs and surplus farm products there, and many farmers drove cattle overland. Even the Winthrops, whose vast farms lay directly on the sea, found the drovers' pay and the cost of fattening in Boston cheaper than shipping the animals.[36]

The success of the Winthrop operations proved that Connecticut had both marketable products and adequate transportation. Running hundreds of cattle on farms operated by hired hands or by tenants, the Winthrops never doubted the feasibility of commercial agriculture. When John Winthrop, Jr., proposed to the Corpora-

[32] *Memorial History of Hartford County*, II, 346, IV, 374-375; Conn. Arch., Trade and Maritime, I, 43. Principal market towns were Hartford, New London, New Haven, and Fairfield (*Conn. Recs.*, III, 297).

[33] Quoted in Judd, 21.

[34] Judd, 36, 94; Larned, *Historic Gleanings*, 135; Bronson, *Waterbury*, 93.

[35] *Conn. Recs.*, IV, 385; see also Edwin Hall, *Norwalk*, 105-106; Larned, *Historic Gleanings*, 137; Judd, 37.

[36] Larned, *Windham*, I, 35; Wait to Fitz-John Winthrop, Sept. 27, 1683, *Winthrop Papers*, pt. IV, 438.

tion for the Propagation of the Gospel a plan for combining religious instruction of Indians with work on a large farm, he said that the farm would pay back the original investment with interest in three to five years and thereafter provide revenue in support of the Corporation.[37] And the small farmer could produce for the market at even lower costs than those of the Winthrops, for payments to laborers and tenants did not cut into his profits; the toil of his sons was free.[38] A Connecticut report to the Lords of Trade in 1680 described the general pattern of economic life: "We labour in tilling the ground, and by that time a yeare's travell and labour hath gathered some small parcell of provision, it is transported to the market at Boston." [39] In that simple round most Connecticut Puritans found their calling.

Nevertheless, not many farmers grew wealthy by working the land, for few commanded sufficient labor to produce more than their families consumed. Could the scale of agricultural production have been enlarged, the markets would have absorbed additional provisions, but farmers lacked the necessary manpower. With land abundant, few individuals were content to work for wages when they might easily be independent. Some small farmers supplemented their income by hiring out, but by English standards the wages were exorbitant. Most men could afford to employ extra hands only at harvest or when constructing a building. Lacking help, they contented themselves with supplying their families and perhaps slaughtering an animal or two to send to market along with a few bushels of grain. Thus they remained at a middling level of agriculture, partly subsistence, partly commercial, but far from the style of the gentlemen farmers or prosperous yeomen of England.

The troublesome shortage of men largely shaped the farmer's strategy in exploiting his resources. He was inclined, for example, to prize timber above other, more labor-consuming crops. Wheat or Indian corn had to be cultivated, harvested, and processed and

[37] John Winthrop to the Governor of the Corporation for the Propagation of the Gospel in New England, *Trumbull Papers,* 45-47.

[38] John Winthrop to Isaac Taylor, May 8, 1721, *Winthrop Papers,* pt. VI, 397-398.

[39] *Conn Recs.,* III, 301.

the soil prepared for sowing by grubbing out the stumps.[40] Timber, by contrast, was fully grown and ready for the harvest; it needed only to be cut and worked, to be saleable.

Until the woodlands were exhausted, farmers were tempted to occupy themselves solely with the lucrative business of lumbering. The tax structure discouraged this concentration, however, for unimproved wilderness land was exempt from levies: everyone received his allotment at the same time, and the town did not tax persons not ready to improve their share. But, once cleared, property was taxed and, unless gainfully employed, was a drain on its owner.

Farmers thus forced to use improved land if only to pay rates concentrated on the product requiring the least labor, cattle. With land plentiful, it took less work to raise animals than grains. By 1690 it was apparent that men's estates were "like to be imp'ved in cattell."[41] Grains fed the family, while cattle provided the surplus sent to market. Throughout the next century the ascendancy of stock raising over all forms of tillage was ever more noticeable.[42]

Even cattle raising made serious demands on the farmers' labor supply, however, for the animals had to be fenced in to prevent straying or damage to neighbors' crops. The Winthrops estimated that "seting up and maintayning fences . . . costs almost as much as the land is worth" and valued island properties where the water served as a barrier.[43] Fencing also hindered the efforts of common men to increase production, and, as the mountain of regulations in the colony and town records attests, farmers were frequently delinquent because of the desire to employ their labor more productively.[44]

Another obstacle to cattle raising was the perennial shortage

---

[40] Judd, 432. Cereals depleted the soil too.

[41] Quoted in Osgood, *American Colonies in the Seventeenth Century*, I, 446.

[42] John Allyn to Wait Winthrop, April 15, 1689, *Winthrop Papers*, pt. VI, 19; Olson, *Agricultural Economy*, 4; Walcott, 240; Caulkins, *Norwich*, 476.

[43] Wait Winthrop to Samuel Reade, Feb. 28, 1700, *Winthrop Papers*, pt. VI, 56.

[44] *Conn. Recs.*, IV, 50, 266.

of hay. Cattle virtually cared for themselves in summer, foraging
in the woods or on partly cleared land, and the ease of such
pasturing tempted men to graze more animals than they could
feed in the winter. To collect winter fodder, farmers had first to
clear a pasture and fence it off from the summer feeding grounds
and then to mow the hay crop, even on the coastal salt meadows
where grass grew naturally. The work involved disposed them to
hope for a mild season and to underestimate persistently the
amount of supplemental feed they would need. As a consequence,
some cattle starved to death before spring.

From the first years of settlement in New England, the hay
shortage impeded stock raising.[45] One of the reasons for migration to Connecticut was the insufficiency of meadows in the Bay
Colony towns. Along the coast of Long Island Sound and beside
the Connecticut River the migrants found the precious meadows
and marshes where grass grew naturally. When people moved
inland, they chose the site for a new town according to its
proximity to meadows rather than to superior tillage land, for a
community could not subsist without "boggy meadows or such
like, that men can live upon." [46] In distributions of land, the
proportion of meadow was carefully rationed to give each man
his fair share.[47]

As the eighteenth century advanced, the insufficient supply of
feed troubled farmers more each year. Every increase in hay
production was matched by an increase in cattle population. At
mid-century, "the scarcity and high price of hay and corn" seriously diminished "the profit of raising and keeping stocks." [48]
Whether a farmer bought additional hay or decreased his herd to
fit the supply, his returns suffered.

The town could be of great service to individual husbandmen
in surmounting these difficulties. Since men were better able to
succeed in market farming as a community than alone, self-

[45] Walcott, 237; Edward Johnson, 114-115; for a contrary opinion, see
Weaver, "Industry in an Agrarian Economy," 83.

[46] Judd, 27, 81; see also Caulkins, *New London*, 82, 169; Andrews,
Beginnings of Connecticut, 19; Relyea, *Green's Farms*, 9; Hunt, *Pomfret*,
5; Bronson, *Waterbury*, 15, 48; Hine, *Lebanon*, 11-12.

[47] *Conn. Recs.*, II, 96; Larned, *Windham*, I, 22.

[48] Eliot, *Essays*, 27.

interest as well as conscience drew them together under the watch and care of ministers and magistrates. The economic necessity of cooperation bound ambitious men to the social order who might otherwise have struck out into the wilderness in pursuit of their fortunes.

Through the authority of the town meeting, for example, roads were built along which farmers carted their barrels of beef or loads of staves to the market. By right of eminent domain, the town obtained passage through intervening property, trading land in its wilderness reserves for the needed strips. The meeting also compelled every inhabitant to work a given number of days each year to keep up the highways, and fines assured the services of delinquents.[49] The residents of Mortlake, a tract in northeast Connecticut, who pleaded with the Assembly to organize them into a town, possessed substantial farms and large stocks of cattle but suffered from one great handicap: "Not being annexed to any town," they had "no convenient highways, and cannot be compelled to lay out nor mend highways." [50]

The town also helped to diminish the labor of fencing. In the first years of settlement it usually agreed to turn its whole area into pasture, fencing out the cattle from the few cultivated acres, and a common herdsman freed the inhabitants for other work. As men enlarged their own holdings, the town continued to assist those who preferred to herd their cattle privately. To decrease the length of fence, groups would cooperatively enclose a plot containing their cultivated lands so that each individual had but a fraction as much fence to maintain as he would have had alone. Though these arrangements were voluntary, the town appointed a fenceviewer to warn persons responsible for faulty sections and, if necessary, to build or repair them at double cost to the delinquent. Thus public supervision made the private arrangement work.

The town was even able to mitigate the difficulties of raising sufficient winter feed. To stretch out the supply, cows were put into the woods to graze in the summer so that hay could grow

[49] Conn. Arch., Travel, I, 12, 101.
[50] Larned, *Windham*, I, 519; Conn. Arch., Towns and Lands, VIII, 222, 225.

on every scrap of pasture where it might be cut. That move made it difficult to find sufficient summer grazing land, however, and towns found it necessary to forbid residents of other communities to put animals on the uncleared outlands, a temptation to men near the boundaries, and to use various expedients for enlarging their own grazing space.[51] When the General Court, for example, gave certain eastern towns liberty to let goats go at large to subdue rough land and bring in pasture "which is much wanted in new plantations," it also recommended that inhabitants clear away "undergrowth and shrubs neer the townes, that soe pasture for cattle and sheep may be increased." The law required the entire town to spend one day a year making pasture.[52] But many communities thought it easier to burn away the brush in the forests and were willing to risk destroying timber to increase grazing lands. In their enthusiasm, the inhabitants of Hadley fired the woods beyond their boundaries and over into Pelham and Belchertown; because so little labor was required, it seemed a happy practice to "Burn the woods for fede of Cattil." [53]

These communal efforts depended on the town's most important source of power over the inhabitants: its common lands. From the huge tracts around the center of settlement which the town owned, all the values, material and intangible, that land represented were made available. A few prominent men received farms directly from the General Court, but, for the most part, each plot came from the town. To qualify, a person of "sober conversation" needed only to possess a freehold valued at 50s. in the common list and be admitted as an inhabitant.[54] The property qualification was a small barrier, and the town gave its approval to virtually all who supported the social order. In effect, those who submitted to the rule of law and authority received in periodic divisions all the advantages that land brought. After the grant of the original home and wood lots, and meadow and upland for tillage, an inhabitant could count on regular

[51] Ashford, "Town Records," 21; *Town Records of Derby,* 119.
[52] *Conn. Recs.,* VI, 491; II, 51-52, 139.
[53] Judd, 98, 194; *Town Records of Derby,* 134; Bronson, *Waterbury,* 57.
[54] *Conn. Recs.,* III, 34; cf. I, 293, 351.

divisions of the town reserve, from which came timber, tillage land for wheat and corn, and pasture for grazing and mowing. Above all, the town gave a man the satisfaction of being a free-holder, of enjoying a degree of independence, and of knowing that his holding linked him with men of property throughout the English world.

Few considered any course but to live within the town. The economic ambitions of the people were attainable only because, living together in a town, they cooperatively mitigated the diffi-culties of exploiting the wilderness. Land distribution, road build-ing, supervision of fencing, supplementation of pasturage, the recruitment and subsidy of millers, tanners, and blacksmiths, and the destruction of pests made the town's participation in the economy crucial to a farmer's success. Without aid from the community, few indeed could have produced a surplus and taken it to market.

Jared Eliot's contention that economic expediency and com-munal order should not cross purposes seemed fully true in Con-necticut in the seventeenth century. The effectual reconciliation of private aspirations with the public good attested to an under-lying harmony. Though sinful men sometimes disturbed that harmony, Connecticut Puritans in 1690 could see no inherent conflict between economic interest and the rule of law and authority.

The flexibility of local government was one reason for the infrequency of serious conflicts. The town was not democratic—the range of candidates for the highest offices was limited to a handful of prominent men—but the meeting was nevertheless popular government. Within the realm of prudential affairs the General Assembly authorized the people themselves to make such orders as concerned "the welfare of the town." [55] The six or seven elected selectmen were not rulers but agents to whom the people legally transferred administrative authority. "It is agreed," reads the *Hartford Town Votes* for 1635, "that the Townsmen [selectmen] for the tyme being shall have the power of the whole

[55] Connecticut Colony, *Book of General Laws, 1673*, 65; cf. *Conn. Recs.*, I, 36. The discussion for Massachusetts in Sly, *Town Government*, largely applies to Connecticut.

to order the Comon occasions of the Towne." [56] They were but the voice and arm of the people who, in important instances, preferred to exercise their power personally. Occasionally the meeting prescribed limits for the selectmen who were forbidden to admit inhabitants, grant land, or levy rates without formal permission, and it sometimes rescinded their administrative actions.[57]

Though in the colony government, rulers, once elected, had no obligation to comply with popular wishes, in the town it was quite different. Despite the fact that prominent individuals always occupied the important offices and exercised a greater influence than lesser men, selectmen were not to govern the people against their will, but, on the contrary, to obey when the people spoke. The records reveal that the participants conceived of the meetings as reflecting majority desires: "The inhabitants of Pagasett mett to gether and granted Joseph hawkings a tract of land"; or "the Towne ordered that an account bee taken of the Indians." [58] Behind the terse summaries the inhabitants can be seen, discussing proposals, consulting their own and the public interests, and reaching decisions by vote. After the New Haven meeting had heard a committee report on the settlement of a new village, the inhabitants were asked to "declare their minds," and "after debate It was by vote declared That the towne graunts the village to those that have ingaged." [59] The discussion sometimes growing intense, it was often ordered "that whoever speaks in town meeting with out leave of the moderator" be fined.[60] The leader was accurately termed a moderator, for while he regulated debate, the inhabitants spoke their minds freely and the majority decided.

The town meetings' accommodation of popular economic interests was reflected in such entries as the "inhabetants mett to-

[56] P. 2; cf. p. 164; Plainfield, "First Book," 17; Ashford, "Town Records," 1.

[57] *Hartford Town Votes*, 258; *Town Records of Derby*, 25, 27; H. R. Stiles, *Windsor*, I, 84.

[58] *Town Records of Derby*, 15; New Haven Colony Historical Society, *Ancient Records*, II, 339.

[59] New Haven Colony Historical Society, II, 255; cf. *Town Records of Derby*, 25.

[60] H. R. Stiles, I, 232.

gether and have made an agreement to Suckure thare corn." [61] Similarly, the meeting might arrange for fencing or highways or for a new division of land. Moreover, public authority readily adjusted to changing circumstances. When, near the end of the century, farmers found sheep raising profitable, they arranged in meeting for a common pound and shepherd. The town granted permission to mine iron, to make turpentine on its lands, and to set weirs in the river as those enterprises attracted inhabitants.[62]

When complaints arose, the troubled parties were heard and action was taken. Farmers too distant to run their sheep in the town pasture were relieved of taxes for the common shepherd and allowed to build pounds nearer their houses. Adjustments were made for individuals treated unfairly in the division of land or in the allotment of common fence to maintain. The town exchanged land to give a man a watering place for his cattle, and it built roads into property without easy access.[63]

The successful rule of the civil authority was due in large part to the town's absorption of minor local discontents. With a community instrument of public authority at their disposal, the townspeople rarely called for assistance on the General Assembly, which, consequently, was relatively free of factional economic disputes. Common men usually struggled to attain their ends in the meeting, where they could seek public help for private needs. The composure of individual desires into order at this level was one reason for the peace enjoyed in the colony.

In the last quarter of the seventeenth century the situation began to change. By 1690 forces were gathering that were destined to debilitate the old order, and alterations in the economy had begun to upset the delicate balance in the social order. The harmony of interests turned gradually to discord as warring parties divided the town. Since the community no longer coordinated the agencies of government, contention in one segment of society could spread to all the others, and church, family, and civil government were

[61] *Town Records of Derby*, 8.
[62] *Town Records of Derby*, 213; H. R. Stiles, I, 233, 180, 234.
[63] *Town Records of Derby*, 213, 17, 220, 216, 34. These examples were gathered from the records of Derby, but any town meeting would have served as well.

all disrupted. At the same time, popular economic interests out-grew the town, which lost its capacity to satisfy the wants of its people.

The colonial government felt the pressure of new demands for land and currency and of uncommon dissension in the churches as well. No longer able to obtain adequate assistance in town meeting, the inhabitants called on the Assembly and governor to step into the breach. But the rulers, accustomed to rule the people and not to comply with their wishes, resisted popular en-treaties. The resulting turmoil seriously eroded the authority of government and shook the entire social order to its foundations.

PART TWO

Land, 1690 – 1740

III

Proprietors

꙳ THE ABUNDANCE OF LAND made it relatively simple to keep peace in the seventeenth-century towns. Discontent and frustration did not arise often when men possessed ample land to realize their ambitions. Moreover, its availability imposed a kind of economic equality on the town and assured a similarity of interests for all inhabitants. Merchants, clergy, and tradesmen as well as farmers owned some land, and even tenants and hired laborers could soon earn enough to purchase a holding.[1] Some large owners leased property to tenants, and many hired extra hands in the busiest season, but very few indeed were sedentary gentlemen farmers. With labor at a premium, virtually every family had to work its own land. Even the very wealthy, if they did not toil in the fields and forests themselves, sent out their sons each morning with plow and axe. Despite all the distinctions in the social hierarchy, the wide distribution of land joined men in common interests which gave a stable base to their commonwealth.

The mere possession of a small freehold, however, did not satisfy the ambitions of inhabitants who wanted to increase their surplus. As Bradford had noted at the very beginning of settlement in New England, "no man now thought he could live, except he had cattle and a great deal of ground to keep them; all striving to increase their stocks." [2] Each needed more pasture for his growing herd and fresh forest lands for timber. In 1690 Nathan Gold and John Staples of Fairfield each owned between 1400 and

[1] In 1705, Norwich was selling forty-acre lots to inhabitants for six shillings (Norwich, Town Votes, 97).

[2] Bradford, *History*, II, 152.

1500 acres within the town. About half the men with dividend rights held over 400 acres.[3] As soon as one tract was cleared and prepared for pasture, a farmer was eager to take on another.

The desire for land mounted also because every father hoped that his sons would prosper at least to the degree he had. In England primogeniture restricted this prospect to the eldest, but in the New World all the sons expected to own a farm. Having far more acres than people, the first settlers fell into the practice of distributing their estates among all the male heirs, with generous portions for daughters too.[4] But in all but small families the sons' estate could never equal the fathers by inheritance; a young man could hope to increase his holding only as his father had, by regular dividends from the town lands.

The town had long been able to satisfy the hunger for land. In the first years of settlement the common practice was to grant virtually every adult male an allotment. Larger grants, in proportion to each person's dignity, observed the proprieties of the social hierarchy, but no one monopolized the land to the exclusion of lesser individuals.[5] As time passed, additional portions of the undivided land were distributed to the people, steadily increasing their estates. This policy permitted everyone to share in the costs of town and church and hurried the conquest of the wilderness.[6] The town fathers also assumed that men with a stake in society would more readily respect the laws protecting order and property.

The form in which the town held its lands gave a legal basis to this generosity. The undivided reserves belonged to everyone, for the colony government bestowed the entire township on the inhabitants collectively, who rightfully divided it among themselves in the meeting.[7] There were no distinctions between inhabi-

[3] Garvan, *Architecture and Town Planning*, 57. Fifty to one hundred acres was a substantial farm in England.

[4] For a retrospective explanation of this practice, see An Act for the Settlement of Intestate Estates, May 1732, *Talcott Papers*, II, 441.

[5] For example, see Judd, *Hadley*, 33.

[6] An Act for the Settlement of Intestate Estates, May 1732, *Talcott Papers*, II, 441; Judd, 89.

[7] *Conn. Recs.*, I, 36. The standard analysis of town proprietorship is Akagi, *Town Proprietors*.

tants and proprietors in the first decades of settlement in Connecticut.[8]

The inhabitants did not hold the town lands as private individuals. They were not, for example, tenants in common, one of the legal ways of owning property jointly, since under this title none of the town's common land could have been sold without the agreement of every inhabitant, and any individual could have demanded his share of the common holdings whenever he wished.[9] Nor was the town a joint-stock company, for then each man would have voted in proportion to the amount of stock owned.[10] Furthermore, under either of these forms of ownership the inhabitants could have alienated their titles, but in Connecticut towns sons did not inherit the right to dividends, nor could the right be sold. Under the technical forms of the common law as well as by New England practice the title to the undivided lands was not a private estate.

Though they never made their position explicit, town inhabitants, judging by their actions, conceived of themselves as a corporation, making by-laws, admitting members, giving and taking property in its own name and acting as a legal person in the courts.[11] The sober, honest men with freehold estates of 50s. in the common list, who were admitted by vote of the majority of the inhabitants, had the corporate power to regulate the town's land.[12]

[8] Except in Hartford, where the proprietors were early set off as a distinct body. Osgood maintains that title actually resided in a small group of town proprietors, but admits that in the first years this distinction cannot be found in the records (*American Colonies in the Seventeenth Century*, I, 462).

[9] Holdsworth, *History of English Law*, III, 126-128.

[10] Although the admitted inhabitants received allotments of land in proportion to their estates, roughly in the fashion of a joint-stock company, this method of distribution was valid only because the inhabitants approved it in a meeting in which each man gave one vote.

[11] Holdsworth, III, 150, 170; IX, 53. See the 1684 case in Fairfield where the power of the town to take a grant was pleaded in court and upheld (The Answer and Defence of Peter Clapham and Isaac Frost, *Trumbull Papers*, 128).

[12] *Conn. Recs.*, III, 34. Town property automatically descended to the successors admitted to the town without any individual deeding or willing his share.

The Crown had bestowed the territory in the Connecticut patent on the corporation created by the charter, but the General Court could not easily make distributions to individuals. Since the towns could judge the worthiness of applicants and give out land as needed, they operated as local corporations, absorbing qualified newcomers and providing land for sons of older residents by the simple process of admitting such persons as inhabitants.

Connecticut towns modeled their landholding procedures after well-known customs in English boroughs. When a village received a grant of land from a manor or monastery, it was obligated to incorporate to take the grant, and all admitted freemen in the borough then determined how to employ the land. Few boroughs owned much property, but where they did, participation in the benefits was an enviable privilege.[13]

Though following well-established precedents, the corporate activities of the Connecticut towns were not technically legal, for under the common law a group of individuals could function in these ways only when formally incorporated. The villages of England applied to the King for their charters, but since one corporation could not create another, Connecticut had no power to bestow the rights it did.[14] The towns, therefore, were not legal corporations and could not rightfully take the grants of land the court gave.

This neglect of formal procedure did not unduly disturb the colonists, because, as a matter of fact, it was a frequent practice to enlarge a partnership to a company and assume corporate

---

Had the inhabitants owned the town's property in fee simple they would have retained possession even when the town was divided. Such was not the case. When Lyme and Glastonbury separated from their parent towns, for example, control of the undivided property in the new boundaries was invested in the daughter towns. Since no individual had a fee simple inheritance in the common property, the old towns and their inhabitants were compelled to relinquish all their former rights to the new corporations (Hurd, *New London County,* 540; S. W. Adams and H. R. Stiles, *Wethersfield,* I, 194; II, 905).

[13] Weinbaum, *British Borough Charters,* xxiv. In Berwick the burgesses or freemen divided the common lands among themselves (Webb and Webb, *Manor and Borough,* 207, 517, 401, 526-527).

[14] Coke said that only the Crown, Parliament, the common law, or prescription could create a corporation (Holdsworth, IX, 46).

powers without seriously risking prosecution. Some English villages had accepted property and managed it as boroughs would
without charters, and corporations had frequently formed sub-
sidiary quasicorporations. Some of the Puritan founders of New
England had actually acted without charter as a corporation to
sponsor reform ministers.[15] Hence the risk for the obscure communities of New England seemed small.

Not until the colony corporation was threatened after the
Restoration did Connecticut worry about the validity of titles.
In 1664 Charles II's patent gave the Duke of York jurisdiction
between the Connecticut and Delaware Rivers, while the Duke
of Hamilton claimed territory east of the Connecticut. Recognition
of these claims would not only put all the undivided lands in
the colony at the disposal of the Dukes but jeopardize all land
held by the illegal town corporations.[16]

In the decade after 1664 various measures were taken to secure
Connecticut land by legally conveying it to individuals, in whose
hands it was relatively safe. The colony extended the boundaries
of many towns, which in turn divided land among individuals.
A law specified that land granted to townships belonged to the
owners, their heirs, successors, or assigns, and not simply to the
successors in the invalid town corporations. West of the river,
where the threat was greatest, four towns transferred ownership
from the town as a corporation to a limited body of proprietors
who held the land in common but as individuals.[17]

After 1680 the hazards of corporate ownership steadily in-

[15] Scott, *Joint-Stock Companies*, I, 227; Holdsworth, IV, 439-440, 478;
Webb and Webb, 156-157; *Activities of the Puritan Faction*, xii, xxiii, xxiv,
4, 126.

[16] For the series of challenges to land tenure, see the narrative of settle-
ment sent to the Crown (*Conn. Recs.*, II, 339-343; cf. The Case of Anne,
Duchess of Hamilton, *Trumbull Papers*, 184). For a secondary account, see
Palfrey, *History of New England*, II, 577-580.

[17] For extension of town bounds, see *Conn. Recs.*, II, 185, 187, 199,
228-229, 155, 175, 176. For division of town lands, Schenck, *Fairfield*,
I, 140, 154-155; Orcutt, *Stratford*, 273; Andrews, *River Towns*, 56-57;
Steiner, *Guilford*, 171-172. The law on the form of inheritance is in the
1673 compilation of laws and not in earlier records (Connecticut Colony,
Book of General Laws, 1673, 38). For towns limiting proprietorship,
Schenck, I, 139-140; Orcutt, *Stratford*, 190; Blakely, *Farmington*, 4.

creased. The King and Council disallowed Massachusetts' law of land tenure, which was very similar to Connecticut's, and *Quo Warranto* proceedings vacated borough and colonial charters throughout the realm. Connecticut officials foresaw that a royal representative would soon rule in New England and feared a repetition of the difficulties experienced in New York, where, after Andros had scrutinized land patents, real estate held or granted illegally was lost. These fears proved well grounded when Andros assumed the governorship of New England, for he scoffed at the presumption of the colonial governments to create corporations. All lands distributed by the towns, he ruled, were the possession of the Crown and would be returned to claimants upon purchase of a quitclaim.[18]

Before Andros' arrival, however, Connecticut had taken measures to secure titles. In 1685 lands in the northwest were granted to Hartford and Windsor, and the Assembly, "for the prevention of future trouble," issued patents to the town inhabitants for their townships.[19] The General Court hoped that Andros would not be able to invalidate titles which assigned colony lands directly to the people, as the charter allowed, without working through the dubious town corporations. Actually, Andros' early deposition prevented him from testing this device in the courts, but Connecticut retained the patents and never returned to corporate ownership of town lands. The succeeding assaults on the charter mounted in England kept the government on the defensive and compelled people to adjust to the new form of ownership.

The patents did not at first displace any inhabitants as proprietors of the undivided lands, for the patentees of 1685 were the accepted town inhabitants. Only the legal form of ownership changed. Before 1685 the town inhabitants held common lands as a group and distributed them to admitted inhabitants, while after 1685 the undivided lands belonged to the individual proprietors as their fee-simple estates. Title was vested in the specific persons

---

[18] Samuel Norwell to John Richards, March 28, 1683, *Winthrop Papers*, pt. III, 435; Haffenden, "The Crown and the Colonial Charters, 1675-1688"; Osgood, III, 407, 406; for the entire Andros episode, Barnes, *Dominion of New England*.
[19] *Conn. Recs.*, III, 177-178, 225.

named or implied in the patents and not in the members of the town corporation.[20] As Bolton was told in 1720, new towns receive all the ordinary privileges, but "it is to be understood they have no power to dispose of any land" within the township.[21]

When the proprietorship of town lands was fixed in the patentees of 1685 and their heirs, the economic and social organization of the community was altered. New inhabitants previously shared automatically in the control of land. Tenants in common, by contrast, could not easily grant a lot to a recent arrival, for it required an unanimous vote to do so.[22] Newcomers could obtain a right to land dividends only by purchase from an older inhabitant.

Many old townsmen welcomed the exclusion of newcomers. Since town lands were nearing exhaustion in many places, and the growing population decreased still further the size of each dividend, the entrenched families probably were happy to shut out future arrivals from a portion of townlands.[23] The strain on

[20] The Court later construed the patents to mean that the proprietor-inhabitants were tenants in common, one of the recognized devices for holding land under the common law and a defensible title in English courts (*Conn. Recs.*, VI, 189; Holdsworth, III, 126-128).

[21] *Conn. Recs.*, VI, 216; cf. *ibid.*, VI, 374; Stark, *Groton*, 74-75.

[22] Because the restricted legal capacities of tenants in common were not well suited to the functions of proprietors, the Assembly, after the crisis passed, bestowed some corporate powers on the proprietors, allowing them to make by-laws, to sue and be sued, and to alienate common property by majority vote (*Conn. Recs.*, VI, 25, 424; VII, 137-138, 337-338). But this discrepancy between legal form and actual functions sometimes embarrassed the Assembly. In 1746 Thomas Hill, a Fairfield proprietor, asked for a partition of common land. According to a colony statute, a tenant in common might compel a division of common land where there was a disagreement among the tenants (*ibid.*, VI, 217-218). The proprietors denied his request on the grounds that they held the lands in a "political" and not in a "natural" capacity, that is, that they were an artificially created person. Only a majority of interest could compel the proprietors to divide. Hill replied that though they administered the lands as a political person and were sued in the courts as such, they held title as natural persons in a partnership, that is, as tenants in common. The controversy stirred both houses, the Upper House agreeing with Hill and the Lower tending to oppose him. Finally Hill won the case and the Assembly allowed him a writ to compel division (Conn. Arch., Towns and Lands, 2nd ser., II, 24; *Conn. Recs.*, IV, 326-327, 367-368).

[23] Certainly Stratford was (Orcutt, *Stratford*, 190).

the available resources in older towns disposed everyone to reserve the outlands for their own families.

Nevertheless, many towns continued to admit new inhabitants and to grant each a portion in the divisions, for there were forces working against limiting the body of proprietors.[24] While a closed proprietary shut out new settlers, it also excluded younger sons of the inhabitants themselves. Previously as each son came of age, the town admitted him to legal standing, granted him land, and awarded him a share in future divisions; a father thus knew that in addition to his sons' inheritance they would receive increases from town lands.[25] Under tenancy in common, on the other hand, new inhabitants did not whittle away the father's portions in each division, but sons had to be content with no more than a portion of their father's estate; they did not receive a dividend of their own by admission to the town. Fathers with small families received a proportionately larger amount, but the father of four or five boys divided his allotment into smaller pieces and saw his sons begin life with an inferior inheritance.

This problem, touching so many families, slowed the establishment of a closed proprietary. Since younger sons who lacked adequate farms were wont to leave the town, men with large families asked for special dispensations, and a variety of compromises to accommodate the children of established settlers resulted. Fairfield admitted children to dividend rights even though they were not freemen of the town when the body of proprietors was fixed in 1668. Stratford admitted new inhabitants as before, devising a rule that excluded outlivers with no family connections in the town plot. Waterbury and Woodbury gave younger sons "bachelor lots" as they came of age, with the provision that they remain in town. Guilford in 1690 made the inhabitants of 1686 the sole proprietors but agreed to give a share in the lands to all children born before the division was ordered.[26] Although

[24] Larned, *Windham*, I, 121-122, 125-126, 215-216; Cothren, *Woodbury*, 77; S. W. Adams and H. R. Stiles, II, 923; Norwich, Town Votes, 78-80; Caulkins, *New London*, 273; Orcutt and Beardsley, *Derby*, 109.

[25] Always before 1685, land allotments had taken family needs into account (Schenck, I, 140; Steiner, 173).

[26] Schenck, I, 140, 154; Orcutt, *Stratford*, 190, 201, 263-265, 284-286 (compare the number of dividends in each list, rising from no more than

contrary to the patents of 1685, these measures successfully accommodated the young men of the community.

Other towns neglected the colony's proprietorship laws in order to attract new settlers. Since the residents of Durham had purchased their property or received it directly from the colonial government (the General Court had never granted them a town plot to be held corporately, as in other plantations), new settlers had to buy their farms from an established proprietor instead of receiving a free allotment. When, as a result, settlement went slowly, the inhabitants obtained permission from the Court to lay down one quarter of their land for "qualified . . . inhabitants according to lawe," thereby reserving a supply of undivided land available to newcomers.[27] Plainfield residents, who also obtained their land by purchase and could not attract immigrants, gave up their unimproved lands to a pool of undivided commons so that they might share their property as a corporation with later settlers. The decrease in taxes as more people contributed to town and society expenses apparently more than compensated for the sacrifice. In Waterbury, where some proprietors were resident and others not, the distribution of land to emigrants provoked an argument between the residents, who wished to encourage settlement by granting land to newcomers, and the nonresidents, who would benefit little from a growth in population and hence could see only the shrinkage in the land dividends. In Windsor the nonresidents also heavily favored limiting the proprietary.[28]

The exclusion of newcomers may also have offended the colonists' sense of economic justice. The early town founders, who had wanted all to share the tax burden but had also taken pride in their kindness toward little men, had distributed land to the poorest and restricted the portion of the wealthiest. Edward Johnson, for example, had boasted of the comparative prosperity of indigent immigrants after a few years in New England.[29] Now,

---

78 in 1676, to 143 in 1699, to 199 claimants in 1738); Bronson, *Waterbury*, 116, 120; Cothren, 78; Steiner, 173-174.

[27] *Conn. Recs.*, IV, 472; Fowler, *Durham*, 3, 15-16, 27.

[28] Larned, *Windham*, I, 121, 125-126; Bronson, *Waterbury*, 118, 120, 150, 243.

[29] *Wonder-Working Providence*, 210.

having once acted on this principle, some people hesitated to exclude poor arrivals.

As the diverse effects of limiting proprietorship became known, quarrels broke out all over the colony. New London's second patent, received in 1699, confirmed its lands to the "inhabitants freeholders," and subsequently the town invited "all freeholders of this town who are desirous to have their names entered" on the patent to subscribe them. This action aroused an extended controversy over the qualifications of proprietors, one party arguing for all legal voters and the other, headed by Gurdon Saltonstall, favoring a more limited group. Finally, the General Court ruled that the patent gave town lands only to the lawful inhabitants before 1703.[30] For a half-century after the issuance of the patents of 1685, similar controversies over the distribution of land split the towns.[31] On the one side were useful customs of corporate ownership and the expediency of admitting all sons to division rights; on the other were the political necessity of securing titles and the ambitions of some to preserve a larger portion in the commons than corporate ownership allowed.

Though the poor and later arrivals understandably favored corporate ownership, this was by no means simply a struggle between rich and poor, or between ancient settlers and newcomers. On the contrary, there were men of eminence in both parties. In Windsor, for example, Roger Wolcott, the town's most honored citizen, took the side of liberality along with Matthew Allyn, one of the wealthiest men in the community. Perhaps Wolcott, the politician, felt obliged to take a stand consistent with popular feelings, and Allyn, the storekeeper, may have foreseen the loss of customers if land-hungry men emigrated.[32] When strong politi-

[30] *Conn. Recs.,* IV, 289; VI, 189; Caulkins, *New London,* 263-263.

[31] Wallingford fell into confusion because the town could not agree on the proper token of proprietary right. Certain purchasers insisted that any owner of town lands received complete division rights with his purchase. The town tried to enforce the rule that land in the town and proprietorship of the common lands might be separated. The town succeeded but not without a struggle (Beach, *Cheshire,* 47-48, 63-64). In Groton the town apportioned land among all inhabitants disregarding the patentees' objections (Conn. Arch., Towns and Lands, III, 243).

[32] Windsor, "Proprietor Acts," 1-16; Conn. Arch., Towns and Lands, VII, 105-127. Only two men protested Canterbury's allotments to all in-

cal and social traditions entered into the controversy, economic
expediency alone did not determine party lines: though both
houses of the Assembly were composed of prominent men, they
could nevertheless not agree on the ownership of town lands,
and year after year the Upper House passed bills to bestow title
on the patentees alone, only to have the measures blocked in
the Lower House.[33]

Many towns settled their arguments by compromise. When in
1700 Norwich, a typical case in some respects, became "sensible
of the Difficulty that may arise with respect unto the disposing
of the undivided lands within this Township for want of a stated
method or foundation for the same," a committee proposed that
the first settlers and their children along with admitted inhabitants
share equally, while other residents receive in proportion to the
taxes they paid.[34] Milford's variation of this procedure was to
limit control of land to the proprietors of 1685 as specified in
law and to give a smaller portion to those who arrived afterwards. Glastonbury voted to divide the land to all inhabitants by
list in 1707 but altered its decision seven years later. Instead,
6,000 acres were first divided among all the inhabitants of 1713
according to the tax list of that year, and then the settlers who
arrived before the meetinghouse was erected received a bonus
of 100 acres. Fairfield limited divisions to proprietors of 1670
but offered land to any dissatisfied persons. Derby gave a per-
centage increase in proportion to the number of years a person
had lived in town. Durham and Killingly admitted new proprietors as the town had once admitted inhabitants. Simsbury granted
dividend rights to certain inhabitants admitted after 1685 but
withheld them from others.[35]

habitants in 1723. All other town leaders concurred in a corporate division
(Larned, *Windham,* I, 156). The fourteen opponents of forming a pro-
prietary body in Norwich were prominent townsmen (Norwich, "Proprietor
Records," 2).

[33] Conn. Arch., Towns and Lands, III, 60, 186, 242; "Journals of the
Upper House," May 13, 1718; Oct. 22, 1718; May 21, 1719.

[34] Norwich, Town Votes, 74, 78, 80.

[35] Labaree, *Milford,* 17, 21; Chapin, *Glastenbury,* 60-61; S. W. Adams
and H. R. Stiles, I, 108; Schenck, I, 243; Orcutt and Beardsley, 109;
Fowler, 26-27; Larned, *Windham,* I, 166, 173; cf. Colchester's system in
Hurd, 386, 388-389; Conn. Arch., Towns and Lands, IV, 101.

Disputes and confusing compromises resulted at last in action in the Assembly in 1723.[36] The purpose was to confirm titles to land granted illegally by the towns since 1685 and then to invest future control of common lands in the proprietors alone. The Court had no choice but to validate grants made in the town meeting because "the said proprietors did, for a considerable number of years in many of our towns, truly consent and agree that the said common lands might . . . be actually divided or disposed of by the major vote of the inhabitants of such towns." Nevertheless, the Act said, the town property was "an undoubted lawful estate of inheritance" of the patentees. They had power to divide it as they wished, "without suffering any other persons, who should afterwards become inhabitants of the said towns, to be concerned." The law now had to be observed: henceforth, no person, "by becoming an inhabitant of such town . . . shall be taken . . . to have any estates, title, right, or interest" in town lands.[37] Thus the line between inhabitants and proprietors was clearly drawn.

Despite the finality of this act, it did not end disagreements. The membership of the proprietor group continued to perplex the towns, for the patents had specified as proprietors only a few prominent individuals and then added "and the rest of the said present proprietors of the township." [38] Some towns organized just prior to the issuance of the patent interpreted this to mean the inhabitants who helped purchase the land and settle the first minister, while others took the list of people in the next land division, that of 1690 or even later.[39] Roger Wolcott insisted

[36] The New London contention, in which the Governor figured, seems to have been the catalyst (*Conn. Recs.*, VI, 161, 189; cf. VI, 76). Love makes a similar claim for Hartford (Love, *Hartford*, 123).

[37] *Conn. Recs.*, VI, 394-397.

[38] *Conn. Recs.*, III, 178.

[39] B. Trumbull, *Extracts of Letters*, 290. Wethersfield decided on the purchasers of new land in 1673 (S. W. Adams and H. R. Stiles, I, 106). Canterbury scaled shares in proportion to length of residency (Larned, *Windham*, I, 156). Norwich established the admitted inhabitants of 1710 as proprietors, since at that date the issue finally came to a head (Norwich, "Proprietor Records," 18, 19, 21, 23). In 1724 Simsbury declared it impossible to determine the lawful proprietors and the number of votes due to each (Conn. Arch., Towns and Lands, IV, 107).

that since the names of the 1685 patentees could not be found, the list of taxables in 1723 must be used.[40] As late as 1754, some Hartford people argued for the inhabitants of 1639 versus the 1685 patentees (the courts finally deciding that the earlier group owned town lands as an inheritable estate and were, therefore, the legal proprietors).[41]

The controversies petered out at last, but the townspeople had to live with the consequences. A new line marked one group from another. The proprietors formed a community within the town, meeting regularly to lay out highways and regulate fences, to survey and distribute land, while other inhabitants looked with envy on this inner group which exercised privileges everyone had once possessed. The town meeting occasionally even had to negotiate with the proprietors for land to provide highways or a common pasture.[42] The task of keeping order became more problematic as the difficulties of obtaining land set apart more definitely those with small holdings from those of larger estates. Since tenants or poor farmers could not so easily increase their inheritances when land was growing scarce, and a fixed group monopolized the town's undivided lands, a clear conflict of interest divided proprietors and non-proprietors.

Differences between the two classes eventually destroyed the fundamental homogeneity of the community and weakened the support it once offered the individual. Younger sons and poor men found themselves in a sense outcasts in their own society, at variance with town leaders and short of land to satisfy their ambitions. In the eighteenth-century situation they could not recreate the lives of their fathers or engage themselves to the community in all the dimensions of the past. They were set free somewhat of older ties, but they lacked the stays and help available in the seventeenth-century town.

[40] Conn. Arch., Towns and Lands, VII, 109.

[41] Love, 129. In 1639 Hartford had invested town lands in a joint-stock company composed of the inhabitants of that year (*ibid.*, 119-120, 124-125; cf. *Conn. Recs.*, VII, 243).

[42] Conn. Arch., Travel, I, 42a, 45a, 46a, 93a.

IV

Outlivers

↜§ THE CHANGE IN THE PATTERN of proprietorship acquired added significance from the reshuffling of settlement that had begun shortly after the foundation of the colony. By the 1680's enough people lived away from the town center to undermine the unity of the town, a change which, in turn, subtly affected community order.

Before 1685, when all shared in land divisions, lots were distributed in a fashion that kept men close to the central settlement. Economically it would have been more efficient to scatter families on sizeable holdings where the farmers would be close to their work, but the social purposes of the community required that everyone live within a small radius so they could easily attend public worship and be subject to the influence of town leaders. The pattern of land distribution reconciled these conflicting principles by enabling the townspeople to live in a compact village on home lots of five or ten acres, the remainder of their land being granted in long strips that began on some road leading into town and stretched off into the wilderness away from the settlement. Usually these strips were from 100 to 1,000 feet wide and two or three miles long. Maps of early towns show sections of these lots pointing like banks of arrows toward the town center, a pattern that was awkward for farming and irregular by English standards but permitted the inhabitants to work at least part of their land conveniently and still live within the town.[1] The farther

---

[1] See maps of Windsor, Hartford, and Wethersfield in Andrews, *River Towns*, 4, 61. Garvan notes that English villages practiced strip farming, but the fantastically long strips projecting from the center were unique to New England (*Architecture and Town Planning*, pp. 56–57). The strips were also a device for evening the quality of the land.

end of the strip was too remote for easy use, but initially this method of distribution prevented economic interest from pulling men away from the center of the settlement.

Eventually the distribution of the back lots disrupted this co-ordination of economics and communal well-being. Once the timber in the nearest section was cleared for pasture, the next length called for attention, and then the next. Before long a farmer either had to walk the two or three miles to the end of his land or neglect it altogether. Neither alternative was attractive, for he soon found most of his land at an uncomfortable distance from his house. As a wedge of pie is wider on the periphery than near the center, so a larger amount of land was eventually distributed three miles from the town than one. Fairfield tried to delay the inevitable by lending forest lands on the outskirts for the space of eight years, hoping that when the inhabitants had cut the timber, they would be content to sow the cleared land in grass and use it for common pasture so that only fences would require their attention. But, unwilling to part with land to which they had given their labor, the borrowers demanded full title. At first the town fined anyone who built on these lands, but at last pressures were too strong and ownership was granted.[2]

In time the attempt to hold men close to the town center by distributing bits and chunks on the periphery of the occupied area defeated its own purpose, for the difficulty of managing these acres disposed men to move out. A typical farmer in Milford owned fourteen lots strung from one end of the town to the other.[3] Driving teams and carts or trudging back and forth with axe or hoe on poorly cleared and pitted roads occupied a large part of the working day. Men short of hands begrudged the toil-some and wasteful travel, and temporary residences soon appeared in the outlands. Some farmers and their sons lived there in the summer while tending their herds or mowing hay; others lived out while working their lands during the week and then re-turned to town on Sundays. Guilford designated such a section where men following this practice could live together Cohabit.[4]

[2] Relyea, *Green's Farms*, 19.
[3] Labaree, *Milford*, 11.
[4] Steiner, *Guilford*, 199.

Since by dwelling temporarily on their lands in the outskirts farmers reduced travel time and immensely increased their efficiency, they were tempted to move out permanently, but usually the town leaders frowned on this course. A concentrated community offered benefits unavailable on dispersed farms. Anyone who moved to the outlands broke away from the circle of virtue and order. He could not easily join in weekly worship, his children would want for education, and he lost touch with all the influences which controlled "a wild and savage behavior." The church could not exercise its watch and care over members too distant for frequent contacts.[5] Neighbors were no longer nearby to observe each day's conduct. Constables, selectmen, and tithingmen had trouble apprehending offenders hidden off in the woods. Encounters with town leaders who occupied the lots of greatest prestige and value near the meetinghouse were necessarily diminished. The lonely man in the wilderness answered only to his own family and the uncritical forest. No one could disregard the overtones of disorder and sin attached to removal from the protecting village.

The first settlers had foreseen that their plantations would not hold all their posterity. In their own generation new settlements spread up and down the Connecticut River and both ways along the Sound, but in all of these towns the immediate gathering of a church and the presence of prominent men to lead had been required. Often in the early days the minister led the migration, and a cross-section of an entire community was transplanted. Social forms were never allowed to disintegrate. If a group of individuals petitioned for a new plantation, the Court was careful to see that "the numbers and quality of those that ingage therein appeare to bee such as may rationally carry on the worke to the advantage of the publique wellfare and peace." [6] Planned

---

[5] Solomon Stoddard warned of the dangers of living so distant that weekly attendance at the meetinghouse was impossible. He declared it unlawful to begin a new plantation without immediate prospect of "obtaining the Ordinances" (*An Answer*, 2). Farmington forbade a prosperous man moving to a new settlement at Waterbury since he had no need for land, and there was no church in the new settlement (Bronson, *Waterbury*, 46).

[6] *Conn. Recs.*, I, 210.

migrations to the outlands, manned by the sons of town plot residents and conducted under the supervision of local leaders, provided some outlet for surplus population.[7]

Apart from these approved departures, some intrepid individuals left the ring of compact settlements and built their isolated cabins in the woods regardless of the warning that their posterity would "degenerate to heathenish ignorance and barbarisme." [8] Among these adventurers were tenants employed by rich men to work lands they could not themselves manage and who did not mind exposing others to the terrors of the wilderness. Newcomers without social connections in the center sometimes settled on the outlands too. The town plot residents in Waterbury were almost entirely first settlers and their descendants, while immigrants from other towns opened the north and northeast sections.[9] Other outdwellers were prominent men, such as Richard Hubbell of Fairfield, a representative to the General Court, who was at odds with one of the town's leading families, the Burrs.[10] Some were religious dissenters, Baptists or Anglicans, who felt uneasy close to the dominant church. James Rogers, father of the founder of the Rogerenes and an enemy of the Winthrops, first settled Great Neck in New London, an area where, later, Baptists of various sorts congregated.[11]

The majority of settlers probably were ordinary men who eventually tired of the long trips to their lands, but they were not a cross-section of the town. The impulse to exchange land with other townsmen so as to bunch acreage in one section tended to leave the rich in the town center as the poor moved

[7] Steiner, 166-167, 170. In 1672 Guilford gave a five-acre premium to families that settled on their new dividend instead of staying in town (Steiner, 172). New Haven's Wallingford and Stratford's Woodbury were carefully supervised.

[8] *Conn. Recs.*, II, 328.

[9] S. W. Adams and H. R. Stiles, *Wethersfield*, I, 189-190, 159-162; Bronson, *Waterbury*, 245.

[10] Hubbell's wife was convicted of selling strong drink without a license, an offense common among outlivers, in a court where John Burr presided. In a rage, Hubbell charged Burr's wife with the same misdemeanor and was thrown out of court for spiting the judge (Fairfield County, "Records of the County Court," I, 200, 204).

[11] Bolles and Williams, *Rogerenes*, 149; Caulkins, *New London*, 202.

to the outlands. Wealthy settlers could afford to buy up the more expensive improved land strategically located near their own home lots and thus assemble more easily worked farms, while poor men gladly sold their central lands and purchased less expensive farms on the outskirts, thereby doubling the size of their holdings. The General Court early forbade this practice, but the law was not enforced. Everyone desired to concentrate his lands, and economic exigencies dictated that the poor should go to the outlands.[12]

All outlivers were to a degree at variance with the community and with the ideal of social order, for they chose to promote their economic interests at the expense of their spiritual welfare. The migration from the town plot involved only those who valued their lands and cattle or their independence more than church worship and participation in community life. When outlivers complained of "the trouble and Danger . . . they are Exposed too by Coming over to the publike worship," the residents in Hartford unsympathetically declared that the outlivers "could not butt forsee" this difficulty before they settled so far away.[13] Springfield, plagued by the same problem up the river in Massachusetts, reminded its outlivers that riding "six miles in a half a Day is more than equal to half a Day's Labour." Since the outlying settlers avoid this travel, they "live with much more Ease and Less Fateague, then those who live in the center of the Parish; who besides the Fateague they have in managing their business at a Distance all the week, are obliged to build and maintain Three Large vessles to Transport the Produce of Their Lands to the stores." [14] Implicit in both of these statements is a rebuke for having preferred convenience to proximity to the meetinghouse. Too often, it was feared, subordination to God was a lesser concern of those who left town to live in the wilderness. As a pamphlet on the problem charged, they "make the Gains of the World their main Aim, End and Design." [15]

[12] *Conn. Recs.,* I, 562-563. In Guilford in 1645 the exchange rate was five to three and two to one, depending on the distance from town (Steiner, *Guilford,* 167).

[13] *Hartford Town Votes,* 236.

[14] Meyer, *Church and State,* 40-41; cf. Conn. Arch., Ecclesiastical Affairs, I, 106, 124; *Conn. Recs.,* IV, 136-137.

[15] *A Word of Advice,* 1-2. From the very beginning the town fathers

Even when the centrifugal movement had become common-place, an aura of dissent remained with the outlivers. A poem composed in the south end of East Windsor during the forming of a new society and addressed to the suspicious disclosed the hidden feelings of the old parish:

> You do account that we Rebel
> And Siscems we do Make
> Thus are we in the talker's mouths
> And of us they do spake.
>
> As if that some new sectary
> We did intend to bring
> We never had the least intent
> To practise such a thing.[16]

The persons most in need of the restraining influence of governing institutions were usually the first to leave, and the town fathers were understandably reluctant to countenance departures to the outlands when the motives of the migrants were so frequently suspect.

In the sequel, the rulers' qualms proved well grounded. Not only was the supervision of the outlivers sporadic and uncertain, but the homogeneity of the town was destroyed. As the interests of inhabitants located in two centers instead of one began to conflict, the town found itself involved in a series of controversies from which its effectiveness as a unit of government inevitably suffered. The outlivers in New London, for example, disliked supporting the town school, which was held in the central plot so far away from them that their children could not easily attend, and felt that they should receive part of an educational endow-

---

perceived carnal motives in the migrations from established settlements. The Cambridge Platform observed the ruin of churches caused by unwarranted departures and severely limited the legitimate grounds for separation. Churches should recognize, the Platform said, only real want of subsistence and not pretended want.

> To separate from a Church, eyther out of contempt of their holy fellowship, or out of covetousness, or for greater inlargements with just greif to the church; or out of schisme, or want of love; and out of a spirit of contention in respect of some unkindness, or some evill only conceived . . . is unlawful and sinfull (W. Walker, *Creeds and Platforms,* 224-225).

[16] H. R. Stiles, *Windsor,* I, 560.

ment fund earlier given to the town and maintain a teacher of
their own. When the town refused, the outlying farmers united
to elect their own candidate as head townsman. Other towns
fought over the same problem. Waterbury divided frequently on
the school issue and other matters, and the outlivers began to
nominate a slate in advance of the election to assure the selection
of sympathetic town officers.[17]

Contentions also arose over the selection of train band officers.
Some militia elections were so hotly contested that the Court
would not confirm the choice. Soldiers withdrew in disgust from
one band in the town and trained with another. Though the
exact issues behind all the disputes are not clear, in Stonington
the contested election pitted men from an outlying district against
men in the town plot. In 1702 widespread strife in the militia
forced the General Assembly to pass a bill establishing the order
of superiority among the train bands organized in various sections
of the major towns.[18] Apparently the outlivers wanted equal
standing in military affairs and would not relent until the Assembly intervened to control the rivalry for precedence that was
disrupting the peace.

Beginning in the late 1670's and in unbroken succession thereafter, quarrels over the locations of new meetinghouses upset
virtually every community, fully displaying the animosities between
town center and outlivers. Both parties submitted petitions to the
General Court explaining their respective viewpoints, delaying for
years the erection of the building.[19] Some towns had to call in
a committee of the Court, at considerable expense, to arbitrate
the dispute when intensity of feeling prevented a local settlement.
The preacher of an election sermon warned that the contention

[17] Caulkins, *New London,* 390-401; Bronson, *Waterbury,* 286; cf.
Larned, *Windham,* I, 232-234; Norwich, Town Votes, 106; Windsor, "First
Congregational Church Records," I, 167; Schenck, *Fairfield,* I, 266-267;
Conn. Arch., Ecclesiastical Affairs, I, 108; Beach, *Cheshire,* 67-68; New
Haven County, "County Court Records," III, 329.

[18] H. R. Stiles, I, 620; Fitz-John Winthrop to the General Assembly,
Sept. 23, 1707, *Winthrop Papers,* pt. V, 404; *Conn. Recs.,* IV, 245, 392-393;
V, 23, 484; for other militia disputes, *ibid.,* IV, 74, 82, 321; VII, 227-228,
399; Steiner, 422.

[19] The petitions for new meetinghouses are preserved in Conn. Arch.,
Ecclesiastical Affairs. The index categorizes them by town.

had risen to such a height in some societies "as to threaten their Ruine." "Such Seeds of Prejudice, Disaffection and Variance Sown, as that many Years to come are not like to Root out." [20]

The outlivers invariably argued that new houses built on the outskirts had shifted the center of population, and that under these altered circumstances, a new site would better suit most of the inhabitants. But, however sincere these petitions, more than that was at stake. Nearness to the town center measured the prestige of a house lot and controlled property values; the cost of land in the center of town had always exceeded peripheral values, sometimes even doubling them. Town leaders, the rich, and the influential had built their homes near the meetinghouse, and a shift in location would inevitably depreciate their property and rapidly appreciate outlying lands. Farmers who had benefited from an exchange when the differential was great saw the possibility of having their cake and eating it too.

Land values near the meetinghouse also went up because the central juncture of town roads was the business center, where farmers met and traded and where merchants most easily sold their goods.[21] With highways expensive and troublesome to keep up, a single focus was necessary, and town meetings felt obligated to lay out highways that would serve farmers on their way to worship. When a meetinghouse went up on a new site, roads planned to some other place were redirected toward the new center, and the value of nearby lands increased.[22]

If the committee from the Court located the meetinghouse apart from the established center of interest, part of the community suffered. When one committee openly expressed its intention to start a new business center by moving public worship, the irate householders who had enjoyed the advantages of proximity

[20] S. Whittelsey, *A Publick Spirit*, 42-43.

[21] The English churchyard was likewise a place for conducting business (Campbell, *English Yeoman*, 298).

[22] Larned, *Windham*, I, 532. The Court ordered Stonington to build roads to a meetinghouse (Caulkins, *New London*, 251; cf. Conn. Arch., Travel, II, 42). Advertisements of property for sale often pointed out that the land was on a road or near a meetinghouse where convenient for a merchant or tradesman (*Connecticut Gazette*, Oct. 1, 1757; March 21, 1761; April 4, 1761; Aug. 22, 1761).

to the old center rose in anger against this threat. And after a commission had settled a Hadley meetinghouse at a distance from the "center of travel," the old residents industriously tore down the frame of the new building as fast as it was put up.[23]

By the time the outlivers were numerous enough to block the erection of a new meetinghouse, it was apparent that they were bent on creating a new community in the outlands. Relocating the place for public worship only temporarily slowed their efforts to achieve independence. In time the town granted them a train band, a school, and a constable, and permitted them to hire a preacher during the winter when travel was especially hazardous. By the 1680's the outlivers in the larger towns began requesting liberty to establish their own parishes, and thereafter every town followed this pattern as the populations on the outskirts grew.

The inhabitants on the periphery exhibited an extraordinary zeal for founding new churches, for independent new towns were notoriously tardy in setting up public worship. Waterbury, for example, did not settle a minister for twenty years after its foundation.[24] Disturbed by such recalcitrance, Cotton Mather pleaded with new settlements to organize a church no matter what the cost.[25] The outlivers in old towns, by contrast, wanted to support a church even before they were financially capable of doing so. While the mother society bewailed the hardship of increased taxes if the outlivers received parish privileges, the outlying farmers themselves bravely insisted on their ability to pay. Poquonock in Windsor, for example, asked for independence when its estates were but £2,000, and the assessments on the remainder of the town amounted to £9,000.[26] The prospect of greatly increased rates, despite the common dislike of taxes, did not deter the movement for a new society.

The motives behind the petitions for independent parishes were the same as in the meetinghouse disputes: desires for more convenient worship and for improved property values. The need

---

[23] Larned, *Windham*, I, 91, 335-340, 525; *Conn. Recs.*, IX, 493; Judd, *Hadley*, 391-393.

[24] Bronson, *Waterbury*, 203.

[25] *Letter from a Gentleman*, 15; *A Word of Advice*, 5.

[26] Conn. Arch., Ecclesiastical Affairs, III, 79; see also *ibid.*, III, 98; XI, 61.

for highways was becoming acute, and the settlers wanted parishes of their own to help improve the situation. The roads laid out by the town, which radiated from the center like spokes from a hub, served the inhabitants in the central plot but were ill-suited for people on the periphery, who often traveled along the circumference, not along lines leading into the center. Moreover, the town had seen no cause to lay out highways to facilitate travel among lots scattered along its outer edge, which hindered everyday work and thwarted the outlivers' yearning for communication with their neighbors. Thè outlivers resorted to cutting across lots to their property or to visit friends, and so frequent were trespasses that the Assembly forbade passage over land where there was no road.[27]

Petitions for highways repeatedly came up in town meeting but were often disregarded. Giving roads to the outlying farmers simply deepened the separation from the community of a group already suspected of disloyalty. Moreover, to lay out and maintain new highways cost the town land and time, and the owners of the requisitioned land objected to highways which increased fencing requirements and left smaller, less easily worked lots. In town meeting proprietors fought hard against the petitions for roads through their outlands.[28]

Once the outlivers obtained a meetinghouse, they could demand

[27] *Conn. Recs.*, IV, 99; cf. Conn. Arch., Travel, I, 38a, 53a, 94a-b; Conn. Arch., Ecclesiastical Affairs, III, 205. The plight of the outlying farmers is illustrated by a petition from Mortlake, an area inhabited by people without town privileges. Like outlivers, residents of Mortlake lacked government power to lay out roads suited to their needs. Once the private domain of Governor Belcher, the tract had never been attached to any town, nor did it pay country rates. Most of the twenty or so inhabitants had "considerable farms and improvements and large stocks of cattle and horses," but suffered from one great handicap. "Not being annexed to any town," they had "no convenient highways, and cannot be compelled to lay out nor mend highways." And they lacked a center. The law said, they pleaded, "that there shall be a sign-post near the centre of each town," but in Mortlake there was none. Though they must then pay rates, they asked to be given to Pomfret so that they could pay taxes "and have a sign-post erected" (Larned, *Windham*, I, 519; Conn. Arch., Towns and Lands, VIII, 222, 225).

[28] I. S. Mitchell, *Roads*, 5-6; Hartford North Meadow Proprietors to the General Assembly, *Wyllys Papers*, 260-261; Conn. Arch., Travel, I, 86b, 302a; II, 10b, 29b, 70a-b, 102c.

better highways. As soon as Thompson parish was set off in Killingly, for example, a flood of requests for roads to the new meetinghouse came in,[29] and the town could hardly deny them when the petitioners ostensibly wanted to ease travel to worship. Foreseeing all that was involved, Farmington agreed to a new society in its bounds, "provided that they shall for their own proportion of labour in the highwayes make and maintain the passages and highwayes they have ocasion for there amongst themselves without involving the towne in generall therewith." [30] If town meeting or county court, where disputes were settled, disregarded the request for highways, the outlivers confidently called on the General Court to order roads to public worship.[31] The government was bound to nurture the piety of all inhabitants, and the sincere desire for convenient access to the meetinghouse coincided with the social and economic need for reoriented roads.

More important than any prudential concerns, however, separation from the town church brought social and psychological independence. The outlivers knew that a parish of their own would remove them from the constant surveillance of the town rulers. Absolved of the responsibility to sit in the central meetinghouse, outlivers could escape the social if not the legal force of authority that radiated from the rulers' persons. Moreover, they would not legally be subject to the discipline of their old minister and of the church dominated by the town fathers. In their outland meetinghouse they could elect their own officers and administer their own discipline. They would themselves be rulers.

The requests were urgent and unrelenting because independence promised great satisfaction. The act of demanding liberty was itself pleasing. Not often could lesser men stand up to their fathers and ask for independence, and the arguments for parish

[29] Larned, *Windham,* I.

[30] *Conn. Recs.,* IV, 528.

[31] *Conn. Recs.,* IV, 314; VII, 130-131, 373-376, 377, 397; East Windsor, "First Ecclesiastical Society, Records," I, 3; I. S. Mitchell, 7; for petitions to the county court, see, for example, Windham County, "Records," VIII, 31, 60, 72, 76, 89, 90, 112, 141, 148, 172, 173, 188, 219, 240, 254, 255, 301, 312, 327, 328, 349, 374, 375, 417, 451, 453; Conn. Arch., Travel, I, 112a; II, 29a-b, 30; for a town sending agents to the Court to oppose a petition for highways, see "Norwich Town Book," 122, 165; *Conn. Recs.,* VIII, 240-298, 474.

privileges were unassailable. It was almost impossible to impugn the motives for separation when petitioners introduced their request by saying:

Apprehending it inconsistant with the designs of our fathers who came into this wilderness that they might injoy the ordinances of God in peace without disturbance . . . that wee should be thereby deprived of the liberty of quietly enjoing god in his ordinances. . . .[32]

Protected by such weighty invocations of the past, the outlivers felt wholly justified in appealing for independence.

Impelled by these complicated motives, outlivers at the end of the seventeenth century began to submit their requests for separation. The first of them met sturdy opposition from the old town residents who mistrusted the intentions of the "handfull of contencious persons" asking for separation.[33] How could the town leaders be sure that this doubtful band of outdwellers would exercise appropriate watch and care over each other, disciplining transgressors and silencing schismatics? What might be the fate of a church in the hands of people who had not scrupled to leave the village nucleus the better to work their lands? One parish received permission to separate, "provided they take care to keep good order in their meetings, and do not neglect to attend the worship of God where they shall agree to meet."[34] Though the ostensible reason for the new society was to ease travel to worship, the towns questioned the sincerity of the intentions. Repeatedly the meeting specified that the new parish must pay rates to the old until a minister was hired.[35]

Opposition to separation also arose because the towns stood to lose a large portion of their taxpayers, thus raising for the remaining residents their proportionate share in the minister's rate. The outdwellers themselves, of course, would no longer contribute, but initially the legal privileges of the town confused the issue in such a way that the inhabitants feared an even

[32] Conn. Arch., Ecclesiastical Affairs, I, 87.
[33] The quoted phrase came up in Fairfield's first separation (Conn. Arch., Ecclesiastical Affairs, I, 125).
[34] Fairfield, "Town Records," B, pt. 2, 276.
[35] For example, Norwich, Town Votes, 127; Conn. Arch., Ecclesiastical Affairs, III, 76.

greater loss. Since towns were privileged to tax all lands within their bounds, the center was apprehensive that parishes would receive the same power and would then collect taxes on property owned by members of the old society, most of whom had farms in the outlands, thus drastically reducing the old parish's revenue.

This prospect enraged Nathan Gold, a colony magistrate from Fairfield. The Court, he said, had granted a township and confirmed it by patent which "wholy reserves to us the inhabitants, all the proffits comodityes, bennifits, priviledges and advantages accruing with Saide Towneship." How then was it possible "without the towns consent, that this Corte shall be able legally to put in so much as there little finger to interpose or medle in any of the prudentiall concerns of our Towne, without apparent violating and brekeing our just and legall libertyes, in an arbitrary manner?" Was it just "that this, one of your first born, a lovely beautiful child, should be disinherited and lose its birthright to an inferior brat?" [36]

Thunderbolts like this did not stop the intrepid outdwellers. Nor did they permanently prevent the Court from dividing the old society, for the petitioners' arguments were composed of the most sacred elements of their tradition. They desired to worship God in peace as had their fathers who left England for the wilderness. Turning the charge of worldliness back upon their opposers, the outdwellers could exclaim with wonder at the controversy raised by their fellow parishioners "only to make their Taxes a little lighter." "We cannot think ourselves justly treated by them," the petition went on, "when they take so much pains to keep us under Such Disadvantages in our Souls concern only to save themselves a little worldly interest." [37]

The Court listened sympathetically to these appeals and eventually bestowed parish privileges on virtually every group of appropriate size which applied. The advancement of religion ranked above all other considerations. To satisfy the opposition, the Court initially empowered the old society to tax lands owned by its residents in both new parish and old, thus exempting the lands

[36] Conn. Arch., Ecclesiastical Affairs, I, 125.
[37] Conn. Arch., Ecclesiastical Affairs, I, 87; II, 62a; Schenck, II, 78-79; Meyer, 41.

owned by center residents, a substantial portion of the whole, from the new society's rates.[38]

The outlivers in Fairfield who joined with nearby inhabitants in Stratford in 1690 to ask for a distinct parish formed the first group to follow the pattern that later became standard for separating societies.[39] As innovators, the Fairfield residents met unusual resistance to their petition, because, apart from the tax problem, the few previous petitions for parish privileges had been only a prelude to requests for full town liberties. The dwellers in what became the town of Preston, for example, began the process of complete separation by complaining of difficulties in attending worship in Norwich.[40] Fairfield wished to block this attempt among their outlivers, because the town stood to lose control of the lands in the new parish. At this time the undivided lands of a town were still thought to belong to the inhabitants as a corporate group, and when the town split, the inhabitants in each portion owned the lands in their part. Glastonbury divided from Wethersfield in 1690, having asked merely for parish privileges the year before, and the inhabitants of the mother town lost all rights to future land dividends in the area occupied by the new community.[41] Fairfield was unwilling to permit its outlivers to become a parish until certain that the lands in the new religious society would not be lost to the town.[42]

The Court soon removed this obstacle to the formation of parishes in Fairfield and elsewhere by adopting the settled policy that parish privileges were not a step toward complete independence and that religious societies were not to control undivided lands within their bounds. The parish in east Windsor, for example, asked for town privileges in 1697, six years after organization as a parish, and was denied. When the eastern part of New Haven, set apart as a village in the late 1670's after enjoying parish privileges for some years, aspired to control the common lands within its bounds, the court ruled that this power was not

[38] Schenck, II, 27; H. R. Stiles, I, 552; Conn. Arch., Ecclesiastical Affairs, II, 63; Conn. Recs., IV, 136-137.
[39] Schenck, I, 263-264.
[40] Conn. Recs., III, 220-221; First Congregational Church of Preston, 14-15.
[41] S. W. Adams and H. R. Stiles, I, 194; II, 905.
[42] Conn. Arch., Ecclesiastical Affairs, I, 108, 124.

within the province of a village.[43] Perhaps foreseeing a similar development in Hartford, the Court warned the east side residents that "common land on that side the river are not intended to belong to that society." [44] After the turn of the century the limitations on parish privileges were clarified, and town centers no longer raised objections to separation on this score.

Not everyone in the town center regretted the establishment of a new parish. Many of the residents sent their sons and daughters to the outlands to make their homes and approved the erection of a meetinghouse nearby. After 1700 new societies multiplied. Any settlement with fifty or sixty families and estates totaling £4,000 could qualify. Once the General Court had estimated that a group of farmers could pay for a meetinghouse and minister, they were granted society privileges. The erection of parishes within the town became a routine procedure, and as time went on, the parish assumed more and more the responsibilities of a self-contained community. Besides its own school and train band, the parish elected constables, surveyors of highways, and sometimes listers and tithingmen. The society chose a clerk, a treasurer, and a managing committee and collected the minister's rate.[45] The outlivers had in a large measure attained their independence.

This achievement did not wholly dissipate the hostility between old parish and new. Squabbles arose, for example, over dividing taxable lands, because newly created parishes bore a heavy tax load. Besides paying a minister's salary, they faced the expense of settling a pastor—at a cost of £100 or more—plus the cost of a meetinghouse. Many societies applied for a temporary cessation of colony rates until they had the unusual expenses of establishing a church behind them.[46] To increase their incomes, some parishes wrangled with the central society over dividing lines, hoping to enlarge taxable lands and thus diminish the rate

[43] H. R. Stiles, I, 551, 556; *Conn. Recs.*, V, 176-177.

[44] *Conn. Recs.*, IV, 381-382.

[45] Norwich, "Proprietor Records," votes for the year, 1723, and p. 3; *Conn. Recs.*, V, 71, 552; VI, 33-34; Schenck, II, 253.

[46] See, for example, Conn. Arch., Ecclesiastical Affairs, I, 127, 130; II, 305; III, 106; Schenck, II, 93.

for each individual. Others looked enviously on parsonage property devoted to support of the town's pastor. New societies argued that these lands belonged to the entire town and that when the town divided, the lands should be similarly divided too, but the old societies claimed that the new parishes relinquished corporate ownership in church possessions when they separated. Often a compromise allocated a small portion of the property to the new society, but for years the issue rankled both sides.[47]

More flammable still was the question of taxes on the parish lands of outsiders. The first new parishes in the colony were forbidden to tax nonresident owners, and the new societies complained that some men abused this privilege by building houses and barns on their lands in the parish and living there from Monday to Saturday, returning to town only for the Sabbath. Seeing some men effectually dwelling in the new society while they paid rates to the old, other residents threatened to follow the same practice and escape the heavier tax burdens in the new parish.[48]

In 1735 the Assembly ruled that landowners who lived outside the town had to pay taxes to the society which contained their property. Likewise, those who lived in one parish and rented their property in another had to pay where the tenant lived.[49] But this compromise did not end the strife: those who hoped to escape onerous ministers' rates still moved over the border, and new societies continued to seek increases in their total list by taxing all nonresident proprietors whether they had rented their lands or not. Arguing that values appreciated because of the church, the new parish thought that all land so benefiting should contribute. Proprietors dwelling in the old parish countered with the assertion that since they did not attend worship in the new society and must pay for their own pastor, they could not in justice be rated. No satisfactory settlement emerged, and mother

[47] See, for example, Schenck, II, 99, 114, 115; *Conn. Recs.*, IV, 528; Conn. Arch., Ecclesiastical Affairs, VII, 172a, 294a, 294b; Fairfield, "Town Records," B, pt. I, 1732, 1733/34, 1755; H. R. Stiles, I, 278, Bronson, *Waterbury*, 229-230, 240.

[48] Conn. Arch., Ecclesiastical Affairs, II, 194.

[49] *Conn. Recs.*, VII, 555-556.

and daughter parishes in town after town carried on the argument, further irritating their prickly relationship.[50]

The antagonisms between the outlivers and the residents in the old town center were in turn duplicated in the new parish, within whose bounds other communities arose, demanding the same privileges and meeting the same resistance its parent had. Districts were formed to supervise schools and highways within parishes, and residents on the edge of the new societies joined in protests against the meetinghouse location, asked for winter privileges, and often became independent parishes. So long as population grew and plots of unoccupied land remained, new societies multiplied. Norwich, for example, a century after its founding in 1660, had added seven churches to the original society.[51]

As a consequence, sections of the town virtually inaccessible for exploitation in the beginning now opened for settlement. With little inhibition people scattered over the township in the confidence that before long a meetinghouse would go up nearby. If a group in some corner of the town was not large enough to form a society by themselves, the Court joined them to settlers over the border in the next town. Society boundaries sometimes encompassed portions of three towns.[52]

Canterbury objected to one such combination, explaining that the town's inhabitants had dispersed themselves in the expectation of soon dividing. If part of their town joined a section of Norwich, the planned division would be impracticable, and distant settlers would suffer. Their complaint illustrated the diminishing social significance of parish bounds: instead of representing a natural geographical unit, the society's limits were haphazard and

[50] Larned, *Windham,* I, 97; Conn. Arch., Ecclesiastical Affairs, VI, 7, 10; VII, 158, 160, 168a, 168b; VIII, 354-357; 2nd ser., IV, 164; "Norwich Town Book," 170; East Windsor, "First Ecclesiastical Society, Records," I, 3; Bozrah, "Ecclesiastical Society, Records," II, 10.

[51] In 1734 precincts with winter privileges were given the power to levy taxes, distrain, and choose a collector and clerk (*Conn. Recs.,* VII, 493). The Assembly decided in 1748 to transfer the responsibility for locating meetinghouses to the county courts (*ibid.,* VII, 334-336; IX, 398-399); Caulkins, *Norwich,* 275.

[52] Conn. Arch., Ecclesiastical Affairs, VIII, 58; XI, 214; Larned, *Windham,* I, 78-79; South Windsor, "First Congregational Church, Records," I, 109-111; Caulkins, *Norwich,* 444.

arbitrary.[53] Convention and theology required that people worship, but many in the congregation might logically have associated elsewhere.

The formation of new parishes loosened the social order of the town in many ways. In each new community each individual had to find his place in the ranks of society, for only a sprinkling of the former town leaders lived among them to fill the new positions. With openings of all sorts available, who was to move up? Who was to organize the petition for winter privileges and then parish privileges? Who was to be clerk of the society and serve on its committee? Who should be elected officers of the new train band? In what order should the meetinghouse be seated? Each of these social decisions represented an opportunity for individual advancement. The physical mobility of the outdwellers gave them a degree of social mobility as well.

On the other hand, malcontents who preferred not to participate in community life now found it easier to withdraw. The position of borderline residents remained unclear for years. Families in one parish often petitioned for attachment to another, and while such cases remained unsettled, neither one society nor the other was responsible for them.[54] The creation of new parishes relaxed the grip of the town on its residents, and the disaffected could locate in out-of-the-way corners, out of sight of the leaders and only vaguely connected to one society or another.

Moreover, the resentments of the discontented found an outlet in the demands of the new parish. In the meetinghouse contentions men tense with animosities confined by social forms directed their hatreds against the town leaders. Taking courage in the legitimate needs of their society, outdwellers loaded their stifled anger into the petitions for privileges. Participants in a separation controversy in Windsor told the court that they foresaw a great "Disturbing [of] the Peace of Societyes to the Disadvantage of Religion by breaking that Love and Friendship that aught to be in Every Community." [55]

That a group within the town spoke in protest at all showed

[53] Conn. Arch., Ecclesiastical Affairs, XI, 119; VII, 126-127, 130-132.
[54] Conn. Arch., Ecclesiastical Affairs, VII, 136a; XI, 55.
[55] Conn. Arch., Ecclesiastical Affairs, XII, 74.

the decline in power of the old order. In the beginning the political, economic, social, ecclesiastical, and military structures were virtually one. Since leaders in one dimension led in all others as well, the influence of church, town meeting, and train band joined to govern the people. After distinct societies arose in the town, the ecclesiastical and social order separated from the political, and the interests of one group ran counter to those of another. As the leaders of one community went to battle with the leaders of another, the overwhelming power of a unanimous social consensus was broken. The loyalties of each individual were divided between the town meeting possessing economic and political control and the parish invested with ecclesiastical jurisdiction. Since the loyalties of each group to some extent nullified one another, a person's total attachment to any community whatsoever diminished. In the interstices, where neither society had complete command, men found enlarged freedom and the possibility of new ways of life.

V

New Plantations

~§ AFTER 1690 MEN LOOKED with increasing intensity for new lands in the wilderness. The same pressures that drove people to the outlands eventually drove them from the town. Seeking space for their sons or for increased production, they spilled over the town bounds into unsettled areas. Those excluded from proprietorship of the remaining town lands hoped to attain in new plantations the economic advantages and the social position of the more privileged.

The towns opened for settlement after the turn of the century were not, however, replicas of those first established in Connecticut. Land was not so easily acquired, nor were individuals bound so effectively to the community. Private proprietorship of undivided land and the scattering of population vitiated the social power of new plantations. Migrants were not absorbed into a society that comprehensively ruled the lives of its members, and, by the same token, men could not achieve the stability once characteristic of community life.

The new form of proprietorship implied in the patents of 1685 crippled certain powers of later towns. Those settled after 1690 accepted private ownership of undivided land as a legal necessity and thereby lost corporate control; title ceased to reside in the town as a corporation after the patents of 1685 conveyed the undivided town lands to the inhabitants as fee-simple estates in the legal form of tenancy in common. Repeated declarations in the ensuing years underscored the proprietors' rights to town lands as "an undoubted lawful estate of inheritance to them and their heirs." [1] The patentees thereafter could sell or will their

[1] *Conn. Recs.*, VI, 395; cf. IV, 433; Josiah Rosseter *et al.* to Robert Treat, Nov. 7, 1703, *Winthrop Papers*, pt. V, 163. The Court's desire to

dividend rights to anyone, whether an admitted inhabitant or not.

The transfer of title from the town to individual proprietors opened enticing possibilities soon to be exploited. After 1690, for example, proprietors' rights could be sold as they could not be earlier. In the eighteenth-century town, lands were assigned to a fixed number of persons who owned their rights as real property. The exact number of acres belonging to a proprietor could be calculated even before the land was divided, and he could legally sell his share or leave it to his children. If he moved away, he retained the right to future dividends, which were as negotiable as a share in a ship cargo or in a manufacturing enterprise. As a result, a proprietor's right before long was obtainable only for a price.

Earlier there had occasionally been some small cost in settling when land was granted by the town meeting or, if the plantation was just beginning, by the committee of the General Court. Though towns often charged the inhabitants for clearing the Indian title and laying out lots—Woodbury until 1693 required that all new residents pay a part of past expenses, and by Court order new settlers in Ashford paid a proportion of the cost of surveying and opening the town[2]—neither the Court nor the town sought to derive revenue from land sales, and the fees attached to admission were small. The chief requisite for becoming an inhabitant was social respectability not capital.

By the end of the century procedures had begun to change. The private proprietorship of town tracts, which removed legal obstacles while increasing demand raised the price of land, provided opportunities for speculators. More and more planting towns became profitmaking enterprises for those privileged to supervise them. Around 1680 the sites of what became Windham and Lebanon fell into the hands of men who proceeded to settle

---

establish fee simple title is disclosed in a declaration of 1686 stating that where county courts in distributions to legatees may have neglected to mention that lands belonged to them, "their heires and assignes forever," the custom of the country intended this meaning (*Conn. Recs.*, III, 217). For the whole story of the 1685 patents, see Chap. III.

[2] Hollister, *Connecticut*, I, 255; Cothren, *Woodbury*, 77; *Conn. Recs.*, IV, 537-538; cf. Hurd, *New London County*, 388.

them with Court approval. The Windham proprietors in 1682 acknowledged that they had to seek the proper ends of plantation work and agreed to ask reasonable terms for proprietor rights. Nonetheless, Richard Bushnell, one of the owners, shortly sold his rights to a thousand acres for £10 10s, not a huge sum, the price of three steers or a horse, but certainly more than his proportion of the planting expenses.[3] The profits were small, but an important precedent had been set: owners of a new town had been allowed to sell the land at a profit.

The General Court for a time discouraged commercialization, sensing a responsibility to distribute the colony lands to the people freely. The Assembly, for example, permitted Durham proprietors to charge for house lots in recompense for laying out and purchasing the town but required that "the land be sold at a reasonable price." [4] Speculation was not to interfere with orderly settlement.

The civil government itself, however, was soon compelled to derive income from land sales. The drain on the treasury for military expenses after 1700 and the popular demand for land persuaded the Assembly to raise revenue from the colony's wilderness reserve. In 1712 the Court ordered land between Fairfield and Danbury sold at auction "to the advantage of the publick treasury which is much exhausted." [5] Returns on sales at Stafford were requisitioned in 1718 for building the state house in Hartford.[6] The Assembly finally agreed to devote the proceeds from a large tract in the northwest to schools and, after hearing two schemes for fair distribution, decided in 1737 that no better method could be devised than to auction shares in the townships, starting at prices ranging from £30 to £60. Six towns were laid out and proprietor rights sold, usually at double or triple the minimum price,[7] the colony realizing a substantial income from the

[3] Larned, *Windham*, I, 64, 66.

[4] Fowler, *Durham*, 14-15; cf. Gov. Law to Johnson, January 1744, Samuel Johnson, *Samuel Johnson*, I, 114.

[5] *Conn. Recs.*, V, 333; cf. *ibid.*, V, 180; VI, 63-64.

[6] *Conn. Recs.*, VI, 91; Willington in 1720 was sold to eight men for £510 (B. Trumbull, *Connecticut*, II, 64).

[7] *Conn. Recs.*, VII, 134-137; IX, 508; Deming, *Settlement of Litchfield County*, 8.

venture. Meanwhile land magnates authorized to lay out townships they owned profited similarly from sales to settlers.

After the practice of selling proprietary rights became legally feasible, speculation in new towns spread. The majority of the purchasers of shares in Kent in the northwest never settled personally but bought for resale. Even those who did settle profited from their purchase: since their initial holdings were at least 1,000 acres, far more than they could use personally, they were bound to sell some and benefit from skyrocketing prices. Virtually everyone who moved to Kent, along with his relatives and many settlers in neighboring towns, speculated in land. When proprietary rights could be bought on credit and prices were certain to go up because of inflation and an expanding population, hundreds frantically bought and sold.[8]

The speculative spirit undermined the order that had earlier been the primary goal of Connecticut towns. Men caught up in speculation were less willing than formerly to settle down to the steady routine of farming and become stable members of the community. Though one speculator in western Connecticut, the largest landowner in his town who could nevertheless not content himself with his farm and tavern, was often elected to important town offices, he left after a dozen years when the General Assembly refused to cooperate in his slightly dishonest schemes to obtain still more land. Economic forces inexorably increased population turnover when profits were made more quickly by buying and selling land than by farming it.[9]

More serious was the altered relationship of the individual to the community under the eighteenth-century system of proprietary purchases. Seventeenth-century land grants had bound the inhabitants to the town, and the vote of admission carried with it solid benefits; farmers depended on the town to enlarge their marketable surpluses and hence identified themselves with the village which provided them the surest avenue to prosperity. This tie was broken when the distribution of land became solely the function of private

[8] C. S. Grant, *Democracy in the Connecticut Frontier Town of Kent*, 14, 58-59.
[9] C. S. Grant, 18, 48-51. Grant believes that Kent was more stable than frontier towns have ordinarily been pictured, but he agrees that there was considerable speculation and that peeople moved in and out frequently.

proprietors. Some new settlers purchased the right to participate in the quasipublic body controlling the undivided land, while others bought land from older residents without obtaining dividend rights. In each transaction money was at the nexus. The inhabitant owned land not by virtue of the town's benevolence, but because he had paid for his acres. His involvement in the community was less an engagement to a social and religious commonweal than participation in a company of landowners.

Private proprietorship also altered the eighteenth-century towns by increasing the number of nonresidents who purchased proprietor rights with no intention of moving to the new plantation.[10] Nonresident proprietors had earlier been unusual, since the meeting consistently stipulated that men admitted and granted land must move to the plantation, failure to settle resulting in forfeiture of the grant. One of the first rules made in the Hartford town meeting required that anyone who moved away must return his allotted lands to the town.[11] Admitted inhabitants at Derby were to build houses on their lots and move to town within two years; otherwise, the town had "power to dispose of the sayd lands and homestead to such as will come and settle with them." [12]

The town had also excluded nonresidents from rights to the undivided lands. Dividend rights could not be purchased by outsiders or inherited by sons who moved away. A share in the periodic divisions could be obtained only by formal admission, which the town never granted to nonresidents. When patents for town lands were issued in 1685, they granted the undivided tracts to the "proprietors inhabitants" of the towns, assuming that none but actual residents would have any claim.[13]

The elimination of corporate ownership removed the legal obstacles to nonresident ownership of dividend rights. Since anyone

[10] The effects of nonresidency have probably been exaggerated, at least in Connecticut's case. In most instances the nonresidents were not greedy speculators monopolizing land and frustrating the plans of resident farmers to develop their plantation. Often they were relatives of the inhabitants or residents in nearby frontier towns who understood the problems of new settlements and willingly cooperated to advance the plantation.

[11] Hartford Town Votes, I.

[12] Conn. Recs., II, 303; cf. Cothren, Woodbury, 39-40; Deming, Settlement of Connecticut Towns, 50; Conn. Recs., I, 351; III, 10, 42; Town Records of Derby, 15, 16, 29, 30, 31, 32, 37.

[13] Conn. Recs., III, 177-178.

could purchase the town's undivided lands, wherever he lived, the number of nonresident proprietors increased steadily. The Durham patent of 1708 was given to "inhabitants and proprietors"—implying that proprietors might not be inhabitants—and specifically referred to nonresidents possessing rights to undivided lands.[14] In 1735 two Stafford men demanded a share in a land division in Norwich. Since they had been residents in 1710 when Norwich decided that the inhabitants of that year were the legal proprietors, the proprietors had to admit them to a share. The right to an allotment was an incorporeal possession that might be carried anywhere or alienated at will. Elsewhere nonresident heirs also petitioned for a share in divisions on the rights of their fathers.[15]

Not all towns concurred in this new arrangement. When a Hartford man in 1708 laid claim to land divisions in Wethersfield on the right of his father-in-law, a resident in 1693 when land had been divided, Wethersfield took the case to court and even empowered the selectmen to appeal to the Crown. It lost the case and was compelled to allow men anywhere in the colony to share in rights that formerly belonged to the inhabitants alone.[16]

Although nonresident ownership contradicted some of the old assumptions about town life, it served the purposes of many. Individuals wishing to acquire large holdings were in a position to obtain land without application to public authority, either the Assembly or the town. By purchase of division rights they could accumulate estates in new towns through land dividends without qualifying as inhabitants, and until the dividend was granted, they paid no taxes on the land due to each proprietor's right. The ambitions of speculators and wealthy men hoping to become gentlemen farmers grew more feasible as cheap wilderness land, rich in timber resources, became available to them in towns other than their own.[17]

[14] *Conn. Recs.*, V, 49-50; cf. *Town Records of Derby*, 459-466.
[15] Norwich, "Proprietor Records," 23; *Town Records of Derby*, 301; Conn. Arch., Towns and Lands, VI, 277; VII, 288.
[16] Conn. Arch., Towns and Lands, II, 259-266; Andrews tells the story in *River Towns*, 91.
[17] In 1709 one-third of Killingly patentees were nonresident (Larned, *Windham*, I, 166; cf. Deming, *Settlement of Connecticut Towns*, 50).

Another and larger group—fathers with sons who would not automatically be admitted to the body of proprietors—also took advantage of the new possibility of reserving estates in new towns. When a boy was too young to work the land, the father was not compelled to pay taxes. A large part of the land in Kent came into the possession of men who did not settle themselves but sent their sons to live there.[18]

The Assembly discouraged nonresidency as best it could. It continued to appoint committees to supervise settlement and directed them to admit "honest and well minded inhabitants." [19] Almost always the Court required buyers either to inhabit or to settle a tenant within a specified time or lose the grant. Purchasers of the colony towns in the northwest, the last tracts in the colony to be disposed of, were to settle within three years or forfeit their rights, with the provision that men with sons of sixteen years might settle them there instead. But the regulations were not always observed, as the multitude of complaints testified.[20]

In those towns where the Court demanded settlement, the purchaser himself was not required to clear the land personally and move in; he could rent his holding. The most important consideration, judging from the statute books and petitions from the towns, was the payment of taxes. Towns were forbidden to tax unimproved lands, and until the owner or his tenant began to work the farm, no revenue was derived from it.[21] This law intended to help men who received a dividend before they were able to exploit it. It seemed unfair to tax land that produced nothing, especially when the owner received it because the majority of inhabitants were ready for a new division. The towns agreed to the exemption on the assumption that the owner would pay on his other lands in the community. But in new towns large tracts of unimproved land owned by nonresidents were tax-free and hence unavailable to men who wanted to settle, work, and contribute to community charges. Purchasers waited to the last

[18] C. S. Grant, 57-58.
[19] *Conn. Recs.*, VI, 62-73; cf. *ibid.*, V, 160, 180; VI, 154-155.
[20] *Conn. Recs.*, V, 121-122, 55-56, 470; VI, 62-63; VIII, 134-137; Deming, *Settlement of Litchfield County*, 8.
[21] *Conn. Recs.*, I, 550.

minute to send a tenant, and meanwhile the town was hard put to meet expenses.

The Assembly agreed that the situation was unjust. As Governor Law explained, the colony "thought it equitable to charge the nonresident proprietors with some part" of town expenses, for the nonresidents "by the settlement of the place have the value of their lands much increased." Law's own property in one town, he said, had been purchased for £70 and was presently worth £500.[22] Accordingly, the Assembly permitted towns to tax unimproved lands within their bounds in the beginning years of their settlement, and constables were allowed to collect rates from persons located anywhere in the colony without waiting for an execution from the courts.[23]

The Assembly thus compelled nonresidents to share the financial burden of opening a new plantation, but the civil authority was not able to restore the community to its former stable and self-contained condition. In a few cases nonresidents refused to pay their taxes or to vote for highways.[24] More important, landownership and inhabitancy no longer went together. Proprietors induced tenants to work the land until a son took it over or until a propitious moment to sell arrived. The renters, though not numerous, were a disturbing element in the community, since they were less subject to government than residents with a firm attachment to the social order; their corrupting influence on the young people and their enjoyment of "tavern-haunting" worried the town fathers.[25] The Assembly could rectify the inequities in nonresidents' tax schedules, but it could not repair the damage to government from the introduction of tenants. All these flaws in the communal order—speculation, nonresidency, the removal of the town meeting's power to grant land—appeared in new plantations because of private control of town lands.

In addition to all this, the move to the outlands that had split older parishes indirectly hurt new plantations too. By distorting the

[22] Law to Johnson, January 1744, Samuel Johnson, *Samuel Johnson*, I, 114; Johnson to W.S. Johnson, June 11, 1755, *ibid.*, I, 219.

[23] *Conn. Recs.*, II, 301, 305, 309; IV, 137, 416; V, 284, 321-332, 322, 356, 382, 469; VI, 154, 208, 216, 123, 465, 541.

[24] Conn. Arch., Towns and Lands, IV, 105; VII, 260-261.

[25] Conn. Arch., Towns and Lands, VI, 146, 356; VII, 21-22, 369-370.

plan of settlement, the impulse to live in the outlands weakened the social power of eighteenth-century communities. Farmers scattered all over the new townships, free of the surveillance of the town dignitaries.

Foreseeing the splits that would occur as men moved to their outland possessions, the proprietors of Windham in 1682 had laid out three centers of settlement that were intended to and did in time become parishes. By setting each man near to his lands and yet within a community, the proprietors hoped to combine social and economic values.[26] Other towns moved in the same direction, but planning was usually not so careful. Because farmers were reluctant to travel to scattered fields, town plots became a patchwork of large farms, sometimes of thirty or forty acres, rather than an intimate collection of smaller home lots. The Coventry proprietors who tried to arrange the home lots in the customary form, along a single street with the farming area stretching out behind, soon abandoned this plan for a system of large tracts because settlers were not attracted to a concentrated village with all the problems it entailed. When the proprietors of another new town tried focusing settlement in a center with long lots stretching away from it, a plan closely following the earliest practices, they had difficulty finding men to farm the awkwardly shaped pieces. Most inhabitants of the later towns preferred the economic advantages of large lots laid out for expediency in farming over the social advantages of the old villages. Observing the trend, the Assembly saw no reason to thwart popular desire and in the northwest towns laid out large farms instead of the thin strips of the first settlements.[27] The futility of attempting to maintain social coherence in the face of the overriding practical advantages of dispersal persuaded the civil authority to bow to the inevitable.

The planting procedures in the colony towns in the northwest reflected all the changes, financial, legal, and geographical, that occurred in the fifty years following the issuance of the patents of 1685. The farmer in search of proprietary rights in a new town

[26] Larned, *Windham*, I, 65.

[27] Garvan, *Architecture and Town Planning*, 62-67, 72, 74-76; compare the map of Cornwall (p. 75) with that of Wethersfield (p. 52), and of Colebrook (facing p. 70) with Coventry (facing p. 67).

had to raise at least £30, and usually he paid much more—occasionally as much as £500—depending on the state of the market.[28] Transplanted to the new township, he lived at a distance from his neighbors, on a large home lot that was a farm in itself, while a portion of the nearby land was reserved for settlers yet to come. Many proprietors sent tenants who were not tied to the soil, as freeholders were, but transients, likely to be replaced from time to time when an owner found someone to pay higher rents or when they purchased land for themselves.

In one way or another the larger portion of the towns settled after 1690 in the northeast and northwest sections of the colony defected from the social order of the seventeenth century.[29] The coordination of government, economics, and geography was disrupted. The inhabitants and owners of the new towns held a motley legal status by comparison with the members of older communities: some were tenants with no political privileges and none of the dignity of landowners, while others owned land and voted but had no rights to the undivided lands and could not attend proprietors' meetings, where a select group made decisions on the fences and highways that affected the whole town. Of the proprietors with division rights, some were nonresident and without political capacity. And all residents lived at a distance from one another, no longer meeting regularly, and able if they wished, to withdraw into some untraveled corner of the town. The social power of the community was far from dissipated, but the yearning to exploit the land was draining the strength of the old order.

[28] The cheapest proprietary share in Kent cost £152, and most were around £190 (C. S. Grant, 175).
[29] The residency requirement was enforced by bond (*Conn. Recs.*, VIII, 134-137); but despite the Assembly's stringency, the colony towns, like plantations settled earlier with a prohibition on nonresidency, petitioned for liberty to tax unimproved land, an indication that some considerable number of proprietors had not taken up their land (*Conn. Recs.*, VIII, 335-336, 404, 470, 560).

VI

The Politics of Land

৩১ NEARLY TWICE AS MANY TOWNS were settled in the thirty years after 1690 as in the thirty years before.[1] The exhaustion of old lands and the closing of proprietary bodies were partly responsible for the intensified search for new farms in the wilderness. When inhabitants could not be assured of adequate holdings for themselves and their sons, they looked beyond the line of settlement for opportunity.

Dramatic population growth was another important factor. From 1670 to 1700 Connecticut's population increased by 58 per cent, and from 1700 to 1730 by 280 per cent.[2] East of the Connecticut River especially, new plantations multiplied as, in addition to the natural increase, a flood of migrants poured in from southeastern Massachusetts, where towns were equally incapable of supporting the younger generation. So acute was population pressure in Roxbury that the town purchased two whole townships in northeast Connecticut on which to settle its surplus. Inundated by the stream of newcomers from the north, the eastern section was fully occupied two or three decades before western Connecticut filled up.[3]

The increase in town planting placed extraordinary pressures on the colonial government. Hundreds of ordinary people whose economic success depended on the opening of new plantations turned to the General Court as they had earlier looked to the town for help. The wealthy were also interested because as the

[1] Twenty compared to eleven.
[2] Garvan, *Architecture and Town Planning*, 3. The older, less reliable estimates in Dexter yield a slightly less extravagant contrast (Dexter, "Estimates," 32).
[3] Larned, *Windham*, I, 13-265.

heightened demand raised land values, it afforded opportunities for speculation. Any move to lay out a town immediately attracted the attention of men whose personal fortunes as farmers or speculators were involved. The legislature, once primarily the playing field of the aristocracy, became an arena anxiously watched by all.

Before the Narragansett War in 1675 the General Court managed the establishment of new plantations. Sometimes private individuals purchased the land from the Indians, and sometimes a committee of the Court, but in every case the Court asserted its jurisdiction over the tract and supervised settlement. Besides the first towns along the coast and the Connecticut River, the tier of communities in the west behind the original string of settlements followed this orderly pattern. Until 1675 the only town-size tract in private hands was a section along the Quinebaug River, near Rhode Island, deeded by an Indian to John Winthrop, Jr.[4]

After the Narragansett War this situation changed radically. Almost the entire country east of the Connecticut River claimed by the Mohegan sachem Uncas came into the possession of a few colonial leaders who were in the confidence of the natives. Changing its policy, the Assembly confirmed these huge tracts to the recipients and allowed them to dispose of the land as they wished.[5] In most of the area the Court imposed no residency requirements and did not regulate prices, on the assumption that the proprietors would see to orderly settlement.

Within twenty years the east was in turmoil. Title disputes raged in nearly every town, government leaders struggled for control of contested territories, and popular factions formed around the warring magnates. Soon after 1700 the Assembly reestablished its supervision over new plantations, in time to save the northwest towns from contention but too late to avert years of controversy in the east.

The confusion arose from the status of Indian titles, which had

[4] Larned, *Windham,* I, 16-17.

[5] The colony continued to nullify purchases made without its permission; but after 1680 it was more liberal in allowing individuals to use Indian lands purchased privately. Later it had difficulty reasserting its former control (B. Trumbull, *Connecticut,* I, 92; *Conn. Recs.,* I, 402; IV, 305; V, 160; VI, 13-14, 65, 355-356).

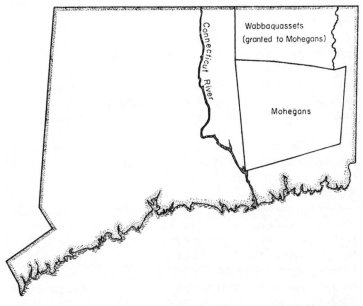

Hereditary Mohegan lands as surveyed in 1705 and Wabbaquasset lands granted to Uncas in 1681.

Source: B. Trumbull, *Connecticut,* I, 356, and Larned, *Windham,* I, 16.

become quite involved. The Mohegans under Uncas claimed as their hereditary lands a huge irregular square north of New London extending from a line on the east a few miles inside the Rhode Island boundary to another line angling south-southeast through Bolton, Hebron, and Colchester to the Connecticut River. North of these Mohegan lands and extending into Massachusetts was the Wabbaquasset country, which the same tribe claimed not as an ancient possession but by conquest of the Pequots.[6] These lands together comprised virtually all of the eastern portion of the colony north of the towns along Long Island Sound. Norwich settlers purchased a nine-mile square north of New London in 1659, but the remainder of this territory went to Uncas's two sons. Owaneco received the eastern half of the hereditary lands plus

[6] B. Trumbull, *Connecticut,* I, 356; Larned, *Windham,* I, 16.

all the Wabbaquasset country, and Joshua inherited the western portion of the Mohegan land. Joshua died in 1676, leaving parcels of land to people in Hartford, Windsor, Norwich, New London, and Saybrook, and to his son Abimilech. All of Windham and Mansfield, for example, were left to sixteen men, mainly from Norwich. Meanwhile, Owaneco, an inveterate drunkard, lost confidence in his ability to control his lands and deeded them in 1680 and 1684 to Captain James Fitch, a magistrate and friend of the Indians.[7] When the Assembly confirmed this vast area to Fitch, it made him the largest landowner in the colony. One of his enemies lamented that Fitch "monopolized to himself more of other men's lands than ever any man did in the Kinges dominions." [8]

Very few Indian deeds to the eastern lands were definitive. Before the English arrived, the Indians had no need to specify the precise boundaries of their hunting grounds. When they passed on their lands to the settlers, they were inclined to go beyond the limits of their undisputed possessions and include generous portions sometimes used by neighboring tribes. Owaneco gave Fitch much of the Quinebaug land which the Winthrops thought was theirs, for example, and in the west Abimilech, Joshua's son, and Owaneco had conflicting rights.[9]

The ambiguous deeds bred a series of bitter disputes, and James

---

[7] Deming, *Settlement of Connecticut Towns,* 53-54; *Conn. Recs.,* II, 291n; *Memorial History of Hartford County,* 78-79; Larned, *Windham,* I, 16-17, 63-64. Probably the Assembly assumed Fitch would hold the lands in trust for the Indians, disposing of them in the public interest. Fitch seems to have thought of himself as acting in this capacity. When Plainfield, a stronghold of the Winthrops, received a patent for their land, Fitch objected that it was "contrary to the nature of granting townships . . . to grant to particular men the whole in fee simple, thereby to exclude others coming into said towns or the impeopling the place and putting stop to the increase and growth of the colony." (Larned, *Windham,* I, 128). Fitch must have thought his operations were of a different character, though similar accusations were leveled at him (Deming, *Settlement of Connecticut Towns,* 59; Samuel Willis to Wait Winthrop, April 21, 1697, *Winthrop Papers,* pt. VI, 38).

[8] Samuel Willis to Wait Winthrop, April 21, 1697, *Winthrop Papers,* pt. VI, 38.

[9] For example, Larned, *Windham,* I, 83; Lebanon, "Deeds," I, 19-20; *Conn. Recs.,* IV, 215.

Fitch was at the center of most of the controversies. The size and position of his holdings and, even more, his truculent nature involved him in endless lawsuits and political struggles. The son of a minister in Norwich, Fitch was consistently elected as an assistant from New London County. In time he became a major in the colonial militia and was recognized as one of the shrewdest legal minds in the colony. But the Winthrops, Wait and Fitz-John, sons of Connecticut's Governor John Winthrop, Jr., considered him an upstart. They were disgusted when Fitch flaunted a plush cape and a signet ring given him by high-placed friends in Massachusetts.[10] Never a member of the inner circle, the Major cast himself as a patriot friend of the people and preferred to harass Connecticut's blue bloods rather than seek an alliance with them.

The Winthrops expected in 1686 to reach an agreement with Fitch on the Indian lands. They wanted a clear title to the Quinebaug country claimed in part by Owaneco, and Fitch probably encouraged their hopes in order to obtain confirmation of Owaneco's bequest. Once the Assembly had acted, however, he refused to conclude the expected arrangements and after 1686 ceased any pretense of friendship for the brothers.[11] Without waiting to settle with the other claimants, Fitch rapidly disposed of Owaneco's property, in about 1686 selling Woodstock in Massachusetts and Pomfret to Roxbury men as entire townships. Since no one else claimed these lands, the Assembly confirmed the Pomfret purchase. Shortly thereafter Fitch began selling land in the Quinebaug country, under protest from the Winthrops, and in the west, where Abimilech claimed title.[12] Subsequent sales by Fitch or Joshua's legatees threw all the land in an arc from Lyme to Stonington into controversy. The areas that later became Colchester, Lebanon, Hebron, Bolton, Coventry, Stafford, Ashford, Canterbury, and Plainfield, as well as sections of New London, were involved. Norwich, Windham, and Mansfield, in the center of this arc, and Stonington, Pomfret, and Woodstock, bordering it, suffered no title

---

[10] Wait to Fitz-John Winthrop, Boston, May 13, 1686, *Winthrop Papers*, pt. VIII, 462.
[11] Wait to Fitz-John Winthrop, Boston, May 8, 1686, *Winthrop Papers*, pt. VIII, 460.
[12] Larned, *Windham*, I, 17, 21; Hunt, *Pomfret*, 4; Hine, *Lebanon*, 52.

disputes over their own lands; but the leaders of these towns were often major purchasers of the Indian lands, buying from Fitch, the Winthrops, or Joshua's legatees.[13] They resold to their neighbors and spread the network of ownership in the contested territory. Residents throughout the entire eastern section became involved in the controversies.

The settlers were pawns in the struggle for control of the new townships. The Winthrops defended their title by prosecuting Fitch's tenants as trespassers, and Fitch did the same to the Winthrop's tenants. As Samuel Cranston said of a similar situation at the Rhode Island boundary, title disputes resulted in "the pulling and halling poor men, fyning and imprisoning." [14]

An illustrative case occurred on the Quinebaug lands which the Winthrops leased to Benjamin Palmer and Samuel Cleaveland. Fitch offered them a lease to the same tract, but they chose to become tenants of the Winthrops. In the fall of 1695 Fitch obtained an attachment on the produce of the farms and, with the aid of the marshal of New London County, forcibly carried away corn and hogs. The Winthrops accused Fitch of using his influence as magistrate to intimidate their representatives and to possess the lands by counterfeiting or deceit. The whole trial which led to the attachment was spurious in any case, Wait said, because the jury consisted "mostly of Norwitch men, or such who are in the same interest with them and depend upon Captain Fitch his bottome." [15]

A number of similar controversies bound Fitch and his followers and the Winthrops and theirs into warring factions. Norwich men joined Fitch's tenants and purchasers in support of the Major, for his political and judicial powers were necessary to defend their titles. Fitch in turn conscientiously used his influence on their behalf, for if their titles fell, all his lands would be jeopardized. In case after case Fitch, acting as lawyer or magistrate, evicted

---

[13] See, for example, the relationship of Saybrook to Hebron and Lebanon (B. Trumbull, *Connecticut*, I, 364; Lebanon, "Deeds," I, 19-20).

[14] Samuel Cranston to Fitz-John Winthrop, May 28, 1701, *Winthrop Papers*, pt. V, 71.

[15] Wait Winthrop to John Gallup, Aug. 6, 1695, and Oct. 19, 1695, *Winthrop Papers*, pt. IV, 504-506; Wait Winthrop to County Court at New London, Nov. 25, 1695, *ibid.*, pt. IV, 514-516; Wait Winthrop to the Governor of Connecticut, April 8, 1696, *ibid.*, pt. IV, 517-522.

Winthrop tenants, prosecuted trespassers, or defended right of title. The Gallups, allies of the Winthrops, even accused Fitch of hand-picking juries to assure favorable decisions.[16] At the same time, the Winthrops, through Gurdon Saltonstall or the Gallups of Stonington, served their allies in the same fashion.[17] In 1702 the Assembly finally divided the contested land, organizing Fitch's followers in the west into the town of Canterbury and Winthrop's men in the east into Plainfield. Although this arrangement quieted the major conflict, lesser boundary disputes and private land controversies continued for years.[18]

The erosion of their land holdings was enough to anger the Winthrops, and the disputes in the county courts were sufficiently disruptive to alarm gentlemen everywhere. But Fitch waged his war on other fronts as well. The land conflict inevitably intruded upon politics, for the judges in the county courts that decided the validity of titles were political appointees of the Assembly. To assure a sympathetic hearing, each party strove to have its own men appointed to the New London bench. The Assembly was also the court of last resort, with power to confirm or negate disputed titles. Since no claimant could hope for success without friends in the legislature, elections became vitally important to hundreds of men whose farms hung in the balance.

The Winthrops and Joshua's legatees, the conservative opponents of Fitch, held an initial advantage. These gentlemen or their fathers had ruled the colony since its founding, and the people

[16] Fitch told the Winthrops that he must stand "as a Norridg man against Pocatanuck and part of Quinabauge" (Wait Winthrop to Fitz-John Winthrop, May 13, 1686, *Winthrop Papers*, pt. IV, 461). The Winthrops chafed at Fitch's ability to be "allways plauging his neibours under countenance of his magistratship" (Wait Winthrop to Fitz-John Winthrop, June 10, 1706, *ibid.*, pt. VI, 141); New London County, "Records," VIII, 320; cf. p. 329.

[17] The Gallups of Stonington were leaders of the Winthrop faction (Larned, *Windham*, I, 108). For attempts of the Winthrops to win over one of Fitch's men, Wait Winthrop to his son John, Oct. 26, 1715, *Winthrop Papers*, pt. VI, 312-313; Wait Winthrop to Fitz-John Winthrop, Oct. 31, 1691, *ibid.*, pt. IV, 499; Larned, *Windham*, I, 118-119, 144; *Conn. Recs.*, IV, 391; Wait Winthrop to John or Adam Gallup, Oct. 19, 1695, *Winthrop Papers*, pt. IV, 505-506; Power-of-attorney from Fitz-John and Wait Winthrop to John Gallup, Oct. 2, 1705, *ibid.*, pt. V, 312-313; Conn. Arch., Court Papers, 513-520, and Private Controversies, VI, 173-175, 180.

[18] Larned, *Windham*, I, 118ff, 133-137.

were conditioned to return them to office almost automatically. But the indomitable Fitch steadily pressed to increase his power, and with surprising success. Willing to connive with enemies of the colony and always an aggressive defender of popular rights, he came near to unseating the aristocratic rulers.

Fitch made his most dramatic move in 1689, when news of the Glorious Revolution in England reached Connecticut. Most colonists assumed that the Andros regime was defunct. A few royalists led by the archconservative Gershom Bulkeley protested the deposition of judges and sheriffs still vested with royal commissions, but the bulk of the people were ready to return to charter government. Fitch agreed but objected to the restoration of the old rulers, who had capitulated so easily to Andros' demands. He called for a meeting of freemen to elect a new government, doubtless expecting that he and his friends who had stood firm against the royal governor would be chosen. The "gentlemen" may have shared Fitch's opinion, for they were reluctant to hold an election and seemed about to prevent it. The insurgent leaders then offered the freemen the choice of three alternatives acceptable to the gentlemen: the restoration of the former magistrates, the continuance of the Andros government, or the selection of a committee of safety. Everyone knew the first would be chosen, but the patriots expected to turn out the gentlemen the next year.

The delay, however, gave the rulers time to frustrate Fitch. In the first session the General Court loosened the requirements for becoming a freeman and altered election procedures so that negative votes (blanks) did not count. Up until then a nominee had needed more favorable votes than blanks—more friends than enemies—but now he simply needed more votes than his rivals. His enemies had to find a candidate well enough known to win more votes, a difficult task when communication was complicated and the incumbent well established.

The men newly introduced to privileges gratefully supported their benefactors, and, notwithstanding the dislike for the gentlemen in certain circles, Fitch and his followers failed to attract enough positive votes to displace the old rulers. Except in the reelection of Fitch himself, the insurgents failed.[19]

[19] Gershom Bulkeley narrates the whole episode in *Will and Doom,*

Defeat in 1689 and 1690 by no means crushed Fitch. Still industriously selling vast tracts in the east, he gained strength in the Assembly. One conservative bitterly complained to Fitz-John Winthrop in 1697 that Fitch was the "principle Minister of State." [20] Fitch's influence was greatest among less prominent politicians and among the common people. A letter to the Winthrops noted that Connecticut was "fallinge into the dreges of a democraticall anarkie." [21] Riding on the crest of popular favor, Fitch was able in some sessions to sweep all before him, and for more than a decade he was a formidable and sometimes dominant force in the government.

Fitch's popularity at the polls gave him an advantage in the contest for Quinebaug lands because, as the elected assistant from New London County, he was chief judge in the county court which heard title disputes. Where he was not in direct control, his imposing person swayed the decisions of lesser civil officers. The Winthrops and their associates knew they would continue to lose ground until they removed Fitch and became obsessed with a passion to break his power in the Assembly and to eliminate his influence in the courts.

At the spring election in 1697 the gentlemen employed Gurdon Saltonstall, a minister in New London and an intimate friend of the Winthrops, to make an outright assault on Fitch in the annual election sermon. Of impeccable pedigree, a forceful preacher, and a man of overawing presence, Saltonstall also possessed extensive knowledge of the law and had frequently handled the Winthrop cases at court. Having observed Fitch at first hand, Saltonstall had developed an implacable hatred for him and willingly took on the assignment of cutting him down in the sermon preached just before the balloting in the annual election.[22]

Saltonstall rehearsed the old Puritan theory of law and authority

154-159. For election procedures, *Conn. Recs.*, I, 22; II, 133-134, 253; IV, 11-12.

[20] Samuel Willis to Fitz-John Winthrop, Dec. 25, 1697, *Winthrop Papers*, pt. III, 31-32.

[21] Samuel Willis to Wait Winthrop, April 1697, *Winthrop Papers*, pt. V, 38.

[22] Biographical information on Saltonstall is in Blake, "Gurdon Saltonstall."

and the relationship of order and liberty. Throughout the sermon he stressed the necessity of electing upright and honorable men, and his list of the requisite qualities of a magistrate was intended to recommend the aristocrats and to deprecate upstarts like Fitch. To make his point clear, Saltonstall directly attacked Fitch's abuse of justice in the New London County courts, warning his listeners to beware of permitting "Flattery or Bribery, Favour or Affection" to influence the course of justice. The poor lacked the means of swaying the court and were easily constrained, while the rich and powerful eluded the law. When "men of a higher Rank . . . scorn to stoop to the Laws" only a courageous man dared rebuke them; judges must brace themselves to resist "the Gifts of the Wealthy, the Favour of Great Ones . . . the Frowns or Threats of the Mighty." [23]

Saltonstall's entreaties had no visible effect on the Assembly until the next year, when the legislature enacted a series of measures to restrain Fitch and his cohorts. His judicial powers as an assistant were removed by a law bestowing the presidency of the county courts on an officer new to Connecticut, the justice of the peace. This office was simply that of commissioner under a new title, but the reorganization prevented Fitch, as an assistant or any elected official, from ruling in the county courts. The courts were composed of justices of the quorum and a judge, all appointed by the Assembly.[24] No matter how popular Fitch made himself by the liberal distribution of his vast land holdings, the control of justice remained in the hands of the legislature, which respected conservative power.

The General Court also passed a law against the maladministration of justice in any inferior court or by any assistant or justice of the peace in a court of small causes. The act allowed an aggrieved person to bring his complaint before the governor and council who could require the accused to appear before the Assembly.[25] Fitch was thus put in the power of the gentlemen who controlled the highest echelons of civil authority. Anyone

[23] *Sermon,* 23, 28.
[24] *Conn. Recs.,* IV, 235, 268.
[25] *Conn. Recs.,* IV, 235, 268.

objecting to Fitch's procedures in small causes or to his exercise of undue influence in other courts could appeal for redress to the governor, from whom Fitch could expect little sympathy.

Even after these alterations in the court structure, the Winthrops were not secure, for such measures were not enough in themselves to neutralize Fitch. So long as he was sufficiently popular in New London County to be returned as an assistant each year, he was a force to be reckoned with. In 1702 a report to Wait Winthrop said that Fitch was leader of a cabal "who much influence the affaires of the uper and lower house at the Genll. Court." His appeal lay in his defense of popular liberties. "He is soe expert in the act of flatery that he makes many of the people beleive that he is the cheife patron of theire charter privelages." [26]

Fitch also had the support of more important people as well, for he was willing to consort with any enemies of the standing order who would help him resist the Winthrops and their allies. With the Masons of Stonington, his relatives by marriage, he revived the claims of the Mohegans to a triangle comprising sections of Lyme and New London and all of Colchester and to other parcels of land in the east.[27] According to the memorials submitted by the plaintiffs, the colony had failed to clear the native title to the lands which the Masons claimed still to hold in trust for the Indians.[28] The Masons knew that if they won, all this land would fall into their hands as guardians of the tribe.

Other eminent enemies of the ruling men joined Fitch at times. The Indian complaint was carried to the crown in 1704 by Nicholas Hallam, one of two brothers involved in a controversy with the Winthrops over the administration of the will of the Hallams' stepfather.[29] Major Edward Palmes, the husband of Wait's and Fitz-John's sister, also supported the complaint, and had appealed

[26] Samuel Willis to Wait Winthrop, 1702, *Winthrop Papers*, pt. V, 111-112.

[27] For Fitch's kinship to the Masons, Caulkins, *Norwich*, 146.

[28] Governor and Council of Connecticut to Henry Ashurst, Aug. 29, 1705, *Winthrop Papers*, pt. V, 310. For the entire Mohegan case, B. Trumbull, *Connecticut*, I, 344-362.

[29] For a summary, *Winthrop Papers*, pt. V, 94n. For Hallam's agency in the Mohegan case, Governor and Council of Connecticut to Henry Ashurst, *ibid.*, pt. V, 304.

to the English courts for a more equitable distribution of the estate of John Winthrop, Jr.[30] The Hallams and Palmes were bitter critics of the Connecticut government. Palmes had signed a testimonial vouching for the truth of Gershom Bulkeley's *Will and Doom,* a royalist condemnation of the colony's rulers written in 1692 shortly after the deposition of Andros.[31]

Thus Fitch assembled a motley but powerful faction. Men with titles derived from Owaneco through Fitch provided a popular base, and the Masons, the Hallams, and Palmes added authority. They offered formidable opposition to Governor Fitz-John Winthrop and his friends, who sometimes scarcely dared speak against Fitch.

The Winthrops were certain that these right- and left-wing leaders were in collusion to subvert the government. In their eyes, Fitch had shown great partiality when taking evidence in the Hallams' suit against the Winthrops.[32] Fitz-John Winthrop also ac-

[30] *Winthrop Papers,* pt. V, 255n; Caulkins, *Norwich,* 226-227. For an early instance of Palmes's offishness, see Gurdon Saltonstall to Fitz-John Winthrop, July 24, 1690, *Winthrop Papers,* pt. V, 123-124; *Conn. Recs.,* III, 193.

[31] Bulkeley, 154, 260.

[32] Fitz-John Winthrop to the General Assembly, May 22, 1702, *Winthrop Papers,* pt. V, 94; Gurdon Saltonstall to Fitz-John Winthrop, March 13, 1703, *ibid.,* pt. V, 123-124; Governor and Council of Connecticut to Henry Ashurst, Aug. 29, 1705, *ibid.,* pt. V, 308-309; Fitz-John Winthrop to the General Assembly, May 22, 1702, *ibid.,* pt. V, 94; Fitz-John Winthrop to Henry Ashurst, July 15, 1703, *ibid.,* pt. V, 133-135; Wait Winthrop to Fitz-John Winthrop, Nov. 24, 1698, *ibid.,* pt. IV, 540.

Both the Masons and the Hallams called Governor Dudley of Massachusetts to their assistance (Daniel Mason to Joseph Dudley, April 13, 1705, *ibid.,* pt. V, 329). Dudley, a long-time enemy of Connecticut, had powerful friends in England and through them obtained an appointment to the commission that sat in judgment on the Mohegan case. Ashurst, the colony agent, was convinced that Dudley used first Hallam's appeal and then the Mohegan complaint to bring Connecticut into disfavor, his aim being to see the charter vacated (Henry Ashurst to the Commissioners of Trade, *ibid.,* pt. V, 383; Governor and Council of Connecticut to Henry Ashurst, Aug. 29, 1705, *ibid.,* pt. V, 304). However well-founded the Winthrops' and Ashurst's suspicions, Dudley did eventually receive a portion of the disputed lands from the Masons. Thus he along with the Hallams and Palmes had a personal interest in the outcome of the Mohegan case. The Winthrops believed that most of the commissioners appointed by the Crown owned land in the contested territory (Fitz-John Winthrop to Henry Ashurst, *ibid.,* pt. V, 353; Henry Ashurst to the Commissioners of Trade,

cused him of claiming lands which rightfully belonged to the
freemen of the colony.[33] But Fitch nevertheless kept his following
for many years and was repeatedly elected an assistant until 1708.

Fitch's influence gradually waned after 1705. He lost friends in
Norwich when an irregular entry in the town book was discovered
and when he supported some Canterbury people in a land dispute.
In 1706 and 1707, after the conclusion of the Mohegan trial, the
Assembly investigated all the Indian claims in the east and took
away some Winthrop lands but deprived Fitch of the entire Waba-
quasset country.[34] After 1707 he was never again elected to the
Upper House.

In 1717 Fitch, coming out of partial retirement, laid out lots
and began selling land in the territory that later was to become

ibid., pt. V, 383; Governor and Council of Connecticut to Henry Ashurst,
Aug. 29, 1705, _ibid._, pt. V, 304-305, 306-308; Joseph Dudley to Fitz-John
Winthrop, Dec. 12, 1704, _ibid._, pt. V, 277; B. Trumbull, _Connecticut,_ I,
361). The commission awarded the land to the Indians in 1704, but the
Winthrops' arguments impressed the Lords sufficiently to persuade them to
suspend the decision (Henry Ashurst to the Governor and Council of Connecticut, _Winthrop Papers,_ pt. V, 324; Wait Winthrop to Fitz-John Winthrop, _ibid._, pt. VI, 139). For an account of the land controversy in the
over-all context of Connecticut politics, see Dunn, _Puritans and Yankees._

[33] Fitz-John Winthrop to Henry Ashurst, July 15, 1703, _Winthrop Papers,_
pt. V, 133-134; Fitz-John Winthrop to the General Assembly, _ibid._, pt. V,
290. The Winthrops referred to Fitch as a snake (Wait Winthrop to Fitz-
John Winthrop, Sept. 17, 1706, _ibid._, pt. V, 144). Fitch's recurring success
in elections appalled them (John Winthrop to Fitz-John Winthrop, June
1706, _ibid._, pt. V, 334). Fitch returned the fire by accusing Governor
Winthrop of carrying on an illegal trade with Canada (Conn. Arch., Civil
Officers, I, 75).

Both Fitch and the Winthrops accused the other party of engrossing
lands to the obstruction of settlement (Samuel Willis to Wait Winthrop,
April 21, 1697, _Winthrop Papers,_ pt. VI, 38; Samuel Willis to Wait Winthrop, April 22, 1702, _ibid._, pt. VI, 112; Larned, _Windham,_ I, 108-109,
128). Some of the colonists thought the government should make no effort
to oppose the Mohegan claims (William Whiting to Fitz-John Winthrop,
Sept. 17, 1705, _Winthrop Papers,_ pt. V, 311).

[34] Larned, _Windham,_ I, 109; Conn. Arch., Court Papers, 525-543; Larned,
Windham, I, 126-128. Fitch and the Masons met hostile measures from
the Assembly as early as 1699 (_Conn. Recs.,_ IV, 305; Wolcott, _Memoir,_
329-330).

When the Assembly undertook to settle Ashford in this tract, Fitch sold
the land in a rush, plunging the township into title disputes which lasted
for decades (Larned, _Windham,_ I, 214-217, 221-227).

Stafford—a tract in the Wabaquasset country which the Assembly had previously removed from his control. When Saltonstall, now governor, issued a proclamation declaring Fitch's presumptions false and calling for the prosecution of trespassers, Fitch countered by asserting the validity of his claims and by boasting that he could easily cut the Governor's proclamation "into as many pieces as the Protestants did the Popish wooden god." [35] Pleading lameness, he brushed off a warrant requiring him to appear before the New London assistant, an ally of Saltonstall's, to answer for these "false and seditious expressions." In May 1717 the Upper House favored dragging him to Hartford, despite the "pretence of lameness." Before it reached an agreement with the Lower House, however, Fitch sent an apology for acting "indiscreetly and disrespectfully." The Upper House still insisted on imposing a £20 fine, condescending to so low a sum only because of Fitch's humble acknowledgement, but the Lower House forced it to count the confession sufficient penalty for his insolence.[36]

The assistants may have been tractable because Governor Saltonstall's part in the disposal of Stafford was itself suspect. When the Governor and Upper House had wanted to sell the land to seven gentlemen for £1,000, the members of the Lower House felt that the colony's best interests were being sacrificed. Even after an investigation cleared the Governor, they refused to accept the vindication. The Upper House had no doubt that this mistrust was due to Fitch's conniving, which aroused "a Spirit against all that assert the Governmts Right in Opposition to their pretences," and the Major demonstrated his power when the deputies insisted that the committee settle the disputed area in Stafford by paying him something for his claims.[37] But the Stafford episode exhausted Fitch's political energies, for he was by that time an ailing old man soon to die.[38]

Fitch's forceful arguments, however, opened the door for a host

---

[35] Larned, *Windham*, I, 151.

[36] Larned, *Windham*, I, 150-153.

[37] Conn. Arch., Towns and Lands, III, 148-150; Conn. Arch., Civil Officers, I, 163; Larned, *Windham*, I, 151.

[38] Palfrey said that Fitch tried to oust Saltonstall from the governorship in 1719 by nominating the deputy governor, Nathan Gold, for the post (*History of New England*, III, 462). I have found no evidence of the attempted displacement.

of smaller claimants, who came to be known as the "native right" men, taking their name from a legal doctrine familiar in New England since Roger Williams dramatized it. They asserted that royal charters granted jurisdiction, the right to govern, but not ownership, which only the Indians could bestow. The rulers of the colony insisted that the Assembly must confirm Indian purchases, which allowed the government to nullify inconvenient claims. This viewpoint was passionately defended by John Bulkley, son of the arch-conservative Gershom and one of the colonial aristocracy. Bulkley charged that the multitude supported the "native right" theory because they had "too much Rubbish in their Brains to think of any thing with distinctness." [39]

The most annoying of the "native right" men were the heirs of John Mason who continued to press the claims made in alliance with Fitch at the turn of the century. Investigating commissions in 1721, 1738, and 1743 were equivocal in their rulings and kept alive the Masons' hopes. They continued to plead their case in England until finally George III awarded the land to the colony. Until then the Masons were doubly disturbing, because the complaint that Connecticut had mistreated the Mohegans provided ammunition for the enemies of the colony who wanted the charter vacated. When the Masons appeared to be losing after the 1738 hearings, one Hartford man thanked the Lord for deliverance from men of violence. [40]

Many other "native right" men were equally violent. A group of Colchester residents deriving title from the Indians engaged in a long contest with Jeremy Addams and his heirs who refused to give the settlers a quit-claim and demanded nearly half the town. The settlers objected that by 1721 the land was greatly appreciated through their improvements and that they had paid taxes on it for many years. When the obdurate heirs sent in surveyors, more than fifty mounted settlers broke the chains and justified their violence by the argument that the common law permitted them to defend their property when illegally threatened. [41]

Still more scandalous was a controversy in Coventry. Jeremiah

[39] Wolcott, *Memoir*, 329; "Preface" to Wolcott, *Poetical Meditations*, l-li.
[40] Caulkins, *Norwich*, 267-268; B. Trumbull, *Connecticut*, I, 340, 356, 363; Wadsworth, *Diary*, 25.
[41] Conn. Arch., Towns and Lands, V, 197, 195.

Fitch of Norwich, a distant relative of the notorious James, bought land there from a Windsor man who gave a title purchased from one of Joshua's legatees. Later John Clark of Saybrook claimed the same land on the basis of a deed received directly from Abimilech, Joshua's heir, but Jeremiah Fitch refused to yield to the judgment of the Superior Court and was imprisoned for resisting Clark's occupancy. Other residents in Coventry, Lebanon, and East Windsor felt threatened, and in 1722 a mob from these towns descended on the Hartford jail and freed Fitch. The sheriff tried to stop the rioters at the ferry, where they were returning across the Connecticut River; but after an exchange of blows, the ferry man was forced to push off, and the mob escaped. The sheriff, sent to arrest them, was repulsed. One Davenport, apprehended as he emerged from the meetinghouse on Sunday, resisted the posse, crying, "Stand off or i will knock your brans out." His friends immediately came to his rescue, and the sheriff returned to Hartford emptyhanded.

Another posse sent from Windham met the same treatment and fled when Fitch and more than a dozen of his cohorts appeared, threatening them with violence. Finally the rioters were rounded up and tried before a special court with a jury made up of men recruited from distant counties because local people were so prejudiced. Fines were levied on the men who assaulted the jail, but Fitch went scot free.[42]

By the time of the Hartford riots the damage done to the political order was disturbingly evident. From 1689, when James Fitch made his first bid for power, through the succeeding three decades, one outbreak after another disclosed how far the spirit of opposition had spread. The magistrates could not even comfort themselves with the thought that the malignant old Major was behind it all. After his influence declined, others arose to defend their claims with new energy.

The gentlemen would have been more comfortable if the government had unitedly quashed the troublemakers, but the Assembly

[42] Conn. Arch., Crimes and Misdemeanours, II, 352. The whole episode is related in *Memorial History of Hartford County*, I, 79-80. Benjamin Trumbull misconstrues the origins of the riot, but adds some interesting details (*Connecticut*, I, 69-70).

itself divided on the issues that split the eastern half of the colony. The assistants sat with the deputies until 1698, and Major Fitch's influence cut across the Upper and Lower Houses. Perhaps to isolate him, the two Houses were separated in the same year that the court structure was remodeled.[43] After 1708 Fitch lost friends in the Upper House but continued to receive strong support from deputies sympathetic to the "native right" cause. In opposing censure of the Major in 1717 and in refusing to vindicate Salton-stall's disposal of Stafford, the deputies fought the assistants to a standstill. When the Upper House passed a resolve that the en-grossment of colony lands under "native right" claims was "the principall bane and Ruin of our Ancient Order and Peace," the Lower House voted down the proposition." [44]

The Assembly was also at an impasse for more than a dozen years because the two Houses disagreed about a forcible entry act. Year after year the Upper House pressed for passage of a bill that would make it easier to prosecute Fitch's tenants as well as other owners holding title by tenuous Indian deeds, but the Lower House refused to concur and in 1716 passed its own version, with a clause authorizing constables to prosecute only those "having no Right to make such Entry." The Upper House foresaw that Fitch's customers and tenants, because they had deeds of sorts, could continue to trespass under this provision on the Winthrops' land, and not until 1722, when the Coventry and Colchester riots shocked the Assembly into strengthening the powers of enforcement officers, was a bill enacted.[45]

The most serious controversy dividing the two houses concerned the power to appoint justices of the peace in the counties and judges of the Superior Court, who were customarily nominated by the deputies of each county and then confirmed by the Assem-

[43] *Conn. Recs.*, IV, 235; B. Trumbull, *Connecticut*, I, 336-337. At least as late as 1702 Fitch's party included men of both houses (Samuel Willis, Hartford, to Wait Winthrop, May 28, 1701, *Winthrop Papers*, pt. V, 71).

[44] Conn. Arch., Towns and Lands, III, 148. The two houses split on other issues too. The Lower House was less inclined than the Upper to give all undivided lands to the patentees of 1685; and in the fight over the location of the College, the two houses again disagreed (above, Chap. III; below, Chap. IX).

[45] Conn. Arch., Civil Officers, I, 93, 150, 357, 461.

bly. No disputes occurred over New Haven and Fairfield Counties, but appointments in Hartford and New London, the counties containing the contested Mohegan lands, caused endless debates.[46] Factions aggressively maneuvered to get their friends appointed to the bench, and Saltonstall informed the Assembly that the ability of these groups to obtain and block appointments gave them an insidious power in the courts. "Justices have been threatened to be Turned out of their places," he said, "by such as Depended upon an Interest among the County Deputys for this End—and Some have been Excluded in that manner." Attorneys elected to the Assembly served their clients by ousting unsympathetic judges not only in the county but in the Superior Court.[47]

Distressed by the annual fracas, the Governor and the Upper House tried to forestall machinations in the Lower House. The assistants refused to confirm partisan nominations, sometimes delaying appointments until a compromise could be reached. Governor Saltonstall eventually proposed that he nominate county judges and that they continue to sit from year to year at the pleasure of the Upper House.[48] The Lower House, on the other hand, sought to enlarge its power of appointment and proposed to settle disagreements, when either house opposed a nominee, by a meeting of the whole Assembly in which each member would possess one vote. This method would eliminate the power of the Upper House altogether, for the twelve assistants and the two executive officers would be vastly outnumbered among the deputies. The Upper House patiently heard this proposal session after session but could not seriously consider relinquishing its only control over appointments. The Lower House claimed that the charter specified this very method for ending stalemates. Furthermore, the deputies said, the fact that Governor Saltonstall had been elected by the Assembly jointly after Governor Winthrop had died in office proved that everyone had once concurred in this procedure. The Upper House replied that the deputies misconstrued

[46] "Journals of the Upper House," May 17, 1721; May 1717; Conn. Arch., Civil Officers, I, 156, 334-343, 366, 368, 374-376, 452, 453.
[47] "Journals of the Upper House," May 17, 1721; May 14, 1723.
[48] Conn. Arch., Civil Officers I, 304; "Journals of the Upper House," Speech of Governor Saltonstall, May 17, 1721.

the charter and distorted the Saltonstall precedent, and the Governor himself called them aggressors. The Lower House answered that they only intended to "Stand for theire Rights and Preveledges by Charter Granted." [49] Throughout the dispute the two Houses saw no other solution than to pass the list of nominees back and forth until a slate agreeable to both could be found.

The deputies were prepared to press for still greater privileges. When in 1716 the colony treasurer died in office, vacating that position in mid-term as the governorship had been vacated upon Winthrop's death, the Lower House at once proposed that the two Houses follow the precedent set at Saltonstall's election and elect the treasurer in joint meeting. In effect it was demanding the right to choose the new treasurer. The Governor and assistants thwarted the proposal in 1716, but it arose again in 1723 and 1724 in more serious circumstances. In 1723 the deputy governor died, and the next year Governor Saltonstall followed him. On both occasions the Lower House pressed for election in a joint assembly. The governorship was at stake in both instances, because the deputy governor customarily became governor upon the incumbent's death. Again the Upper House refused to join the Lower, thereby retaining a check on the deputies, but only after an exchange of resolves revealed the temper of the town delegates. The Lower House declared that the Assembly as a whole represented the freemen in whom the right of election was vested, and that since all the freemen could not be canvassed, the whole Assembly was to act for them. The will of the people was not to be frustrated by a small group of aristocrats, no matter how wise or prominent.[50]

Governor Saltonstall was less troubled by specific disputes over land or appointments or the deputies' power than he was by the erosion of law and authority. Repeatedly he complained that there was "little Order and Government left among Us." [51] He knew that there were complaints abroad that he was "to Strict, Severe and Lordly" and was pained by such reports, for he felt

[49] "Journal of the Lower House," May 1717; Conn. Arch., Civil Officers, I, 145, 322, 173, 476, 84, 364.
[50] Conn. Arch., Civil Officers, I, 257, 439-442, 457, 470, 474.
[51] Conn. Arch., Civil Officers, I, 285.

it his duty to make the unruly sensible of their failure not only to uphold "the Honour but the Usefullness and even Being of Government." "If the Quarrels and Factions, the Bad Temper and Murmurings, which have been of late, should grow or pre-vaile, We can expect no Good, either from God or from Man." [52]

Roger Wolcott, an influential magistrate and later governor, attributed the corruption in government solely to Major Fitch and his party. Wolcott's memoir, written in 1759, stated that "the public men unanimously promoted the public interest" until the end of King Phillip's War and that then some of them set up the "native right" theory and bought and sold Indian lands, using their great power in the Assembly to impart legality to their ventures. Their conniving divided and undermined civil authority.[53] The other assistants largely agreed with Wolcott. The schemes of the "native right" men, the Upper House had declared in the middle of the troubles, were "the principall bane and Ruin of our Ancient Order and peace." [54] The aristocrats were convinced that Fitch made "the Kings Authority and Govt. vile and Contemptible in the Eyes of All men." [55] The *"Principles of Rebellion and Opposition to Government"* for which Fitch stood were danger-ously infectious.[56] All manner of "Discontented and Illdisposed Persons," blinded with their own passions, were won over to his party, for "Lesser Piques and Quarrells Run into that as Smaller brooks into a great River." [57] In the channel of opposition cut by Fitch and the "native right" men, ordinary people voiced their complaints, protected against the wrath of authority which they could not withstand alone. By the same token, divisions in the Assembly encouraged "others to all Contempt of Government and they will think if Some of us Should be for Calling them to Account for any faults the party that are against us, would stand by them." [58] Opposition within the Assembly gave rebels every-where courage to speak up against their rulers.

[52] Conn. Arch., Civil Officers, I, 163.
[53] Wolcott, *Memoir*, 329-330.
[54] Conn. Arch., Towns and Lands, III, 148.
[55] Conn. Arch., Crimes and Misdemeanours, II, 136.
[56] Bulkley, "Preface" to Wolcott, *Poetical Meditations*, xiv.
[57] Conn. Arch., Towns and Lands, III, 148.
[58] "Journals of the Upper House," May 14, 1723.

What had begun as a conflict between a few land magnates in 1686 had by now corrupted hundreds of ordinary men. The struggle between James Fitch and the Winthrops over the Quinebaug lands quickly drew into it the tenants and purchasers who dwelt in the contested area along with speculators from outside. The settlers in Coventry and Colchester who resorted to violence in defense of their lands were not associated directly with James Fitch or the Winthrops but, like the men at Quinebaug, were sucked into politics. Their cases were typical of dozens in which the rulers decided the disposal of farms and woodlands.[59] The dissidents' claims were refuted in the courts, the Assembly saw to their punishment, and the gentlemen in charge were usually acknowledged enemies. The outcome left a feeling of deep bitterness toward civil authority. Opposition became alarmingly widespread, vocal, and open. The division among the legislators extended deep into society, and defenders of the older order recognized that respect for authority was deteriorating both in the population at large and in the Assembly. Politics was becoming a contest of factions.

After 1724 the political wars abated, and not until the decade following the Great Awakening were there controversies of comparable magnitude. But the battles of the 1720's left scars. The conflict over eastern lands changed men's attitudes toward government, preparing the way for the more drastic actions of the 1740's. The quest for land imbued Connecticut farmers with political consciousness and simultaneously diminished in their minds the unassailable sanctity of civil authority. When next rulers aroused popular ire, men acted with an audacity unthinkable in 1690.

[59] For a sample of land disputes not described in this chapter see *Conn. Recs.*, IV, 333; V, 331, 381-382, 510-511; VI, 63-64, 75, 218-219, 343 345-346, 491; Conn. Arch., Towns and Lands, III, 45-47; Norwich, "Proprietor Records," 3-7; Larned, *Windham*, I, 221-227; Deming, *Settlement of Connecticut Towns*, 53, 70.

PART THREE

Money, 1710–1750

PART THREE

VII

New Traders

৶ IN SEVENTEENTH-CENTURY Connecticut towns there were no pronounced incompatibilities among the interests of farmers, tradesmen, and merchants. No recurring economic conflicts put one portion of the populace out of harmony with another. Rather, economic interest drew men into the unifying social order and induced peaceable subjection to the rule of ministers and magistrates. Everyone wanted land, and the town provided it, along with the roads, pasture, and common fencing which enabled individuals to prosper.

Changing economic circumstances destroyed this stability after 1690. Restrictions on new land broke up the old pattern and led to struggles over proprietor rights, division of parishes, and titles to Indian lands. And almost simultaneously another, though lesser, force began to undermine the social order: the appearance of new traders with interests different from those of established merchants.

Before 1690 farmers and merchants had lived at peace because they understood their interdependence. After 1690 more and more farmers entered trade, and a common interest in commerce had the opposite effect from a mutual involvement in agriculture. No farmer conceived of himself as a competitor, for the increase in his output did not seem to hurt his neighbor. But the growth of one trader's business perceptibly diminished another's, heightening social and political friction.

Farmers began to trade on the side because they raised no staple like tobacco or indigo which brought high profits. Lumber and ship's stores were in demand, beef and pork always could be sold, but there were difficulties in expanding the output of both.[1]

[1] Until the Revolution, wood and cattle products (after fish) predominated

Woodlands were becoming so scarce in long-settled communities that town meetings had to prohibit the export of staves or lumber to reserve a sufficient supply for local use. By the middle of the century the bulk of timber exports came from the unsettled forests to the north. Everyone raised meat, but an English visitor estimated that prices were 50 per cent below those in the mother country, while labor costs were 300 per cent higher. The hay shortage continued to limit production.[2] More acres were cleared, but the available land had to support a rapidly increasing population.

Throughout the eighteenth century the Connecticut farmer was a marginal producer. Both his profit and the surplus products he could spare for the market were small. Most people lived comfortably, but frugally.

Their farms yield food—much of cloathing—most of the articles of building—with a surplus sufficient to buy such foreign luxuries as are necessary to make life pass comfortably: there is very little elegance among them, but more of necessaries.[3]

The products of Connecticut agriculture provided a lean existence.

The lack of a satisfactory staple induced farmers to seek any work that promised to supplement their incomes. Weirs to catch fish were set up in the Connecticut River and its tributaries. A Windsor man did a small business in cider and brandy and, instead of raising cattle, sold his hay and grain in the late winter, when feed was running short, thus making the most of the shortage. Others rented out cattle and sheep rather than worry about winter feed. All the traditional crafts provided opportunities for profitable sidelines. Each town had its artisans: at least one weaver, carpenter, blacksmith, tanner, shoemaker, glazier, wheelwright, and stonemason.[4]

---

among New England exports. In 1765 Governor Fitch told the Board of Trade that if anything was a staple in Connecticut it was beef and pork (*Conn. Recs.*, X, 622; cf. *American Husbandry*, 44; Bidwell and Falconer, *History of Agriculture*, 135-136).

[2] *Conn. Recs.*, V, 434-435, 499-500; *American Husbandry*, 65, 66.
[3] *American Husbandry*, 50.
[4] Judd, *Hadley*, 306; Ellsworth, "Account Book," *passim*; Hartford County, "Records," 14, 15; for a representative list of artisans, Steiner, *Guilford*, 250; for other industries, Weaver, "Industry in an Agrarian Economy."

Men without tools or skill sold their labor with no difficulty. For many years 2s. a day in the summer had been the standard wage, but during the inflation of the late 1740's two days work making a wall and digging stones earned £1 8s. and a day carting wood brought £1 5s. Merchants regularly hired help. Jonathan Trumbull in Lebanon employed laborers to operate his farm, to help construct and run his malt house and flour mill, and to drive cattle to Boston; and Dwight of Springfield in Massachusetts let men pay their debts by carting produce, slaughtering and packing animals, and coopering.[5]

Public funds offered income to some. The bounty on rattlesnakes, though small, was helpful, and large numbers of birds and snakes were killed each year in Norwich to earn tiny sums. Ebenezer Grant ran up credit for £142 with the Windsor proprietors by surveying and laying out lots. A parish in Killingly paying 3s. a day hired three dozen men to work on the new meetinghouse. In a letter to the wife of an influential Hartford man, one good woman, alert for ways of enlarging the family income, asked to have her husband selected as a builder for the meetinghouse. Expenditures in town meeting and parish added to the income of people at every level.[6]

A common form of expansion was construction of a saw- or gristmill. Distilling rum was so profitable that the colony discouraged excessive production. Shipbuilding appeared in nearly every town along the coast or up the Connecticut River. A poor person could not invest in these enterprises, but people in the middle range could. A one-sixteenth share in a Windsor vessel in 1748 entailed an investment of less than £14.[7]

Trade was one of the important expedients for earning some money beyond the farm income. Young Samuel Nott, whose father had lost his property in a debt case, went off in the winter, when

[5] Ebenezer Backus, "Acct. Book, 1744-1747," Feb. 16, July 9; Weaver, *Jonathan Trumbull*, 14-16, 21; Martin, *Merchants and Trade*, 155-156.

[6] Caulkins, *Norwich*, 297-298; *Conn. Recs.*, V, 563-564; E. Grant and R. Grant, "Account Books," I, *passim;* Larned, *Windham*, I, 308; Elizabeth Belknap to Elizabeth Wyllys, April 14, 1722, *Wyllys Papers*, 400-401.

[7] *American Husbandry*, 49; *Conn. Recs.*, VII, 138, 565; Bailyn and Bailyn, *Massachusetts Shipping*, 106-109; H. R. Stiles, *Windsor*, I, 767-768; for the distribution of commercial investments in Massachusetts, see Bailyn and Bailyn, 56-59.

he was not needed at home, to sell buckles, pins, buttons, pamphlets, and other sundries. Later he opened a small trade in New Haven, where he accumulated enough to put himself through Yale. Others found ready markets for cider and liquor in the Indian villages on the outskirts of nearly every town. The Assembly forbade this trade but admitted in its repeated prohibitions that restrictions were not observed, even by respectable persons. Control was ineffective because the barter was at a distance from the town, where it could not be easily discovered, and because almost anyone could make a start with beverages purchased on credit or manufactured at home. One man indicted for selling liquor was so poor that the assembly agreed to amortize his £8 fine over four years.[8]

The sale of liquor to English settlers also enticed aspiring men of commerce. In 1676 the clergy rebuked the colony for its excess of tippling houses where evil flourished "for filthy Lucres Sake." [9] The ministers did not propose to close all taverns, which were necessary for travelers' comfort, but the clergy did disapprove of the small retailer who illicitly sold to apprentices, servants, and the dissolute. The Assembly forbade the unlicensed to sell liquor in the small quantities that the poor men could afford and regretted that such large numbers of "illdisposed and indigent persons" were often "so hardie as to presume to sell and retail strong beer, ale, cyder . . . and to keep tipling houses." Despite the law, illegal retailers supplied with smuggled rum remained in business. Frequently the offenders were so poor that they could not pay the fine without hardship to their families, and whipping had to be substituted.[10] The Legislature also complained that undue pressure was put on county courts for tavern licenses and that altogether too many were issued.[11]

[8] Nott, "Life of Nott," 45, 46, 50, 52, 59-61, 75, 77, 79; *Conn. Recs.*, I, 263, 344; VI, 31; VII, 472; Caulkins, *Norwich*, 278-279; Caulkins, *New London*, 247, 372; Judd, 64-65; petition of Ben Uncas to the General Court, Oct. 1773, *Talcott Papers*, I, 292.

[9] Ministers of Connecticut to the Church of Connecticut, *Wyllys Papers*, 237.

[10] *Conn. Recs.*, IV, 437.

[11] For liquor laws, *Conn. Recs.*, II, 133; IV, 136, 145, 436-438; V, 319; VI, 31, 156-157, 221, 223-224, 282-283, 350, 392; VII, 110, 472, 561-562, 565; VIII, 57, 276.

Tavernkeeping often was the beginning of a larger trade. The son of one of the first tavernkeepers in East Windsor became the largest retailer in the parish. Alexander Pygan, who began life as a ne'er-do-well, turned to innkeeping and died a prosperous merchant. Examples like these set the course for others who saw the beginnings of their fortune in a small liquor business.[12]

Craftsmen also stocked a few commodities to retail among their neighbors. Samuel Nott's father, a tanner, became a merchant of sorts shortly after setting up his tanning shop by filling his store with goods purchased on credit; later on he bartered goods for horses which he drove to New Jersey to sell. Thomas Clark, a weaver in Waterbury, having found customers for the products of his loom and deciding to sell other goods as well, obtained sugar, salt, wine, rum, molasses, tobacco, and nails from Derby and New Haven and also took in boarders and occasionally victualed soldiers; prospering in commerce, he rose in society and became justice of the peace, selectman, deputy, and town treasurer. Men like Clark and Nott, discontented with farming, were quick to enter trade whenever they saw an opportunity.[13]

The opportunities for chapmen, storekeepers, and taverners multiplied as the town expanded. After 1690 small communities four or five miles from the center of business appeared in every township. In each of these new parishes there was at least one licensed tavern and many small, illicit liquor businesses. Forbidden by law from idling in taverns, apprentices, servants, and the shiftless gladly patronized more secretive retailers.

Legal trade in the outlying parishes also flourished as the long road to shops in the town plot created new opportunities for the enterprising. Farmers with small surpluses—a couple of barrels of pork, a few bushels of corn—would share a cart to transport their produce, and the man who drove would make small purchases for the others. Before long someone saw that a stock of

---

[12] H. R. Stiles, *Windsor*, I, 418, 427; Caulkins, *New London*, 341. The men chosen for inn-keepers in Fairfield were prominent figures (Fairfield, "Town Records," B, pt. 2, 245). The combination of farming, tavern-keeping, and a small retail trade was common in England too (Campbell, *English Yeoman*, 26, 158-159).

[13] Nott, "Life of Nott," 10, 14, 19; Bronson, *Waterbury*, 144-145.

store goods in the parish would be a convenience to neighbors and bring a small profit.

The opportunities for trade multiplied in the new towns which sprang up after 1690. Lines of communication with nearby markets had to be set up, and men were needed to collect, transport, and sell produce. To open trade, a merchant already established in a market town required a connection with someone living in the new settlement. Almost every purchaser bought on credit, and only a person well acquainted with the inhabitants knew how far to trust each customer. From the buyer's point of view as well, trade in a strange town was awkward. As Stoddard pointed out, not only was travel costly, but "the Man is also in a strait because strangers will not trust him, and the Seller takes that advantage to oppress him." [14] Town residents therefore preferred to deal with a local tradesman.

These conditions induced some of the new settlers to become tradesmen and shopkeepers. No great capital was needed, since established merchants in nearby towns, knowing that sales in the country towns were often more profitable than elsewhere, readily supplied goods on credit. The difficulty of importing goods encouraged the inhabitants to pay more, and their ignorance of the market sometimes allowed chapmen to raise prices excessively. "Crafty Men" abused the ignorant. "In Country-Towns, Men sometimes give a shilling for that, which at the Market Town, might be had for six pence." [15]

Trade brought prosperity to many settlers in new plantations. William and Roger Sherman, sons of a Massachusetts shoemaker of small estate, moved to New Milford in the 1740's and jointly bought a store in 1750; shortly afterwards Roger opened a branch in New Haven, and began his rise to prominence there. Joseph Trumbull, who came to Lebanon from Suffield in 1705, collected small herds of cattle from the nearby towns and drove the animals overland to Boston, bringing back imported goods which he retailed at home; his son Jonathan expanded the business, prospered, and eventually was elected governor. [16]

[14] Stoddard, *An Answer*, 2.
[15] Stoddard, 1.
[16] Boardman, *Roger Sherman*, 15, 37; Weaver, *Jonathan Trumbull*, 3-5, 12.

Men of smaller fortunes sold to scattered settlers who often preferred to buy from peddlers on the back country roads rather than journey into town. In Woodstock, the first settlement in the present Windham County, the earliest attempt to trade with Providence was by a "Butter-cart" which picked up small products from housewives in exchange for minor luxuries. In the next generation this enterprise grew into a large store, selling a complete line of West India goods. Carts went all over the country picking up pork, beef, and ashes for potash, to be exchanged in Providence for molasses and rum.[17]

Peddlers prospered so well that larger merchants complained. An act of 1717 levied a duty of 20s. per £100 of goods carried by every "hawker, pedlar, petty chapman, or other trading person, going from town to town travelling either on foot, or with horse or horses."[18] In 1721 the Assembly prohibited itinerant retailing altogether, but in 1757 they gave way again and issued licenses for £5. This amount did not adequately discourage peddlers, however, and in 1765 the fee was increased to £20.[19]

Established merchants in market towns profited at least as much as the petty traders in the rising settlements. Ebenezer Backus in Norwich, for example, was able to expand his retail business into wholesale lines because of his connections with men north of Norwich who purchased large quantities of merchandise and repaid in cash or produce. Andrew Minor bought £30 worth of cloth on one month's credit, Eleazer Fitch of Windham received two month's credit on 222 panes of glass, and Eliphalet Dyer purchased £92 worth of hollowware, nearly a half a ton. In addition, Backus conducted some legal business and loaned out money.[20] Involving as many men as it did, Backus' firm and others like it made Norwich more and more of a mercantile

[17] Larned, *Historic Gleanings*, 143-144.
[18] *Conn. Recs.*, VI, 23-24.
[19] *Conn. Recs.*, VI, 276-277; VII, 166; Hooker, *Colonial Trade*, 37-38; Conn. Arch., Trade and Maritime, I, 93-95; II, 50, 81.
[20] Ebenezer Backus, "Account Book, 1748-50," July 7, July 11, July 31, June 23, 1749; cf. July 1747, June 14, Nov. 12, 1748, and "Acct. Book, 1744-1747," June 11, Sept. 28, May 19, 1744. For Jonathan Trumbull's wholesale business, Weaver, *Jonathan Trumbull*, 18; for a similar operation in Windsor, E. Grant, "Account Books," I, *passim*.

community. One of the parishes, Chelsea, the port at the head of navigation on the Thames, was almost wholly devoted to commerce. "There is but very few in that Society," declared a petition in 1752, "but what Depend on Trade and Navigation for their livelyhood." [21]

Transportation improved with the greater flow of commerce, since inland towns were forced to find outlets on the water for their produce. From 1700 to 1750 dozens of new roads linked the towns east of the Connecticut River to markets in Providence, Hartford, and Boston. In 1740 Norwich, Lebanon, and Windham inhabitants argued that the amount of carting and traveling justified a new road to the north, and from 1751 to 1761 Norwich submitted three petitions for a lottery to build a cart bridge near the landing, explaining that most of the eastern part of the colony marketed their produce there. Preston inhabitants asked for a better road to Stonington, where they marketed their lumber. [22]

After the 1730's the coast towns in the west also enlarged their harbors, wharves, and warehouses. A petition for a bridge over the Saugutuck River in Fairfield spoke of the need to "relieve and remedy so public an inconvenience, in so great a road to so great a market and where is so great connection." In 1724 a large group of Wallingford men cleared the river down to New Haven to carry vessels to the sea, and in 1761 two Waterbury residents requested that the town employ highway workers to clear the Naugutuck River, "it having been conjectured that the river from Waterbury to Derby might be made navigable for battooing." [23]

Expanding markets for provisions matched Connecticut's population growth and stimulated new commercial ventures. The British West Indies absorbed more and more cattle, horses, and staves, and after 1717 trade with the French islands also thrived. Newfoundland remained a good market for provisions and timber products, and in the 1720's the English colonies took over a large

[21] Conn. Arch., Ecclesiastical Affairs, VIII, 356a.

[22] I. S. Mitchell, *Roads*, 13, 20; Conn. Arch., Travel, I, 104; *ibid.*, II, 299, 301, 338.

[23] Fairfield, "Town Records," B, pt. I, 1733, 1766, 1749, 1758, 1760, 1761; Federal Writers' Project, *Milford*, 39-40; Steiner, *Guilford*, 218; cf. Bronson, *Waterbury*, 98, 99, 101; Boardman, *Roger Sherman*, 28-29; I. S. Mitchell, 29, 30; *Conn. Recs.*, VI, 463.

part of the commerce with Nova Scotia. The rising export of fish to European, South Atlantic, and Caribbean ports supported a growing fleet which consumed provisions from Connecticut. The expansion of these staples and the development of whaling served farmers and petty traders all over New England.[24]

The intermittent expeditions to Canada and against raiding Indians, characteristic of the entire period from 1690 to 1763, also aided trade. Military campaigns increased demands for provisions: vast quantities of flour and barrelled pork were sold to the army, and victuallers and innkeepers along the line of march housed and fed individual companies of soldiers.[25]

The campaigns also compelled the Assembly to issue currency, an immense boon to trade. The strain of excessive spending when money was scarce was more than the colony could bear. Officers complained that no one trusted the colony's credit because the government paid so meanly. Taverners refused to serve the soldiers unless the officer in charge personally guaranteed payment of the bill. The colony hoped for reimbursement from England but was disappointed until after the middle of the century. Consequently, the Assembly was forced to issue bills of credit in 1709 and thereafter partially financed all of its campaigns by deficit spending.[26] The bills rapidly dispersed throughout the colony as salaries to civil officers and soldiers spread the money widely. More went to the commissioners obtaining supplies, from them to friends who assisted in collecting provisions, and thence to small traders and farmers. In one year's time the new currency was so widely

[24] E. R. Johnson, *History of Domestic and Foreign Commerce*, I, 95. The author of *American Husbandry* thought the West Indies would absorb as much cattle as New England could possibly produce (pp. 58-59). Weeden, *Economic and Social History*, II, 595; Weaver, *Jonathan Trumbull*, 99-100; Instructions to Jonathan Belcher, Dec. 19, 1727, *Talcott Papers*, I, 145; *Colonial Currency Reprints*, III, 377; see also *American Husbandry*, 41, 44; Bidwell and Falconer, *History of Agriculture*, 111. For a suggestive comment on the expansion of New England in these years, see Morison, "A Generation of Expansion," 272; see also E. R. Johnson, I, 85.

[25] Direct purchases by the British fleet, when they occurred, were a great boon (*Colonial Currency Reprints*, II, 194).

[26] B. Trumbull, *Connecticut*, I, 354; John Chester to Fitz-John Winthrop, Aug. 16, 1703, *Winthrop Papers*, pt. V, 140-141; John Chester to Fitz-John Winthrop, Aug. 20, 1703, *ibid.*, pt. V, 148; Gurdon Saltonstall to Henry Ashurst, Jan. 30, 1710, *ibid.*, pt. VI, 211; Weaver, *Jonathan Trumbull*, 37.

distributed that the Assembly could equitably require everyone to pay his taxes in cash instead of produce.[27]

After 1744 hostilities with France rapidly increased military expenditures, and the opportunities for enterprising traders multiplied. In a very few years a poor man might rise to considerable wealth. Solomon Mack of Lyme, a person of small estate reared in indentures as a farm laborer, enlisted in the army in 1755 and was able, after a year's service, to come back to Lyme and pay £80 for a house and a tract of land. In 1757 he returned to the army, this time as a teamster with his own oxen. The next year he purchased more land in Lyme, married, and the following spring set up a sutler's shop at Crown Point. Through a misfortune, he lost his profits but managed nevertheless to buy 1,600 acres in Vermont and another tract in Lyme. Around 1760 he freighted a vessel for New York and sold his cargo for high prices. Damage to the vessel ate up his profits and compelled him to move to Vermont, where he recovered by engaging in trade once more and by speculating in land.[28] Eventually Mack became a prominent figure, and his career served to illustrate how a poor man by moving in and out of military service could accumulate enough capital to enter commerce.[29]

Though not on so large a scale, the earlier wars had provided similar opportunities. From the first decades of the eighteenth century onward, military expenditures, new markets, and growing old markets in New England and abroad quickened movement along the lines of trade. Especially in new communities where commerce was fluid, men dissatisfied with the returns from agriculture competed for the trade of their neighbors.

Commercial prosperity, exciting and rewarding as it was for individuals, did not increase the peace and order of Connecticut society. New traders, whose interests ran counter to those of the old, plagued the established merchants and agitated the colonial government, and because both groups included men of force and

[27] *Conn. Recs.,* V, 157, 166.
[28] Bennett, "Solomon Mack," 631-632, 713-714.
[29] A newspaper notice in 1758 declared that most of the carters in service with the army were poor men trying to get out of debt (*Connecticut Gazette,* Dec. 30, 1758).

ingenuity, the clash badly shook the social order. The central issue was paper money. Small traders, operating on a shoestring, needed capital to begin a venture, to expand it, or to recover from one that had failed. Usually they began on borrowed capital, and they were always short of money to satisfy their creditors. Overconfident factors of British merchants, in order "to clear their Warehouses and Shops of Goods the faster and make room for a new Store, and Enliven Trade," were "very fond of Trusting out great quantities of Goods with almost any Body that would take them." [30] Other traders in European wares "encouraged people to take them up, giving large prizes for the produce of our Country." [31] Confident that sales would continue, smaller merchants, country traders, chapmen, and hawkers went deeply in debt. A single calamity could destroy the trader in this precarious financial position; a ship lost at sea or a drop in prices might drastically reduce his capital. Without a reserve to meet his debts as they came due, he had no alternative but to borrow further, hoping to restore his finances.[32]

Beginners were solidly behind the movements for land banks and inexpensive government loans. Mortgage loans facilitated the exchange of land for a medium of exchange usable in trade. Men on the borderline of agriculture and commerce gladly risked losing their land, which earned small profits, in order to stay in trade, which promised more. Possible depreciation of money, being all to their advantage, did not worry them. As the "hard money" men claimed, the one to complain of a stable currency "is the Man that has little or no Stock, that runs largely into Debt, and depends upon paying *One Hundred Pounds* with *Seventy five*." [33]

In Connecticut, as elsewhere in the colonies, cheap currency was considered the best encouragement for a discontented farmer inclined to start a small business. As one antibank man said, easy money was a boon to a husbandman, who "besides his Farm . . .

[30] *Colonial Currency Reprints*, I, 421.

[31] *Colonial Currency Reprints*, II, 282; cf. II, 342.

[32] The standard description of currency in the early eighteenth century is Nettels, *Money Supply*. I am indebted to Hammond's *Banks and Politics* for useful insights.

[33] *Colonial Currency Reprints*, I, 126-127; III, 71.

wants to be fingering of Trade, or to keep a Tavern."[34] Benjamin Franklin saw that available currency drew out all those eager to enter trade who had been held back for want of capital: "Many that understand Business very well, but have not a Stock sufficient of their own, will be encouraged to borrow Money; to trade with when they can have it at moderate Interest."[35] An advocate of paper money argued that "men of Projecting Brains," who often helped the commonwealth, needed money to work out their schemes. "Every Body almost would be Improving his talent, if Money were stiring."[36] One bank advocate in Massachusetts accused the "hard money" men of hoping to discourage the "many Persons who now run into Trade and Shop-keeping, and Shipping, and Fishing" and to force them back to cultivate the land by decreasing the medium of exchange.[37] In 1749 Deputy Governor Roger Wolcott received a letter from Massachusetts urging currency stabilization, in which the writer lamented that when "men could pay £100 with £75, they have been tempted to leave Industry and labouring with their hands and turn Jockys and Hucksters to live by their wits and sharping upon their neighbours by money they have borrowed and could pay so easily."[38] No one doubted that easy money produced new traders.

The issuance of paper on the scale advocated by new enterprisers horrified older merchants, who often benefited from the scarcity of currency. When money brought 10 per cent interest without the risks of commerce, the wealthy preferred to lend rather than trade, and many great merchants had huge sums owed to them. More than half of the Dwight estate in 1768 was in bonds and notes. When Timothy Thrall of Windsor died in 1724, he owned store goods amounting to £411, land worth £1,145 and mortgages, bonds, and notes for £2,923. Men with estates divided

[34] *Colonial Currency Reprints,* II, 325.

[35] *Colonial Currency Reprints,* II, 337.

[36] *Colonial Currency Reprints,* I, 406.

[37] *Colonial Currency Reprints,* III, 129.

[38] Samuel Welles to Roger Wolcott, Jan. 31, 1749, *Law Papers,* III, 289. Governor Hunter of New York said the circulation of paper money "enables the many to trade, to some small loss to the few who had monopolized it" (quoted in Weeden, II, 477; see also *Colonial Currency Reprints,* II, 80).

in such proportions took a huge loss when currency depreciated, and for them cheap money was of course anathema.[39]

Paper money also threatened the established merchants' trade. Under the barter system, a farmer could hardly escape dealing at the same store year after year. Once indebted, he was obligated to turn over his surplus to his creditor to pay for past advances; if he traded with someone else, he faced prosecution and imprisonment for debt. The merchant could therefore set prices as he wished. A Connecticut statute of 1734 noted the disposition of "many ill minded persons" to force their debtors to "trade further with them, upon unreasonable advance, to the great oppression and undoing of many families."[40] In a barter economy even "good men" were "laid open to temptations, and opportunities given to bad ones, that exact from those who must crave Credit, or cannot make suitable pay."[41]

A new merchant in the town buying for cash could easily take over the business of his entrenched competitor. With the money received from the new trader, the farmer could then pay old debts and free himself to sell his produce to the highest bidder and to purchase imported goods at the lowest price. Where there was plenty of money, one pamphlet commented, "no *Buyer* will be bound to one Person, or Market; nor purchase Credit at the Grantor's price; nor be necessitated to become Servant to the Lender."[42] When paper money was in circulation, John Wise of Massachusetts observed, there was always a better market for farm produce.[43]

In 1765 a series of vituperative articles in the *Hartford Courant* revealed precisely why new traders paying cash were feared and despised. When, just before harvest, Thomas Davidson, a new

[39] *Colonial Currency Reprints,* III, 55, 168-169, 139; Lisbon, "Newent Congregational Church, Records," II, 6; *Conn. Recs.,* VI, 316, 320; Martin, 95. Thrall's is in the Hartford Probate Records, Connecticut State Library, Hartford.
[40] *Conn. Recs.,* VII, 514. For the workings of a country store, Weaver, *Jonathan Trumbull,* 18-19.
[41] *Colonial Currency Reprints,* I, 113.
[42] *Colonial Currency Reprints,* I, 112.
[43] *Colonial Currency Reprints,* II, 185.

merchant, began advertising his goods for sale at low prices, offering to pay cash for farm produce, sixteen Hartford merchants signed an article in the next issue warning the inhabitants to avoid Davidson. They asked readers to "inform those who are any ways so indebted to us, as above, that we expect after so long Patience used with them, that they discharge their respective Ballances due to us, forthwith." Any debtors trading with Davidson "may depend on being immediately sued without Exception, or farther Notice."

A "Letter from a Farmer" refused to accept this threat. The merchants were saying, the "Farmer" rejoined, that "no stranger in the mercantile Way shall stand among us; the People shall buy only of us, and at our Price, and we will have their Produce as we please." He urged everyone to join him in patronizing the "generous dealer": "Carry him your Produce for his Cash or his Goods, with his moderate Advance." Do not fear "such Combinations as mean to enslave us," he reassured his readers, "for if you have got in Arrear to any of them, before their Bailiff, Dun, or Suits can o'er-take us; meet them with that which answers all Things," meaning, of course, cash. Then the farmer could with satisfaction see his "debts cancelled; bid Defiance to their Oppressive Designs," and in turn exact a righteous price for his own produce.[44]

This episode illustrates the reasons why paper money divided small and beginning traders from large and established ones, the outsiders from the insiders. Bills threatened the settled merchant's control and opened a source of commercial power to the new enterpriser. Neither side explicitly discussed competition, since a frank defense of undiluted private interest was unsuitable for public petitions. Instead, the opponents of cheap bills argued that a depreciating medium permitted dishonest debtors to cheat their creditors, while supporters of paper money emphasized the value to farmers of a brisker market, the need for commercial capital, and the easing of all transactions when there was an ample medium of trade.

The fact remained, however, that new merchants jeopardized

[44] *Connecticut Courant*, Aug. 19, 1765; Aug. 26, 1765; Sept. 2, 1765; Sept. 9, 1765.

the positions of older ones. Established traders opposed rapid loosening and expansion of the economy and preferred gradual growth. Backed by capital of their own and supplied with more by their connections in Boston and New York, they needed no more government aid than their influence with the Assembly already afforded. Both groups were energetic and ambitious, and both argued their cases in the name of the public good. Inevitably their disputes invaded the Assembly, where the paper money question had to be finally settled. In the resulting ruckus, new traders were not wholly triumphant, but older magnates were compelled in part to give way to their competitors.

VIII

East versus West

‿ঌ PETTY TRADERS were not in themselves a political threat in the first half of the eighteenth century. Power and social status were so closely linked that one man of rank offset numerous discontented storekeepers. The pleas of peddlers and chapmen for paper money could not alone overcome the stolid conservatism of the civil rulers. New traders became a formidable force only because important social and political figures also advocated paper money and argued for it in the Assembly.

East of the Connecticut River merchants of all ranks, many of the well-established along with new ones, agitated for paper money. Rapid growth there accounted for the general interest in currency issues, for the same population explosion that inflated the value of Fitch's lands stimulated trade. Eastern Connecticut was settled doubly fast because of immigration from Massachusetts. Governor Law said in 1749 that the largest proportion of the residents of northeastern Connecticut came from that province.[1] Fed by the influx, twenty towns were organized in the east in the forty-five years after 1690, while only five appeared in the west. New communities and a swelling population opened vast new markets. Expanding their operations to make the most of the opportunities, large merchants and small alike required capital.

The increase in the wealth of the east was phenomenal. The prosperity of Norwich is a useful index of eastern growth because most of the trade from the central portion of the section centered there. In 1690 Norwich's tax assessment was eleventh largest out of twenty-six towns, near the middle of the list, while in 1742

[1] Larned, *Windham*, I, 491; cf. pp. 49-95, 110, 324; Garvan, *Architecture and Town-Planning*, 13. For growth in the east, see Appendix I.

it was first among forty-seven towns, so greatly had it prospered from trade with the back-country that had grown up behind it in five decades.[2] Petitions from Norwich in the 1730's observed that many of the inhabitants seemed "with fixed Eye to be Set upon Trade and Commerce." [3]

Other eastern towns shared the prosperity. Traders in Preston, Windham, and Lebanon all operated ships out of Norwich, and both Windham and Lebanon petitioned the Assembly for the privilege of holding market days for people in the surrounding towns. Woodstock became a comparable trade center on the road to Boston. Middletown and older market towns on the Connecticut River also profited from the inland trade. The fact that eastern Connecticut's share of the colony's tax assessments more than doubled between 1690 and 1740 gives a rough measure of its relatively rapid growth.[4]

Abundant economic opportunities encouraged merchants to expand. They strove to win a share of the traffic in the new settlements and had to stretch their resources to enlarge their business. The established merchant in the east needed additional capital as sorely as his smaller competitor, and all united to ask the government for aid. The imposing names of Huntington, Saltonstall, and Leffingwell appeared on the petitions for government loans received in the Assembly.[5] Their influence eventually persuaded the legislature to lend paper to the traders.

Much opposition had to be overcome before the eastern men had their way. From the middle of the 1720's onward bills introduced in the legislature authorized colony loans to anyone who could offer land as security. Paper money proponents argued that it was needed "to procure the Commodities which in this Country are Sutable to Send abroad to the West India Islands." In 1726 and 1728 the Lower House passed bills setting up such a land bank, but in both instances the conversatives in the Upper House de-

[2] *Conn. Recs.*, VIII, 507-508, 528-529.
[3] Conn. Arch., Trade and Maritime, I, 101.
[4] Conn. Arch., Ecclesiastical Affairs, XII, 139; Travel, II, 339; Trade and Maritime, II, 73, 75; Larned, *Windham*, I, 45. Tax assessments by town are listed annually in *Conn. Recs.* See Appendix II.
[5] Conn. Arch., Trade and Maritime, I, 101, 103-105.

feated the measures. Refused a public bank, men from New London proposed to erect a private trading company authorized to loan bills secured by mortgages, but this petition was also rejected.[6]

Undiscouraged, the New London merchants petitioned for a charter creating the New London Society for Trade and Commerce, whose ostensible purpose was to accumulate sufficient capital to open a trade with Europe. Though the subscribers probably had more in mind, they sincerely intended to engage in international commerce, and they knew that the Assembly was willing to charter a company for foreign trade.

For years Connecticut merchants had sought to bypass middlemen in Boston, Newport, and New York in order to earn for themselves the profits of direct commerce with Europe. Governor Talcott told the Lords of Trade that Connecticut was always studying ways of dealing directly with Britain.[7] Such wishes were not easily fulfilled, however, for Connecticut men were dependent on Boston and New York in the same way that farmers were tied to merchants under the barter system. Each cargo had to be shipped to creditors in the great ports to pay for the goods advanced on the last journey. English merchants were willing to risk shipments only to American traders they knew and trusted, and few in Connecticut enjoyed such connections. Their only hope was to accumulate a surplus beyond the required payment to their creditors and ship that to England, and few merchants could spare enough to make up such cargoes. Obligations in Boston or New York required that every shipment go to one port or the other. The stated aim of the New London Society for Trade and Commerce was to pool the capital of a large number of merchants to make possible direct shipments to England.

Fifty-eight men first petitioned for the charter, and nearly eighty eventually subscribed. They declared that their company would advance the public good by starting an independent trade with Europe and so was worthy of government backing. The Assembly

[6] Conn. Arch., Finance and Currency, I, 314; II, 49, 50, 140, 150; A. Davis, "A Connecticut Land Bank."

[7] Feb. 12, 1733, *Talcott Papers,* I, 272; cf. Hooker, *Colonial Trade,* 7; *Conn. Recs.,* III, 301; IX, 283-285; Conn. Arch., Trade and Maritime, I, 97, 103, 110; Caulkins, *New London,* 229.

responded favorably, and in 1732 the New London Society for Trade and Commerce was in business.[8]

Perhaps the subscribers planned all along to issue bills once their charter was granted, or perhaps they discovered that even eighty of them were unable to accumulate the capital necessary to purchase a ship and buy a cargo. In either case, during its first year the Society began to issue bills of credit. These were simply promissory notes given to the subscribers in return for mortgages, and with such notes, circulated as money, the company built a ship and fitted it with a cargo, becoming in the process a land bank. Without the supplementary capital, the trading company would have collapsed; by going beyond the limits of their charter to issue bills of credit, they had a fair chance to succeed.

Before any profits were realized, however, the government destroyed the enterprise. As soon as it became known that the New London Society was issuing bills of credit, Governor Talcott halted its operations, declaring that the charter of 1732 granted no authority to print money and that the bills were contrary to the peace of the Crown and a great wrong to purchasers.[9] Although ordered to divide their stock and reimburse the holders of the notes, some of the subscribers privately covenanted to add £50 apiece to the existing stock and to carry on the ventures already afoot. They were finally ruined when their schooner was shipwrecked, and the Spaniards captured another ship.[10]

Talcott's suspension of the New London Society's charter relieved western merchants, who feared inflation and the increase of new traders. The New London Society also opened the alarming prospect of a wholesale commercial invasion from the east. With its cheap money, the New London Society threatened to win business in areas which western merchants had long controlled.

Westerners were apprehensive because they had seen Rhode Island's paper money enable its merchants to engross the trade of Massachusetts, a frightening example of how ambitious traders

[8] A full account of the Society and its fate is in A. Davis.

[9] Governor Talcott to the Sheriff of Hartford County, Feb. 9, 1733, *Talcott Papers*, I, 269.

[10] Conn. Arch., Trade and Maritime, I, 186, 200, 203. Petitions for relief from interest payments are in Conn. Arch., Trade and Maritime, I, 195-233.

supported by government power could wreak havoc in the settled commercial order. In the seventeenth century Rhode Island, like Maine and Connecticut, was a commercial outpost of Boston. But the decades after 1700 brought economic independence, and Rhode Island vessels roamed the Atlantic and Caribbean as widely as did Bay Colony ships. By the Revolution Newport was the fifth largest city on the mainland. Rhode Island merchants penetrated the Massachusetts and Connecticut countryside buying provisions, and their carts moved along the highways carrying local produce one way and imported goods the other. Connecticut ships went to Newport almost as frequently as to Boston. By 1730 Rhode Island had largely achieved what the New London Society aimed at: a foreign trade of her own and consequent dominance of a large hinterland.[11]

Rhode Island's fertile Narragansett country and the whaling industry partly accounted for the little colony's prosperity, but contemporary observers stressed the effect of its loan bills. Boston merchants, accustomed to dominance in New England's overseas trade, lamented the power of Rhode Island's cheap money: "We may speak as contemptibly as we please of the *Rhode Islanders* emitting Bills, they have found the Sweet of it, for they have eaten up half our Trade with it, and will soon eat us out of all." [12] Supplied with cheap bills, Rhode Island traders crossed the border to buy provisions that formerly went to Boston. Stocking their ships with Massachusetts produce, they took over a large share of the West Indian trade and eventually imported goods from England.[13] Benjamin Franklin stated the general principle precisely:

If in two Neighbouring Countries the Traders of one, by Reason of a

[11] Bailyn, *New England Merchants*, 99; *Colonial Currency Reprints*, I, 424; III, 146, 211; Larned, *Historic Gleanings*, 132-146; J. Eliot to Stiles, June 8, 1762, E. Stiles, *Extracts*, 481; *Conn. Recs.*, VII, 582.

[12] *Colonial Currency Reprints*, III, 146; cf. III, 318; II, 440-441.

[13] *Colonial Currency Reprints*, I, 424; II, 440-441; III, 51, 146, 170-171, 211, 315, 318. Stonington, on the Rhode Island border, had a similar complaint. Merchants there reported in 1727 "Multitudes of foreign or Perigrine Pedlers" flocking into the colony, underselling Connecticut merchants (quoted in *Memorial History of Hartford County*, I, 321). The main worth of colonial currency was for use in local markets since it suffered such an immense discount abroad (Jeremy Dummer to Governor Talcott, Oct. 12, 1725, *Talcott Papers*, I, 64).

greater Plenty of Money, can borrow it to trade with at a lower Rate than the Traders of the other, they will infallibly have the Advantage, and get the greatest Part of that Trade into their own Hands.[14]

The New London Society explicitly intended to follow Rhode Island's course, hoping to free itself of Boston's control.

But the New London Society also threatened Hartford and New Haven merchants. With cheap money its members could enter the trade areas of the older centers exactly as Rhode Island had those of Boston. A Connecticut clergyman, writing before the Revolution, explained that Hartford and New Haven merchants, jealous of New London, obtained goods at reduced prices from New York or Boston, which also feared the rise of that rival and thus undersold their competitors.[15] The western towns could never allow New London the advantage of its own paper money.

Talcott's suspension of the New London Society charter temporarily stopped the threatened invasion from the east, but the agitation for paper money continued. Many merchants still felt that the colonial government should make loans to enterprising traders. James Packer of Groton, a town just east of New London, wrote to the Assembly in 1733 asking that Connecticut issue a large sum of paper money. With these bills the colony could escape the domination of Boston merchants, "Ingross their trade and consequently Riches, and thereby . . . Shift the immence burthen of Debts which now lie upon our Shoulders on to theirs." One-fifth of the colony, Packer computed, was under mortgage to Boston and Newport. With its own bills Connecticut could "Balance our Accounts . . . soon gain our debts, and Inrich ourselves with foreign Commodities by fair trading." [16]

Debt-ridden farmers joined the eastern merchants in the desire for a bank, hoping that loans would ease the pressure on them. Everything farmers purchased was advanced on credit because not enough currency was available for cash dealings. The storekeeper carried the debts on the books until the next harvest, when the borrowers evened the accounts as much as they could. A government loan could help farmers when crops failed or when they contemplated large capital expenditures.

[14] *Colonial Currency Reprints,* II, 337.

[15] Peters, *Connecticut,* 270-271.

[16] James Packer to Governor Talcott, Groton, May 7, 1733, *Talcott Papers,* I, 279-280.

In the seventeenth century indebtedness had seldom amounted to much. Farmers dared not go beyond their limit to pay and risk losing their houses and lands, and shopkeepers were cautious in advancing goods. A poor farmer who produced little for the market received and probably asked for little credit, but storekeepers were much more generous with the prosperous, who regularly brought in cattle or lumber to sell. The men most deeply involved in debt were those with high expectations; borrowing came as a result of bright, not dim, economic expectations. Farmers sought loans when they wanted to increase their holdings and improve their style of life, hopes that not many entertained during the first century of settlement.

Indebtedness increased in the eighteenth century as good markets and more money in circulation eased the difficulties of repayment. Jared Eliot deplored the unbounded confidence growing prosperity induced: "We know indeed our present Ability, but we depend greatly on what we think may be hereafter. Thus many run into Debt without measure, and without end, hoping they shall be able to Pay next Year, when they have no visible means for a ground of their hope." [17] In the steadily improving economy farmers grew sure of their ability to meet obligations, and traders were willing to trust their customers with more goods for long periods.

Farmers also went into debt to buy new land. They had no choice when the free town plots once available to all inhabitants were controlled by the proprietary and when rights in new places were costly. Few had sufficient liquid capital to purchase a share; almost everyone had to borrow to buy. John Wise in Massachusetts argued that an emission of bills would be the best stimulus to settlement of the wilderness, and an opponent of the bank agreed that government loans would be used for stocking farms and buying new land.[18] Farmers, like traders, wanted capital for expansion.

---

[17] *Give Cesar his Due,* 43. One observer, appalled by the misery of indebted families, thought a shortening of credit would by itself heal the economy (*Colonial Currency Reprints,* I, 427-429; cf. I, 421; II, 282).

[18] *Colonial Currency Reprints,* II, 187-188, 325.

Immigrants to the northwest colony towns in the 1740's, for example, bought their land on credit. Many later asked for relief, for they found it impossible to open the new town and pay interest too. Sharon told the Court that if it were required to pay interest, it would be forced to rent its lands to rich merchants "at their own prices." When Salisbury residents felt themselves in danger of losing their lands, they asked for a loan without interest, suggesting that if the colony treasury was low, more money could be printed.[19]

The spread of indebtedness inclined farmers everywhere to want easier credit. If prices fell in 1680, they could simply take in their belts and deny themselves a new axehead or their wives a strip of ribbon, but in 1740 a fall in prices brought hundreds of farmers into court. At best they might give a bond or a mortgage to their creditors, at worst they would lose their farms. When driven to the wall, they borrowed from whoever would assist them, though the interest rate was 10 to 20 per cent. A loan from the colony was far more desirable, for the Assembly charged reasonable interest and was more likely to be lenient about repayment.[20]

Looking back in 1759, Roger Wolcott thought that the pressure for more currency had come from "the debtors, which make the greater part of the people" and who were "continually calling and contriving for new loan bills."[21] Debtors did in fact comprise the larger part of the population because so many needed money— farmers to buy or stock land, traders with little capital extended beyond their ability to repay, extravagant men indebted for store goods they could not afford. There was some justice in William Douglass' judgment that the "paper-money-making assemblies" had been "legislatures of debtors, the representatives of people

[19] Deming, *Settlement of Litchfield County*, 13. The colony did not suspend interest payments, but before the bonds fell due, men in straitened circumstances were given extensions, and, as a special favor, Sharon received a £200 loan (*Conn. Recs.*, VIII, 472-473).

[20] Connecticut was very lax about collecting outstanding loans (Bronson, "Historical Account," 59). Some Massachusetts borrowers hoped the government loans would never be collected (*Colonial Currency Reprints*, I, 431).

[21] Wolcott, *Memoir*, 332.

who from incogitancy, idleness, and profuseness, have been under a necessity of mortgaging their lands." [22] Douglass and Wolcott failed to consider, however, that the prevailing indebtedness and extravagance were the results of an expanding economy which stimulated people to take risks in venturesome enterprises.

The combined weight of farmers and traders at last compelled the Assembly to make loans available "to those Persons who shall desire to have the same to promote Trade." [23] The stress on commerce was to be expected because the immediate pressures on the Assembly were from merchants. In 1733 the legislature felt compelled to print and lend £15,000 to help the New London Society subscribers repay its obligations so that the creditors would not suffer.[24] In the same year a petition from eastern merchants persuaded the Assembly to lend money to other persons too. When, in a lengthy memorial, Norwich petitioners complained of the hardships suffered in trade with Boston and Newport and asked for loans to help them bypass the great ports, they warned that excessive interest rates, rising sometimes to 20 per cent, along with other difficult commercial conditions, "occasioned very great uneasiness in the people." They themselves had suffered rather "than to make a tumult in the State," yet the basis for disturbance was "Still increasing and tending to prejudice the whole body in regard of the trade Husbandry and all business." If not prevented in time, "more open ill Consequence" might result.[25] Perhaps moved by these thinly veiled threats, the Assembly voted to lend £35,000 "to promote Trade." [26]

The money was divided among the towns in proportion to their estates, to be loaned in sums between £50 and £100, secured with mortgages of double the value. There were at least 500 initial borrowers, and, in addition, the towns reissued sums repaid before they were due. In 1740 another £22,000 was provided on the same

[22] Douglass, *Summary*, I, 310; cf. *Colonial Currency Reprints*, II, 323; III, 327; *A Letter From a Gentleman*, 6-7.

[23] Conn. Arch., Finance and Currency, II, 364; III, 57, 208.

[24] *Conn. Recs.*, VII, 452-453.

[25] Conn. Arch., Trade and Maritime, I, 103.

[26] Conn. Arch., Finance and Currency, II, 364; *Conn. Recs.*, VII, 449-456, 479-480.

basis, and much of the 1733 money was loaned again after the notes fell due in 1741. In 1747 £55,886 old tenor and £24,687 new tenor were outstanding.[27]

Much as they disliked paper money, western merchants preferred a bank that distributed its loans evenly about the colony to one that supplied only their eastern competitors. The westerners also partly controlled the size of public issues, while only the dubious judgment of its subscribers had limited the New London Society. The conservative Upper House agreed to the bank in hopes of stilling eastern complaints without sacrificing the control of trade in the Connecticut Valley.

The public loans of 1733 did not end the threat of eastern competition, however. Inflated Rhode Island currency flowing in from across the border gave New London and Norwich merchants almost the same advantage Society bills had. Eastern merchants acquired large quantities of Rhode Island money, while the westerners employed New York money, which held its value better. To the dismay of dealers in Hartford and New Haven, Connecticut people, unused to discounting, passed Rhode Island money without allowing for depreciation. With this cheap currency, eastern traders and Rhode Islanders outbid the westerners in purchasing farm produce.[28]

When complaining of their competitive disadvantage, the western merchants mentioned only the Rhode Islanders, who "by their present Large unequal proportion of outstanding bills are Enabled Annually to buy off A great part of the produce of this Colony." But only New Haven and Hartford were aggrieved; west opposed east on this issue as on bank loans.[29] William Douglass in 1760 commented on this division: "Their eastern townships have been tainted by the adjacent paper-money-making colonies of Massa-

[27] *Conn. Recs.*, VII, 503; VIII, 320; Bronson, "Historical Account," 59, 56.

[28] Memorials from New Haven County and Hartford County Merchants, May 6, 1751, *Wolcott Papers,* 60-66; cf. Roger Sherman's argument against Rhode Island money in *A Caveat.* Sherman was in New Milford when he wrote.

[29] New Haven County Merchants' Memorial, May 6, 1751, *Wolcott Papers,* 61-62; cf. pp. 60-66.

chusetts-Bay and Rhode-Island, and followed that fraud instead of
going into the better currency of their western adjoining province
of New-York." [30]

In 1747 a committee of the Assembly recommended that only
Connecticut currency be accepted for payments to the government and on all executions by sheriffs. The Assembly was at
first not so strict, leaving open the possibility of paying debts
in Rhode Island money though requiring Connecticut currency
for payments to the colony. But in 1752 Rhode Island bills emitted
after December 1750 were banned as legal tender unless otherwise
previously agreed, a move that partially neutralized the advantage
of New London and Windham counties. [31]

At the same time the English Parliament called a halt to all
emissions of paper. When the Currency Act of 1751 forbade land
banks, creditors were of course happy with this intervention from
abroad, as were the conservative and well-established merchants
who objected to the swarms of hucksters dependent on cheap bills.
Many others also wanted a check on depreciation, for the inflation
that once stimulated trade had by mid-century got out of hand.
The value of an ounce of silver worth 8s. in 1708 had risen to
55 or 60s. in 1749 and was still increasing. [32] Moreover, the
presses did not stop altogether: to finance the numerous expeditions in the war with France between 1755 and 1764, the Assembly
issued bills of credit amounting to £359,000. [33] Currency for war
expenditures satisfied those elements whose fortunes depended on
easy money. There were few complaints when the flow of paper
money was curtailed after 1750.

During the half-century from 1710 to 1750 not a shortage of
goods but enterprising and speculative traders had been chiefly
responsible for currency inflation. The actual demand for New

---

[30] Douglass, *Summary,* II, 158.

[31] Conn. Arch., Trade and Maritime, I, 130; *Conn. Recs.,* IX, 282; Bronson, "Historical Account," 71.

[32] By the late 1740's, some eastern merchants, who had to compete for
produce with Rhode Island men, complained of their "pernicious bills of
credit." However, they never petitioned for exclusion of the bills (Samuel
Lynde and others to Jonathan Law, Feb. 16, 1748, *Law Papers,* III, 213-
214). In 1755 a conservative was still complaining (Gale, *Present State,* 2).

[33] Bronson, "Historical Account," 65, 81-82.

England products in foreign markets, as measured by their prices in silver, remained almost constant; only a few commodities, notably fish and oil, rose in real value. Paper money alone had changed in worth, constantly depreciating as it came from the colony presses in increasing quantity.[34]

The marginal traders wanting capital were chiefly responsible for the excesses. At the slightest encouragement, hundreds of men branched into commerce with the resulting "*needless* multiplying [of] Taverns and Retailers." [35] "It was *this Increase* of Trade," complained a Boston man, "which at first Introduced into our Province the fatal Necessity of paper Money." [36] To establish a business and keep it going when profits were slim, new traders created demand for money. They called for banks, bid up prices to win business from older merchants, went bankrupt when their returns were small, and then demanded more money. Depreciation of government bills was the price New England paid for protecting intrepid enterprisers.[37]

Connecticut rulers worried about depreciation and conscientiously tried to support the value of money.[38] Acts to issue bills of credit for public expenditures always included provisions for taxes sufficient to redeem the bills, and public loans were scheduled for collection in a specified time. By comparison with Massachusetts and Rhode Island, Connecticut's money policy was conservative. The pressure for loans was comparatively light because Connecticut lacked opportunities for the expansion of fishing, whaling, and lumbering, which offered investment incentives in Massachusetts, Rhode Island, and New Hampshire.

The close relationship of commercial opportunities and the demand for paper money was shown in the geographical correlation

[34] For commodity prices adjusted to silver, Judd, *Hadley*, 368-372. Judd's prices are in dollars at six shillings to the dollar. Depreciation of bills is given in Bronson, "Historical Account," 52. See also *Colonial Currency Reprints*, I, 419-420.

[35] *Colonial Currency Reprints*, I, 355; cf. I, 390; Eliot, *Essays*, 137.

[36] *Colonial Currency Reprints*, III, 81.

[37] *Colonial Currency Reprints*, I, 418-420, 423, 425. It should also be noted that the market for provisions they created kept the farmer's hand to the plow and hurried the development of the wilderness.

[38] Gov. Law to William Shirley, March 3, 1749, *Law Papers*, III, 294; Gov. Law to Eliakim Palmer, Oct. 4, 1745, *ibid.*, II, 89.

of land bank advocates with the new markets. In Massachusetts paper-money men were distributed rather evenly throughout the colony because new towns in the back country were equally accessible to the coastal ports; the split over the currency was not sectional but divided small and enterprising from established and conservative merchants. In Rhode Island the situation differed: Providence, the rising port, was the center of paper-money advocacy because its trade with new towns in the northern part of the colony was growing, while Newport, the center for established merchants, fought the emission of bills. Since Providence was politically dominant, Rhode Island was extravagant with its issues. The eastern portion of Connecticut corresponded to the Providence district: both eagerly sought to exploit the back country. Since eastern Connecticut was politically subordinate to the west, however, the colony as a whole followed a comparatively conservative money policy.

By 1750 the currency issue faded from Connecticut politics, but east and west were arrayed in permanently hostile camps. In succeeding decades new issues, stemming in part from the currency struggles of the 1730's, were to perpetuate the split. East and west remained fixed political factions for years to come.

IX

Covetousness

~§ MANY FACTORS—more markets, more traders, more debts, and more money—accelerated the economy along an upward spiral of prosperity. In the 1750's Jared Eliot noted the general enrichment: the colony was "Improving and Advancing very much"; there was "a great deal of Silver and Gold in the Country," and folk had "better Houses, Publick and Private, richer Furniture, better Food and Cloathing; better Bridges and Highways, fatter Cattle and finer Horses, and Lands bear an higher Price." [1] The social order, however, suffered from the increase of wealth. Old values were no longer binding, and the relations of man to man were enflamed. Even at the beginning of the century a Middletown minister had declared that God had a quarrel with "many of his people of this land for their love of filthy lucre in their Indean trade and in these and those covetings to have licenses for selling of drink." [2] In 1771 Ezra Stiles questioned the overall effect of trade on virtue: "How far the principle of Righteousness and Moral Virtue was affected in the mixt scenes of Commerce, God only knows." [3]

The clergy everywhere in New England lamented the depreciation of the currency. A sunken medium, Jared Eliot warned the Assembly, tended to "destroy the natural notions of *Right* and *Wrong,* to deface the lines of *Justice* and break down the boundaries fix'd between *Good* and *Evil.*" [4] A decline in money values

---

[1] Eliot, *Essays,* 41n; cf. Wolcott, *Memoir,* 332; *Colonial Currency Reprints,* II, 177.

[2] Samuel Stow to Wait Winthrop, June 9, 1696, *Winthrop Papers,* pt. VI, 34-35; Hosmer, *A Peoples Living,* 28-29; Chauncey, *Faithful Ruler,* 46-47; Saltonstall, *Sermon,* 63-64.

[3] *Literary Diary,* I, 92.

[4] Eliot, *Give Cesar his Due,* 40; cf. T. Edwards, *All the Living,* 35-37.

opened the door to oppression of all sorts: debtors cheated creditors, creditors extorted excessive interest, employers and laborers
wrangled over wages.[5] Blatant unrighteousness was the consequence: "Injustice in Prices, delays and dishonesty in Payments,
Deceit, Falseness, and Unfaithfulness in Bargains, Contracts and
Betrustments, griping Usury, Evading and Baffling the Laws made
for the Security of men from that Oppression." Men dragged each
other into court, saying, "Pay me What thou Owest." [6] They lived
beyond their means and then sank into poverty. "That we have
over lived the Extravagant Expence of Strong Liquor; and our
multiplied Debts, are flagrant Proofs and Evidences of this sad
Truth." [7]

If "multiplied debts" were a measure of social deterioration,
the ministers had good cause for complaint. In the first three
decades of the eighteenth century population increased about
three and one-half times, while the number of debt cases in the
county courts increased nineteenfold.[8] In the flush of prosperity
men ventured further than before to exploit the possibilities of the
expanding economy, and storekeepers and merchants extended
credit ever more liberally. The immense rise in debt cases perceptibly increased day-to-day social frictions. For every case taken
to court, many more pleas and threats had been directed at delinquents, and many more debtors excused themselves and squirmed
away to escape legal action. Indebtedness embittered relations all
across the complex web of credit.

The experience of a rather prosperous storekeeper and tanner
east of the Connecticut River illustrates the ill feelings generated
by debt. The tanner, named Nott, had borrowed from one of the
Webbs, a prominent Wethersfield family. When Webb died, his
widow married Silas Deane of Revolutionary fame. The tanner's
son later complained that the "mercenary" Deane had "no bowels
of compassion," for he began to seize Nott's property; and as
other creditors learned of it, they moved in before nothing re-

[5] Stoddard, *An Answer,* 193-194, 206.
[6] W. Russel, *Decay of Love,* 24-25; see also Stoddard, *An Answer,* 206;
T. Edwards, 34.
[7] Eliot, *Give Cesar his Due,* 43; see also Stoddard, *An Answer,* 197-198.
[8] See Appendix III.

mained. As a result, "many who had been friends now became enemies." Unable to extract full payment, Deane had Nott imprisoned for debt. Nott, until then a lawabiding subject, cast aside compunction, broke out of prison, and went to sea on a fishing vessel in hopes of recovering his fortunes.[9]

The ministers saw behind this perversion of personal relationships a rottenness in the soul. "There has been a great Cry of *Poverty, Debt, Bondage, Oppression, hard Usage in the Land of late,*" Jonathan Marsh said in 1721, and men attributed this to *"the want of a Medium of Trade."* The real source of misery, however, was *"Our changing our God, our Glory,* for the *Creature that can't satisfy us or make us a happy People."*[10] Men had thrown over religion for the world. They no longer talked of doctrine but of "how they shall get Estates." "The Concern is not as heretofore to accomodate themselves as to the Worship of God, and get under an Edifying Ministry; but where they can have most Land, and be under best advantages to get Money." [11] Men were more avid to get "Land and Money and Stock, than they be about getting Religion revived, and securing the Salvation of their Souls." [12]

Little more could be expected of the ordinary people when their leaders were worldly and covetous. *"The Unexamplariness of Men that make a Principal Figure, in the Places where they Live"* deeply wounded religion and virtue.[13] The corruption of the people was too general for the Assembly to check. "If the more Accomplished minded nothing but Earthly things, the Simple are in great danger of erring in their Spiritual Converses, and Degenerating with them." [14]

Major Fitch, when battling the government for control of colony lands, had accused the Council itself of self-seeking. Other eastern men, hurt by official suspension of Fitch's land title, had shared his opinion.[15] Gershom Bulkeley in 1692 had openly accused

---

[9] Nott, "Life of Nott," 20-21.
[10] *Essay*, 46-47.
[11] W. Russel, 21-22.
[12] Marsh, *Essay*, 15-17.
[13] Hosmer, 16.
[14] Hosmer, 18; cf. Marsh, *Essay*, 16.
[15] Larned, *Windham*, I, 131.

the magistrates of employing public funds to their own advantage. Court fines, he reported, went to the corporation, and "doubtless some or other find a way to feather their nests" with them. The governor rigorously enforced the navigation laws because he received one-third of the proceeds. When a case was about to be settled out of court, he insisted on a trial in order to obtain the forfeit for himself. Furthermore, Bulkeley charged, the expedition against the French had no military purpose; it was merely an excuse to increase government activity and the consequent emoluments to officials.[16]

John Whiting, treasurer of the colony and member of one of the most distinguished Connecticut families, darkened the suspicions attached to high officialdom. When Whiting died bankrupt in 1717, he was indebted to the colony in the amount of £2,060. While he was treasurer, a government grant to Yale of £100 had "by mistake" never been transferred to the College. Though administrators of his will argued that some of the money was stolen at the time of his death, the Lower House refused to believe them. Already mistrusting Whiting, it had some time before passed bills to regulate the Treasury, though the Upper House, perhaps to guard the reputation of an honored family, had refused acceptance.[17] One preacher of the election sermon, besides admonishing the people, felt obliged to warn the rulers themselves against covetousness.[18]

The most damaging result of corruption was the erosion of civil authority. Malfeasance by any official hurt the entire body of rulers, whose authority rested on popular confidence in their superior wisdom and virtue. And on no point were colonists more sensitive than on the expenditure of tax money. James Fitch nearly succeeded in blocking a payment to Sir Henry Ashurst, Connecticut's agent in London, because the Assembly thought that his defense against the charges of Hallam and Palmes was Governor Winthrop's personal litigation and not colony business.[19] The

[16] Bulkeley, *Will and Doom*, 110, 196, 215-216, 203-204, 257, 262.

[17] *Conn. Recs.*, VI, 28, 79, 91, 544; Conn. Arch., Finance and Currency, I, 384; "Journals of the Upper House," Oct. 9, 1715; "Journal of the Lower House," May, 1717.

[18] *All the Living*, 19.

[19] Wait Winthrop to Henry Ashurst, June 1704, *Winthrop Papers*, pt. VI, 128-129; cf. Robert Treat to Fitz-John Winthrop, Nov. 10, 1703, *ibid.*,

least suspicion of corrupt use of funds aroused bitter feelings, and as rumors multiplied, the prestige of the ruling men dwindled.

Governor Saltonstall's behavior did not pacify the opponents of the government. While Fitch accused Saltonstall and the Council of self-seeking in the disposal of Stafford lands, the Assembly suspected the Governor of mismanaging colony money. In his message to the legislature in 1717 Saltonstall asked to be cleared from the "false and base Aspersions, of having never rendered any Account of that publick Money, which I have recd, to be remitted to our Agent." [20] Though he seems to have refuted these imputations, doubts of his disinterest remained. Saltonstall demanded that he be paid his £200 salary in silver at full value rather than in depreciated bills of credit. Counting it a point of honor and dignity to receive an income appropriate to his station, he repeated the request until his motives came into question and he was accused of "Oppression and Covetousness." When he finally was granted £300 in bills of credit, he insisted on recompense for the deficits in past wages, but even the Upper House refused.[21] Whatever the truth about the scandalous reports "industriously scattered among the people," civil authority lost some of its prestige for having been criticized.[22]

The belief that political power was a source of personal gain spread and influenced the motives of officials and people. Suspicion undermined Saltonstall's popularity, yet a widening circle of men moved by ambition began to act on the same premise as he. The colonial government had at its disposal approximately £4,000 in annual taxes as well as the emissions of bills of credit. Treasury expenditures along with a variety of other privileges—proprietary grants, licenses to fish or peddle, and liberty to build a bridge—were the envy of those who regarded political favor as the means of making their fortunes.

Military expenditures, for example, excited interest all along

---

pt. V, 161; Fitz-John Winthrop to the Legislature of Connecticut, *ibid.*, pt. V, 384; Wait Winthrop to Fitz-John Winthrop, July 8, 1700, *ibid.*, pt. V, 69; Henry Ashurst to Gurdon Saltonstall, June 27, 1709, *ibid.*, pt. V, 196.
[20] Conn. Arch., Civil Officers, I, 163.
[21] Conn. Arch., I, 285, 353; *Conn. Recs.*, VI, 268, 443; Conn. Arch., Finance and Currency, 251; "Journals of the Upper House," May 15, 1721; May 15, 1723; May 18, May 19, 1724.
[22] *Conn. Recs.*, VI, 546-547; V, 491.

the lines of trade. The commissions allowed contractors were not large: the commissaries of the Cape Breton expedition were strictly instructed to charge no more than 2.5 per cent; but when the British partly paid the cost, the returns were in silver, valued for its purchasing power abroad. Moreover, the commissaries' profit spilled over to their friends. Even before Jonathan Trumbull was appointed commissary, he received large orders from a friend in the next town who held the post. A single person in an influential position was an advantage to his whole town and the surrounding countryside. In a set of accounts from the recent war, submitted in 1711 by Roger Wolcott, half of the costs were incurred in his native Windsor itself and another quarter in neighboring Hartford. Wolcott, his friends among the storekeepers, and dozens of nearby farmers benefited, and all backed his efforts to turn expenditures in their direction.[23]

The struggle for government favors became more intense in the second decade of the eighteenth century, when the eastern and western sections of the colony split over a large expenditure of public money for the maintenance of Yale College. The chief contenders for the location of the school were Hartford and New Haven, although Saybrook objected mightily to a removal from the original site. Both Hartford and New Haven were very serious about the issue, and each raised hundreds of pounds toward the erection of a building. For a number of sessions the Assembly disagreed, and at one point the Lower House voted to settle the institution in Middletown. Finally New Haven won, but even then some students deserted and took up their studies in Wethersfield for a period.[24]

The stakes involved in the contention became clear later, when men were more frank about their motives. The ostensible ground for the debate was convenience in travel, and the Hartford supporters argued that the college would be most accessible if located on the Connecticut River. But John Winthrop came nearer to the

[23] *Conn. Recs.*, V, 262; X, 623; IX, 143; Weaver, *Jonathan Trumbull,* 35, 36. For the excitement war expenditures caused among merchants, see John Ledyard to Governor Law, June 13, 1746, *Law Papers,* II, 233; Reflections upon the Affairs of New England, *Wyllys Papers,* 333; Palfrey, *History of New England,* IV, 152-153.

[24] Clap, *Annals of Yale,* 28-29, 17; *Conn. Recs.,* V, 550-551; VI, 30n, 83-84, 98-100.

center of the issue when he wrote his father Wait that "Mr. Stonington Noyes was violent for keeping it at Saybrooke, or else they should lose the old Govenor's legacy to it." Besides the income from special endowments, Yale annually received at least £100 from the colony, most of it to be spent locally.[25] In addition, the presence of so many rich men's sons in town a good part of the year provided a large business for local provisioners.

In later disputes over the location of colleges, the contestants were less reluctant to reveal their true feelings. In 1770, when Providence and Newport were fighting over the location of a college in Rhode Island, Providence appealed to the surrounding towns for support and explained that "the building the college here will be a means of bringing great quantities of money into the place and thereby of greatly increasing the markets for all kinds of the countries produce; and, consequently, of increasing the value of all estates to which this town is a market."[26] Following the same reasoning, Jonathan Trumbull strove to keep Wheelock's Indian school in Lebanon because he hoped to sell it some of his land.[27] New Haven and Hartford saw in Yale College a rich supplement for their normal sources of income and perhaps a boost for land prices.

The northern and eastern parts of the colony stood behind Hartford, since they would gain little from location at New Haven. Both Houses at one time voted to fix at Hartford, but the weight of the imperious Governor Saltonstall, who owned property in New Haven, swung the decision in the opposite direction and prevented the vote from being recorded. Talcott and Pitkin in the Upper House, both distinguished citizens, also sided with the western party "to secure their Interest." The Upper House then conformed to Saltonstall's will, and, with great reluctance, the Lower House concurred. Perhaps the earlier decision to hold the General Assembly in Hartford persuaded less involved deputies to give New Haven the college. In any event, in order to soothe the defeated parties, the Assembly in 1718 granted Saybrook £50 for their school and Hartford £500 to build a state house. This allot-

[25] *Conn. Recs.*, VI, 30n; VII, 523; Clap, *Annals of Yale*, 16n; Blake, "Gurdon Saltonstall," 17. For the religious side of the question, Winslow, *Jonathan Edwards*, 60; Peters, *Connecticut*, 205.

[26] Quoted in Thompson, "Ward-Hopkins Controversy," 371.

[27] Weaver, *Jonathan Trumbull*, 132.

ment of colony funds was some recompence for the loss of the profits from college expenditures.[28]

Throughout the debate the Hartford and New Haven men cloaked their purposes in the language of public good and at least sustained a surface appearance of subservience to the social order. More upsetting were the desperate characters who plunged into politics purely to advance themselves. Especially dangerous, Jared Eliot warned, were "persons deeply involved and greatly in Debt." Men once prosperous and now poor were "prone to grow uneasie and disaffected to the Government." "Men of broken fortunes, men who have made shipwreck of a good Estate and a good Conscience, they are fit for any rash adventure. Being full of discontent and despair, adhere to any Party, and fall in with any Interest, tho' it be never so contrary to the true interest of the Government."[29] Combining with others of an "Aspiring Spirit," they wished "for a Change, hoping that in the Change of the State, they shall Change their Situation in it."[30] In the ministers' views, these outcast debtors and ambitious politicians had abandoned the public good altogether; they no longer saw the government as the conservator of order, but as a power to help them satisfy personal interests.

The temptation to manipulate government for personal ends touched men of all classes. Settlers disputing a title to Indian lands, small traders asking for a land bank, farmers and retailers hoping to supply a military expedition, all pressed for favors. In the previous century the town meeting had served their economic needs, while the civil authority stood above the populace, exercising its commission to rule men's evil passions. After 1690 the people outgrew the towns, and interests in lands and trade beyond the borders engaged men in enterprises over which the meeting had no control. Ordinary people, not just the local aristocracy, looked to the colonial government for help; their ambition to prosper, whetted by improving economic conditions, moved them to exert

[28] Clap, *Annals of Yale*, 19, 21-22; E. Stiles, *Extracts*, 204; *Conn. Recs.*, V, 328, 381; VI, 36, 83-84.
[29] *Give Cesar his Due*, 44.
[30] S. Whittelsey, *A Publick Spirit*, 31; cf. Hosmer, 31, 34; Stoddard, *Gods Frown*, 19.

pressures on the civil authority out of keeping with its traditional function.

Until 1740, at least, no one in Connecticut recognized that the old conceptions were outmoded. If anything, the responsibility to keep order and the dignity of rulers were affirmed more fervently than ever. But the theory of government and the practice of politics were increasingly contradictory. The civil authority, which was intended to control the people, was itself the subject of a contest for control. The conflict raised questions that, if never articulated, were keenly sensed. How could the government restrict and direct men and at the same time respond to their desires? The earlier division of responsibility between town meeting and colonial government had minimized the difficulty: the people governed within the bounds set for the town, while the governor and magistrates ruled from above. Would the people now obey a master at one moment who was their servant at another?

For a time, religious sanctions were able to prevent the collapse of civil authority. In a moment of stress Timothy Edwards reminded the colony of its obligation to obey magistrates—"Let us not dare rashly to censure and reproach them that God hath set over us in the capacity of Rulers, and Fathers in our Civil State" [31] —and his oft-repeated injunction still carried weight in the 1730's. Yet the ministers' frequent admonitions revealed that unruly elements were speaking out against the government. The fact that they could "make some fair colours" for their revilings evoked the fear that "ungrateful and ungovernable Spirits" might eventually disregard the religious limitations on political activity.[32] Without denying the legitimacy of the office, their criticism could undermine authority, or they could turn out an official on account of his personal shortcomings.

The government was unable to restrain the inhabitants at the very time when a firm hand was most needed. A change in men's hearts had brought on a general deterioration. People loved wealth more than religion, and that spirit had destroyed the peace of society. Many ministers believed that only some inward transformation could restore social order.

[31] *All the Living,* 46.
[32] Hosmer, 29, 35; Eliot, *Give Cesar his Due,* 14, 17; Russel, 28-29.

Sam! H. Bryant · 1967

Drawn from

Connecticut in 1765

A Scale of Miles

0   10   20   30

...nard Romans · CONNECTICUT and Adjacent Parts · Amsterdam, 1777 and by Cóvens, Mortier & Cóvens, Jr.

PART FOUR

Churches, 1690–1765

X

Clerical Authority

◄§ THE CONGREGATIONAL POLITY in England was at first designed not to sustain a social order, but to disrupt one. Part of the impulse behind the Puritan movement was resistance to the Establishment. Psychologically the Independents as a group were trying to shake off the onerous burden of ecclesiastical authority, and their church organization gave this desire institutional expression. Ultimate authority was transferred from the King and Bishops to the members.

In America, however, Congregationalism had to transform its polity from an instrument of rebellion to one of control. The church carried the responsibility of subduing men to the social order, a task that was not simple when the members themselves had the final voice in the discipline of transgressors. If the pastor and the people concurred, offenders were easily restrained; but if the church divided into factions, the minister and his allies could not easily repress the rebellious. Furthermore, only the small group of saints who identified themselves as the elect were members and subject to discipline; the remainder of the population escaped the watch and care of the church. To offset these weaknesses, clerical authority was enlarged and consolidated at the expense of the powers of the congregation. As a result, a century after settlement Congregationalism had reverted to many practices of the very Establishment the Puritans had once sought to escape.

The Synod of 1662 in Massachusetts took the first important step to enlarge clerical control. The Half-Way Covenant, which the assembled divines approved, brought under church discipline the grandchildren of members, without requiring evidence of conversion in the parents. Until that time only visible saints had been admitted to the church on the basis of evidence of regeneration

as demonstrated by persistent good conduct and a personal experience with the Holy Spirit. The children of communicants automatically received baptism, became subject to ecclesiastical discipline, and were expected eventually to manifest the signs of divine
grace in order to qualify for full communion. But after two decades
in New England a dismaying number of these baptized persons,
failing to discern the effects of grace in their lives, remained half
in and half out of the church; and it was uncertain whether they
could rightfully claim baptism for their own children. Baptizing
them would enlarge the number of half-way members and alter
the distinctive character of a church of visible saints, whereas
refusal to baptize them would swell the ranks of townsmen inaccessible to church discipline. The clergy had to choose between
simple purity of the congregation and control of the children.
After a protracted argument, the Synod chose control over purity.[1]

For years the Covenant divided congregations and separated
entire blocs of church members from their pastors. The stiff resistance it encountered partly cancelled the advantages gained by
the advocates of greater ministerial authority. The debates in the
Synod spread to the towns, where the innovation in procedure
received bitter criticism. In Hartford, Windsor, Wethersfield, and
Stratford dissatisfied parties withdrew from the church to form
separate societies or to move to new plantations where they might
shape polity to their own convictions. In Greenwich the majority
favored the Rev. Mr. Peck's refusal to baptize the children of non-
communicants, but protestors were sufficiently powerful to force
his dismissal. The Fairfield Church carefully inquired after the
principles of a ministerial candidate on the question of baptism
before they agreed to settle him. The inconsistency between the
Half-Way Covenant and the consensus of the founding fathers
concerning the biblical mode of church organizations so appalled
John Davenport of New Haven that he transferred his ministry
to Boston in order to oppose the innovation more effectively.[2]

[1] Miller, *The New England Mind: From Colony to Province,* chaps. vi,
vii, viii.
[2] G. Walker, *First Church in Hartford,* 184-209; H. R. Stiles, *Windsor,*
I, 190-217; S. W. Adams and H. R. Stiles, *Wethersfield,* I, 143-162; *Contributions to Ecclesiastical History,* 515; D. Mead, *Greenwich,* 72-73;
Fairfield, "Town Records," B, pt. 1, 98, 105; Miller, 106-107.

In time most of these dissident voices were hushed. The General Assembly explicitly urged all churches to adopt the Half-Way Covenant and asked whether it were not the duty of the churches to accept in "fellowship, by an explicitt covenant" all goodly men who understood the Gospel, thereby qualifying their children for baptism.[3] Evidence of grace was not mentioned. When, at the turn of the century, Solomon Stoddard mounted arguments to support this practice, some Connecticut congregations followed his lead and thus obliterated the distinction between the merely upright and those who had evidence of grace.[4] All were admitted to communion in order that the word and the sacraments might draw them toward holiness. The restraining influence of the church on all was more important than the preservation of a congregation of visible saints. The Half-Way Covenant thus introduced a flaw into Connecticut's ecclesiastical system, which was later to give way at the point where theory and practice did not coincide.

After the Synod of 1662 pastors assumed even greater prerogatives, and the privileges of the congregation dwindled proportionately. Perhaps the introduction of graceless men into association with the church justified the encroachment on the powers of the laity, but congregations nevertheless noticed and protested their losses. Little was said when ordinations under the hands of church members were discontinued, but as time went on, many ministers neglected or refused to ask for the church's consent to important decisions, an open departure from the fundamental Congregational principle that authority rested ultimately with the saints. Among many protestors, Hartford dissenters asserted that a regularly organized group of visible saints "hath all power and privileges of a church belonging to it." The power of "guidance or leading" was regarded as the Elder's prerogative, while the "power of judgment, consent, or privilege, belongs to the fraternity, or brethren in full communion." [5] Durham, after delaying the ordination of Nathaniel Chauncey for five years, finally compelled him to ask for some sign from the church when deciding weighty affairs.[6]

[3] *Conn. Recs.*, I, 438.
[4] Caulkins, *New London*, 380; E. Stiles, *Extracts*, 280; I. Backus, *History of New England*, I, 461; B. Trumbull, *Connecticut*, II, 111.
[5] Quoted in G. Walker, *First Church in Hartford*, 206-207.
[6] Fowler, *Durham*, 41-43; *Contributions to Ecclesiastical History*, 44-45.

Aware that lay power was declining, the members wanted to check the growth of clerical authority.

The ministers remained discontented, however, and strove to buttress further their own authority. The right of appeal from the church's disciplinary action was the most annoying weakness in the system. The church under the pastor's guidance could excommunicate a dissenter, but the Cambridge Platform allowed an appeal to a council of ministers and lay members from other churches. By choosing carefully, the accused could assemble a group sympathetic to his cause and have his sentence rescinded; but the friends of the pastor could then find a technical flaw in the proceedings and call a council of their own. The possibilities for appeal and counterappeal were endless.[7] Meanwhile the transgressor, instead of being properly humiliated, advertised his arguments against the pastor. Appellate councils thus institutionalized resistance to clerical control.

The General Court, aware of this failing, proposed in 1666 that a synod answer the question, "Unto whom shal such persons repaire that are grieved at any Church process or censure, or whether they must acquiesce in the Churches sentence unto which they doe belonge." [8] About this time the ministers began convening in informal associations where they could discuss reproofs and censures, though these groups had no authority to decide cases.[9]

Finally the clergy, prompted by Governor Saltonstall, adopted at Saybrook in 1708 a platform for reinforcing church discipline. The most significant article fixed the composition of appellate councils.[10] To end the confusion and to strengthen discipline, the Platform organized the churches of each county into consociations composed of the ministers and lay delegates. These bodies alone were to hear appeals: neither the church nor the individual had the option of selecting a favorable council.[11]

The Saybrook Platform added substantially to the minister's authority. He thereafter confronted dissenters and their allies with

[7] C. Mather, *Ratio Discipline*, 183.

[8] *Conn. Recs.*, II, 55.

[9] B. Trumbull, *Connecticut*, I, 407-408.

[10] This was the judgment of Thomas Clap some years later (Clap, *Annals of Yale*, 13).

[11] The Platform may be found in B. Trumbull, *Connecticut*, I, 410-414.

the backing of the elders and churches of all the surrounding towns. For as long as he was in harmony with the consensus on a given issue, his authority was indisputable. Moreover, even an entire church could not defect from its minister: if it disregarded the decision of a consociation council, it lost the legal right to raise taxes to support its pastor.[12] In conjunction with the Half-Way Covenant, the Saybrook Platform imbued Connecticut churches with much of the strength of the establishments in Scotland or England.

This step toward Presbyterian government undermined the ideology of the ecclesiastical order, however. The Saybrook Platform clearly transferred sovereignty from the congregation, where the Cambridge Platform had placed it, to the consociation, where the lay members had virtually no power since, though they could speak, the vote of the clergy alone was decisive. The complete dominion of the elders under the Saybrook Platform contrasted sharply with the distribution of power described in the Cambridge Platform.

Some societies, among them Windham and Stratfield, accepted the Platform at once. Fairfield County ministers interpreted the Platform to give them even greater powers than were intended by the framers. In New Haven County, on the other hand, which clung to the tradition of strict Congregationalism stemming from John Davenport and preferred to read Presbyterianism out of the Platform, the clergy gave the lay messengers in the consociations equal voting strength with the elders, a majority of both groups being requisite for the acceptance of any act. New Haven also specified that before declaring noncommunion with any congregation, with the consequent loss of taxing privileges, the consent of the churches in the consociation had to be obtained.[13]

A number of individual congregations renounced the platform altogether. Joseph Moss persuaded his Derby church to remain on the Cambridge Platform. The church in Woodstock, adopting the Cambridge Platform as its rule of discipline at its organization,

---

[12] *Conn. Recs.*, V, 37.
[13] Larned, *Windham*, I, 92; Bridgeport, "United Congregational Church, Records," I, 1; *Contributions to Ecclesiastical History*, 41, 42; E. Stiles, *Extracts*, 335-337.

dismissed a pastor inclined to favor the Saybrook Platform and thereafter demanded that ministerial candidates clarify in advance their attitude toward the two forms of church government.[14] In 1723 Lisbon parish in Norwich rested its discipline on the Cambridge Platform. Ecclesiastical administration was to proceed "after the Manner of a mixt administration So as No Church Acts Can Be Consummated or compleated without the Consent both of the Elder or Elders and Brotherhood." [15] A Harwinton church in 1738 did the same and, in addition, allowed excommunicated members to call their own councils. Jonathan Parsons, settled in Lyme in 1731, immediately renounced the Saybrook Platform of his own volition. A member of the Canterbury church informed the newly settled minister in 1723 that if he had not signed a statement favoring Congregationalism over all other forms of church government, he would have been no more trusted than a "Papish Jesuit." [16]

The angriest protest occurred in Norwich, where after the Rev. Mr. Woodward, secretary of the Saybrook convention, had managed to obtain a majority to support adoption of the Platform, two of the town's most influential men withdrew from the church taking a minority with them. In 1714 the majority changed its mind and voted to dissent from the Platform; a year later it dismissed the pastor who had already had difficulty getting his wages. The next minister, Benjamin Lord, healed the rupture by not joining the New London consociation and by meticulously observing the privileges of the brethren.[17]

The Norwich opposition was formidable because it was soundly reasoned. Backus, a leading dissenter, traveled to Ipswich to consult with John Wise, who was distinguishing himself as a defender of the Cambridge Platform in Massachusetts.[18] Other Connecticut

[14] Shipton, *Sibley's Harvard Graduates,* IV, 484; Larned, *Windham,* I, 36, 60-61, 365, 372, 380.

[15] Lisbon, "Newent Congregational Church, Records," I, 10.

[16] E. Stiles, *Extracts,* 179-180; *Law Papers,* III, 350n; Larned, *Windham,* I, 292; cf. E. Stiles, *Literary Diary,* 147-148; Conn. Arch., Ecclesiastical Affairs, III, 264; VII, 315; VIII, 330.

[17] Caulkins, *Norwich,* 285-286; Norwich, Town Votes, 102, 119, 120, 124-128; Conn. Arch., Ecclesiastical Affairs, II, 2, 4, 5; *Conn. Recs.,* V, 555-556.

[18] I. Backus, *History of New England,* I, 475.

men formulated their own arguments that chipped away at the Saybrook Platform. If the Establishment in theory still commanded support, informed men seriously questioned clerical administrations within it.

The opponents could not simply argue that the Saybrook Platform was a departure from the pure Congregationalism of the first settlers, for the reasoning behind the Platform did not in fact apply to many eighteenth-century churches. In 1715 numerous Half-Way members were attached to virtually every church, and few congregations could claim to be the divine institutions described in scripture. Nearly everywhere standards of admission were appreciably relaxed; some towns had gone so far as to admit all upright and orthodox men to communion and full church privileges, as Solomon Stoddard had proposed. Furthermore, by act of the Assembly in 1699, every inhabitant, whether church member or not, had a voice in the selection of a new minister, a development that seemed to abandon the privileges of the covenanted church. Any argument for congregational polity based on the tenets of the Cambridge Platform was hopelessly outdated.[19]

The most comprehensive effort in Connecticut to prepare a brief against Presbyterian government came from the pen of Roger Wolcott. One of the colony's favored sons, he had come up through the ranks of town office and the Lower and Upper Houses. A term on the bench of the Supreme Court and service as a major-general in the militia were later to take him to the summit of colonial officialdom: in 1741 he was elected lieutenant governor and in 1750 governor. Aspiring also to be a man of letters, he wrote a small book of didactic religious and political poems that was the only publication in verse by a Connecticut author in the first half of the century.[20]

Wolcott wrote his treatise on church government during the 1730's, when the East Windsor church was contesting the actions of Timothy Edwards, its pastor and father of Jonathan Edwards. When Timothy Edwards disciplined a young man for marrying the daughter of William Stoughton without her father's permission, Wolcott and many others disagreed with the decision and with

[19] *Conn. Recs.*, IV, 316.
[20] Biographical information is in the Introduction to *Wolcott Papers*.

Edwards' handling of the case, especially his disregard of the rights of the congregation. Edwards stood by his guns, however, and for years refused to hold communion. In the midst of the controversy Wolcott penned a long statement, apparently intended for publication though fated to remain in manuscript, which condemned Connecticut's Presbyterian church government and the enlargement of clerical authority at the expense of the congregation.

Like Wise, Wolcott organized his case largely around analogies with secular government. Puritan political theory rested on the conception of rule by law and the restraint of arbitrary power, principles that experience with Andros and the threats to their charter had reinforced. Wolcott charged that the minister's veto and the subordinate role of laymen in consociational councils invested the clergy with a dominion to which they had no title. In effect, "the whole power of church order [is] put into the hands of the clergy, which experience hath taught us is not safe." If the pastor could negate the judgments of the brethren, there would be no check on the ministry, however misled.[21] The minister's purported rights invested him with the same authority over messengers and the church as the King of England had over the Dean and chapters or the Pope over the Roman Church. "Understand us not, that we speak against clergyman as such," Wolcott made haste to add, but "it is not safe to trust the whole power of order in their hands." [22]

In Wolcott's argument the brethren who were to check and guide the clergy were not described as a covenanted fraternity of visible saints, worthy to be the mouthpiece for the divine will. Laymen were to be trusted because they had proved themselves capable of judgment in secular affairs: men allowed to rule the civil state were perfectly able to act in church councils. The pastor, while making much of his own rights of conscience, callously neglected those of the brethren: "The consciences of the Brethren are mere puny things, and of that flexible nature that if the Pastor should cast out one or all of them against their declared right, they can be easily well satisfyed with it." In short, lay members

[21] Wolcott, "Narrative," 13-14, 82, 20-21.
[22] "Narrative," 103-106, 82-83.

had the right to a voice in church councils not as saints, but simply as men.[23]

Wolcott's clinching argument was that all present troubles resulted from the alterations in Congregationalism. The churches should return to the order taught by the founding fathers, because departures from that order had brought the colony to division and distractions "that so awfully Threaten the Subversion of our church and Reducing us back into bondage unless we Keep our Constitution."[24]

Though Wolcott's statement never got into print, its circulation in East Windsor worried the clergy. Frank opposition by one so distinguished was a symptom and a cause of profound disaffection. More than 100 pages of passionate and carefully reasoned argument by an eminent magistrate hurt badly. Wolcott's opposition showed how unpopular the clergy were, and it threatened to rally lesser enemies of the Establishment. Backus and Bushnell, the Norwich opponents of the Saybrook Platform, were important men too, repeatedly elected deputies and among the town's wealthiest inhabitants. The clergy lamented that their enemies were found not only "among the more Base and Vile among us, but even among such as would hold a place among those of Rank and Quality."[25]

The ministers felt themselves under constant attack by their congregations. The election sermon of 1721 complained that even minute departures from the Cambridge Platform were "Suspected by some Religious and Holy men and cryed out against, as Innovation and a Degree of Declension and of Apostasy, as the way to invest the Ministers with the Sole power of Church Government, and to cut off the Privilege of the Brotherhood."[26] Timothy Cutler told the General Assembly in 1717 that the clergy were well aware of the resentments of the people: "We know the Vile Words that are cast about, of *Priest-Craft,* and Priest-Ridden, and an *Ambitious* and *Designing Clergy,* and the like Effusions

[23] "Narrative," 15-16, 80-108, 66, 53-56.
[24] "Narrative," 100, 92-93, 4-5.
[25] Bulkley, *Necessity of Religion,* 45. For a full discussion of controversies between ministers and congregations, see Winslow, *Meetinghouse Hill.*
[26] Marsh, *Essay,* 38-39.

of Men's Corrupt Minds, and the Jealousies the World hath of us." [27] In almost every congregation, Thomas Clap said, "there are some disaffected and uneasy Spirits, that seem to envy the tranquile State of the Church; and are ready to take all Opportunities and Advantages, to stir up Opposition and Contention." [28] These *"Cavillers* and *Opposers,"* an ordination sermon objected, had "much Pride and Spirit and Self-Conceit" and easily found pretexts for raising a tumult. "They can't relish such and such Doctrines, They can't approve of such and such Practices, They don't like such and such Orders or Methods of Discipline." [29] They went out of their way to take offence at the minister: "Some Men seem to take a Pride in discovering some Error and Imperfection in their Minister, because that seems to imply as if they were wiser or could see further than their Teachers." [30] "How little are Ministers set by, lookt upon with a Diminutive Aspect; their Persons are Slighted, Undervalued and Despised by many; their Ambassy Disregarded and Trampled under Feet; their Word of little or no account." [31]

Ministers suffered materially from this antipathy. "Some Persons," Clap said, "especially when they conceive themselves to have been any ways injured," went about secretly building prejudice against the preacher, trying to "blacken his Reputation; and disaffect the People towards his Ministry." When the dissenters had a party behind them, they openly demanded his dismissal.[32] In Greenwich and Hebron slanders on pastors who favored one of the competing sites for the location of the meetinghouse led to their unwilling resignations.[33] Few clergymen were actually dismissed, but frequently party divisions resulted in a diminished salary. Whenever contentions arose in the parish, the pastor was likely to be short-changed on his yearly income. If censure and excommunication were his ultimate sanctions, popular control over wages was the congregation's restraint on its pastor.

[27] *Firm Union,* 55.   [28] *Greatness,* 16.
[29] E. Adams, *Gracious Presence,* 37.
[30] Clap, *Greatness,* 16-17.
[31] A. Mather, *Gospel Minister,* 13.
[32] Clap, *Greatness,* 23; cf. p. 17.
[33] D. Mead, *Greenwich,* 81-83; *Sketches,* 55-56; cf. Judd, *Hadley,* 389-390; S. W. Adams and H. R. Stiles, I, 151-153.

Societies were notoriously miserly, even under ordinary circumstances. "Are not Allowances generally too short," the preacher of an election sermon queried, "and they too brought in, (if not in a considerable part unfairly withheld) much to disadvantage!" [34] "Surely, our leaders, cannot be such Strangers in our Israel," exclaimed another, "as not to know there is in many Places too great a Neglect as to the Maintenance and Support of such as Represent Jesus Christ." [35] When choosing a minister, it was charged, people paid no attention to his learning or preaching abilities. "A cheap Minister is the great Article in desire of too many." Although the parish contracted for a fair salary, it often fell behind in payments, until the pastor was forced to sue for his just due.[36]

In any case, salaries did not cover the rising cost of living. Inflation steadily reduced the value of the minister's income and forced him to turn to the people, hat in hand, for a raise. Timothy Edwards in 1735 carefully compared the prices of commodities with those of 1698, when he had been settled; his congregation was unsympathetic, however, because of a controversy over a discipline case, and Edwards pondered the possibility of resigning. Other ministers complained that "the Credit of that *Little Paper* they come at, is sunk wretchedly Low and is now of little Value." [37] Of the ministers in New England and northern Long Island between 1680 and 1740, 12 per cent were involved in serious financial disputes with their congregations, and 5 per cent of them left their pulpits as a result.[38]

The problems of collecting a salary increased when other contentions divided the society. In the seventeenth century the Windsor pastor received little or nothing from parishioners who disagreed with his position on the Half-Way Covenant, and the dissenting party in Norwich refused to pay Mr. Woodward's salary during the Saybrook controversy. Governor Saltonstall, while still a pastor, had trouble obtaining his salary when the parish was

[34] Woodward, *Civil Rulers*, 41.

[35] A. Mather, *Good Rulers*, 34, 39.

[36] *Conn. Recs.*, VIII, 105; Lisbon, "Newent Congregational Church, Records," I, 7.

[37] Stoughton, "Windsor Farme," 59-65; A. Mather, *Good Rulers*, 34.

[38] Shipton, "Clergy," 50.

discontent. Dissatisfaction with the minister's action in a discipline case led Norwalk to stop its pastor's salary. There were similar experiences in New London, Woodstock, and East Hartford.[39] Aware of the disposition to hold back on rates, clergymen were reluctant to displease their people. "Ministers may be under Temptations," a pastor warned a new preacher, "to go too far in seeking to Please the People, least they shut their Liberal Hands and close their Purse strings." [40]

The only apparent solution was to stiffen the laws for the ministers' support. The Assembly mobilized the tax-collecting machinery of the colony to assist the beleaguered clergy. A 1697 law gave magistrates the right to empower collectors to distrain the property of defaulters on ecclesiastical taxes, and in 1708 the Assembly gave the minister the privilege of having his salary collected with the country rate if he wished. Even this legal backing did not guarantee payment, however. Among the Norwich dissenters of 1716 were the collectors and the selectmen who refused to perform their duties so that the Assembly had to order the county sheriff to collect the rates. To hurry tardy parishioners, the Assembly in 1735 directed the selectmen or the society committee to see that the rates were collected within two months after the end of the year and to take out a distress on the collectors if they failed to deliver then. If there was no action, the King's Attorney was to attach their property.[41] The Assembly knew by this time that virtually no one in the community was immune from dissent.

The vehemence of the protests against ministers was in part at least another expression of Puritan character. To this highly defensive temperament any superior authority threatened destruction; and when it invaded the individual's realm of autonomy, he lashed out furiously. The very respect and awe in which each congrega-

[39] Selectmen of Windsor to the General Assembly, Oct. 17, 1676, *Wyllys Papers*, 262; *Conn. Recs.*, V, 555n; IV, 241-242, 389; Edwin Hall, *Norwalk*, 115, 119; *Talcott Papers*, II, 239n; Larned, *Windham*, I, 59-61; 380; Goodwin, *East Hartford*, 127; cf. Huntington, *Stamford*, 136-137; *History of the Town of Litchfield*, 28.

[40] A. Mather, *Gospel Minister*, 26.

[41] *Conn. Recs.*, IV, 198-199; V, 50; VII, 554-555; Conn. Arch., Ecclesiastical Affairs, II, 2, 4, 5.

tion held its clergyman made it sensitive to the limits of his power. When he trespassed beyond the accepted boundaries, it opposed him in self-defense.

Congregations were, however, not simply playing out a psychological drama with cathartic value. Since the minister's power of church discipline sharply affected an individual's standing in the community, the outcome of church trials had important consequences. A censure from the pulpit before the entire congregation was stiff punishment; a public and authoritative reproach humiliated the proudest individuals. In addition, the excommunicated member was treated *"as an Heathen or a Publican";* he was not denied any human needs, but he was rarely employed in public office and was generally avoided. Small wonder that some individuals moved without a letter transmitting them to the care of another parish, and that town residents often quibbled about the jurisdiction of the church over their lives.[42]

The requirements of social order dictated that discipline be thorough and severe. Congregations frequently voted to include all baptized members in the watch and care of the church.[43] Thomas Clap labored hard to bring all in his Windham parish under the covenant so that they might be subject to church courts; a committee helped gather information on offenders, since the "business of the Pastor of a Church is very great and extensive, and particularly the enquiring into Public Scandals and procuring evidence thereof is laborious and burthensome." [44] Ministers were conscience-bound to bear down hard on offenders, for leniency was a sign of weakness. Samuel Peters of Hebron, who defected to Episcopacy, wrote that New England ecclesiastical courts were more "severe and terrible than ever was the star-chamber under the influence of Laud, or the inquisition of Spain." [45]

Church members willingly, even maliciously, reported the mis-

[42] E. Adams, *The Work of Ministers,* 33-34; Hartford North Association, "Register," 9; C. Mather, *Ratio Discipline,* 155-156, 138, 140; Hartford North Association, "Register," 10; "Windham Association Book," 26.

[43] Larned, *Windham,* I, 229, 158, 100; Norwich, "First Congregational Church, Records," II, 23.

[44] Dexter, "Clap," 251; Larned, *Windham,* I, 286.

[45] *Connecticut,* 148.

demeanors of their brethren. One of Roger Wolcott's strongest memories was the people's disposition to be censorious.[46] A Hartford pastor, troubled by a discipline case, wrote in his journal that he wished he could "quiet the minds of those fierce and wrathful people." [47] Enemies of a candidate for church membership often used the occasion of his application to air scandal about him. The preacher of an election sermon rebuked the people for "an Unaccountable Stiffness" in affecting "to lay Obstructions in the way of those who are Approaching to the Lord's Table." [48]

A pastor's actions in the church courts therefore could always draw criticism, no matter how carefully he proceeded. When, after accepting the services of the Reverend Stephen Buckingham for thirty years, the town of Norwalk voted to sever its contract with him, the opposition cited some suspected scandal; but the friends of the minister said that the real reason was that Buckingham "would not suffer disorder and Evil manners in his flock which ocationed most of the principle actors against him to make their publick Acknowledgments for misdemeanors Either in themselves or Relations which we verily Belive to be the first grounds of their Envy against our Reverent Minister." Smarting under his censures, the opposers wanted a minister "they might better Command" than Buckingham.[49]

After 1690 changing conditions in the economy and in communal life made the minister's task virtually impossible. The excitement and hardships of exploiting the new country strained human relations at many points, and within the small world of the Connecticut town social and economic controversies became personal feuds, which the minister was expected to settle. A sample case mentioned in Windham County's ministerial association was the charge that, as a device for obtaining credit dishonestly, one man falsely told another that someone owed him £10. Another question handled in Windham was whether or not it was censurable to say, "I do really think that you and all your blood relations would sell your souls to the devil for the lucre of land." [50] As

[46] *Memoir*, 332.
[47] Wadsworth, *Diary*, 46; cf. 47, 110.
[48] E. Adams, *The Work of Ministers*, 33-34.
[49] Conn. Arch., Ecclesiastical Affairs, III, 207.
[50] "Windham Association Book," 81, 68.

the occasions for conflicts of this kind multiplied, the administration of discipline got wholly out of hand. The minister could not contain within the law the explosive social forces generated by economic expansion, and after the turn of the century he was more maligned than ever.

Controversies in any area of community life spread to the church. Unsuccessful candidates for town offices formed schisms in the congregation, and in Haddam opposing parties in an ecclesiastical dispute battled over the election of selectmen as well. New London's debate over the legal proprietors of town lands threatened to break the peace of the church. Title disputes in Ashford forced the minister to take great care in discipline cases lest he hurt inflamed feelings. Roger Wolcott led one party in an East Windsor controversy involving the daughter of another town leader, William Stoughton, in the same years that the two men were also leading groups disputing proprietary rights to town lands.[51]

The meetinghouse became the battleground for all the issues dividing the town. Persons of high standing were often involved in discipline cases along with the less reputable, and then all the animosities that centered on them for economic and social reasons focused on the church.[52] The ministers well knew that not all the charges sprang from concern for religion. "It is oftentimes apparent," Thomas Clap said, "that Persons Judgments are influenced by Affection or Disaffection towards Men's Persons, and not from a sincere Regard to the Honour of Religion and the Good of Souls."[53] One of Samuel Johnson's objections to Congregational government was that "discipline was often on mere human frailties and made a means to revenge little private quarrels."[54] Joseph Bellamy complained that "a number of the more elderly

[51] Peters, *Connecticut*, 62; Jeremiah Hobart to Timothy Woodbridge, Jan. 3, 1699, *Wyllys Papers*, 354-355; Conn. Arch., Towns and Lands, III, 175; Larned, *Windham*, I, 386; "Windham Association Book," 23; for the ecclesiastical dispute in Windsor, H. R. Stiles, *Windsor*, I, 569-574; for the land controversy, Conn. Arch., Towns and Lands, VII, 105, 109, 110.

[52] Larned, *Windham*, I, 142, 154, 363-364, for cases involving important people.

[53] Clap, *Greatness*, 10. For an example of this in Windsor, see Dissenting Church Members of Windsor to the General Assembly, Oct. 9, 1668, *Wyllys Papers*, XXI, 183-184.

[54] Samuel Johnson, *Samuel Johnson*, I, 11-12.

people being ambitious and having a grudge at each other are continually fomenting contention, strife and division about society affairs." [55] A censured man gathered a group of sympathizers about him, the church broke into parties, counsels were called, and quarrelling and contention spread.[56]

Thomas Clap recognized that personal controversies "usually End in a Quarrel and Contention in the Church . . . which unavoidably centers upon the Minister at last." As the arbiter in disputes, the pastor often made enemies among those he reproached. "It is very distressing to the Minister," Clap said, "to have the Parties come to him, expressing a censorious and uncharitable Spirit, and exclaiming against one another." No matter how impartial he was, both sides were apt "to be jealous of him, and he must unavoidably get the Ill-will of one Party, and very frequently of both." When the minister used any authority to prevent contention, "the Clamour of *Korah* and his Company is revived against them . . . *Ye take too much upon you, seeing all the Congregation are holy.*" Clap thought that factional disputes were the chief source of antiministerial sentiments: "I believe there are but few Instances, where People are generally uneasy with their Ministers, but it originally sprung from some such Jealousy, or party Spirit among themselves." [57]

Perceptive as Clap was, no pastor was prescient enough to perceive fully the vicious predicament of the ministry. Economic expansion after 1690 gave occasion to innumerable small disputes and party fights in every community. Bound by his duty to quiet the turmoil and censure offenders, the minister inevitably made

[55] Cothren, *Woodbury*, 243.
[56] E. Adams, *The Work of Ministers*, 33-34; Clap, *Greatness*, 10.
[57] Clap, *Greatness*, 10, 22-23.
Under the circumstances it was difficult for the minister to maintain the appearance of complete impartiality. The Reverend Mr. Heaton of Goshen was accused of supporting one party in a church controversy. His accusers charged that he treated "a number with Titles of Friendship, in Distinction from, if not in direct opposition to others," while "keeping at an unchristian Distance from others." Heaton was considered guilty of urging men to join the church to vote for his party in a case where certain members were under censure. The consociation council found the charges inadequately supported, but in the eyes of his enemies, Heaton was a partisan in the feud ("Litchfield Consociation," 11-12).

enemies who resented his authority. Like the magistracy, the ministry sought to uphold the traditional standards of social order in the midst of unprecedented economic growth, when all the restraining institutions were under extraordinary strains.

Widespread opposition placed the ministry in an uncomfortable position. If troubled by disorders, Clap's first impulse was to make laws to crush them. When he encountered difficulties in the administration of discipline, he thought the chief problem was "the want of more full and particular Rules." [58] When ministers' salaries were cut, the proposal was to fix them by law and "not to depend upon the arbetrary humors of the vulgar sort of people." Yet grudging salary payments and criticism such as that from Wolcott indicated that the people would not tolerate more power in clerical hands. While ministers habitually turned to civil authority, they recognized the drawbacks of coercive support. "It is well known," one pastor commented when discussing salaries, "that Compulsion of Men to their Duty in this Point is a very Tender thing, and sometimes Disaffects Men to their Ministers so as they never afterward Profit by them." [59]

By the 1730's the century-long movement to strengthen the Congregational Establishment had come to a halt. A series of alterations, most notably the Saybrook Platform, had reshaped the Connecticut churches without increasing the actual power of the ministry. Legal reinforcement of the Congregational Establishment could not compensate for the decline of voluntary loyalty. Under such circumstances the responsibility of the clergy to keep order was more and more difficult to fulfill.

[58] Clap, *Greatness*, 13; cf. Billings, *A Warning*, 23; Estabrook, *Sermon*, 41.
[59] Cutler, *Firm Union*, 52.

XI

Dissent

⮑§ DURING THE SEVENTEENTH CENTURY the Congregational Establishment was free of sectarian competition. In 1680 the Governor reported to England that "there are 4 or 5 Seven-day men, in our Colony, and about so many more Quakers." [1] The remainder of the population spread no further along the religious spectrum than from strict Congregationalist to moderate Presbyterian. The consensus gave great weight to the prevailing faith.

After the turn of the century organized groups of Baptists and Episcopalians appeared, largely as the result of the work of proselyting missionaries from Rhode Island and New York. During the 1720's a spate of conversions forced the colony to take notice of these dissenters. Thereafter, critics outside the Establishment constantly harried the clergy and threatened to lure away their parishioners.

In 1674 a group of seventh-day Baptists in Newport convinced John Rogers, one of the richest men in New London, that the scriptures did not teach infant baptism and Sunday worship. Around Rogers and his family collected a small number of radicals who blatantly transgressed the colony's Sabbath rules and bore noisy testimonies against the Congregational pastor while he tried to preach. The Rogerenes were the first indigenous dissenters to appear in Connecticut, and prosperous and well-connected converts lent an impetus to the movement that kept it going until the Revolution. The beliefs of the sect changed, however: it broke with the Newport Sabbatarians, gave up long formal prayers, and began practicing faith healing. Borrowing from the Quakers, the Rogerenes also forbade participation in war. Their faith was thus a concoction of deviant doctrines common in Rhode Island.[2]

[1] *Conn. Recs.*, III, 299.
[2] Caulkins, *New London*, 152, 201; Bolles and Williams, *Rogerenes*, 173,

More conventional Baptists began to hold meetings in Groton in 1705, under the guidance of Valentine Wightman of Rhode Island. In 1726 Stephen Gorton was ordained pastor of a congregation in New London, and other groups appeared in Wallingford, Farmington, Lyme, and Saybrook. The Baptists did not raise the furor that the Rogerenes did, but John Bulkley considered Wightman a sufficient threat to meet him in a debate at Lyme in 1727 and to publish a long argument against the dissenters.[3]

Though Quakers had demonstrated in Connecticut during the seventeenth century, they made few inroads in the colony after 1690. The only organized group appeared at New Milford, where in 1727 the church experienced a revival and some young men began private meetings for worship. Four years later nineteen of them declared themselves Quakers. They apparently mixed other heresies with their beliefs, however, for the pastor in New Milford, John Graham, devoted the larger part of a pamphlet officially condemning the defection to a defense of Sunday worship.[4]

The first invasion of Anglicans came from New York during the first decade of the eighteenth century.[5] A layman from across the border preached to small groups settled nearby, and the pastor at Rye ministered to Stratford Churchmen. In 1731 a Stratfield minister, while pronouncing the funeral sermon of a stalwart Congregational pastor in Stamford, thanked heaven for his long establishment "near the western limits of New England as a bulwark against any irruptions of corrupt doctrines or manners."[6]

During these early years Episcopal congregations were small and composed of "the poorer sort of people," recent immigrants from England or New York with only occasionally a wealthy individual among them.[7] They struggled to raise money to build a church and relied on the Society for the Propagation of the Gospel

177, 213, 280-291. John's father, however, was at variance with the Winthrops (Caulkins, 91).

[3] Newman, *History of the Baptist Churches*, 231; I. Backus, *History of New England*, I, 519-521, 525; II, 32.

[4] Orcutt, *New Milford*, 59, 110; Graham, *The Christian's Duty*.

[5] The growth of Episcopacy is best followed in Beardsley, *Episcopal Church in Connecticut*, I.

[6] *Contributions to Ecclesiastical History*, 12.

[7] B. Trumbull, *Connecticut*, I, 405; Schenck, *Fairfield*, II, 10, 89; Samuel Johnson, *Samuel Johnson*, I, 13; Episcopal Clergy of Connecticut to the Secretary of the Society, *ibid.*, III, 234, 235; Beardsley, I, 112.

to support their ministers. In 1720 the Church at Stratford was the only organized body of Anglicans in Connecticut.

The Anglicans dated their firm entrenchment in the colony from 1722, when four Congregational ministers declared for the Church of England and three others expressed strong approval of Episcopal government. Among the converts were the rector of Yale, a College tutor, and two of the colony's most distinguished clergymen. Their ordination and the sympathy for Episcopacy expressed by the three other prominent young pastors opened the way to a series of similar declarations in subsequent years. After 1722 former Congregationalists from Connecticut supplied virtually all the missionaries sent by the Society to the colony.[8]

Growth in the two decades after the Yale defection caused Samuel Johnson, one of the converts, to look back with pride in 1742. When "I came alone into this colony a few years ago," he reminisced, "there were but 70 to 80 adult Church people in the whole government, and now there are above 2,000." The communicants, however poor, had managed to erect ten churches and to begin three more, and seven priests, ordained in England after a hazardous ocean voyage, ministered to them.[9] Episcopacy, having spread through the western towns and to seaports in the east, was securely established in Connecticut.

The laws reflected the growing acceptance of these dissenters. Until 1708 the civil government forbade heresy and proscribed even the introduction of books containing condemned ideas. But the Crown ordered Connecticut to rescind the law against Quakers, and in 1708 sober dissenters, with the exception of Roman Catholics, were given the legal right to worship as they pleased. Dissenters still had to appear before the County Court to obtain permission to worship and were required to pay taxes for the established ministry; and, despite the ostensible liberty of conscience, the civil authority stifled such extreme deviationists as the Rogerenes. But within broad limits the state thereafter countenanced doctrinal variations.[10]

[8] Beardsley, I, 32-43.
[9] Johnson to Roger Price, July 5, 1742, Samuel Johnson, *Samuel Johnson,* I, 106.
[10] Greene, *Development of Religious Liberty,* 187; *Conn. Recs.,* IV, 546; V, 50. Laws against unauthorized worship were passed in 1721 and 1723 especially to stop Rogerene meetings (*Conn. Recs.,* VI, 248, 401-402).

Anglicans and Baptists were never prosecuted for heresy, but even after 1708 the government compelled them to help pay for Congregational worship.[11] Since religion guarded civil peace, all were expected to contribute to the protecting institutions. The Connecticut magistrates agreed with Cotton Mather that the pastor in a town was really the King's minister, and taxes for him were therefore collected in the name of the Crown.[12] Everyone had to support the church for the same reason that they paid for bridges or the militia.

The Baptists and Anglicans objected. In the tradition of Roger Williams, the former believed that no secular government could act in the name of God. John Rogers' son stated this position succinctly: "When the worldly rulers take upon themselves to make laws relating to God's worship, and thereby force men's consciences, and so turn their sword against God's children, they then act beyond their commision and out of their jurisdiction."[13] Only individual consciences could discover the truth in religion, and the state was not to interfere in the process. The New Testament method of supporting the ministry, Valentine Wightman declared, was "the free-will offerings of the people."[14]

Although Anglicans made no objections to government surveillance of faith, they believed that "there could be no such thing as a regular establishment of any one denomination of Christians in Connecticut . . . without an explicit consent of the King's Majesty." Furthermore, they argued that the Church of England deserved official support for the benefit of the social order. Episcopacy excelled Congregationalism in promoting "the public good of society" and taught men "to be good Christians, kind neighbors, upright magistrates, and dutiful subjects."[15] Thus the Anglicans contended that, given all the premises of Connecticut's ecclesiastical laws, the Church of England merited at least equal treatment with Congregationalists.[16]

The government at last relented on the taxation issue. English

---

[11] Bulkley, *Impartial Account*, 131-133.

[12] *Ratio Discipline*, 21.

[13] Bolles and Williams, 364.

[14] I. Backus, *History of New England*, I, 520.

[15] Beardsley, I, 109, 108.

[16] Anglicans wished to receive precisely the privileges granted to Congregational societies (Bronson, *Waterbury*, 296; Schenck, II, 162).

friends of the dissenters exerted pressure at a time when the charter was in danger and the colony dared not resist. Since Anglicans and Baptists argued that their religious beliefs also protected social order, the civil authority, with only slight misgivings, in 1727 and 1729 freed them from supporting the Establishment.

The exemption took different forms. Anglicans, who believed in establishment, received a portion of the minister's tax proportional to their numbers. The Baptists and Quakers, rejecting the conception, were simply freed from paying taxes and left to their own devices to support their worship.[17]

Although the toleration laws met little opposition, the Congregational clergy did not welcome the dissenters. The ministry knew from experience that an Anglican or Baptist meeting in town disrupted discipline, since an individual under censure could fly to the arms of the dissenters. When John Graham of New Milford charged that the Episcopal Church served as a "Sanctuary to the contentious, refractory and ungovernable," [18] he knew whereof he spoke, for the New Milford Quakers had separated from his congregation, four of them later transferring to the Anglicans, where they were safe from his reproaches. Hezekiah Gold, pastor in Stratford, berated Samuel Johnson, the Anglican minister there, for "fishing in troubled waters.":

You have been very officious in visiting particular persons and families from time to time, that were under disgust with another, or with myself, [and endeavoring] to win them over to be your followers. [Many of your communicants] were members of our church, who left us in a very unrulable and disorderly manner [to avoid the humiliation of discipline].[19]

Dissenters everywhere offered the same challenge to authority. The opponents of a New London pastor threatened to turn Churchmen, Baptists, or Quakers if the minister were not dismissed.[20] The Congregational churches could never keep order in their households if dissenters dissipated the terrors of excommunication by welcoming those cut off for misconduct.

The established clergy also felt keenly the loss of power as a

[17] *Conn. Recs.*, VII, 107, 237, 257.
[18] Graham, *Some Remarks* (1733), 35.
[19] Gold to Johnson, July 14, 1741, Samuel Johnson, *Samuel Johnson*, III, 135-136.
[20] *Dialogue*, 26.

result of opposition from these minority churches. Anglicans and Baptists could not exist peacefully alongside the established churches; they had to dissent volubly and persistently. Oversensitive to aspersions because of opposition within their own churches, the ministers fought back vehemently. The incessant warfare diminished the dignity of the clergy and raised doubts about its authority.

The dissenting spirit was most pronounced among the Rogerenes. Isaac Backus, who lived in Norwich when the Rogerenes flourished in the next town, said "their greatest zeal has been . . . to testify against hireling teachers, and against keeping the first day of the week as a sabbath." [21] Their moments of greatest pleasure came when they interrupted a Congregational meeting to condemn the pastor. The Quakers in New Milford impressed John Graham, the Congregational pastor there, as the inveterate enemies of order in church and state; these antinomians, he charged, wanted to "overthrow all *Civil* and *Sacred Orders* of Men, *Magistracy* and *Ministry*." [22]

John Bulkley, the champion of Congregationalism in the debate with Valentine Wightman, discerned the same temper in the Baptists, who charged that the established ministry were "hirelings, they Teach for Hire and Divine for Money . . . Yea and what is worse, they are Greedy Dogs and Ravenous Wolves that devour their Flocks: Therefore come not nigh them." Bulkley thought that the Baptists were obsessed with the desire to "bring an Odium on the Ministry in the Land, and hurt their Reputation and Interest with their People" and had no sincere religious purpose in converting the people. "If they can but gain them to their *Senseless Opinions,* furnish them with some Objections against the Established Religion of the Country, render them Prompt and ready at Invective and Railery against Ministers, and prevail on them to forsake our Assemblies, neglect Family Prayer, Prophane the Sabbath etc., Tis enough, and there they leave them, they are now Good Christians." [23] Bulkley's frantic rhetoric must be discounted —the Baptists were not the saboteurs he depicted—but his panic reveals the clergy's loss of nerve in the face of opposition.

Though far more respectable intellectually and socially than the

[21] *History of New England,* I, 381.
[22] *The Christian's Duty,* 42.
[23] J. Bulkley, *Impartial,* 143-145, 185.

left-wing dissenters, the Anglicans also disparaged the Establishment. Hezekiah Gold of Stratford accused Samuel Johnson of doing everything possible "to discredit and undervalue our ministry, suggesting that our ordinations were groundless and unwarrantable." [24] John Graham chastised the Anglicans for "unsetling Men's Principles" by "railing against our Ministry and Administrations." [25] In the election sermon following the fateful Yale commencement when the tutors declared for Anglicanism, the preacher lamented that "those sad things" have "stumbled some and prejudiced others against the Ministry of the Land, and confirmed them in their Wicked and Groundless Jealousies concerning the Ministry." [26] The Congregationalists perceived Anglicans as the dedicated enemies of the established order that in fact, though perhaps not so violently, they were.

The Anglican attacks were especially disturbing because they frankly questioned the ability of the existing polity to keep order, voicing the very doubt that had long worried Congregationalists. Samuel Johnson's experience with contention in the Connecticut churches while he was growing up in the first two decades of the eighteenth century convinced him that Congregationalism was incapable of controlling the laity. The "great animosities" and "virulent separations" prevalent throughout the colony appalled him. "A way so entirely popular could but very poorly and he thought not long subsist." The country was in such a "miserable state, as to Church government" that it needed reformation and alteration.[27]

Johnson believed that the church had to draw greater strength from civil authority and to use that power decisively. "An external uniformity ought to be agreed on and established by the authority of the church, and the measures of such an external and visible uniformity, being themselves lawful and established by lawful authority, ought to be held as sacred and inviolable." All Connecticut conservatives agreed with this view to the extent that the Saybrook Platform attempted to improve ecclesiastical order by the

[24] Gold to Johnson, July 14, 1741, Samuel Johnson, *Samuel Johnson*, III, 136.

[25] Graham, *Some Remarks* (1733), 34-35.

[26] Eleazar Williams, *Essay*, 46.

[27] Samuel Johnson, *Samuel Johnson*, I, 11-12, 63.

enactment of strict laws to enforce uniform discipline. The clergy believed that the charter invested sufficient powers in the colonial government to protect the "peace and unity of the church" if only the Assembly would cooperate.[28] But Johnson and his fellow Anglicans had lost faith in Connecticut government and were prepared to abandon the charter as a pernicious instrument of democracy.

Anglicans denied that the charter bestowed any right to establish religion and cited as proof an opinion of the Lords Justice.[29] Connecticut should relinquish its false claims to self-government in ecclesiastical affairs, Johnson said, and submit their churches to the dominion of the Crown. "For whatever Constitution they may have thrown themselves into, they are Parts of the Nation, and bound to pay Obedience to the National Laws." Since the "Church established by King and Parliament" was the lawful establishment in the colony, objections to Anglican rites and ceremonies were irrelevant. The sole issue was "whether what you are required to comply with, be *Lawful?* and if it be found so, it is sufficient to bind you to Obedience, that 'tis injoyned by Lawfull Authority." How else was order to be protected? "Men may think themselves wiser than their Governours" and still be bound "to Obedience, for the Preservation of public Peace and Order." [30] Subservience to the undoubted legitimacy of the Crown was the cure for Connecticut's ecclesiastical ills.

Anglicanism also sought to sustain ecclesiastical order through the imposing power of Bishops through whom apostolic authority had descended. Without episcopal ordination no one was believed to be authorized to act in the ministry; vested with power from a Bishop, the pastor's legitimacy was regarded as beyond question. In Samuel Johnson's mind Congregational clerics were weak figures indeed, established by a spurious interpretation of the charter and devoid of apostolic authority. The people understandably trampled on their ministry. Because episcopacy commanded respect, it was

[28] Samuel Johnson, *Samuel Johnson*, III, 4.
[29] Samuel Johnson, *Second Letter*, 44; cf. the Episcopal Clergy of Connecticut to the Society, Nov. 15, 1738, Samuel Johnson, *Samuel Johnson*, I, 95.
[30] Wetmore, *Letter*, 18-19, 26; Samuel Johnson, *Letter*, 21.

of "the most direct and best tendency to promote, preserve and maintain the peace and unity" of the Church.[31]

For Johnson and others conversion to episcopacy signified a transfer of allegiance from a deficient charter and clergy to King and Bishops,[32] whose exalted offices would restore order to Connecticut's troubled churches. Sensing the revolutionary transformation contemplated by the Anglicans, the preacher of the election sermon in 1730 warned that enemies of the colony intended to "disparage your Constitution Civil and Ecclesiastical, and urge a change." [33]

The Connecticut clergy in 1720 could not reply as the founders of the colony might have. The Congregations had been steadily shorn of their power, and the clergy had become more and more independent of the covenanted elect. Half-way members, admission of the merely upright, the voice of the town in calling ministers, and the contentions between clergy and people had led many ministers to look beyond the congregation for their authority; they no longer trusted the affirmations of the Cambridge Platform. Instead, the defenders of the faith accepted the need for episcopal authority, claiming that Congregational pastors were Bishops too. The pamphlets asserted that in the New Testament presbyters or elders held the same office as Bishops and that any pastor in the colony had the same authority to ordain as the Archbishop of Canterbury. Congregationalism was simply the New England version of the English Establishment.[34]

[31] Samuel Johnson, *Samuel Johnson*, III, 6.

[32] Johnson to the Archbishop of Canterbury, May 3, 1737, Samuel Johnson, *Samuel Johnson*, III, 88.

[33] Russel, *Decay of Love*, 30-31.

[34] The controversy hinged not on the powers of a congregation but on the nature of a Bishop. The Anglicans claimed that in the primitive Christian churches, he supervised more than one congregation and held an office different from that of elder. The Presbyterians said that Bishops led but one congregation and were equivalent to the elders in the churches of the present day. "Single Churches which are under the Conduct of a single Bishop or Presbyter," argued one pastor, "are to be owned and acknowledged to be true Churches of Christ." "Diocesan Episcopacy, according to the modern Notion of it," on the other hand, "is not of Divine, but of Humane Institution" (N. Eells, *Evangelical Bishop*, 23-24). Neither case could be proved conclusively, but at least the Establishment had grounds for resisting Episcopal claims. So long as the scripture and early

The new defense of the Congregational polity, however, had a
serious flaw: the ordinations by laymen, which had fitted perfectly
with the conceptions of the founders, now were embarrassing. The
intervention of non-Presbyters destroyed the contention that ministers were linked with apostolic authority as solidly as priests of
the Church of England. "The notion of these ordinations by
laymen" Joseph Webb complained, "do us more damage than all
the arguments than can be brought for the necessity of Episcopal
ordination." The founders of Connecticut had gladly accepted
laymen into the ordaining circle as a means of signifying that the
minister's authority came through the congregation, but this conception was dim or repugnant to Webb. "What led those eminent
men, who first settled the country to allow laymen to act in such
affairs is not for me to say." [35]

To make the best of the situation, John Bulkley asked for
tolerance. No "Positive laws," he said, limit calling and separation
"to any particular Mode or Modes." Biblical precedents proved
that any succession of men "so furnished with Light and Grace
as to be capable of the Ends of the Ministerial Work," when called
and set apart, were bona fide ministers. Moderate Episcopalians,
another pastor said, "acknowledge Presbyterian Ordination to be
Valid: And no man can give any reason from Scripture, or the
most Ancient Antiquities, why it should not be so accounted by
all." [36] Somehow the Congregationalists had to persuade the colony
that they possessed sufficient authority to keep order in the churches.

The radical dissenters presented a different challenge altogether.
The Rogerenes, Baptists, and Quakers were not concerned about
the historical origins of a Bishop's authority or the relative merits
of the King or charter to sustain an establishment. Indeed, they
objected to any form of establishment. Their distinguishing doctrines implicitly criticised Congregational piety, a matter of greater
concern to them. Sunday worship or baptism by sprinkling were

church history provided examples of Bishops whose "whole Diocese was
only One single Congregation," one clergyman assured his readers, "we
need not be moved at the Customs that have obtained in the following
more Corrupt Ages" (*ibid.*, iv).
[35] Schenck, II, 70.
[36] Bulkley, *Impartial Account*, 142, 154; N. Eells, *Evangelical Bishop*, 44.

evidences of orthodoxy's departures from the truth and of the
clergy's lack of spiritual understanding.

The Baptists, Rogerenes, and Quakers sensed in Congregationalism a lack of that spiritual power and knowledge which superseded
all worldly learning. The Baptists, who claimed "to have the Holy
Spirit and an uncommon degree of Illumination and Sanctity," rejected the established clergy because they lacked "immediate, extraordinary" light from heaven. The Rogerenes practiced faith healing
as a demonstration of their spiritual superiority, while the New
Milford Quakers held that sinless perfection was attainable in this
life and charged that Congregational pastors substituted spurious
human wisdom for spiritual enlightenment. Defects in piety along
with government interference with religion were the dissenters' warrant for separation from the Establishment.[37]

The weaknesses of Congregationalism lent force to these objections. Ministers feared sectarian criticism because the long internal
conflict over clerical authority had prepared Congregationalists to
sympathize with complaints about deficiencies in order or piety.
The Saybrook Platform had divided them into two groups: some
wished the government to strengthen external controls and crush
all disturbances, while others regretted any departure from pristine
Congregationalism and considered order less important than piety.
The dissenters attracted critics from within the Establishment at
both extremes. The Anglicans urged total control by the overawing
authority of King and Bishops, while the others advocated the
elimination of all legal support for religion. Ministers worried most
about dissent because it focused attention on existing discontents.

The conversion of many Congregational ministers and church
members to Anglicanism showed the appeal of the stability promised by the rule of King and Bishops. Like Johnson, these pastors
feared that they were usurpers in "the House of God."[38] His conversion and the arguments he and others later propounded cast suspicion on the authority of all. Under Anglican pressure, an East

[37] Graham, *The Christian's Duty*, 36-37, 39; Colton, *Two Sermons*, 64;
Bulkley, *Impartial Account*, 146.
[38] Samuel Johnson, *Samuel Johnson*, I, 61. When Johnson announced
his conversion in 1722, there were other Congregationalists who admitted an attraction to Episcopacy, though they were persuaded to remain
with the Establishment (Beardsley, I, 38-39).

Guilford pastor lost confidence in his right to officiate because one of his ordainers had been ordained by laymen. In 1734 Ebenezer Punderson in North Groton could not be persuaded "that his ordination was good," and he left to take orders in England.[39]

The established ministers frankly admitted that they feared the Anglican attacks because episcopacy appealed to discontented elements in their own congregations. Perverse criticisms of Congregational ordinations were spread, perhaps, as one sermon implied, "on a design of drawing away Disciples." [40] Shortly after the defection at Yale, Joseph Webb of Fairfield wrote Cotton Mather that "the axe is hereby laid to the root of our civil and sacred enjoyments, and a doleful gap opened for trouble and confusion in our churches." [41]

The other dissenters won fewer converts, but their stress on piety was also attractive. In two scandalous disturbances at Guilford and Milford in the 1730's church members renounced the Saybrook Platform and separated from their pastor because of spiritual deficiencies such as those the Baptists disparaged. In both cases resistance to authority was linked to a yearning for a more vivid experience with God.

At Guilford a dozen of the chief men disapproved of Thomas Ruggles, Jr., the ministerial candidate favored by the majority. The minority thought that he lacked piety and, besides being a party man, was not an "experimental and animating preacher." [42] When Ruggles was settled in 1729, the dissenters withdrew, rejected the Saybrook Platform, and asked to be made a separate society, free of restrictive ecclesiastical controls. The New Haven County Court was sufficiently sympathetic to recognize them as sober dissenters, and the petition for parish privileges, which asked for exemption from taxes to the old society, then went up to the General Assembly.

The Assembly was unwilling to countenance the Guilford separation, however, and in 1731 called in a council of ministers to restore order. Indignant that the minority had qualified as sober dissenters,

[39] E. Stiles, *Extracts*, 292; W. Hart to Stiles, Jan. 17, 1769, *ibid.*, 497.
[40] Buckingham, *Moses and Aaron*, 49; cf. N. Eells, *Evangelical Bishop*, 44.
[41] Beardsley, I, 39.
[42] B. Trumbull, *Connecticut*, II, 86; Steiner, *Guilford*, 305.

the council declared that the "pretended qualifying was an abuse of the law, and unjustifiable." "Setting up a separate assembly for public worship," it ruled, was "disorderly and sinful." [43] Ruggles' church was directed to suspend the dissenters unless they apologized and returned. The Assembly was forced by law to release them from paying taxes to the old society but rejected the petition for recognition as a distinct parish. To block the loophole through which the minority had slipped, the Assembly then ruled that no persons of "congregational or presbyterian persuasion" could thereafter qualify as sober dissenters.[44] It was clear that the toleration law was for the benefit of dissenters not schismatics.

Though heavily criticized, the Guilford minority nonetheless received support from outside the parish. Azariah Mather and Joseph Moss, both distinguished ministers, openly gave comfort, the latter, one of the pastors who had himself rejected the Saybrook Platform, assuring the dissenters that they had good cause for separating. The Saybrook Platform was "very wide" of the Cambridge Platform "in many essential things," and the dissenters' desire for "the bread of life in an edifying ministry" was rightfully a matter of conscience.[45] The efforts of the Establishment to preserve order at all costs, Moss told the Guilford people, were wholly unjustified, and the ordination of Ruggles in the face of the minority's objections "looked too much toward that prelatical tyranny, from which our fathers fled, . . . and a breaking in upon the natural liberty, which belongs to all the churches and Christians." Moss's dislike of ecclesiastical tyranny was as strong as that of Roger Wolcott, but he went some distance further than Wolcott in repudiating controls. "No civil power upon earth," he said, "hath any authority to make any laws about ecclesiastical matters." The dissenters had a perfect right to incorporate into a church "without being set off by the General Court." [46] Like the Baptists or Rogerenes, Moss rejected the legal basis of the ecclesiastical order altogether and made conscience and piety supreme. Concurring with him, the Guilford men argued in their petition that the civil magistrate had no right to legislate in matters of conscience.

[43] B. Trumbull, *Connecticut*, II, 94.
[44] *Conn. Recs.*, VII, 309.
[45] Steiner, 307; B. Trumbull, *Connecticut*, II, 92.
[46] Steiner, 303, 309–310.

As the dispute dragged on, the minority won other supporters. At least half the members of one of the councils that debated the question of allowing a distinct ecclesiastical society considered the cause just. Within Guilford itself the minority comprised fully half of the church by 1732. Concluding that reunion was impossible, six leading ministers urged the formation of a distinct society.[47] Moss encouraged the dissenters with the report that "the scale is turning in the Country and . . . the great men, both civil and sacred, seem to be less smart in their opposition to you." Meanwhile, he was arguing publicly that though "ill consequences" might "attend such a liberty for separation," yet the peace of the society demanded it.[48] At last acquiescing, the Assembly in 1733 permitted the organization of the Fourth Society in Guilford within the same bounds as the First.[49]

In 1738 a minority in Milford, perhaps encouraged by events at Guilford, objected to the settlement of Samuel Whittelsey, whom they accused of leaning toward Arminianism. That label was applied to an indefinite composite of opinions that exalted the worth of human activity and gave a theological basis for demanding that men perform good works and was probably associated with a style of preaching as well. The minority at Milford complained that Whittelsey was not evangelical enough and that, instead of preaching the gospel, he taught a "system of morals."[50] Whittelsey, like Ruggles, apparently lacked animation and warmth.

After considerable pressure from the older men in the ordination council and from Deputy Governor Law, the minority agreed to hear Whittelsey for six months, after which, if they were still dissatisfied, the society was to choose a colleague who would preach half the time. When, after two years, the minority asked for the appointment of the second minister and were refused, they separated from the church in 1741, during the Great Awakening, qualified as legal dissenters, and joined the presbytery of New Brunswick, a more fervent body than the New Haven County Consociation. Although the Milford dissenters built their own

[47] B. Trumbull, *Connecticut*, II, 99; Steiner, 318.

[48] Steiner, 309, 303.

[49] The whole story is told in detail in Steiner, 301-328; and B. Trumbull, *Connecticut*, II, 85-103.

[50] Federal Writers' Project, *Milford*, 52; B. Trumbull, *Connecticut*, II, 86.

meetinghouse and had regular preaching, the Assembly refused until 1750 to exempt them from paying rates to the first society. Nonetheless, the minority followed Guilford's example and remained separate, feeling that their yearning for a more pious preacher warranted their disorderly course.[51]

The problem of order had existed before the sectarians appeared. Discontent with legal controls was no more the result of agitation by Baptists and Rogerenes than the attempts to strengthen clerical authority were the consequence of Anglican criticism. Congregationalists differed on the question of civil support for the ministry for reasons quite apart from sectarian opposition. The Anglicans and Baptists were simply additional expressions of discontent with the Connecticut solution. Criticism of excessive clerical authority was indigenous and not the product of propaganda.

The conflict between order and piety manifested itself among the clergy also. The yearning at Guilford and Milford for "experimental and animating" preaching was not a mere echo of Baptist or Quaker dissent. Congregational supporters of piety were independently urging a greater fervency in the pulpit. Indeed, judging from the sermons on homiletics in these years, a number of ministers were earnestly debating the value of emotional preaching as contrasted to cold rationality.

Solomon Stoddard opened the controversy in 1724 with a sermon on *The Defects of Preachers* which blamed the pastors for the spiritual lassitude of their congregations. There was "a great want of good Preaching; whence it comes to pass, that among Professors a spirit of Piety runs exceeding low." Stoddard did not question the ministers' learning or morality; many were eminently well prepared intellectually and were zealous against sin. They lacked, however, the experience of saving grace. "Every Learned and Moral man is not a Sincere Convert, and so not able to speak exactly and experimentally to such things as Souls want to be instructed in." Without personal knowledge, their sermons on grace were bound to fail, because "Experience fits men to Teach others." [52]

---

[51] B. Trumbull, *Connecticut*, II, 281-285; Federal Writers' Project, *Milford*, 51-54.
[52] Pp. 8-10.

Ministers lacking experience made mistakes that detracted from the piety of their hearers. They persistently appealed to the listener's reason, expecting him to believe the Bible, for instance, because of the probable evidence instead of the divine glory that must be perceived intuitively. Or they explained justifying faith as working in reason alone when all the scriptures on faith "imply not only an act of the Understanding, but also an act of the Will." Stoddard emphasized that men must be moved emotionally as well as intellectually, that effective preaching humiliated people by driving home the hopelessness of the human condition under the law. Men had to be shown the horrors of damnation. "A little matter will not scare men, their hearts be as hard as stone." "It is well," Stoddard said, "if Thunder and Lightning will awaken them." To melt those obdurate hearts, "men need to be terrified and have the arrows of the Almighty in them that they may be Converted." "Reason will govern men in other things," he warned, "it is Fear that must make them diligently to seek Salvation." [53]

Stoddard's counsel was well received. The introduction to the published version of *The Defects of Preachers,* written by a Connecticut pastor, Salmon Treat of Preston, sympathized with Congregations "under Dull Preaching" and advised them to "Lament it before GOD, and Pray Night and Day for your preacher, that the Lord will enlarge him with Grace and Ministerial Gifts." Foreseeing that the desire for evangelical preachings would disrupt churches, Treat warned his readers to "take heed of a froward Mouth and wrangling Carriage." Dissatisfied as they might be, they should do no more than entreat their pastor "as a Father, to strive and Pray for Enlargement of his Work." [54] On this point Azariah Mather, another Connecticut minister, apparently thought differently, for he stood by the right of the Guilford minority to separate. He concurred, however, with Stoddard's declaration that "such as have not passed the New-Birth themselves" are inadequate for the ministry.[55]

The evangelical preachers believed that out of a full heart a pastor spoke to the hearts of his audience. Learning touched the

[53] Stoddard, *The Defects of Preachers,* 18, 15, 12, 13-15.
[54] P. ii.
[55] A. Mather, *Minister,* 21; cf. Marsh, *God's Fatherly Care,* 21.

rational faculties, but to sway men, emotions had to be stirred. In times of spiritual lethargy ministers served best by "speaking piercing words to their hearers." When men are asleep, they "stand in great need of Terrour." *"Smoothness of Language, Exactness of stile,"* were of less weight than the message and "the *strength and pungency of their motives."* [56] The seat of piety was in the heart more than the mind, and preaching had to penetrate the will as well as the understanding.

Some of the most prominent pastors in the colony took issue with Stoddard and his Connecticut followers. The opponents of evangelical preaching believed the mind a more creditable instrument than Stoddard allowed. Indeed, Samuel Whittelsey thought it the only faculty the preacher could reach. Only God could "change the Heart"; the minister had to address men simply as "rational and intelligent" beings.[57] John Bulkley argued that the pastor would have more success if he persuaded the understanding: "To make Addresses to the *Affections* of our Hearers is but to Storm the Out-works"; impressions made there were easily erased, "whereas due Conviction of the reasonableness of Religion will abide with and have a permanent Influence." [58] For Jared Eliot also the rational faculty was the control center, where religion could best direct human life, and the passions were not the source of piety but a dangerous force to be restrained. "There is a vast deal of mischief," Eliot warned, "that ariseth from our suffering the inferior Power to usurp dominion over Reason, which should be the governing Principle." [59]

Advocates of these contrasting preaching styles tended to fall into the two groups already defined by the stress on order or on piety. As at Guilford and Milford and among the Baptists, evangelical preachers opposed the Saybrook Platform and strong civil control of religion. Fervent preaching emphasizing human helplessness and free grace was associated with piety.[60] By contrast, rational

---

[56] Marsh, *Essay,* 37; cf. S. Whitman, *Practical Godliness,* 40.

[57] S. Whittelsey, *Sermon,* 11.

[58] Bulkley, *Necessity of Religion,* 56-57.

[59] *Two Witnesses,* 19.

[60] Stoddard was unusual in enjoining Presbyterian controls while advocating warmer preaching. In a series of revivals in Northampton, he proved his own ability to evoke piety.

preaching had doctrinal connections with Arminianism. Samuel Whittelsey's dissenting parishioners accused him of Arminiansm as well as lack of fervency in the pulpit, and when the Guilford separates said that Ruggles neglected the "distinguishing" doctrines of Christianity, referring to human depravity and divine grace, they implied that he also was tainted with Arminianism.[61] Jared Eliot, the champion of reason and natural religion in the colony, had revealed his willingness to flirt with Anglican Arminianism when he nearly converted to Episcopacy along with Samuel Johnson in 1722. Rational preaching and Arminian leanings both rested on the assumption that reason could alter human conduct. Those who believed that man might rationally direct his behavior without waiting for grace addressed their sermons to the human understanding as Eliot and Bulkley advocated.

Both components fitted into the order syndrome because confidence in rationality made human control of society feasible. Samuel Johnson asserted that the Congregational doctrines of depravity and grace undermined moral effort: order was tenuous unless men were responsible for their actions, as preaching addressed to the understanding implicitly assumed they were. Arminianism, rational preaching, and stress on ecclesiastical order fell into a single pattern.[62]

Throughout the 1730's signs multiplied that people were dividing into two camps, the supporters of order in one and of piety in the other, with the Anglicans and the other dissenters the extremes of each position. Anglican reliance on the authority of King and Bishops attracted those who favored even stronger support for clerical authority than the Saybrook Platform, while the Guilford and Milford controversies revealed the determination of other Congregationalists to reject all external controls and, like the Baptists or Rogerenes, to stress piety at the sacrifice of order. The pastors' debate over rational and evangelical preaching disclosed

---

[61] B. Trumbull, *Connecticut*, II, 87.

[62] Arminian doctrines did not always imply a stress on order. Arminianism seems to have been characteristic of some Baptists before the Great Awakening as it was of later Methodists, and yet did not prevent either group from emphasizing piety. A degree of rational control of will equipped a man to accept Christ as well as to live a moral life. Some revival preachers leaned toward Arminianism for pious reasons.

a fundamental difference in conceptions of human psychology, conceptions that put a premium on either order or piety. The same issue in different forms ran through the entire religious sphere.

In the middle of the decade two episodes up the Connecticut Valley in Massachusetts further crystallized opinion. In 1735 the proposed ordination of Robert Breck in Springfield aroused the wrath of some Connecticut ministers who objected to the installation of a notorious Arminian. Breck was settled, but, as Jonathan Edwards noted, the case spread the fear of Arminianism. That same year Edwards, who believed that conversion, an immediate experience of grace, was the best antidote for the Arminian poison, led his congregation in a revival of piety such as New England had never before seen.[63] As the revival moved down the valley into Connecticut, the emotions it released fed the prevalent hunger for greater piety.

Though the Breck case and the revival deepened the difficulties between the friends of order and the friends of piety, the cleavage was not fully apparent at the time. Jared Eliot or John Bulkley would deny they were Arminians, but their stress on reason certainly separated them from the followers of Stoddard. Joseph Moss would resent the imputation that order was unimportant to him, but he opposed the Saybrook Platform and supported the minority in Guilford in their search for an experimental preacher. The colony was not yet split into distinct parties as it was to be in 1750.

Nonetheless, a cleavage did in fact exist. If sectarians were few in number before 1740, their objections to Congregationalism were symptomatic of a deeper division. The election sermon of 1733 told the ministers to take care that they did not "break into parties and draw different ways, and one party as Industriously pull down what another builds up." [64] The conflict between order and piety defined a fissure along which the religious quakes accompanying the Great Awakening split Connecticut society wide open.

[63] Byington, "Breck Controversy"; J. Edwards, *Works*, III, 233.
[64] E. Adams, *Discourse*, 71.

XII

Awakening

◄§ IN 1721 an extraordinary number of conversions occurred in Windsor, Windham, and two parishes in Norwich. For the first time a rash of revivals occurred instead of individual instances spotted across the face of the colony at wide intervals in time. Another series, beginning in Northampton in 1735, followed the same pattern on a much larger scale. Religious excitement moved down the Connecticut Valley, eastward from the river into the back country, and in both directions along the coast.[1]

The conversion spirit spread rapidly because religious tension was high. Edwards said that news of the 1735 revival struck "like a flash of lightning, upon the hearts" of the people.[2] Throughout the decade ministers often had to comfort *"Souls in Distress under Inward Troubles."* [3] Clap found this pastoral work the most difficult of his duties: "Persons are oftentimes under great Trouble and Distress of Mind," he wrote in 1732, "and sometimes brought almost to Despair." [4] A colleague in 1737 offered suggestions on the best method of leading persons under concern "thro' the Work of Humiliation . . . unto Christ." [5] The tide of conversions was already rising in 1740 when Whitefield visited New England.[6]

The need for an Awakening to heal society as well as to save men's souls was widely acknowledged. For eighty years the clergy had deplored the declension of piety. As vice, injustice, pride,

[1] M. H. Mitchell, *Great Awakening,* 8-9; Larned, *Windham,* I, 330; B. Trumbull, *Connecticut,* II, 104.

[2] J. Edwards, *Works,* III, 234, 236.

[3] Marsh, *God's Fatherly Care,* 25.

[4] Clap, *Greatness,* 13.

[5] S. Whittelsey, *Sermon,* 9-10.

[6] For increasing conversions in 1739, see Orcutt, *New Milford,* 48-59; Cothren, *Woodbury,* 820-821; Norwich, "Fifth Congregational Church, Records," 59ff.

contempt for authority, and contention in church and town became
more prevalent, law after law was added to the books to restrain
corruption but without appreciable effect. "There have been many
Enquiries after the *Cause of our Ill State,*" lamented the election
sermon of 1734, "and after proper *Means* and *Methods* of Cure:
Yea, and many *Attempts,* but alas, to how little purpose!" [7]
Ministers pleaded with their congregations "*to awake out of
Sleep.*" [8] Privately they sought ways "to revive a Concern about
religion." [9] Congregations fasted and prayed to humble themselves
"before God Under the sense of Leaness and bareness . . . and
to Implore the divine Graces to be poured out." [10] After the
Windham revival in 1721, the pastor exclaimed, "Oh! that the
same Good *Spirit from on High* were poured out upon the rest of
the Country." [11] Hearing of Whitefield's success in the middle and
southern colonies, several leading New England ministers invited
him to visit and preach, and Governor Talcott gratefully welcomed
him to Connecticut in 1740.[12]

For six weeks in September and October Whitefield toured New
England, releasing a flood of religious emotions wherever he went.
Along his route from Boston to Northampton, down the Connecticut Valley, and westward along the Sound hundreds were
converted, and the itinerants Gilbert Tennent of New Jersey and
James Davenport of Long Island continued the work through 1741
and 1742. Local ministers, adopting Whitefield's style of preaching,
started revivals in their own congregations and aided neighboring
pastors in theirs. The increase of admissions to full communion is
a measure of the volume of religious experience.[13]

The revivals occurred throughout the colony. Even though some
areas, such as the first parish in Fairfield, did not respond, religious

[7] Chauncey, *Faithful Ruler,* 49-50.
[8] Marsh, *God's Fatherly Care,* 22.
[9] Wadsworth, *Diary,* 20.
[10] Norwich, "First Congregational Church, Records," II, 19.
[11] E. Adams, *Sermon,* iv.
[12] B. Trumbull, *Connecticut,* II, 120.
[13] For example, *Records of the Congregational Church, Franklin,* 13-14;
Lisbon, "Newent Congregational Church, Records," I, 26; Cothren, 820-821;
Orcutt, *New Milford,* 48-49; Norwich, "Fifth Congregational Church, Records," 59ff; C. Davis, *Wallingford,* 301; *First Congregational Church of Preston,* 134.

activity flourished all around them. Coast and inland towns, new and old towns, towns in the east and in the west participated in the Awakening.[14] Although it was probably more intense in the east than in the west and on the coast and large rivers than inland, no area was immune to the contagion.

The Awakening affected people of all classes. One clergyman reported that men of "all orders and degrees, or all ages and characters" were converted.[15] Edwards marveled that "some that are wealthy, and of a fashionable, gay education; some great beaus and fine ladies" cast off their vanities and humbled themselves.[16] In town after town leading citizens participated along with more common people. A comparison of the taxes of persons admitted to communion in two Norwich parishes from 1740 to 1743 with the taxes of the town as a whole shows that economically the new converts represented an almost exact cross-section of the population.[17]

The revivals Whitefield precipitated seemed to fulfill all the hopes placed in him. Vicious persons repented of their sins, inveterate absentees from worship returned, love for the minister waxed strong, contention in the town died away, and interest in worldly pursuits shifted to the scriptures and the state of one's soul. People could not get enough preaching: meetings were added to the regular schedule, and worshippers met privately to discuss religion. When the Hartford County Association in June 1741 urged ministers to hold extra meetings, preaching alternately for each other if necessary, it declared that the "awakening and Religious Concern, if duly cultivated and directed may have a very happy Influence to promote Religion and the Saving Conversion of Souls." [18]

A few ministers were dubious from the start, however, and their

[14] Schenck, *Fairfield*, II, 131; *Bi-Centennial of Green's Farms*, 9; Fairfield, "First Congregational Church, Records," 7. For the location of revivals, B. Trumbull, *Connecticut*, II, 103-219; *Christian History;* Tracy, *Great Awakening;* Larned, *Windham*, I, 396, 431-432, 434, 444, 450, 464.

[15] Pemberton, *Duty*, 28.

[16] *Works*, III, 297.

[17] B. Trumbull, *Connecticut*, II, 109; Gilman, *Historical Discourse*, 45; Larned, *Windham*, I, 397; "Norwich Town Rate"; *Records of the Congregational Church, Franklin; Manual of the First Congregational Church.*

[18] Wadsworth, 66n.

doubts steadily darkened into dislike. The news of enthusiasm on Long Island made Daniel Wadsworth, pastor of the first church in Hartford, uncomfortable even before Whitefield arrived. Upon seeing him in October 1740, Wadsworth was uncertain "what to think of the man and his Itinerant preachings," and by the following spring "irregularities and disorders" in the town worried him. In August 1741 the Hartford Association declared against itinerants and their unjust censures of other ministers. The clergy agreed that no weight was to be given to "those screachings, cryings out, faintings and convulsions, which, sometimes attend the terrifying Language of some preachers," nor to the "Visions or visional discoveries by some of Late pretended to." The following month, after reports of Davenport's conduct had reached Hartford, Wadsworth concluded that "the great awakening etc. seemes to be degenerating into Strife and faction." Itinerants had turned people "to disputes, debates and quarrels." "Steady christians and the most Judicious among ministers and people," he observed at the end of September 1741, "generally dislike these new things set afoot by these Itinerant preachers." [19] By the end of 1741 open opposition appeared to what had at first been considered to be a work of grace.

At the request of several ministers, the Assembly in October 1741 underwrote the expenses of a general convention of ministers to stop the "unhappy misunderstandings and divisions" in the colony and to bring about "peace, love and charity." [20] Probably in response to the resolves of the clergy, the Assembly enacted a law in the spring of 1742 forbidding itinerants. Ministers were to obtain permission from the congregation and the pastor of a parish before preaching there. If a complaint was lodged against a pastor for preaching outside of his parish, the magistrates were not to enforce collection of his salary, and unordained persons and ministers without congregations or from other colonies were required to obtain permission before preaching. Realizing that one consociation might be more favorable to revival preachers or contentious individuals than another, the Assembly forbade any to advise or to license candidates to preach in the jurisdiction of another. Thus

[19] Wadsworth, 49, 56, 66, 70n, 71, 72, 73.
[20] Conn. Recs., VIII, 438-439.

this act outlawed itinerancy, the primary method of spreading the revival, and thereby officially denounced the Awakening. When Whitefield next visited Connecticut in 1744, most pulpits were closed to him.[21]

Conversions waned after 1743. Only sporadic and isolated revivals occurred in the next fifty years, and none was comparable in size to the Great Awakening. But the impact of the experience was felt long afterwards. The converted were new men, with new attitudes toward themselves, their religion, their neighbors, and their rulers in church and state. A psychological earthquake had reshaped the human landscape.

What had happened to prepare so large a portion of the population for this momentous change? What power was there in the words of a sermon to plunge a person into the blackest despair and then bring him out into light and joy, a new man? The answer lay in the revivalist's message. He told his listeners that they were enemies of God and certain to be damned. When sufficiently crushed by their sinfulness, they learned that good works would never save them but that God's free grace would. This idea lifted men from their misery and restored them to confidence in God's love. Men who had come to believe that they were damnably guilty were ready to rely on unconditional grace.

The peculiarities of the Puritan personality partly account for the listeners' conviction that they were worthy only of damnation and hence wholly dependent on God's favor. Hypersensitive to overbearing authority, and always afraid of its destructive power, Puritans instinctively resisted whenever it threatened—but not without guilt. Since they could not avoid conflicts, surrounded as they were by rulers and laws, they lived in the consciousness of multiple offenses. They did not separate earthly clashes with authority from sins against God, for they believed the rulers and laws derived their power from the heavens. With life so structured, deep feelings of guilt inevitably grew.

These tensions had existed long before 1740, but despite pleas from the clergy, conversions had been few. Not until 1721 were any appreciable number of men sufficiently overpowered by their

[21] *Conn. Recs.*, VIII, 454-457; Wadsworth, 130; B. Trumbull, *Connecticut*, II, 152.

own sinfulness to rely wholly on God's grace and be converted. Two conditions prepared men for conversion: an increased desire for material wealth that ministers called worldly pride or covetousness, and the growing frequency of clashes with authority entailed in the pursuit of wealth. Both were the results of economic expansion, and both were, in the Puritan mind, offenses against God.

The Puritans' feelings about wealth were ambiguous. Even the most pious associated it with a secure place in the community and divine approval, and everyone accorded great respect to rich men, numbering them among the rulers of society. Prosperity was a sign of good character: all were expected to practice industry and thrift, the virtues that brought the rewards of wealth. To some extent worldly success was a token of God's favor: none felt constrained to stint their efforts to prosper in their callings.

Yet the dangers of riches also were well known. The rich were prone to *"fall into Temptation,"* Cotton Mather warned, and be *"drowned in Perdition."* "There is a venom in *Riches,"* he said, "disposing our depraved Hearts, to cast off their *Dependence* on *God.*" [22] It was a maxim of the Jeremiads that "where a Selfish, Covetous spirit and Love of this world prevails, there the Love of God decayeth." [23] When Connecticut's first published poet, Roger Wolcott, occupied himself with the theme of the divine wrath visited on seekers of earthly honor and wealth, he explained that he might have chosen the path of pride himself, "but that I see Hells flashes folding through Eternities." In this world money answered everything but a guilty conscience. [24]

The contradiction in the prevailing attitudes toward wealth perplexed both the ministers and the people. Pastors complained that men excused avarice as justifiable enterprise. "They will plead in defense of a Worldly Covetous spirit, under the colour or specious pretence of Prudence, Diligence, Frugality, Necessity." [25] Cotton Mather lamented that even the farmer was grasped with worldliness, yet he turned away rebukes with the assertion that he was merely pursuing his calling as a husbandman. The people could

[22] C. Mather, *Agricola,* 59, 64.
[23] Russel, *Decay of Love,* 11.
[24] Wolcott, *Poetical Meditations,* 18, 12.
[25] Marsh, *Essay,* 15-17.

not distinguish respectable industry from covetousness: their ambitions drove them on year after year, while self-doubts were never far below the surface. Robert Keayne, the wealthy Boston merchant of the early period, built a fine fortune, but at great cost. When censured by the clergy for acting against the public good, he was crushed and, in a document written to clear himself of guilt, poured out the tensions he had long felt.[26]

Throughout the seventeenth century a few Puritans experienced Keayne's miseries, but the temptations of worldly pride were too remote to hurt the consciences of most. The opportunities for gain were largely inaccessible to ordinary men until after 1690, when economic expansion opened new prospects to many more farmers and merchants. Common men could take up a small trade or invest in a ship sailing to the West Indies, and land purchased in a new plantation doubled in value within a few years. The expansive economy of the early eighteenth century unleashed ambitions restrained by the absence of opportunity. Everyone hoped to prosper; the demand for land banks and the 300 per cent increase in per capita indebtedness were measures of the eagerness for wealth.[27] An indentured farmhand in the 1740's complained that his master never spoke about religion: "His whole attention was taken up on the pursuits of the good things of this world; wealth was his supreme object. I am afraid gold was his God." [28]

In the midst of this economic growth, the ministers faithfully excoriated the spreading worldliness. It was obvious, one minister wrote, "that the Heart of a People is gone off from God and gone after the Creature; that they are much more concerned about getting Land and Money and Stock, than they be about getting Religion revived." [29] "The Concern is not as heretofore to accommodate themselves as to the Worship of God," it was said in 1730, "but Where they can have most Land, and be under best advantages to get Money." [30] These accusations were put aside with the usual rationalizations, but so long as the ministers re-

[26] C. Mather, *Agricola*, 71; Bailyn, "The Apologia of Robert Keayne."
[27] See Appendix III.
[28] Bennett, "Solomon Mack," 631.
[29] Marsh, *Essay*, 15.
[30] Russel, 22.

minded men that riches cankered their souls, a grave uncertainty haunted everyone who pursued wealth.

The desire to prosper also precipitated clashes with law and authority, adding to accumulating guilt. With increasing frequency after 1690 people fought their rulers or balked at the laws, usually as a consequence of their ambition. Such friction wore away confidence as it convinced men inwardly of their own culpability.

Under more peaceful circumstances law and authority protected the Puritan from the asperities of his own doctrines. Taken seriously, Puritan theology kept men in unbearable suspense about their standing with God: He chose whom He would to be saved, and the rest were cast into the fires of hell. But the founding fathers had qualified this pure conception of divine sovereignty by stressing the authority vested in the social order. Since civil and ecclesiastical rulers were commissioned by God and the laws of society were an expression of His will, obedience to Connecticut's government was in effect obedience to divine government, and the good will of the rulers was an omen of God's good will. So long as man complied with the law and submitted to authority, he was safe from divine punishment.

After 1690, in their ambition to prosper, people disregarded the demands of social order. Nonproprietors contested the control of town lands with proprietors, and outlivers struggled with the leaders in the town center to obtain an independent parish. In the civil government settlers fought for a clear title to their lands and new traders for currency. Church members resisted the enlargement of the minister's power or demanded greater piety in his preaching. All these controversies pitted common men against rulers and the laws.

Under these circumstances the social order became a menace to peace of mind rather than a shield against divine wrath. Just as conformity gave an inward assurance of moral worth, so resistance, even in spirit, was blameworthy. Dissenters, in politics or economics as well as religion, could not oppose the community fathers whom God had set to rule without feeling guilty. Even when a move to the outlands or complaints about a minister's arrogance were well justified, the participants in the action feared that they sinned in resisting.

Few men in 1740 were outright rebels, for strong loyalties still bound almost all to their communities. By comparison to their forebears of 1690, however, this later generation was estranged. It could not comfort itself in the recollection of a life of conformity to the divinely sanctioned order. In part it was emboldened by the wealth it had sought and often gained, but that provided an unsteady support when the pursuit of riches was so often condemned. However hardened the contentious appeared, guilt generated by an undue love of wealth and by resistance to the social order had hollowed out their lives.

East of the Connecticut River, in the most rapidly expanding section of the colony, turmoil was greatest. Extravagant growth plunged the towns into strife over land titles, currency, and religion. The party battles loosened the social structure and alienated men from their social and religious leaders. Economic opportunity also aroused the hunger for land and commercial success. Here the revival was noticeably most intense. "Whatever be the reason," Ezra Stiles commented later, "the eastern part of Connecticut . . . are of a very mixt and uncertain character as to religion. Exhorters, Itinerants, Separate Meetings rose in that part." Around three-quarters of the separations between 1740 and 1755 occurred east of the Connecticut River. The greatest number in any town—four —were in Norwich, the commercial center of the east. Nearby towns—New London, Groton, Stonington, Lyme, Windham, and Preston—had similarly prospered, and a third of the separations in the colony took place in these towns and Norwich.[31] These departures, roughly measuring the fervor of the Awakening, were the outcome of the personal instability eastern men felt after a half-century of extraordinary expansion.

Before Whitefield arrived, ministers sensed the shaky state of their parishioners' confidence. One pastor noted the grave uncertainty of people under spiritual concern: "They want to know they shall be sure they believe, that they love God, that they are in the right way, are sincere and the like." [32] As the ministers recognized, an outward show usually covered somber doubts:

---

[31] E. Stiles, *Extracts*, 299; Goen, *Revivalism and Separatism*, 302-309; cf. Brainerd, *Life*, 358.
[32] Wadsworth, 7.

reprobates disguised or fled from their real condition while inwardly they suffered from a consciousness of guilt.

Whitefield broke through this facade. Though he stood apart from the established clergy, he was accepted by them. He did not represent the repressive ministerial rule which entered so largely into the conflicts of the period but nevertheless came clothed with acknowledged authority. The revivals he started in the middle colonies also imbued him with a reputation of extraordinary power. "Hearing how god was with him every where as he came along," one awakened person later reported, "it solumnized my mind and put me in a trembling fear before he began to preach for he looked as if he was Cloathed with authority from the great god." [33] Besides, he was an impassioned and fluent preacher.

Whitefield moved his hearers because excessive worldliness and resistance to the divinely sanctioned social order had already undermined their confidence. He told men what they already knew subconsciously: that they had broken the law, that impulses beyond their control drove them to resist divine authority, and that outward observance did not signify loving and willing submission. Confronted with truth, his listeners admitted that they were "vile, unworthy, loathsom" wretches. "Hearing him preach," a converted man said, "gave me a heart wound. By gods blessing my old foundation was broken up and i saw that my righteousness would not save me." [34]

This confrontation of guilt, the first part of conversion, drove men to despair, but the revivalists did not leave their hearers there to suffer. By publicly identifying the sources of guilt and condemning them, the preachers also helped to heal the wounds they first inflicted. Converts were persuaded that by acknowledging and repudiating their old sins, they were no longer culpable. The reborn man was as joyful and loving when the process was completed as he was miserable at its start.

Converts were told, for instance, that wealth held no attractions for the saintly. The business of Christ's disciples, one preacher taught, "is not to hunt for Riches, and Honours, and Pleasures in this World, but to despise them, and deny themselves, and be

[33] Quoted in G. Walker, *Some Aspects*, 91.
[34] Quoted in G. Walker, *Some Aspects*, 91.

ready to part with even all the lawful Pleasures and Comforts of the World at any Time." [35] In a dramatic gesture expressing a deep impulse, Davenport had his followers gather the symbols of worldliness—wigs, cloaks, hoods, gowns, rings, necklaces—into a heap and burn them.[36]

Converts responded eagerly, casting off with great relief their guilt-producing ambition. The pious David Brainerd spontaneously broke into poetry:

> Farewell, vain world; my soul can bid Adieu:
> My Saviour's taught me to abandon you.[37]

After Isaac Backus was converted, he felt that he "should not be troubled any more with covetousness. The earth and all that is therein appeared to be vanity." [38] His mother, also a convert, felt ready to "give up my name, estate, family, life and breath, freely to God." She would not relinquish her peace of soul "no, not to be in the most prosperous condition in temporal things that ever I was in." [39] For many the choice was to enjoy peace of soul or prosperity. The pursuit of wealth and an easy conscience were incompatible. Jonathan Edwards noted a temptation among converts to go to extremes and "to neglect worldly affairs too much." [40] They were unwilling to jeopardize their newfound peace by returning to worldliness.

The revivalists undermined the social order, the other main source of guilt, not by repudiating law and authority, but by denying them sanctifying power. Estrangement from rulers and the traditional patterns of life was demoralizing as long as the social order was considered divine, but Awakening preachers repeatedly denied that salvation came by following the law. No amount of covenant owning, Sabbath observance, moral rectitude, or obedience to rulers redeemed the soul. Praying, Bible study, and attendance at worship might result solely from worldly motives, to avoid disgrace or to pacify a guilty conscience. "Civility and ex-

[35] S. Williams, *Christ*, 70.
[36] Tracy, 248-249.
[37] *Life*, 82.
[38] I. Backus, "Account," 22-23.
[39] Denison, *Notes*, 28-29; Hovey, *Memoir*, 27-28.
[40] *Works*, III, 234-235; cf. 296-297.

ternal Acts belonging to Morality," one revivalist taught, "are no Part of the Essence of the Religion of Christ." [41] Without grace, "tho men are adorn'd with many amiable qualities, and lead sober, regular, and to all appearance religious lives, yet they remain under the condemning sentence of the Law, and perish at last in a state of unsanctified nature." [42] Reborn men were expected to practice moral virtues, but their salvation was not at stake. Obedience brought no assurance of grace, and disobedience did not entail damnation. Though still driven to resist rulers or to depart from the approved pattern of community life, believers in the revival message felt little guilt.

In this fashion the Awakening cleared the air of tensions. Men admitted that they had lusted after wealth, condemned themselves for it, and afterwards walked with lighter hearts. They ended the long struggle with the social order by denying its power to save and hence to condemn. After a century of Puritan rule, law and authority were burdens too heavy to bear. All the anxiety they evoked was released when men grasped the idea that salvation came not by obedience to law.

In the converts' minds the escape from guilt was possible because of God's grace. The idea that the law could not condemn if God justified contained the deepest meaning of the Awakening. The rules and rulers, who governed both externally and in the conscience, had judged men and found them wanting until God out of His good grace suspended the sentence of damnation. The authority of Christ nullified earthly authority. Edwards said that converted men exulted that "God is self-sufficient, and infinitely above all dependence, and reigns over all." [43] In the inward struggle with guilt, God's infinite power overruled the older authority that had stood over every Puritan conscience, judging and condemning.

In that moment of grace the Awakening worked its revolution. Henceforth a personal relation with God governed reborn men who were empowered by faith to obey the God they knew personally

[41] Frothingham, *Articles*, 8; S. Williams, *The Comfort*, 19-20; Tennent, *The Danger*, 4.
[42] Pemberton, *Knowledge*, 17.
[43] *Works*, III, 303.

above the divine will manifest in earthly law and authority. It was characteristic of the converted to "renounce all confidence in everything but Christ, and build all their hopes of happiness upon this unalterable Rock of Ages." [44] "I seemed to depend wholly on my dear Lord," Brainerd reported following his conversion. "God was so precious to my soul that the world with all its enjoyments was infinitely vile. I had no more value for the favor of men than for pebbles. The Lord was my ALL." [45] Though the old authority was still a substantial force in every life, it did not structure the identity of converts as much as their own bright picture of God.

Under the government of this personal, internal authority, converts experienced a peace and joy unknown under earthly fathers and their old conscience. God's grace dissolved uncertainty and fear. The convert testified to the "sweet solace, rest and joy of soul," the image of God bestowed.[46] "The thought of having so great, so glorious, and excellent a Being for his Father, his Friend, and his Home, sets his heart at Ease from all his anxious Fears and Distresses." [47] The power to replace oppressive authority figures with faith in a loving God was the ultimate reason for the revivalists' success.

Thus the men affected by the Awakening possessed a new character, cleansed of guilt and joyful in the awareness of divine favor. Unfortunately for the social order, however, their personal redemption did not save society. In making peace with themselves, converts inwardly revolted against the old law and authority, and, as time was to show, they would eventually refuse to submit to a social order alien to their new identity. Conservative suspicions of the revival were confirmed when reborn men set out to create a new society compatible with the vision opened in the Great Awakening.

[44] Pemberton, *Knowledge*, 9.
[45] *Life*, 84.
[46] J. Edwards, *Works*, III, 300.
[47] S. Williams, *The Comfort*, 15. Radicals carried this confidence to the point of asserting the new principle in them was perfection. "All Doubting in a Believer is sinful . . ." (Windham Consociation, *Result*, 7; cf. 18).

XIII

The Church and Experimental Religion

❧ THE EXPERIMENTAL RELIGION of the Awakening put new wine in old bottles, and they could not contain the ferment. Reborn men first sought to reform the churches and then left in large numbers to create new ones more to their liking. Conservatives were powerful enough to prevent a radical reformation of the established churches, but even there experimental religion altered the ecclesiastical structure. Everything from preaching styles to theology and consociation government received the impress of the new enthusiasm.

The issues the Awakening raised were not new. The conflicts between the New Lights—the friends of the revival—and the Old Lights—its enemies—were essentially an extension of the earlier contest between piety and order. Milford and Guilford in the 1730's were fighting over the same points that divided churches after the Awakening: the minister's cold preaching, the neglect of the Calvinist doctrines of depravity and grace, and the restraints of the Saybrook Platform. Because of the similarities, the Milford dissenters, when they finally broke away in 1741, were classed with the Separates. The Milford minority identified itself at once with the New Lights by joining the pro-revival New Brunswick Presbytery in New Jersey and by inviting Samuel Finley, a revivalist so offensive to conservative civil authorities that they forcibly carried him from the colony, to preach. Like other Separates, the Milford dissenters were refused exemption from paying taxes to the old society, and for nine years they supported both the conservative minister and their own pastor.[1] The Milford case thus connected the conflicts of the 1730's to those of the 1740's.

[1] The whole story is told in B. Trumbull, *Connecticut*, II, 281-285. For a reservation on this point, see note 2, Chap. XIV.

The Awakening, however, intensified the strain between order and piety. As the forces of piety grew in size and fervency, those of order, in reaction, took a firmer stand against emotional religion and ecclesiastical confusion. Both groups clarified their views and moved to more radical positions, and this polarization itself produced controversy which ineluctably remodeled ecclesiastical organization.

In propounding their view, the New Lights illuminated the nature of the piety that had been somewhat obscure at Milford and Guilford. From the flood of sermons published in the revival and after, there emerged a clearer picture of the insatiable hunger for certain exquisite emotions which underlay experimental religion. Rather than bringing permanent satisfaction, conversion only whetted the appetite for holiness. Fading spiritual joys and the return of guilt and uncertainties led awakened men to repeated renewals of the experience which was for them the heart and life of religion. "Committing the soul to Christ is not barely a single act," one preacher said, "but is the frequent practice of every christian." [2]

The newborn divided their experience into three categories. The first was cold, dull, heartless, lethargic, a state associated with worldliness or carnal security. While at Yale, Brainerd lamented that his yearning to excel brought this distemper on him. "I grew more cold and dull in religion, by means of my old temptation, namely, ambition in my studies." [3] This lack of any concern for religion he detested above all else. So long as the soul was in turmoil, there was hope that grace might be working; the absence of a sense of danger put men in greatest jeopardy.

Relief came through humiliation. When Brainerd found himself "declining with respect to . . . life and warmth in divine things," he prayed: "Oh, that God would humble me deeply in the dust before Him!" He was pleased when after being "remiss and sluggish, without any great convictions of sin," despair seized him more violently: "And though my distress was sometimes thus great, yet I greatly dreaded the loss of convictions, and returning back to a state of carnal security, and to my former insensibility of impending wrath." [4] Samuel Hopkins, another New Light leader,

[2] Pemberton, *Duty*, 17.
[3] Brainerd, *Life*, 74.
[4] Brainerd, 75, 61.

reported the same recurring sense of "awful depravity." [5] Frothingham, the leader of the Separates, said this "great Sense of his
own Nothingness, and great Vileness and his intire Dependance
upon God" was also his daily experience. He and his friends rejoiced that they had "seen much of God's Power, and their own
Nothingness and Vileness." [6] Humiliation was a purgative, a sign
of grace, and in itself a joyous sensation.

Humiliation was the prelude to the third category of experience,
exaltation in God. Brainerd's vivid faith created in him a "divine
temper, whereby the soul exalts God and treads self in the dust."
The converted sought constantly to repeat the sequence of humiliation and exaltation. Speaking of a time of spiritual joy, Brainerd
said,

my soul was exceeding melted, and bitterly mourned over by exceeding
sinfulness and vileness. I never before had felt so pungent and deep
a sense of the odious nature of sin as at this time. My soul was then
unusually carried forth in love to God and had a lively sense of God's
love to me. [7]

The Separates also were "up and down from time to time, sometimes under bitter Desertions, and then in Divine Light and
Power." [8] Hopkins was "often sunk in darkness and despon-
dencey" and then again "raised above all doubts, and to high
religious enjoyments in the exercise of those affections which appeared to be truly gracious." [9] Lowness and misery led to those
moments of "sweet calm" when the converted felt their hearts
"swallowed up in God" and approached that ecstatic mysticism
Brainerd described: "I never felt it so sweet to be nothing, and
less than nothing, and to be accounted nothing." [10]

New Light preaching corresponded to this sequence. "The exer-
cises and experiences" of Hopkins' heart were the "ground of his
preaching" and "led to those passages of scripture and subjects"
he chose for his discourses.[11] Like all New Lights, he aimed to

[5] *Sketches*, 59. [6] *Articles*, 427, 388.
[7] *Life*, 353, 72-73.
[8] Frothingham, 430.
[9] *Sketches*, 59.
[10] *Life*, 88, 87.
[11] *Sketches*, 59-60.

shock men out of their worldly lethargy and to lead them first
into humiliation and then to exaltation. The renowned New Light
Eleazer Wheelock told preachers they must first "set before Sinners
the *Wretchedness, Miseries,* and *Necessities* of their State by Nature," without which they were blind to "the Glories of the Media-
tor." Men had to "see, and feel, and know *that they are wretched,
and miserable, and poor, and blind, and naked;* or they never will
have a Cure." Then, when prepared, the audience could receive
the doctrines of Christ: "The greatness of his Love and Conde-
scension, his *Bowels,* and *Mercies,* his Fulness and All-sufficiency
. . . his Power and Faithfulness to keep, and conduct to Glory,
all such as believe and trust in him." [12] The value of Gospel
knowledge, Ebenezer Pemberton said, was that "it humbles the
sinner before God and fills him with a deep sense of his own un-
worthiness." [13] After that he could be lifted up to exult in the
glory of free grace bestowed through God's mercy.

The New Lights cultivated a violent style of preaching to make
men "measure the misery of their apostate state." The minister
spoke to sinners "in the voice of terror," one pastor said, "that
they may be awakened to fly *from the wrath to come.*" [14] The
clear intent of Edwards' *Sinners in the Hands of an Angry God*
was to strip men of their confidence and prepare them to rely on
God alone for salvation. Although "disagreeable to the sentiments
and inclinations of a secure world," the preaching of terror was
"the most successful method of promoting the interests of real
and vital religion." [15]

The content of this preaching, the New Lights insisted, had to
be Calvinism at its harshest. Belief in utter depravity and complete dependence on grace corresponded perfectly to the delight
in debasement and union with God. Calvinist doctrines correctly
taught, Tennent said, are "Nature-humbling." [16] They "exalt the
Throne of God and abase the sinful Creature." [17] Human corrup-

[12] Wheelock, *Preaching,* 6, 5.
[13] *Knowledge,* 7.
[14] Pemberton, *Duty,* 7.
[15] Pemberton, *Sermon,* 12.
[16] *The Danger,* 9.
[17] J. Parsons, *Wisdom justified,* 42.

tion, justification by faith alone, and the sovereignty of God produced the humiliation at which the preachers were aiming. The "Sovereignty of Divine Grace," one preacher urged, "is indeed mortifying to the haughty and proud Sinner, and may it give a fatal Stab to the letting out of the very Hearts-Blood of damning Pride and Self Righteousness." [18] The doctrines of humiliation destroyed carnal security and forced men to the self-reproach which preceded the sweet calm of faith. Stress on these doctrines became the hallmark of New Light preaching.

The Old Lights, who organized their own religious feelings differently, reacted strongly against these extremes in style and content, fearing that emotional ecstasies would obscure the importance of good works and that men would stop with the assuring sensation of faith and not prove themselves by "gracious Actings, and sincere Obedience." [19] Without other virtues no man could count himself converted, "notwithstanding any possible degrees of Terror and Transports of joy." [20] Those who waited passively for gracious emotions would think that "the Work is God's and we need not take pains . . . it will be Presumption in us, and really disadvantage the Work." Sinners pretended to honor God in acknowledging His sovereignty, "but they are not honest and upright herein, for they Excuse themselves from duty, hereby." [21] When men believed that the assurance of salvation was all the faith needed to unite them to Christ, they naturally *despise all Means of Conviction, and attribute all Endeavours for it to* Ignorance *of God.* [22]

In order to redress the balance that was weighted too heavily on the side of emotion and grace, the Old Lights enlarged upon the importance of reason and good works. The Spirit ordinarily worked through man's reason. "IT is by leading us to a *true Knowledge, and firm Belief,* of the great Truths of the Gospel, that the *Holy Spirit* does regenerate us." [23] As the Spirit moved men to examine the scriptures in the light of reason, the inducements to obey gradually became overpowering. "The more we ponder

---

[18] Cooke, *Divine Sovereignty*, 32.
[19] S. Williams, *Vindication*, v, 41.
[20] Hart, *Holy Scriptures*, 19.
[21] Russell, *Man's liableness*, 5.
[22] S. Williams, *Vindication*, v, 41.
[23] Hart, *Discourse*, 10-11.

upon . . . the Blessings held forth in the Promises of the Gospel, the more valuable are they wont to appear . . . and so they will have the greater Influence on our Minds." [24] This knowledge sanctified a man's life. "By thus inlightning the mind in the knowledge of *God,* of *Jesus Christ* and of the *Way of Salvation* by him; the *Holy Spirit* does renew the *Will* and sanctify the *Affections* and *Tempers* of the *Heart.*" [25] Since religion was essentially intellectual, reformation of the total man began in the understanding. "The more religious, the more rational are we." [26]

Because the Spirit entered through the reason, a man could put himself in the way of grace by studying the scriptures and ordering his life according to the divine will. Admittedly sinners could do nothing to merit God's favor, "BUT yet, we have *no* Reason to think God *backward* to work this Great Work in us; if we seek it of him in a *becoming* Manner." [27] The assurance that grace would usually follow the employment of means was not a promise but a declaration of God's purpose. "The general Rule of the divine Conduct as the moral Governour of the World," declared Chauncey Whittelsey, Old Light tutor at Yale, is "to grant *more Grace, more Power and richer Advantages* to those who have been faithful in their past Improvements." [28] What must a man do to obtain grace? "Let him be in as much Earnest in using his persevering Endeavours, in God's own appointed Means." [29] Good works were no guarantee of divine favor, but they were not wholly useless.

The Old Lights defended their "lifeless" preaching with the argument that before grace could work a sinner needed above all a clear understanding of Christ and of the gospel. The clarity of a preacher's doctrine and the cogency of his arguments best prepared men for the Holy Spirit. A well-stocked head, not an overflowing heart, was the first qualification for the ministry. Education was more important than a violent experience with the Holy Spirit. Since direct inspiration had left the Christian Church in the first century, God had expected his servants to obtain

[24] C. Whittelsey, *Sermon,* 21.
[25] Hart, *Discourse,* 16-17.
[26] Russell, 49.
[27] Hart, *Discourse,* 25-28, 8.
[28] *Sermon,* 18.
[29] Dickinson, *Discourse,* 17; cf. p. 20.

knowledge by study, and, accordingly, the emotional power of the pastor was of little importance. The telling question was: Does he "preach the Truths of the Gospel of Jesus Christ"? No one could rightfully object to an upright minister with sufficient knowledge.[30]

Without deprecating education altogether, the radical New Lights believed that Old Lights exaggerated its importance. Tennent encouraged the organization of private colleges, and a New Light school held forth in New London until the Assembly forbade unauthorized academies.[31] But learning was at best a tool for converted men with an inward call. Unfortunately, Backus pointed out, multitudes, puffed up by erudition, made "more of human Wisdom and Learning, than of the Spirit of God."[32]

The New Lights gave no credence to the Old Light version of religious experience. Conversion obliterated all understanding or tolerance of milder varieties of piety. New Lights dismissed Old Lights who slighted Calvinist doctrines and preached bookish, unmoving sermons as having never tasted grace. An unconverted pastor's "cold and sapless" sermons were a serious hindrance to the work of God. "Pharisee-Teachers," Tennent said, "having no Experience of a special Work of the Holy Ghost, upon their own Souls, are therefore neither inclined to, nor fitted for, Discoursing . . . upon such important Subjects."[33] Jonathan Parsons of Lyme was persuaded that "no publick Teacher of the Church is like to do much real Service to the Souls of his People, whom they have reason to think a Stranger to a saving Work of divine Grace upon his own Soul." Sanctifying grace was a "necessary Qualification in a publick Teacher of the Gospel Church."[34] Strangers to Christ entered the ministry "under the influence of Carnal motives."[35] Ministers should aim at the glory of God, Tennent said. "And can any natural man do this? No! no! Every Skin of them has an Evil Eye."[36] Unconverted pastors were "the

---

[30] Beckwith, *Christ*, 61, 54; cf. 68-70.

[31] I. Backus, *All true*, xii; Tennent, *The Danger*, 11; *Conn. Recs.*, VIII, 500-502.

[32] *All true*, 16, 72.

[33] *The Danger*, 6.

[34] *Needful Caution*, 20, 7-8.

[35] Pemberton, *Knowledge*, 25.

[36] *The Danger*, 5.

plagues of the Church and the Unhappy occasion of the damnation of multitudes." [37]

Tennent warned that false teachers often disguised themselves in a pretended piety. Some modern pharisees "have learned to prate a little more Orthodoxly about the New Birth." [38] They "pretend Orthodoxy in Principle, appearing in a Mask," while actually their teachings "encourage Presumption, or build up their Hearers in a fatal hope of Acceptance before God by the righteousness which is of the Law." [39] Since "Openness will not bear . . . the Poison has been guilded over, that so it might be received without being distinguished from pure Gospel." [40] These lifeless ministers could be detected by a number of revealing clues. For example, "they put their Sermons into a conect Form, so smooth, and in such general Terms, that no Conscience is awakened, or Saints quickened." The sermons go "round about Religion, and never can get into the Heart and Life of Religion." Their eyes rove about the meetinghouse or follow persons from the door to their seats. They offer the same prayer from Sabbath to Sabbath and always preach "in a legal old Covenant Spirit." [41] Under the inspection of so critical an audience a minister was forced to weigh every intonation and gesture. "A Wigg, or a new Coat," it was observed, "is many Times offensive to the tender Consciences of young Converts." [42]

Small wonder that conservatives opposed the Awakening when they saw the growth of this critical spirit which assaulted more violently than ever the already weakened foundations of ecclesiastical authority. Any pastor who did not preach terror and emphasize justification by faith was labeled dead and unaffecting. Rational preachers were utterly rejected, and even moderately evangelical sermons dissatisfied the more radical New Lights. Moreover, religious differences were the vehicle for social resentments. The radicals seemed often to direct their warnings of "the terrible Justice and Holiness of GOD" "to personal Applications, and to

[37] Pemberton, *Knowledge*, 25.
[38] *The Danger*, 11.
[39] J. Parsons, *Needful Caution*, 11.
[40] J. Parsons, *Wisdom justified*, 13.
[41] Frothingham, 109, 118.
[42] J. Parson, *Wisdom justified*, v.

be terminated on particular Objects whom they think to be Opposers, and with vehemence to treat them as discovered to them to be the Objects of Divine Displeasure." [43] "Intemperate, indiscreet zeal" led even the saintly Brainerd into rash judgments about "others whom he looked upon as better than himself." His epithet on Chauncey Whittelsey, the Yale tutor, contained a dose of venom: "He has no more grace than this chair." [44] When some New Lights declared that lack of grace made ministers greedy, the conservative clergy understood how serious were the revivalists' discontents. A plea for higher wages could be interpreted as an admission of the pastor's unregenerate state.

Radical statements convinced the Old Lights that a plot was afoot to remove them. "It was notorious," Thomas Clap, the Rector of Yale, said in 1745, "that Mr. *Whitefield,* and *other Itinerants* did endeavour to perswade People, that the *generality* of the Ministers were *Unconverted* . . . from whence it necessarily followed, that People ought to *discard* them." Clap believed that during the Awakening "there had been a *Design* to turn the *generality of Ministers in the Country out of their Places,* and where they could not make the Party strong enough to do that at once, they would, in the mean Time set up a *Separation."* [45] The itinerants, the Old Lights thought, inadvertently or not, wished to "crowd their Brethren out of the Vineyard or fill their People with those Prejudices against their own Teachers that will quite indispose them for being benefitted by their Teaching." [46] In defense of their positions and the peace of their congregations, the conservative clergy requested the Assembly to forbid itineracy and explicitly asked Whitefield not to visit a second time.[47]

Neither laws nor arguments, however, prevailed against the New Lights' pious urges. In order to hear experimental preaching, radicals left their educated pastors and went where the Spirit was to be found. Tennent advised men to cross parish lines to hear a moving preacher. Other radicals counselled separation from Old

[43] Windham Ministers, *Letter,* 44; cf. Worthington, *Duty of Rulers,* 38.
[44] *Life,* 381.
[45] Clap, *Letter to a Friend,* 5, 4.
[46] Beckwith, *Christ,* 63.
[47] *Conn. Recs.,* VIII, 454-457; Tracy, *Great Awakening,* 367.

Light ministers who jeopardized a congregation's "precious never-dying souls." [48] Religion required people to "break over the Bounds that have been set . . . by the Traditions of Men." [49] Tennent agreed that departures from convention caused disorder, but, he asked, "must we leave off every Duty, that is the Occasion of Contention or Division? Then we must quit powerful Religion altogether." [50]

Radicals therefore departed from lifeless, unconverted ministers to form separate congregations that were taught by preachers qualified by experience with humiliation and grace. The resulting turmoil, the Separates insisted, arose from the wicked opposition of worldly men. "There has never been the vital Power of true Godliness visible," one of them declared, "but there was more or less Opposition against it, and Divisions made by the carnal World." [51] The pursuit of holiness inevitably set the saints in conflict with ecclesiastical order.

Radical New Lights recognized that their piety challenged church authority, for they denied that God worked more than incidentally through the formal structure. Divine power descended directly in a personal encounter with the Spirit. A license from the consociation or ordination by other pastors, for example, was no assurance of authority.[52] "The Essence of the Call of all God's Messengers," Isaac Backus said, consisted in being "by the Work of his Spirit, on their Hearts, commissionated, and sent forth in his Name." [53] Ordination was a trivial human exercise, insignificant by comparison with that inward call. The government of religious affairs belonged not to ecclesiastical institutions but to the God within each reborn man.

This external revolt reflected the inward revolt that occurred in conversion. The reborn man set his guilty conscience at ease by denying all divine authority to the social order and relying wholly on Christ to redeem him. The converts' peace of mind depended

[48] Tennent, 12, 14; Frothingham, 119.
[49] I. Backus, *All true*, 85.
[50] Tennent, 16.
[51] Frothingham, 363-364.
[52] Conn. Arch., Ecclesiastical Affairs, XV, 225; I. Backus, *A Fish Caught in His Own Net*, 32-33; cf. Goen, *Revivalism and Separatism*, 54-66.
[53] *All true*, 25.

on God's overruling the earthly fathers, whose ordinances brought terrifying guilt; conversion prepared him to defy the law whenever it interfered with his new holiness. Radical New Lights circumvented earthly government and claimed authority directly from the heavens, rejecting the mediating agency of any institutions connected with the old order. Laymen with no other qualification except "some Conviction of their Minds about Preaching," Backus said, are to obey "God in what has been made clear Duty" to them.[54]

The Old Lights, bound to conventional law and authority, still believed that ecclesiastical institutions were the "plain revealed Will of Christ." [55] Arguing that "the Validity of Administration depends not upon the Faith and Holiness of the Minister . . . But on a man's having Christ's Commission" received in a proper ordination,[56] they foresaw chaos if men judged the validity of authority for themselves. The notion that everyone who was "persuaded he has an inwd Call, is Sufficiently Authorized for Such an Undertaking" had "a direct tendency to Subvert the Whole Institution of the Gospel Ministry, and to Open a Door to let in all Ignorant and Superstitious Teachers in the Churches." The end of it all was "Quakerism and open Infidelity and the Destruction of all the Christian Religion." [57] It was impossible to manage the "affairs of Christs Kingdom Decently, without Observing Some *Order* or Rules of Conduct," and the Separates were enjoined not to "break over the *Good Order* that has already obtained" in the churches.[58]

The Separates adamantly asserted that "Christ is not bound to any Order that Men think fit to Come into Among them." [59] The Old Lights' claims to authority "set aside the Work of God's Spirit, and the Kingly Authority of Jesus Christ" and "set up mortal Man in his Room." [60] The immediate experience with God was suffi-

---

[54] I. Backus, *All true*, 97.
[55] Elihu Hall, *Present way*, 73.
[56] Beckwith, *Christ*, 59.
[57] "Windham Association Book," 120, 121.
[58] Joseph Fish, Stonington, to Joseph Parke, Westerly, Dec. 9, 1743, Lane Memorial Collection.
[59] Joseph Fish, Stonington, to Joseph Parke, Westerly, Dec. 9, 1743, Lane Memorial Collection.
[60] I. Backus, *All true*, 79.

ciently vivid to structure their lives and churches, and they happily accepted the commission of pastors whose only authority was an inward call.

The Separates' revolutionary attitude also revived the notion of congregational autonomy. Just as motions of the Spirit authorized anyone to preach, the gift of grace authorized congregations of reborn men to act independently. The Separates confidently returned to the pristine Congregationalism affirmed in the Cambridge Platform because their churches, excluding half-way members and merely upright men, consisted entirely of visible Saints, as the first in New England had. The Separates demanded of each candidate the relation of a concrete experience of grace, and qualified candidates were not scarce after the Awakening. The Separates were confident too that they could discern "not meerly of moral Sincerity," but "Saintship itself, or real Grace and true Holiness." They claimed an "eye of Grace, or Divine Light shining into the Soul, that sees in Kind as God seeth, because it is a Ray of Divine Light from God," [61] and with that eye they identified the true saints who would make up their churches.

A congregation so constituted deferred to no one. The Holy Spirit in each man made him the agent of God, and, collected in a church, the saints were sovereign. "All Power given by God, for the well-being of his Church" worked "Instrumentally" through the members, "according to the Grace and Gift of God given to each." Divine authority was located only in Christ in heaven and in the congregation of Saints on earth. "All Power and Rule of every Kind, that is Needful for the Well-being of the Church of Christ, is either in the Head, Christ, or given from Christ to the Members, as a Body or Church, to be exercised by the Church." [62]

Consequently, the Separates rejected the system of checks on the congregation built up over the past century, beginning with the minister's veto over church actions. Christ and the regenerate Saints were to govern ecclesiastical affairs without interference. "No Room can possibly be found for a third Power of Rule to be exercised in this Church," a Separate preacher said. "That Church that suffers or allows an Elder or Minister to have the negativing

[61] Frothingham, 49, 100-101.
[62] Frothingham, 181, 212.

Power intire, has two Heads, and so is a Monster." If it was not a monster, he went on, then "Jesus Christ is not a Head in it, but a human Creature; and so consequently it is an Anti-christian Body or Church." [63] Separate churches revived the practice of allowing lay members to officiate in ordinations as a symbol of congregational authority.[64]

Consociations were anathema. Since God worked only through congregations of the reborn, the powers of clerical councils were "the Powers of Darkness." [65] Saltonstall, by urging adoption of the Saybrook Platform, "did as much Mischief as almost any man that ever was in the Colony." [66] One Separate said that at first converted men sought more fervent preaching, but later they left primarily because of the unholy authority consociations exercised over congregations of the elect.[67] The established ecclesiastical order had no divine commission, for the Saints themselves were supreme.

Ecclesiastical discipline against these rebels was doomed to fail. The Assembly forbade recognition of Separates as sober dissenters, thus compelling each church to treat them as schismatics. Pastors called in the wayward members for trial, but the Separates treated the church representatives with disdain, failed to come to the public hearings, and refused to admit that the congregation had any jurisdiction over them. Those who appeared and stated their reasons used the trial to advertise their cause, airing in detail their objections to the pastor or the Connecticut Establishment. The ministers occasionally recovered a few members, but the departure of a large group, undismayed by their excommunication, showed the failing strength of such sanctions.[68]

While ostensibly the Separates caused these disturbances solely for the sake of experimental religion, their motives were mixed. They were moved not only by a genuine piety generated in the

[63] Frothingham, 212, 217-219.
[64] Goen, 76; cf. 168, 194.
[65] Frothingham, 253.
[66] I. Backus, *All true,* 89n.
[67] I. Backus, *A Fish Caught in His Own Net,* 32-33; cf. Conn. Arch., Ecclesiastical Affairs, XV, 225.
[68] *Conn. Recs.,* VIII, 522. The vicissitudes of trying Separates are illustrated in Norwich, "First Congregational Church, Records," I, 37ff.

Awakening but also by the familiar struggle with authority. Judging a minister "as an Hypocrite, and Carnal," the Old Lights thought, was a way of "Despising, and setting him at Nought." Cries of *"Carnal, Carnal,* Unconverted, Hypocrites, Pharisees" showed more hate than love.[69] The Separates' own words revealed their animosity. There was a vindictive pleasure in leaving a church "stuffed full of Hypocrites or Dissemblers." [70] Piety thinly covered antagonism and permitted the safe release of pent-up bitterness.

The New Lights divided into distinct camps over the question of opposition to the old order. Moderates, the majority among supporters of the Awakening, reproved the radicals' animosity and their disdain for ecclesiastical order. Such men as Jonathan Edwards and Solomon Williams believed that experimental religion could flourish within the Establishment and deplored the disrespect for ministers, fearing that people would condemn the work of grace in its entirety because of the violence of a minority of the New Lights.

The moderates formed a middle party between the Old Lights and the Separates, distinguished not by a unique conviction but by their compromise between order and piety. To foster separations from ministers was "to teach Rebellion in Israel." [71] They remembered that "there's scarce any thing more fully and strictly Enjoin'd in the Gospel than Charity, Peace and Unity among Christians; and scarce any thing more plainly and frequently forbidden than Divisions, Schisms and Separations." [72] Separate churches and lay preaching would "destroy all Order, and throw the Churches into *Anarchy,* and *Confusion.*" [73] Separations were to be avoided and constituted authority respected.[74]

At the same time, the moderates shared the Separates' sense of glory and power in the new birth. Edwards and Williams and their friends agreed that vital religion might necessarily overstep the

[69] Beckwith, *Christ,* 48-49; cf. I. Stiles, *A Prospect,* 55ff.
[70] Frothingham, 342.
[71] Beckwith, *Christ,* 53.
[72] *Judgment,* 7.
[73] Beckwith, *Christ,* 63-64.
[74] Clap, *Letter to a Friend,* 5-6; J. Parsons, *Needful Caution,* 48-50; *Wisdom justified,* v; Windham Ministers, *Letter,* 34; J. Edwards, *Works,* I, 86-87.

bounds of traditional propriety. Williams, for example, signed a petition protesting the law against itineracy, and upon the passage of this legislation, Joseph Bellamy, Edwards' follower, promptly issued an open invitation to all itinerants to preach to his congregation in Bethlehem whenever they wished. Edwards relaxed his resistance to unauthorized ministers enough to admit that lay exhortation was sometimes permissible and urged a colleague to tolerate men who separated from his congregation because of a tender conscience.[75]

While denouncing tumults, Edwards tried to make the conservatives understand that confusion and uproar inevitably accompanied so magnificent a work of God as the Awakening.

Many that are zealous for this glorious work of God, are heartily sick of the great noise there is in the country, about imprudences and disorders: they have heard it so often from the mouths of opposers that they are prejudiced against the sound; and they look upon it that that which is called being prudent, and regular, which is so much insisted on, is no other than being asleep, or cold and dead in religion, and that the great imprudence that is so much cried out of, is only a being alive and engaged in the things of God.[76]

Though Edwards acknowledged that piety should not overthrow order, he agreed with the Separates on the supreme value of the new birth and the necessity of preaching doctrines which prepared men to experience it, and, with the other moderates, insisted that the church must at certain points conform to the dictates of experimental religion.

On a number of questions their common emphasis on rebirth forced moderate New Lights and the Separates to similar conclusions. Working from within, the former gradually effected some of the changes in ecclesiastical policy favored by the latter. In the long run the moderates altered the church more drastically than the radicals.

After considerable soul-searching, Edwards asked his Northampton congregation to require evidence of conversion for admission to communion. The proposal was difficult for him because his own grandfather, Solomon Stoddard, had begun to admit moral and

---

[75] Shipton, *Sibley's Harvard Graduates*, VI, 354; Cothren, *Woodbury*, 247; J. Edwards, *Works*, III, 397; S. E. Dwight, *Edwards*, 204-209.
[76] J. Edwards, *Works*, III, 349; cf. p. 291.

sincere applicants unsure of conversion. Still more embarrassing was the Separates' advocacy of the same procedure. Edwards foresaw that the radicals would claim him as their own and use his arguments to justify their departures from the established churches. In the introduction to the defense of his position, Edwards repeated in the most forceful terms his opposition to separations, but the radicals rejoiced nonetheless in his support of their views.[77]

Most New Lights refused to follow Edwards at first, though he was an acknowledged leader among the revivalists. Solomon Williams, Edwards' kinsman in Connecticut, spoke for his opponents among the moderates. Williams' lengthy rebuttal charged that Edwards' scheme of reform was unscriptural, unworkable, and destructive of good order. Not until a decade after Edwards first argued for a church of true Saints did he begin to win any appreciable number of followers. Then his disciple and successor as leader of the New Lights, Joseph Bellamy, published two tracts against half-way members and merely moral communicants. Bellamy's advocacy won others to the position, including the entire Litchfield Consocation.[78]

Many moderate New Lights, like their more radical brethren, were also chary of the Saybrook Platform. The Old Lights often used the consociations to dampen the Awakening. Philemon Robbins of Branford encountered difficulties with the New Haven Consociation for preaching to a Baptist congregation in Wallingford without the permission of its regular pastor. Robbins was willing to apologize, but he would not admit that his visit was sinful, for he felt he was doing his part in spreading the revival spirit. When the association censured him, his Church withdrew and returned to the Cambridge Platform. Robbins published an account of his case to which was appended a letter by some anonymous defender who argued that "if a Church does not give away *their Right of private Judgment* in Matters of Religion, when it consents to act by a particular *Platform,* which they never can do; then you had a Right to do what you did, in refusing *that Platform.*"[79]

Since the New Haven Consocation actively harried all the New

[77] J. Edwards, *Humble Inquiry,* iv-v.
[78] S. Williams, *True State;* "Litchfield County Consocation," 35.
[79] Robbins, *Plain Narrative,* 40.

Light ministers, their sympathizers criticized consociational controls.[80] Elisha Williams, writing anonymously for the New Lights in 1745, asserted that synods and ecclesiastical officers were not to legislate rules of faith or practice for Christians in any sense. Though a congregation voluntarily subjected itself to guidance, it retained the right to judge all cases for itself and could withdraw without fear of penalty.[81] Jared Ingersoll said that New Lights generally refused to submit to consociations, thinking "every Particular Church to have an inalienable Power within itself to act and determine in the affairs of the Church." [82]

Although most moderates did not follow the Separates in repudiating the Saybrook Platform altogether, certain aspects of it were particularly offensive. The ministerial veto in the consociation was unwarranted when lay delegates also possessed the grace of God. The Litchfield County Consociation, dominated by Bellamy, ruled in 1752 that a major vote of both laymen and elders was required for the passage of any measure, whereas previously ministers could act alone. Bellamy, like the Separates, believed that the minister had no right to negate the wishes of the laity. Windham County soon followed suit, and nearby in Cornwall the church adopted articles of discipline, probably drafted by Edwards, putting their minister on an equal footing with the members in making important decisions.[83]

Neither the abandonment of Stoddardeanism nor objections to clerical control aroused many moderate New Lights against the conservatives, however, and the major impact of the moderates was felt elsewhere. A cause better able to summon their energies was the exposition of the "distinguishing doctrines of Christianity." The New Lights' devotion to experimental religion gave them, as it did the Separates, a special affection for the Calvinist doctrines of depravity and grace. The New Lights felt an urgent desire to force upon men a conviction of sin. Brainerd discoursed repeatedly on the necessity of "that humiliation, self-emptiness, or full convic-

[80] B. Trumbull, *Connecticut,* II, 157-158.

[81] Elisha Williams, *Essential Rights,* 50, 53, 46-48.

[82] "Historical Account," 8.

[83] "Litchfield County Consociation," 35; "Windham Association Book," 158; cf. p. 135; E. Stiles, *Extracts,* 182, 180-181.

tion of a person's being utterly undone in himself, which is necessary in order to a saving faith." The doctrines of divine sovereignty and human helplessness were necessary to prevent men from assuming some "self-righteous appearances" of grace.[84] A religion without power "to break Men's carnal Peace, may safely be set down for a false Religion." [85]

The New Lights were frustrated because the theological distinctions between the Old Lights and themselves were not always clear. Most conservatives held to the same orthodoxy as the friends of the revival and made no objection to the Calvinist conceptions of depravity and salvation by grace alone. On the other hand, an extreme New Light like Isaac Backus insisted that he did not mean "to beat Souls off from the Use of Means" and also agreed that the Holy Spirit worked on men by enlightening their minds. The issue again was one of emphasis and balance. Backus said he would not beat men off from the use of means, but he "would beat them off from resting in any Thing short of a living Union to Christ, by which alone they can have any Safety." By "Driving, Driving, to Duty, Duty," Tennent said, Pharisee teachers "fix a deluded World upon the false Foundation of their own Righteousness; and so exclude them from the dear Redeemer." [86]

The traditional statement of Calvinist doctrines would have suited the moderates perfectly had not the Old Lights misconstrued orthodoxy. Men talked all too easily of depravity and grace without undergoing the terrifying experience of humiliation and the joyous experience of exaltation in God. "A felt Christ, or a Christ revealed in their Souls, they know nothing about." [87] An immense gulf separated an abstract intellectual knowledge of Christ from experimental knowledge. The New Lights thought the Old Lights failed to perceive the full power of the Calvinist doctrines ostensibly accepted by both parties.

The Old Lights' complacent mouthing of beliefs about man's vileness and God's justice forced some of the New Lights to an exaggerated statement of Calvinism. Their effort produced the first major theological innovations in 100 years. Jonathan Edwards and his followers eventually hammered out concepts that represented the experience of conversion they had known, in contrast to the regeneration of reason taught by the conservatives. Understandably, the debates that ensued centered on the doctrines of humiliation —original sin, free will, and the sovereignty of God. Edwards and his colleagues struggled against all "those doctrines that tend to exalt the creature in his own conceit," and defended "those that establish the absolute Sovereignty of God." [88] The main intent of the New Divinity, as their formulation came to be called, was to put in theological terms the sense of man's degradation and God's exaltation, the attitudes that lay at the heart of the newborn man's life. They drove each concept to its ultimate extreme in an effort to unsettle the stolid conservatives. The acute awareness of having known God in His overwhelming power compelled the New Divinity men to try for the remainder of the century to distinguish that experience from the fraudulent or trivial perceptions of worldly men.

For a time in the 1750's and 1760's the New Lights were convinced that they opposed not mere complacency but outright heresy. In the decades when Calvinism was revived by the religious experience of the Awakening, Arminianism and a train of other heresies were spreading in Massachusetts. The New Lights, unwilling to tolerate doctrinal deviations that quieted the excruciating emotions leading to rebirth, mounted a campaign to preserve the distinguishing doctrines of Calvinism, an effort that ultimately altered the Establishment more radically than conscious reforms.

Bellamy and others suspected that Connecticut Old Lights were of the same mind as more open heretics in Massachusetts but hid their beliefs to keep their pulpits. The reluctance to elaborate on depravity and grace covered an actual disdain for those doctrines. The Old Lights showed their true feelings in their sermons on reason and the use of means. In a parable of his own making, Bellamy likened the suspected Old Lights to one *"Authades,"* a Socinian of some unspecified earlier time. To obtain a settlement in a Calvinist church, Authades concealed his convictions by generally preaching on noncontroversial "moral subjects." Once in-

[88] Cary, "Revival Experiences," 738.

stalled, he realized he had to continue to delude the congregation or lose his salary and behind the scenes, after making a few proselytes to the Socinian scheme, began his attack. He "slily dresses up *Calvinists,* as *bigots,* and *vital piety* as *enthusiasm."* His lot was hard, for he knew that "if his church and congregation could strip off his false colours, and get legal proof of his true character, he must lose his £100 *per annum."* An honest man would declare himself and retire, Bellamy said, but Authades' love of money compelled him to cheat his people.[89]

In his own consociation of Litchfield, Bellamy was careful to see that only candidates with undoubted devotion to the "distinguishing doctrines of Christianity" were licensed.[90] He advocated that every minister subscribe to a creed that would put his orthodoxy beyond question. Then if a congregation mistakenly hired a heretic, they could "find him out, and prove him to be a *Socinian,* and as such, have him silenced, and take away his £100 *per annum."* [91]

Not content with purging heresy in Litchfield County, Bellamy attempted to enlist the united powers of the General Association in the cause. His strategy was to revive the proposal for a General Consociation made by Old Lights in the 1740's, when they had been dominant. The association of Connecticut ministers was merely an advisory body, but the proposed consociation was to include lay representatives as well as ministers and thus to represent the churches fully. Though the Old Lights had wished this body to possess final judicial authority in all ecclesiastical disputes in order to be able to stamp out antinomian impulses released in the Awakening, Bellamy, of course, wanted to use the consociation to crush Arminianism. The Old Lights had abandoned the idea by 1752, after three New Light associations had persistently refused to cooperate, but in 1754 Bellamy's Litchfield Association revived the plan as if it were a continuation of the Old Light recommendation, asking first that the General Association adhere to a Calvinist confession of faith. The next year the General Association reaffirmed its orthodoxy and went on to urge ministers to bear testimony against the prevailing doctrinal errors. Socinianism,

[89] Bellamy, *Letter,* 15-18.
[90] "Litchfield County Association," 86.
[91] Bellamy, *Letter,* 15-18.

Arianism, Arminianism, Pelagianism, and Antinomianism were condemned—all the heresies, with the exception of the last, in which New Lights suspected Old Lights of indulging.

Thereafter, however, Bellamy's plans met stiff opposition, both from Old Lights who saw through the scheme at once and from eastern New Lights who had some misgivings about more ecclesiastical controls. To the relief of conservatives, the General Consociation was never organized. The most Bellamy could obtain was a recommendation to all county associations to review periodically the licenses of candidate preachers so as to nip in the bud any heretical tendencies.[92]

A New Light triumph at Wallingford in 1758 and 1759 soon offset this disappointment. A minority of church members there objected to the appointment of a candidate preacher, James Dana, sent down from Cambridge, whom they suspected of heretical tendencies. When Dana was less than congenial to inquiries about his orthodoxy, the New Light minority complained to the New Haven Consociation. By this date New Haven County had fallen to the New Lights, as the Old Lights of the 1740's had been replaced by younger pastors; and the Consociation was quick to descend on Wallingford to block Dana's ordination. The church, however, had carefully chosen its ordaining council, which disregarded the Consociation's request to examine Dana and proceeded with the ordination. The infuriated Consociation ministers called in New Light allies from Hartford County and pronounced a sentence of noncommunion against Dana, his church, and the members of the ordaining council, declaring the minority party to be the First Church in Wallingford. The Old Light ministers of the ordaining council announced their independence by breaking their ties with the Consociation. Dana's voice was not hushed, but his influence and that of his Old Light friends was curtailed by the imposing array of New Light ecclesiastical authority.[93]

[92] *Records of the General Association,* 26, 28, 32-34, 37; Hunn, *Welfare,* 28-29; "Windham Association Book," 136-137; Fairfield East Association, "Book of Records," 42, 53-55; "Litchfield County Association," 93; Hart, *Remarks,* 48.

[93] For a detailed account of the Wallingford controversy, with pertinent documents, B. Trumbull, *Connecticut,* II, 408-449; cf. *Records of the General Association,* 41, 43, 44.

In the aftermath, when the parties to the controversy attempted to rationalize their positions, a new set of attitudes toward the Saybrook Platform became apparent. To justify their defiance of the Consociation, the Old Lights argued for a strict interpretation of the Platform. No considerations of general welfare, even where laudable, authorized enlargements. The right of approving ordinations was given to councils chosen by the churches, not to the consociation. The New Haven Consociation had stretched its authority beyond constitutional limits when it interfered at Wallingford.[94]

The main intent of the Old Light pamphlets was to defend the liberties of individual churches and to minimize the consociational power now in the hands of their enemies. These onetime protectors of order now dilated on the advantages of liberty. One pamphleteer verged close to the Separates' way of thinking when he contended that Christ gave to each church power to exercise government over itself and that "no church can divest itself of the authority, or release itself from that duty, by assigning, giving up or transferring the same to another." [95] Another, impressed with Locke perhaps, began with the premise that because men are rational they have "a natural and unalienable Right to search, examine, and judge for themselves," and came to the conclusion that it was the right of every church as well "to see and judge" for itself.[96] Even the framers of the Saybrook Platform were invoked in behalf of the churches' liberties.

The truth is, that our constitution is in a great degree congregational. And the formers of it, were attentive to secure the essential rights and liberties of particular churches, especially of vacant churches, and to guard them against the encroachments of ambitious clergymen, and protect them from the tyranny of the consociated churches.

This author thought it fortunate that the framers were so farsighted as to guard against a day like his own when "too many of the clergy are disposed to ride hard, and urge on the unwilling jade, with the spur of zeal for orthodoxy." [97] By whatever means, the

[94] Hart, *Remarks*, 5, 11, 17-19; Hart, *A Few Remarks*, 29; Fitch, *Explanation*, 10.
[95] Fitch, *Explanation*, 11; cf. p. 14; Bartholomew, *Some Remarks*, 12.
[96] *Letter to the Clergy*, 5; cf. Fitch, *Explanation*, 22, 23, 33-34.
[97] Hart, *A Few Remarks*, 11, 12.

Old Lights were bent on defending and enlarging congregational autonomy as against consociational control.

The New Lights, on the other hand, took to arguing much as the Old Lights had during the Awakening. The New Lights became the friends of "Order, Unity and Peace," seeking to crush disruptive nonconformity.[98] The impulse in the two instances was not exactly the same, however: the New Lights made greater capital out of their protection of orthodoxy than out of the preservation of order and were unable to disregard the accusations of tyranny as lightly as had the Old Lights in the 1740's. They claimed that the New Haven Consociation acted fully within its constitutional rights at Wallingford and agreed that the controversy should be fought on the grounds of liberty alone. The main New Light protagonist recognized that "the grand objection against the scheme I am pleading for, is 'That it establishes a tyrannical power in councils, and destroys the liberties of particular churches, and the members of them.'" "As I am a sincere friend to liberty," he said, "and detest tyranny of every kind, ecclesiastical as well as civil, I freely consent, that the whole controversy should turn on this single point." The Consociation, he said, had protected the rights of the minority against the heretical majority at Wallingford; hence it was the bulwark of liberty and free conscience.[99] That argument had not been heard among Old Lights when Tennent was in the colony's pulpits.

The tone of the entire argument was an indication of the Connecticut temper in 1760. The New Lights admitted that the objection to tyranny was "popular." The appeal of liberty was so great that one New Light defender conceded that if his principles did "not more effectually promote and secure the rights and liberties of mankind, than the opposite scheme" did, then he would be "content that they be exploded." [100] Those who spoke for liberty against authority in 1760 did so with far more courage and effect than was possible at the beginning of the century. Moreover, the terms of the Wallingford argument—constitutional powers, volun-

---

[98] Hobart, *An Attempt*, 12, 44.
[99] Hobart, *The Principles*, 38-40; Dickinson, *Some Remarks*, 22; E. Eells, *Some Remarks*, 23.
[100] Hobart, *The Principles*, 38, 39; Hobart, *Vindication*, 68.

tary compacts, and natural rights—rang more with the rhetoric of the post-Revolutionary age than with that of the era of Gurdon Saltonstall.

The great Difficulty in civil and ecclesiastical policy is to fix the Balance between Authority and Liberty. Authority is apt to degenerate into Tyranny, and Liberty into Licentiousness and confusion . . . . The Constitution of the consociated churches in Connecticut is in my opinion the true medium between these Extreams.[101]

Conditions of life in Connecticut had made these characteristically American notions about liberty and authority appropriate for use in 1760.

Neither religious party put liberty at the center of its thought. Both were quite willing to exercise power for the sake of the public good when they could,[102] and liberty was desirable mainly to protect some more vital interest—experimental religion for the New Lights and morality and a measure of their old status for the Old Lights. But, while ecclesiastical liberty was not the chief aim of Old or New Lights, it was the salient result of their dispute at Wallingford. The Old Lights were too firmly entrenched in colonial society for the New Light consociations to bring them to task, and the censured ministers carried on without any ill effects. Unable to enforce its will, the consociation's power declined and congregational liberty grew.

Furthermore, the New Lights east of the Connecticut River, perhaps because of Separate influence, chafed at supracongregational authority. Many churches there set aside the Saybrook Platform and returned to the Cambridge Platform, while others adopted their own combinations of Presbyterian and Congregational control. Undermined on every hand, the Platform was silently dropped from the colony's statue book in 1784.[103]

[101] Hobart, *An Attempt*, 43.
[102] Cf. Dickinson, *An Answer*, 14. One reversal was particularly striking: The same Old Lights who censured Philemon Robbins objected strenuously when their turn for rebuke came; and this same Philemon Robbins sat on the consociation council that chastised his former oppressors.
[103] C. Whittlesey to Stiles, Jan. 20, 1762, E. Stiles, *Extracts*, 583; Norwich, "First Congregational Church, Records," I, 45-46; *Contributions to Ecclesiastical History*, 62, 122. For churches electing to follow the Cambridge Platform or some variety thereof, see H. R. Stiles, *Windsor*, I, 595; Franklin, "Congregational Church, Miscellaneous Documents," 3a,

Thus experimental religion gradually diminished ecclesiastical authority. The eventual result of all the New Light reforms was a diffusion of power from pastor to people. The Separates' holy and fervent preachers, convinced of the graciousness of their people, relinquished their veto over the laity and dropped consociational controls almost entirely. Their objections accustomed Connecticut to trenchant and pious criticism of leaders previously considered sancrosanct, and successful separations further undermined the power of the Establishment.

Experimental religion worked through the moderates in a somewhat different fashion. Their elimination of the Half-Way Covenant and Stoddardeanism tended, as with the Separates, to give the laity more voice in church affairs. Moreover, their theological pronouncements provoked thought on questions once considered closed and introduced an era of imaginative speculation and lively discussion. But, most important, moderate New Lights split the established church and created conflicts that made consociational controls unworkable. Because the division was so nearly even and the balance of power shifted from one party to the other, both factions at one time or another committed themselves to ecclesiastical liberty.

The truly revolutionary aspect of the Awakening was the dilution of divine sanction in traditional institutions and the investiture of authority in some inward experience. Thereby the church lost power, and individuals gained it, using it to reform the old order in both principle and practice. The final outcome, though largely unintentional, was to enlarge religious liberty.

4a; *Contributions to Ecclesiastical History,* 392-393; Caulkins, *New London,* 489; East Windsor, "First Ecclesiastical Society, Records," I, 3; E. Stiles, *Extracts,* 308, 456; I. Backus, *History of New England,* II, 82; Norwich, "First Congregational Church, Records," II, 43-48; Norwich, "Second Congregational Church, Records," I, 10-17; "Hanover Congregational Church, Records," I, 4; Fairfield East Consociation, "Book of Records," 63, 70; Conn. Arch., Ecclesiastical Affairs, XI, 156, 158, 159, 164, 176; VIII, 44, 330.

XIV

Church and State

&§ POPULAR SUPPORT for the Establishment had declined after adoption of the Saybrook Platform, but the state continued its active regulation of religion. The law required everyone to attend a Congregational society and to contribute to the minister's salary unless specially exempted to worship with Anglicans, Baptists, or Quakers. Whenever ecclesiastical disorder threatened, as at Guilford in the 1730's, the legislature intervened. The Assembly's law against itinerants in 1741 was only consistent with the customary practices of the civil government.

The Awakening brought the privileges of the Established churches under heavy fire, because the multiplication of dissenters increased the difficulty of enforcing ecclesiastical laws and spread a new sense of their injustice. A number of prominent and articulate persons began to criticize the colony's religious policies and to propose changes in the traditional relations of church and state.

The most troublesome dissenters were the Separates, some thirty or forty of whose churches had sprung up by 1755.[1] A number of them were fanatical and bitter in spirit, but others attracted stable and even distinguished supporters. In New Haven and Canterbury, for example, the dissenting congregations contained some of the town's most respected residents, and a majority of Canterbury's inhabitants separated from their pastor.[2] In these

[1] Goen, *Revivalism and Separatism*, 302-309. The exact number of separations is difficult to count because some began with disputes reaching back to before the Awakening and were not wholly in sympathy with later more radical Separates (see note 2). Others were so ephemeral they had little effect on their communities.

[2] For prominent men among the Separate leadership, Larned, *Windham*, I, 459-463; Caulkins, *New London*, 452; I. Backus, *History of New England*, II, 77; Orcutt, *New Milford*, 191. Professor William G. McLoughlin has

places where the good faith of the dissenters was beyond question, requests for relief from ecclesiastical laws fell on sympathetic ears.

Many Separates gravitated toward the Baptist churches, which the Awakening thus indirectly strengthened. Adult baptism of believers was a logical extension of the New Light belief in a church of visible Saints. Once the ordinance of the Lord's Supper had been reserved for the converted, it was a small step to the belief that only reborn men were worthy of baptism.[3] Furthermore, the Baptists' exemption from ecclesiastical taxes in Connecticut was a sign of community respect, and Separates, who were not completely callous to public opinion, felt more comfortable worshipping with them.[4] The number of Baptist churches rose steadily after the Awakening until there were sixty in 1796.[5]

The Anglicans also gained new members, though they were drawn from the conservatives rather than from the New Lights. Samuel Johnson reported that the revivals "occasioned endless divisions and separations, so that many could find no rest to the sole of their feet till they retired into the Church, as their only ark of safety." Far from hurting the Church, the revivals "proved the greatest means of its increase and enlargement." [6] Throughout the colony, prominent families entered the Anglican communion.[7] Offended by New Light preaching, eleven of the principal men in a Waterbury parish became sensible of the unscriptural worship of the Established church "and of the weakness of the pretended

---

drawn my attention to an important distinction between these respectable dissenters and more radical Separates. The former wanted recognition as independent parishes within the Establishment; the latter withdrew entirely, repudiating all state intervention, even that in their favor.

[3] I. Backus, *History of New England,* II, 113-114; I. Backus, "Isaac Backus's Book," II, 57-58; I. Backus, "Account," 79-80.

[4] One of the themes of Backus' *History of New England* was the orderly freedom enjoyed in Baptist-dominated Rhode Island. See, for example, I, 408-409.

[5] Gaustad, *Great Awakening,* 122.

[6] Samuel Johnson, *Samuel Johnson,* I, 28; Johnson to the Archbishop of Canterbury, July 12, 1760, *ibid.,* I, 293-294; E. Stiles, *Extracts,* 290.

[7] For example, Beardsley, *Episcopal Church in Connecticut,* I, 154; Johnson to Dr. Burton, Dec. 1, 1762, Samuel Johnson, *Samuel Johnson,* I, 326; Johnson to Dr. Bearcroft, March 25, 1742, *ibid.,* III, 230; Caulkins, *Norwich,* 452.

constitution of the churches (so called) in this land; whereupon we fled to the Church of England for safety." [8]

The increasing numbers of Anglicans, Baptists, and Separates changed the relationship of dissenters to the Establishment. Before the Awakening withdrawal from the Established churches marked a person as alien, while afterwards it took little effort to become a Baptist or Anglican. The conversion of many respectable men opened a wide and easy road out of the Establishment, for scarcely a parish in the colony comprehended all the people living in its bounds.

The Anglicans and Baptists soon lost their predominantly dissenting character. Before the Awakening their writings had focused on the differences between their faith and that of the majority, but after 1740 membership required less and less justification. Men of differing persuasions continued their pamphlet controversies, but as dissent became simply a matter of religious taste, internal affairs steadily assumed more importance. Thus Samuel Johnson began to argue for a Bishop to discipline the Anglican ministry as well as to attract Congregationalists, the Baptists in 1766 set up an association to strengthen their communion and guard against errors, and even the Separates formed associations to settle ecclesiastical disputes and to aid in the ordination of ministers.[9] After 1765 the Anglicans and Baptists and to a lesser degree the Separates were not simply dissenters but denominations.

As these groups achieved stature, ecclesiastical laws that had always been taken for granted seemed unjustly to favor one variety of Christianity at the expense of another. Even the basic law requiring everyone to pay taxes for the minister's salary met occasional protests. As legal dissenters, Anglicans and Baptists could obtain exemption from ecclesiastical taxes. Baptists who did not believe in enforced religious contributions were simply excused from payment, and the rates levied on Anglicans helped support their own missionaries. Though the Anglicans sometimes objected to the interpretation of the law which specified that in order to qualify they must live near enough to a minister "conveniently" to

[8] Beardsley, I, 132-133; cf. Steiner, *Guilford*, 293-294.
[9] I. Backus, *History of New England*, II, 413; Goen, 167-174.

attend worship,[10] the magistrates refused to relax the provision until the increase in the number of Anglican missionaries ended the problem.[11]

The position of the Separates was far less favorable, however. Without legal status, they were taxed to support the Established minister and fined for breaking the laws against nonattendance at public worship and against unauthorized church services. The Separates refused to pay and either went to jail or, more frequently, forced the constable to distrain and auction their property.[12] As law officers and tax collectors harried them, they in turn bothered the Assembly with petition after petition demanding relief.

The legislature usually disregarded these petitions, however, for collecting clerical salaries was difficult even without legal exemptions. If Separates were included in the tax list and apportioned a share of the levy, collections were delayed or never made. If the Separates were omitted, a greater burden fell on the faithful members, and even they tended to default. In Lyme, where one-third of the town were dissenters, the rest of the inhabitants paid 50 per cent more taxes than when all contributed. Where the number of dissenters was small, they sometimes included men of large estate, the loss of whose rates made a substantial difference in the taxes of everyone.[13] Benjamin Lord of Norwich complained that he was one of those ministers "who by Means of the late religious unhappy Dissentions and Separations have often met with Great Difficulty to obtain their Just dues and proper Support." [14] The Assembly hesitated to relieve Separates in the face of such appeals.

At the same time, sympathy for the suffering of the dissenters aroused lay opposition to compulsory ecclesiastical taxes. A

[10] *Conn. Recs.*, VII, 107; Johnson to Governor Law, May 14, 1750, Samuel Johnson, *Samuel Johnson*, I, 139-140.

[11] Wolcott to Ebenezer Punderson, Jan. 30, 1752, *Wolcott Papers*, 146.

[12] Conn. Arch., Ecclesiastical Affairs, X, 61; B. Trumbull, *Connecticut*, II, 191-192.

[13] E. Stiles, *Extracts*, 267; Conn. Arch., Ecclesiastical Affairs, XII, 114; XIII, 64; Hopkins, *Sketches*, 49. For salary controversies, *Conn. Recs.*, IX, 23, 27, 124-125, 253, 280-281, 397, 406, 566-567, 574. Rapid inflation eased the parish's difficulties in meeting its contractual obligations, but the depreciated salary poorly satisfied the pastor.

[14] Conn. Arch., Ecclesiastical Affairs, XI, 52.

Guilford society reported that gathering rates from the Church of England was accompanied with "the effusion of so much blood" that no one would act as collector.[15] When, after 1747, the Assembly had to compel men in Norwich to assume the unpleasant work of collecting from the Separates, some refused to serve on principle, believing "that it cant be right to force Men to that (in matters of Religion) which they declare to be against their Consciences," [16] and one society in Norwich wrote into its articles of discipline the provision that "it is not expedient for the health of this Church to compel any by civil power contrary to their minds to pay anything to the support of the Gospel." [17] The Separate leader Frothingham observed in 1750 that many solid men so objected to auctioning Separates' property for taxes "that they had rather pay twice their Part of the Rate, and so let the oppressed Party go free." [18]

Objections to state regulation of religion had begun with the act against itinerants, for the law forbidding ministers to preach outside their parishes unless invited by the pastor and his church made it appear that the civil authority intended to crush the work of God. When the Assembly punished Benjamin Pomeroy, the zealous New Light from Hebron, for declaring that the law against itineracy was a foundation for persecution and contrary to God's word, many powerful New Light friends in the Court spoke in his defense. Pomeroy had also been indicted earlier for illegally preaching in Ripton with James Davenport, and after the two had appeared before the Assembly, a mob in Hartford, outraged at the arrest, nearly tore the ministers away from the authorities.[19] Some New Lights felt that the civil authority's opposition to the revival warranted violent action, and even such moderates as Solomon Williams petitioned for the repeal of the law because it impeded the progress of the Awakening.

The unpleasant experience with the itineracy law and the mount-

[15] Steiner, 381-382.
[16] Conn. Arch., Ecclesiastical Affairs, XI, 35, 37, 43, 48, 50.
[17] Lisbon, "Newent Congregational Church, Records," I, 132.
[18] *Articles,* 301; cf. p. 302; Ashford, "Town Records," 79; Conn. Arch., Ecclesiastical Affairs, XI, 67, 216, 238.
[19] B. Trumbull, *Connecticut,* II, 139; Wadsworth, *Diary,* 84; cf. I. Backus, *History of New England,* II, 66.

ing disapproval of compulsory ecclesiastical taxes raised doubts about the felicity of such rigorous magisterial support of the church and compelled a reexamination of the arguments for state control of religious affairs. The standard case for the Establishment rested on the belief that the magistrates, as "nursing Fathers to the Church," were to promote godliness out of regard for the best interests of the people and to maintain order in the community.[20] Without state support religion would collapse, and "there would not be ('tis probable) one regular visible Church left subsisting in this Land *Fifty* Years hence." [21] In light of recent events, the New Lights felt compelled to reassess these traditional assumptions.

The Separates advanced the most radical opposition to civil support by making a distinction between "the Revelation of Jesus Christ, and the Gospel Plan of Salvation," on the one hand, and "the moral Law, and the Rule of Equity and Righteousness," on the other. The Gospel ruled the church, while the moral law protected all society. Since Christ alone was governor of the church and judge of those who disobeyed the Gospel, magistrates usurped His authority when they made ecclesiastical laws; their function was to punish men for breaches of the moral law and not to impose taxes for the support of worship or fine men for failure to attend. The church was a gospel kingdom set apart from the world and under Christ's direct leadership, and civil rulers were to restrict their government to the rules of equity that applied to all men.[22]

Though not so extreme, Solomon Williams, a leader of the moderate New Lights during the 1740's, argued similarly. The kingdom of Christ ruled only the "inward Frame of Men's Minds, their most secret Thoughts," and external actions were significant only as a representation of inward devotion. If men worshiped "from any worldly Motives, that's no Obedience to Christ at all; nay, 'tis Disobedience, 'tis Rebellion, and Hypocrisy." Men erred when they thought to honor Christ by inducing obedience with worldly incentives. Promises of "Reputation, Esteem, and Honour" and

[20] For example, Elihu Hall, *Present Way,* 51; E. Whitman, *Character,* 22; Devotion, *Civil Ruler,* 51; Dickinson, *Sermon,* 33-34.
[21] Elihu Hall, 45.
[22] Frothingham, *Articles,* 296-297; Gaustad, 109.

threats of imprisonment, fines, and whippings were alike inimical to Christ's kingdom. "The *Weapons of Warfare* in this Kingdom *are not carnal but spiritual.* Christ never directed any secular Force to be used either to maintain, or advance it." The employment of worldly means was "not only ridiculous, and nonsensical," but sinful; "for it tends to hinder a Man from loving and obeying Christ" for the proper reasons. The use of force was "the most likely Means to advance the Kingdom of Satan," because it probably would "make Men Hypocrites." Compelled by the civil government to observe the external acts of religion, men ceased to seek for the new birth.[23] Thus the fines imposed on the Separates degraded rather than elevated their spiritual condition.

Elisha Williams, brother of Solomon and former rector of Yale, came closer to being a rationalist than any New Light. He was not a fervent revivalist, but when the authorities failed to reappoint him to the Superior Court in 1744, he became embittered against the Old Light hegemony and wrote a long tract on the essential right to liberty of conscience. Closely following Locke, Williams criticized ecclesiastical laws on two grounds. The first was that the proper realm of civil authority was the protection of personal rights and property. In the social compact, the state was given responsibility for these secular affairs but received no mandate to regulate beliefs. The right of judging and choosing remained with the individual. The second reason for opposing supervision was that man's reason gave him the power to discern for himself. God blessed man with freedom of will for the very purpose of allowing his understanding to guide his actions, and man could not give up the right to choose without destroying his essential nature. "This *Right of judging every one for himself in Matters of Religion* results from the Nature of Man, and is so inseparably connected therewith, that a Man can no more part with it than he can with his *Power of Thinking.*" Forced obedience was not truly religious. ."No Action is a religious Action without Understanding and Choice in the Agent." [24]

Williams therefore opposed many of the controls over the Established churches. He believed that the itinerancy law rested on the

[23] S. Williams, *Christ*, 65, 78, 79, 101, 67, 102.
[24] Elisha Williams, *Essential Rights*, 7-8.

false principle that "civil authority hath Power to establish a Form of Church-Government by penal Laws" and argued that the right of the minister to forbid visits from other preachers stripped Christians of "an invaluable Branch of Liberty Christ has vested them with" and lodged it in a single order of men. Synods and ecclesiastical officers were not intended to legislate rules of faith or practice for Christians, and the Saybrook consociations had no ultimate authority. Though congregations voluntarily subjected themselves to the guidance of an association, each maintained the right of private judgment for itself. "If on Experience of such a Method of Regimen . . . there is good Reason for them to forbear practising farther in that Form," the congregation could withdraw. Indeed, individuals within a church could, if they judged best, withdraw and form one of their own. The rational nature of man warranted divisions in Established churches and required all men to tolerate Separates.[25] These were radical views for a man still closely identified with the Establishment, and Williams had to write the pamphlet anonymously.

Among the New Lights, only the Separates advocated that the civil authority abandon all interest in religion. Elisha Williams believed there were grounds for excluding Roman Catholics from the colony, for a Papist "by his very Principles . . . is an Enemy or Traytor to a *Protestant State*: and strictly speaking *Popery* is so far from deserving the name of *Religion,* that it is rather a Conspiracy against it." Moreover, Williams thought it not worth the time to prove that the civil authority was obliged to collect wages for the ministry. As one of the clergy himself, he well knew that without compulsion salaries would not be paid or the burden would lie unequally on a few.[26] The New Light campaign for liberty of conscience did not include complete repeal of ecclesiastical taxes, without which public worship would cease, but held that religion was necessary to the "Political Happiness of Communities." Only belief in immortality and judgment restrained men when circumstances permitted them to injure or oppress without fearing detection.[27]

At most the New Lights sought to repeal the law against itin-

---

[25] Elisha Williams, 50, 53, 46-49.
[26] Elisha Williams, 40, 56-57.
[27] Hobart, *Civil Government,* 24-25.

eracy and to relieve men of differing faiths from paying for worship they did not attend. The Establishment was to rest "upon such a broad Bottom, and understood in such a Latitude," a New Light said in 1755, "that all good Christians notwithstanding their different Sentiments, may receive Benefit by it."[28] New Lights wanted the same toleration for Separates as the Anglicans or Baptists had achieved in 1727.

The Assembly gradually enacted such measures. In 1750 a legislature in sympathy with New Light views dropped the law against itineracy and exempted the societies in Milford and Guilford formed during the controversies of the 1730's from taxes imposed by the older parishes. Between 1755 and 1760 the Assembly also relieved the Separates in South Killingly, Canterbury, Plainfield, and Wallingford from ecclesiastical taxes.[29] Each of these was a somewhat exceptional case—the Canterbury Separates, for example, were the majority of the society—yet the recognition of these groups prepared the way for concessions to others.

Probably not all New Lights concurred with the thinking of either of the Williamses on this subject. Bellamy was not tolerant of Separates, for example, and many others of his party opposed disorderly withdrawals.[30] New Light ministers had their own salaries to worry about too. Nevertheless, the argument for toleration had been made, and many of the party were committed to it. One purist in Norwich accepted dismissal rather than wages collected by public rates. Lay members offered to pay the rates of conscientious Separates to prevent forcible distraint. The Plainfield church voluntarily recognized the Separate church in the town and allowed it a third of the annual levy.[31] Finally, in 1770 the Assembly exempted all dissenters, including Separates, from penalties for nonattendance at public worship and, after the Revolution, from ecclesiastical taxes for established ministers.[32]

The tracts on liberty of conscience, however, were even more

[28] Dickinson, *Sermon*, 31-32.

[29] Greene, *Development of Religious Liberty*, 269; *Conn. Recs.*, IX, 516-517, 520; Steiner, 330; Blake, *Separates*, 124; *Letter to the Clergy*, 20-21.

[30] Bellamy complained of the people in his parish who pleaded for tolerating the Separates (*Contributions to Ecclesiastical History*, 348).

[31] Lisbon, "Newent Congregational Church, Records," II, 110, 129; Larned, *Windham*, I, 537-538.

[32] Greene, 327-328, 333.

significant for their new conceptions of church and state than for the legislation they stimulated. The New Lights were willing to argue that toleration enhanced social order more than did uniformity of religion. Magisterial support of one party in "oppressing and persecuting another," an election sermon declared in 1750, aroused "Animosities and Quarrels." When the magistrate protected all equally, people were "most likely to act the Part of good Subjects toward their Rulers, and that of good Neighbours toward one another." [33]

A new view of religion diminished the usefulness of political support. Both Elisha and Solomon Williams thought that religion consisted not so much in specific beliefs and practices as in a process. Elisha stressed the importance of personal judgment: unless a man chose his beliefs freely, he had not acted religiously and was not responsible for his convictions. Solomon, recognizing that no amount of lip service paid to true doctrines prepared a man for heaven, believed the only important matter to be the experience of new birth. Tenets and institutions, all the trappings of public worship, were at best an expression of a strictly personal experience, and forcing men to conform brought them no closer to the essence of religion. Government intervention was even potentially dangerous, for it impaired the integrity of religious experience.

The Separates favored the complete abandonment of the Establishment; the Williamses and the New Lights proposed severe modifications. Elisha meant not to oppose the Establishment if that word signified "only an *Approbation* of certain Articles of Faith and Modes of Worship . . . or *Recommendation* of them to their Subjects," but to make the Establishment "a Rule binding to the Subjects, on any *Penalties* whatsoever, seems to me to be oppressive of Christianity." [34] The Establishment was to be an expression of religious sentiment and not a militant engagement to the church. Not all New Lights went so far, but their consistent advocacy of liberty of conscience in the 1740's tended to move in this direction. [35]

---

[33] Hobart, *Civil Government*, 29; cf. Elisha Williams, 40-41; S. Williams, *Sad Tendency*, 25.
[34] Elisha Williams, 19.
[35] Samuel Peters thought opposition to oppressive ecclesiastical laws was

In conception and reality, the colonial Establishment was there-fore a far different institution in 1765 than it had been in 1690. In the election sermon of 1697 Gurdon Saltonstall had conceived of ecclesiastical and civil government as concentering on the re-ligious interests of the people, but the New Lights thought of these two jurisdictions as distinct realms ruling the segments of life they were qualified to govern, the civil authority almost wholly secular, the church a kingdom unto itself. By 1765 the Establish-ment was neither an agency of social control nor a symbol of community coherence, but only the religion of the majority. Ever larger numbers of people were outside the jurisdiction of Congre-gational discipline, and even members brought up for trial lightly disregarded ecclesiastical censures, turning to a minority church for religious sustenance.[36] The Establishment was not even able to set the intellectual and moral tone of the colony, for no single, authorized intellectual system overarched all of society. Led by preachers of varying opinions, Connecticut men could agree only on a few Christian fundamentals.

The only effective instrument of social control remaining to the ministers was the power to persuade, and even that was vitiated. The voices of the Established clergy reached only a portion of the community and were weakened by years of harsh debate. "Nothing sinks the Reputation of the Ministry more," one layman warned the clergy, "than for them to revile and reproach each other. No wonder in that Case, if we of the Laity have a low Opinion of you, when you seem to have so very low an Opinion of your-selves."[37]

After 1765 the civil authority was the sole institution binding society. The state was the symbol of social coherence, as once the Established churches had been. Group solidarity depended on loy-alty to the government.[38] United action in the wars of 1745 and 1756 restored a society rent with religious schisms. The triumph at Louisburg and the subsequent celebrations were balm for the

---

the salient characteristic of the New Light party (*Connecticut*, 288-289).

[36] For example, H. R. Stiles, *Windsor*, I, 301; Hartford North Associa-tion, "Register," 63.

[37] *Letter to the Clergy*, 21.

[38] The dissenters' pleas for toleration were attempts to regain their standing in the community, but on an independent basis.

anxieties aroused by contention within the churches. In a sense those celebrations were rituals that assured religious dissenters they were not totally isolated from their community. Patriotism helped to heal ecclesiastical wounds.

Concentration of community loyalties on the state intensified devotion to those principles on which all could agree. The contents of the social compact—liberty and property—became the rallying cry of the social order. When the opportunity to defend the common interests arose, men responded with religious fervor.

PART FIVE

Politics, 1740–1765

XV

New Lights in Politics

&> THE GREAT AWAKENING transformed politics as it did all aspects of life centering on authority. Until then, factions operated beneath the surface, for the most part disguising their disaffection.[1]
The revival broke the seal on political controversy. Besides creating new causes of resistance, the nature of the discontent imposed
an obligation to speak out to further the work of God. First in
sermons, petitions, and pamphlets, and later through conscious
political organization, the New Lights worked to overthrow their
conservative rulers.

The attitude toward the Awakening itself was the first issue in
dispute. New Lights thought poorly of all the critics of the revival.
At best, those who cast reproaches "upon the good Work of the
Lord" were "the more carnall and profane part of the World," [2]
while at worst, as Philemon Robbins said, opposers were guilty of
the unpardonable sin and lost to the devil.[3] These ill feelings
were directed against the Assembly when it passed the law against
itineracy. Since the New Lights believed that itinerants since
Whitefield had been divine agents in bringing the Awakening to
America, to forbid their preaching was to fight against God. The
itineracy law thus became the symbol of the rulers' stupidity or
malevolence. Many years later, the New Light Benjamin Trumbull,
writing his history of Connecticut, still felt the bitterness the itineracy law evoked in men of his party: it "manifested, in a strong
point of light, the exceeding hatred, rancour and opposition of
heart, which there was in the Arminians and old lights, to the

---

[1] Eliot, *Give Cesar his Due,* 13.
[2] Fairfield East Consociation, "Book of Records," 13.
[3] *Plain Narrative,* 19.

work of God, and all the zealous and faithful promoters of it." [4]

At the time, bolder New Lights were not reticent to express their wrath. When Benjamin Pomeroy, disregarding the law, preached in another minister's parish without permission and was arrested, he defiantly charged that the statute was "made without reason and contrary to the word of God." "The great men had fallen in and joyned with those that are on the devil's side and enemies to the kingdom of Christ." [5] During the trial James Davenport, who had been arrested along with Pomeroy, attempted to preach to the crowd gathered outside the church where the hearings were held. When the sheriff tried to lead the protesting Davenport away, Pomeroy in a fierceness of righteous indignation thundered, "Take heed how you do that heaven-daring action; the God of heaven will surely avenge it on you." [6]

To some degree all the New Lights shared Pomeroy's anger. The Fairfield East Consociation unanimously adopted a resolution asking the Assembly to repeal the act against itinerants, and Solomon and Elisha Williams printed discourses to demonstrate its odious character. [7] Until the end of the decade the existence of the itineracy law reminded New Lights that the men in power were enemies of religion.

Instead of defending the law against itinerants, the Old Lights castigated their critics as despisers of order and government. The New Lights' frank criticism was a shock to rulers accustomed to the protection afforded by their exalted stations, who naturally interpreted resistance as an assault on authority. Warnings against "Disloyal seditious" ministers began to appear in the Old Light election sermons. [8] "If there shou'd be a Religion Advanced," one election sermon said, "which is inimical to civil Authority (as if that was all Usurpation and Imposition) and that sets People a praying against, and blaspheming the Rulers: And that teacheth them to resist the Power that be Ordained of God," that religion damaged society. "When once the way is so prepared," the preacher

---

[4] *Connecticut*, II, 131.
[5] *Conn. Recs.*, IX, 28.
[6] Wadsworth, *Diary*, 84.
[7] Fairfield East Consociation, "Book of Records," 16; see Chap. XIV.
[8] Hunn, *Welfare*, 28.

continued, "that Men think it is Religion, and what they have immediate Warrant for from God; why then, they will be Lawless, and disobedient to lawful Authority, under colour of Obedience unto God." [9]

The Old Lights sensed a general rebelliousness that went beyond the dislike of a specific statute. Philemon Robbins was so conscious of the disposition to criticize government that he carefully wrote out those portions of his sermons relating to magistrates, but, despite his care, he was accused of undermining civil authority.[10] John Owens, a pastor in Groton, was convicted of defaming the government and its laws, though the court was lenient in consideration of the times and in the charitable hope that Owens spoke "from a misguided conscience and over-heated zeal." [11] Though resistance at this point remained verbal, the Old Lights were persuaded that the New Lights were plotting "a great change in the civil government." [12]

The Old Lights also took steps to eliminate the influence of their enemies. Just as the Old Light consociation in New Haven County purged the most active supporters of the revival, so the Old Light governor and Council, with some support from the deputies, removed troublesome individuals from political office. Elisha Williams, the vocal opponent of the itineracy law, was dropped as judge of the Superior Court in 1743 and as justice of the peace in Hartford in 1745. Williams never forgave the Old Lights for this affront; as a former rector of Yale, sometimes mentioned as a candidate for governor, he expected to be honored with the highest offices in the colony. Others of comparable status fell along with him: for example, Hezekiah Huntington, prominent enough to be elected an assistant in 1742, was eliminated as a justice of the peace because he befriended religious radicals. And lesser men suffered the same fate: all the justices of the peace in Hartford who refused to execute the laws against irregular preaching were turned out as early as 1742.[13] Pomeroy was reported as saying in

[9] Lord, *Religion and Government,* 34, 20; cf. Worthington, *Duty of Rulers,* 20.
[10] B. Trumbull, *Connecticut,* II, 173.
[11] *Conn. Recs.,* IX, 20.
[12] Quoted in Beardsley, *Episcopal Church in Connecticut,* I, 148.
[13] Conn. Arch., Civil Officers, I, 86; III, pp. 11, 8, 14, of the Index;

1744 that "if there be but a faithful man in civil authority he must lose his honore and usefulness." [14]

Opprobrium and political persecution failed to crush the New Lights, however, for too many powerful individuals stood in their ranks. The Williamses in Connecticut and Jonathan Edwards up the river in Northampton were social and intellectual powers. The entire Fairfield East Association, ministers holding some of the most ancient and honored pulpits in the colony, came forward in defense of Whitefield and the Awakening. The ministers in the northeast who shortly formed the Litchfield Association were solidly in the New Light camp, as were clergymen from the east, although the latter had long been wary of radicalism. When Pomeroy was censured after a trial before the General Assembly in 1744, the New Lights were "a numerous and strong party, and great efforts were made to save him." [15] When he had been arrested along with Davenport in 1742 for preaching illegally, the two were nearly torn from their captors' hands by an unruly Hartford mob, and forty militia men were called out to keep the peace.[16]

Throughout the 1740's the New Lights concentrated their political energies on obtaining relief from Old Light oppression. Their strategy was to argue for less state control of the church, and their influence was strong enough so that even before the brothers Williams published their discourses Old Light election sermons gave space to a rebuttal. "Some indeed are disposed," the preacher said in 1744, "to deny the Magistrate any right to make laws about, or take Cognizance of Religious affairs; as if every man had a good right to follow his Conscience how dreadfully soever it Errs." [17] Two years later, after the New Lights had formally made their case for the dangers of coercing belief through external pressure, the election sermon noted that "some will say, *That Religion and Vertue is nothing worth when Forced*. Be it so, yet what is begun in Force, may end in Choice: What is begun in Fear, may end

B. Trumbull, *Connecticut*, II, 138, 190; Jared Ingersoll, "Historical Account," 12. The process of nomination and elimination or appointment can be followed in Conn. Arch., Civil Officers, III.

[14] *Conn. Recs.*, IX, 28.
[15] *Connecticut*, II, 139.
[16] Wadsworth, 84.
[17] Worthington, 11-12; cf. pp. 10-13.

in Love." Arguing in the traditional fashion, the preacher added, "besides it's not small Advantage to the common Cause of Vertue, that men can be brought to be visibly or externally Good and Vertuous." [18] Subsequent reiterations of the same theme disclosed the impact of the New Light campaign for toleration.[19]

At the end of the decade the New Lights were forging ahead in the contest for power, and by 1748 sympathy for their cause had overcome dislike of the religious confusion they caused. In that year the freemen returned to the Assembly many friends of the revival who had been dropped earlier,[20] and, for the first time, the preacher of the election sermon, Nathanael Eells, adhered to the New Light line on toleration, arguing with the Williamses that "the Magistrate has no power to bind Conscience in matters of Religion." "Some thro' the Ignorance that is in them," Eells contended, disposing of the Old Lights in one thrust, "fondly oppose the Peace and Order of this world, to the *Kingdom of Christ which is not of this world*: These ought to consider that here is no Opposition; that as Christ's Kingdom is purely spiritual, so it stands opposed *only* to the Kingdom of Sin and Satan. . . . It molests not the State." [21] Acting upon the implied injunction, the Assembly reappointed some of the justices stricken off earlier by the Old Lights, restored the daring Benjamin Pomeroy to his pulpit in Hebron, and gave a group of dissenters in New Haven permission to build a meetinghouse. In 1749 a proposal to acknowledge all Congregational and Presbyterian churches as established in law was too radical for the Assembly, but its submission was a straw in the wind.[22]

With their increased strength in 1748, the New Lights must have played a part in the significant skirmish that arose in the Assembly when Roger Wolcott, the incumbent deputy governor, failed to receive a majority of the votes cast, though he did have a plurality. The Lower House claimed that he was not elected, and that the

[18] S. Hall, *Legislatures Right*, 20; cf. pp. 19, 26.
[19] Todd, *Civil Rulers*, 13, 24, 26, 27n.
[20] B. Trumbull, *Connecticut*, II, 191.
[21] *Wise Ruler*, 25, 27.
[22] B. Trumbull, *Connecticut*, II, 191; Conn. Arch., Civil Officers, III, p. 12 of Index; *Conn. Recs.*, IX, 375; Tucker, *Puritan Protagonist*, 135; Conn. Arch., Ecclesiastical Affairs, XI, 257.

Assembly must make the choice. Governor Law objected vociferously; insistence on a majority, he warned, besides making elections "always very precarious and uncertain," would transfer the power of election from the freemen to the Assembly, in contradiction of the charter.[23] Wolcott argued that until this time a plurality had been sufficient, but the Lower House had in its favor a decision of 1742 concerning the choice of colony treasurer in which the Assembly had ruled that when an officer lacked a majority, the legislature was to make the final choice. The Lower House therefore demanded that both houses vote as one body, thus giving the deputies preponderant power, but the Upper House refused to concur, referring to the disputes of the 1720's when the Assembly had eventually voted separately. Though the Lower House held out for a time, it suddenly capitulated and acquiesced in the selection of Wolcott.[24]

The episode raises tantalizing questions, most of them unanswerable. Wolcott unlovingly called the advocates of a majority vote simply "active" men,[25] and perhaps they were opponents of restricting the currency of paper money, a measure Wolcott endorsed.[26] Probably the New Lights entered into the controversy too, though there was no apparent reason for them to dislike Wolcott.[27] They were chiefly concerned to increase their bargaining power against the Upper House, where Wolcott's supporters and Old Lights predominated.

The New Lights were looking for political leverage because of their interest in the revision of the colony laws, which they hoped would give them an occasion to revoke the itinerancy statute. A revision committee, appointed in 1744, had come to a standstill precisely because of disagreements over this issue. When in the October session of 1748, with New Lights present in large numbers, the Lower House nominated Elisha Williams, the advocate of tolera-

[23] *Wolcott Papers,* 479–480.

[24] Wolcott, *Memoir,* 334; Conn. Arch., Civil Officers, III, 142, 147, 166, 167. The whole business is summarized in *Conn. Recs.,* IX, 385n.

[25] *Memoir,* 334.

[26] Conn. Arch., Trade and Maritime, I, 130; Wolcott, *Memoir,* 332.

[27] Indeed later they were partial to him, berating the Old Lights for having contributed to his defeat in 1754 (Hobart, *Congratulatory Letter,* 3).

tion, to serve on the revision committee, it left no doubts about its sentiments on the itineracy law. But the Upper House refused to concur, thereby making its stand similarly clear. Since the debate over Wolcott's election proceeded in the same sessions, the New Lights may possibly have been willing to support the anti-Wolcott men in order to pressure the Upper House into agreement on omitting the itineracy law. In any case, the Lower House suddenly accepted the proposal for separate voting and chose Wolcott. Meanwhile, the work of revision had begun again, and when the new law book appeared in 1750, the itineracy measure was conspicuously absent.[28]

In 1750 the New Lights also obtained Assembly recognition of the minority society in Milford, which since 1741 had refused to listen to the Old Light Chauncey Whittelsey and instead had entertained such men as Samuel Finley, whom the authorities had evicted from the colony under the provisions of the itineracy law. This relief was by implication a repudiation of coercive methods in religious affairs.[29] Thus on certain issues of toleration, the New Lights commanded a majority.[30]

Their ascending influence attracted the attention of everyone whose ambitions or well-being depended upon government favor. The most important of those who in 1750 revised their first impressions of the New Lights was Thomas Clap, the imperious and influential rector of Yale. In time he was persuaded to throw in his fortunes with the New Lights and earned the epithet the "New Light Pope." [31]

Little in Clap's record in the 1740's foreshadowed such an alli-

[28] Conn. Arch., Civil Officers, III, 175. Regulation of intestate estates and the rules for stating fees, fines, and penalties were the other points of contention (*ibid.*, III, 57, 174). In 1749 the election of both deputy governor and governor were thrown into the Assembly because neither obtained a majority, but both incumbents were reelected. Wolcott accused the "active" men again of reducing the officials' votes to a mere plurality. (*Memoir,* 334).

[29] Recognition as sober dissenters relieved the society from paying taxes to the First Church. Full establishment as a society with power to tax its own members was delayed another ten years (B. Trumbull, *Connecticut,* II, 283-284).

[30] J. H. Trumbull, "Sons of Liberty," 350.

[31] For a discussion of Clap's conversion, Morgan, *Gentle Puritan,* 103-104.

ance. Indeed, he had been an unyielding opponent of revivalism, both in the College and in the colony as a whole. Among the New Light students whom he had severely punished were David Brainerd, expelled for invidiously comparing tutor Whittelsey's grace to that of a chair, and John and Ebenezer Cleaveland, expelled for attending a Separate meeting in Canterbury, where the Separates comprised a majority of the town. Clap's reproval of some of the Cleavelands' Yale friends for reprinting Locke's *Essay on Toleration* had revealed that he was committed to the harshest repressive measures. His removal from the College Corporation of Samuel Cooke, an eminent New Light who had aided in the separation of dissenters from the New Haven church, had carried on at Yale the purges begun in the government and in the New Haven consociation. Thus no one in 1745 could have predicted his eventual conversion to the New Light party.[32]

Clap never did come to accept New Light views on toleration; he was as fully committed to the use of power, civil or ecclesiastical, in behalf of his new religious convictions as he had been earlier. Nor was he won over to New Light fervor and Bellamyan theology. While emphasizing the new birth, original sin, and grace much as New England Calvinists had always done, he was not drawn to the extremes of the New Divinity and the religious passions those doctrines were meant to evoke.[33] It was the New Light political power that attracted him.

Clap's dominant concern since his appointment as rector in 1739 had been to win independence for the College Corporation and to assure his own control within it so that he could shape the College into the strictly Calvinistic, character-building institution he wanted it to be. In 1745 the new charter he obtained from the legislature granted a large measure of the independence he sought, but the College had not yet become financially autonomous. For major outlays the Assembly allowed it a lottery, and to cover yearly expenses, a legislative subsidy remained an important part of the budget.[34] Forced to maneuver amid the shifting political align-

---

[32] B. Trumbull, *Connecticut*, II, 142-146. Clap's part in regulating New Lights is described in Tucker, 133-143.

[33] For a summary of Clap's theology, Tucker, 148-154.

[34] Tucker, 73-74, 203-204.

ments in the legislature in order to assure the College its annual appropriation, Clap by 1750 was calculating means for making friends of the men he had so thoroughly alienated before 1745 but who now were a force to be reckoned with in the Assembly.

Careful politician that he was, Clap would not have abandoned the Old Lights so precipitously between 1750 and 1755 were the New Lights' political promise their only virtue. The Old Lights were still firmly entrenched in the Upper House, and the New Lights had their way in the Lower House only occasionally. Moreover, he understood that the New Lights would not rally to his cause upon the first overtures of friendship; he would have to live down his dark past first.

Nevertheless, after 1750 Clap boldly declared his enmity toward the Old Lights and his friendship for the New. He entertained Whitefield in New Haven, for example, and invited him to preach to the students, in marked contrast to the hostility expressed in 1745. By 1753 no doubt remained but that Clap meant to sever the old ties completely.

His defense of orthodoxy left Clap no other choice, for he had always hated theological disorders as passionately as ecclesiastical ones. He had thrown himself into the fight against Robert Breck, the Springfield Arminian, as fervently as he had disciplined the Cleavelands for their association with the Separates.[35] Until 1745 the Old Lights had appeared to be the best allies in both struggles, but when the open publication of Arminian and Arian heresies in Boston had planted suspicions that his colleagues were departing from the faith, a fierce determination to protect the traditional orthodoxy had estranged him from his former friends.

The fear of heresy at once put him on common ground with the New Lights, whose champions, Edwards and Bellamy, were concurrently turning their guns away from the Calvinist opponents of the revival toward more dangerous enemies. New Light objections to state interference in religion diminished in no degree their willingness to see Clap purge Yale or to use the consociations to screen heterodox ministerial candidates. On his part, Clap no

[35] Tucker, 143n, 47-58. In the early 1740's Clap permitted his students to toy with Enlightenment heresies, confident he could gently restore them to orthodoxy (Morgan, 108).

longer worried over New Light disturbances of ecclesiastical order, for the division of the New Lights into moderates and separating radicals had distinguished those members of the party who were a threat to the churches from those who were safe. With the path cleared and strong forces pulling him that way, Clap became a New Light.

For a few years the New Lights doubted Clap's sincerity, but his persistent support of their cause and his opposition to the Old Lights eventually satisfied both parties as to where he stood. A hint of his inclinations came in 1749, when Solomon Williams, an eminent if moderate New Light and a prominent spokesman for toleration, was appointed a fellow of Yale. As if to prove his sincerity, Clap in 1753 offered Williams the Professorship of Divinity.[36]

The establishment of a chair of Divinity, a project close to Clap's heart, confirmed his alienation from the Old Lights. The idea of such a professorship had been current for some years after the threat of heresy had made it urgent that students receive instruction in orthodox theology. The Old Lights took offense at once because the proposal cast a slur on one of their number, the Reverend James Noyes, pastor of the New Haven church which Yale students attended. It was rumored that Clap, along with others in the colony, suspected Noyes of Arminian leanings, and these suspicions were strengthened when Clap withdrew all students from Noyes's church and established separate worship at the College. The Old Lights were stung again when Clap invited Williams to occupy the chair of Divinity, a clear indication that the President preferred New Light preaching to Old. Publicly he explained his actions otherwise, but his private correspondence with Williams, expressing his fear of Arminianism, sustains the Old Light interpretation.[37]

Clap meanwhile was also fighting heresy on other fronts. In 1753 he persuaded the Yale Corporation to pass an orthodoxy act empowering it to examine any college official suspected of heresy and requiring new appointees to subscribe to a confession of faith and

---

[36] E. Stiles, *Extracts,* 6; Morgan, 105.

[37] Tucker, 183-189; *Letter to the Clergy,* 10-12; Conn. Arch., Ecclesiastical Affairs, XI, 89; Clap, *Religious Constitution,* 11; Thomas Clap to Solomon Williams, June 6, 1754, Williams Papers.

submit to a verifying examination. The Fellows themselves were to subscribe to the same confession under an oath which bound them to resign if their beliefs changed. The objections of the four members of the Corporation who were staunch Old Lights and among those reputedly heterodox were in vain. New Lights of course were delighted with the purge.[38]

President Clap and the New Lights both benefited from the entente. The New Lights were not sufficiently numerous in the Assembly to assure Clap success in every venture, but their sympathy strengthened his hand. In 1753 the Assembly, while not appropriating funds for the Professor of Divinity, did authorize a subscription, and most of the contributions came from New Light territory in the north and east. On their side, the New Lights received Clap's stamp of approval, clearing them of any remaining taint of disorderliness. Wavering conservative ministers, confused by the Old Light drift toward Arminianism, swung over in Clap's wake. Alerted to the presence of heresy by his dramatic actions at Yale, church members elsewhere began to demand thoroughgoing New Light Calvinists in their pulpits. Clap's entourage and New Light forces from Litchfield and the east also won supremacy in the General Association. The advantages to both were demonstrated in 1755, when the Association officially supported Clap's proposal for a Professor of Divinity and accepted the Litchfield recommendation that all county associations reaffirm the confession of faith.[39]

Clap's triumphs eventually led to a change in the character of the New Light party itself, which had been distinguished by its toleration of dissenters and experimental religion. Clap did not embrace those tenets, and, because he was so imposing a figure, the center of gravity shifted in his direction. After 1753 the protection of orthodoxy, the principle in which he and the New Lights concurred, became increasingly important as his zeal dramatized the struggle against heresy.

[38] Clap, *Annals of Yale*, 61-65; *Brief History*, 13-17; Tucker, 192-193; E. Stiles, *Extracts*, 6.

[39] Morgan, 105; B. Trumbull, *Letter*, 15-16; Clap, *Annals of Yale*, 99-100; Dexter, *Biographical Sketches*, I, 196; John Devotion to Ezra Stiles, July 14, 1769, E. Stiles, *Extracts*, 477; C. Whittelsey to E. Stiles, Jan. 20, 1762, *ibid.*, 584; *Records of the General Association*, 33-35; Gaustad, *Great Awakening*, 135.

In 1755 Clap broadened the New Light campaign when he announced in a pamphlet that heresy was to be found in all corners
of the colony, even among the ostensibly orthodox. A "New Scheme
of Divinity" was spreading, he declared, which exalted human
abilities, deprecated the doctrines of grace and original sin, and
made Christ less than God. Its proponents were all the more insidious for not being frank. They twisted the meaning of words in
order to preach in the familiar language of Calvinism while their
real beliefs were far from orthodox. Scrutinize candidate pastors
rigorously, he urged, to verify their orthodoxy.[40]

Outraged Old Lights felt personally attacked by these accusations, and rightly so. When Bellamy and his New Light allies in
the General Association voted in the same year that all ministers
were to reaffirm the traditional confession of faith, the Old Lights
recognized the danger to any of their number who held reservations
about Calvinist doctrine. As the party of orthodoxy, the New Lights
were now on the offensive, ferreting out heresy among their former attackers.

Events to the end of the decade confirmed the new image of the
New Lights. After the students were withdrawn from the New
Haven church and given over to the Professor of Divinity, James
Noyes, the pastor, remained on the Corporation of the College, in
seeming contradiction of Clap's own pleas for a purge of heretics.
In 1757, however, Clap demanded that Noyes be examined, and
after a stormy session of the Corporation, he was ordered to appear.
At sixty-nine still a match for Clap, Noyes stoutly refused, in the
process indicting the legality and morality of the Orthodoxy Act.
Perhaps fearful of appearing too inquisitorial, Clap backed down,
and Noyes remained on the Corporation to his death.[41]

Hardly had that excitement subsided when in 1759 the New
Lights in New Haven County raised a cry against James Dana in
Wallingford. The strenuous efforts to prevent the ordination of a
man suspected of heresy by now came as no surprise to the Old
Lights, for it continued a campaign begun in 1750, when the New
Light legislature had made denial of the Trinity a felony.[42] In the

[40] *Brief History*, 19ff, 34-37, 40-41.

[41] Tucker, 189-191.

[42] Hart, *A Few Remarks*, 35-36; *Remarks*, 46-52; Greene, *Development of Religious Liberty*, 305.

unprecedented number of pamphlets the controversy produced, the New Light authors all advertised themselves as the party of order and orthodoxy.

The Old Lights were neither amused by the irony of this reversal of roles nor content to let it pass. By implication they had been made to seem the party of heresy. It was true that many who found the doctrines of original sin and salvation by grace alone inadequate to imbue men with morality toyed with varieties of Arminianism and rationalism. One Old Light had even been daring enough to declare publicly that Calvinism must not be embraced simply because it was the faith of the fathers.[43] But for the most part, Old Lights denied the least taint of heresy and insisted that New Light charges were a factional design to "blacken a Number of Gentlemen in the Government." They ridiculed Clap's pamphlet on the "New Scheme of Divinity," declaring categorically that not "one Man of that Persuasion" existed in New Haven, where Clap located the headquarters of heresy.[44]

One Old Light summarized the charter his party preferred when he said, "I am a friend to orthodoxy, and a friend to liberty too." [45] The New Lights, on the other hand, were "animated by a love of dictating, and lust of pre-eminence and power." [46] Their policies from Clap's imposition of an orthodoxy test at Yale in 1753 to the censure of James Dana at Wallingford in 1759 gave ample support to the indictment. Clap's "Desire of Power and Grandeur" was "boundless," [47] and his actions served "covetous designs," since he was skilled in the "art of making *gain by godliness.*" [48] These charges were meant to establish the Old Lights not as the enemies of Calvinism, but as friends to liberty. "Our whole guilt consists in this," one Old Light summed up, "that we have censured, and, in a lawful way, opposed unconstitutional measures, and the exertions of arbitrary power, in ecclesiastical affairs." [49] With the controversy thus described, "Love of Equity, and generous

[43] Morgan, 63-64; Darling, *Some Remarks,* 51-56; "To the Freemen of the Colony," *Connecticut Gazette,* Oct. 15, 1757; Darling, 7.

[44] Darling, 36, 31; *Letter to the Clergy,* 9.

[45] Hart, *Remarks,* 52.

[46] Hart, *A Few Remarks,* 37.

[47] Darling, 45.

[48] Gale, *Letter,* 22.

[49] Hart, *Remarks,* 52.

Zeal for Liberty, and just Abhorrence of every Species of Tyranny, both civil, and ecclesiastical" became peculiarly Old Light virtues.[50]

As for practical politics, the Old Light strategy was to curtail Clap's power at Yale. Many of the party's most prominent men— Jared Eliot, Joseph Noyes, Thomas Darling, Chauncey Whittelsey — were closely associated with the College either as members of the Corporation or as former tutors and, long accustomed to dominance, were incensed to have a dogged and resourceful opponent in so exalted a position as the Yale presidency. Their instincts moved them to seek his removal, as they had removed New Light justices during the revival, but opposition strength in the 1750's made the use of brute force impossible and forced them into political maneuvers more appropriate to the nearly equal division of power in the legislature.

The most outspoken Old Light initially was Benjamin Gale, a Killingworth physician and magistrate and son-in-law of Jared Eliot. Gale dedicated his trenchant mind and sharp tongue to convincing "the World that the President was an Assuming, Arbitrary, Designing Man; who under a Cloak of Zeal for Orthodoxy, design'd to govern both Church and State and Damn all who would not worship the Beast." Such tactics were a new departure in Connecticut's politics. Clap was openly assailed at a time when, as Gale confessed later, "it was disreputable, to oppose one, esteem'd a Man of God." [51]

In 1755 Gale's pamphlet entitled *The Present State of the Colony of Connecticut,* written anonymously though the name of the author was soon well known, accused Clap of designing to enlarge his power illegally and to prevent the Assembly from supervising the College.[52] The undisguised purpose of the pamphlet was to persuade the Assembly to refuse Yale its annual £100 appropriation,

[50] Gale, *Letter,* 1. The Old Lights also deprecated New Light claims to be the upholders of ecclesiastical order. Old Lights occasionally reminded the public of the confusion New Lights caused in the 1740's when separations were common. New Light toleration of Separate churches later on provided the Old Lights further ammunition (Gale, *Present State,* 5; Darling, 50-52; "To the Freemen of the Colony," *Connecticut Gazette,* Oct. 15, 1757; *Letter to the Clergy,* 20).

[51] To Jared Ingersoll, Aug. 9, 1762, Jared Ingersoll, "Selection," 276.

[52] *Present State,* 10-14.

and when Gale marshaled figures to prove that the colony had been overly generous already and that Clap was misusing funds,[53] his candor was a startling departure in political technique. Discontented groups had previously submitted memorials bringing inequitable conditions to the Assembly's attention, the clergy had discoursed on general principles bearing on legislative business, and during the 1740's the New Lights had even made comments that barely concealed their dislike of the itinerary law; but the adversaries always seemed to be dueling at a distance, following a convention that forbade the contestants to touch one another. Gale, however, engaged his foes at close range, unmistakably and publicly directing his attack at a specific person and issue. Instead of presenting politics as high-level deliberations of wise and dispassionate men who applied divine principles of right to the colony's affairs, he implicitly recognized that the feelings of constituents affected decisions. His pamphlet was an attempt to mobilize public opinion in a legislative controversy, using specific facts and accusations to impugn the motives of an acknowledged ruler, and his unconventional and disturbing techniques stunned his colleagues. As he reported later, looking back on the time when he fired his opening shot, "I was Alone; them who wish'd me well, dare [sic] not appear for me." [54]

Standards of political decorum shifted abruptly, however, when the Assembly voted down the Yale appropriation in 1755. Gale's successful sally released bitterness on both sides, touching off a long series of slashing attacks and counterattacks as the leaders of both parties freely vented their wrath in the public prints, becoming far more direct and vituperative than Gale had first dared to be.

Gale and his Old Light friends began to act on the assumption that the Assembly's votes were the outcome not of dispassionate adjudication but of a power struggle. If Clap were to be removed from the Yale presidency, the Old Lights needed a majority among the deputies. The scheme they chose was to reduce the number of deputies by about half. They proposed in 1756 that the colony pay for one representative from each town instead of for two.

[53] *Present State*, 4-10.
[54] To Jared Ingersoll, Aug. 9, 1762, Jared Ingersoll, "Selection," 276.

The option of sending another if the town meeting paid his salary was left open, but, penurious as Connecticut men were, not many communities were expected to assume the added expense. The reduction of colony expenditures when war was straining the treasury, and increased efficiency in the Lower House were the purported advantages of the change.[55] The partisan reasons for the proposal can be understood if it is remembered that eighteenth-century men presumed that electors would always choose the most distinguished members of the community to represent them. Elimination of the second choices would keep out of the House lesser figures whose sympathies might not lie with the aristocratic Old Lights.[56]

The Old Light effort was nearly successful. Proposing their scheme just before the spring session of the Assembly in 1756, they persuaded twenty-three towns to send only one representative to the fall session. But the bill to limit deputies was defeated by a vote of thirty-nine to thirty-eight. The Old Light strategists had not planned their tactics carefully enough, for had the towns with a single representative been represented in double strength, the measure probably would have passed. The Old Lights began a newspaper campaign again before the May session in 1757, but their efforts were fruitless.[57]

After 1757 the Old Lights dropped their limitation proposal in the face of the growing popularity of their antagonists. Instead, at the May session in 1757, three Old Light members of the Yale Corporation, Joseph Noyes, Thomas Ruggles, and Jared Eliot, asked the legislature to investigate the College. The petitioners argued that separation from the New Haven society, establishment

[55] "An ADDRESS to the Freemen of the Colony of Connecticut," *Connecticut Gazette,* March 20, 1756. In 1755 Gale mentioned the plan in his *Present State,* 3.

[56] The same assumption underlay the conviction that the indirect election of Senators under the federal Constitution would make the upper house a more aristocratic body. The assumption was grounded in fact too, for even in Massachusetts and Connecticut where the governors' councils were directly or indirectly chosen by the people, the councils were consistently at variance with the lower houses.

[57] *Connecticut Gazette,* March 20, 1756; May 1, 1756; March 26, 1757; *Conn. Recs.,* X, 553-554; W. Williams, "Rough Sketch," 8, 27. Another account says twenty-five towns sent only one (*Connecticut Gazette,* March 26, 1757). For the 1757 campaign, *ibid.,* March 19, 1757.

of an independent church, and appointment of the Professor of Divinity showed Clap's "unwarrantable thirst of Power and Dominion." [58] Fearful both of the precedent and of Old Light meddling, Clap steadfastly fought efforts to review his policies. Though he had nothing to hide, he objected to legislative intervention on principle. The purpose of the prized charter of 1745 was to make Yale independent of the civil government against the day when some corrupt legislature might try to subvert orthodoxy and good order in the College.

The petitions were pigeonholed in 1757, but the Old Lights were not content to abandon the strategy. In 1759 Benjamin Gale renewed the effort by entering a motion for visitation supported by a pamphlet which exposed Clap's villainy. His major argument was that Yale was blessed with a surplus of funds for its rather small expenses and that no appropriation was needed. Gale went on to indict the President's entire administration, contending that Clap was sapping the College treasury for his own use, exacting exorbitant fines from the students, and, in the face of their increasing disorder, cruelly punishing them. All this demanded immediate investigation. Gale's vituperation, however, fell on deaf ears, for more than three-fourths of the Assembly, now heavily New Light, voted against his motion.[59]

The New Lights, of course, did not supinely accept this onslaught. Clap found a pen as vitriolic as Gale's to reply. John Graham, minister from Woodbury and ardent New Light, hammered back, ceaselessly driving home the point that Old Light enmity was rooted in their dislike of orthodoxy.[60] But, like the Old Lights, Clap and his associates were not confident that words alone would assure Assembly backing. Sometime after their setback in 1755 they began a more immediate campaign to win support at the grass roots, though it is difficult to determine how actively they worked to elect candidates because the Old Light reports on the electioneering are clearly exaggerated. A newspaper article in 1756, for example, charged the New Lights with "artful and indefatigable Industry" among the freemen "to carry on some Re-

[58] Conn. Arch., College and Schools, I, 338; Tucker, 222.
[59] Gale, *Letter; A Calm and full Vindication;* Tucker, 222-223.
[60] *Letter; An Answer to Mr. Gale's Pamphlet;* Tucker, 213-214.

ligious Controversy, or to obtain the Governments Money to enable them the More powerfully to Tyrannize and Insult them." [61]
Later Gale publicly stated that the New Lights had engaged in a
series of plots to turn the elections in their favor, making plans
in 1757 and willfully trying to deceive the public the next year.
When the colony printer had died before issuing the list of nominees
for the Upper House, the written lists that were sent around in
1758 had New Light preferences at the top.[62]

Clap, through his spokesman Graham, indignantly denied the
charges in an October 1759 issue of the *Connecticut Gazette,* but
this repudiation unluckily played into Gale's hands. In February
1760 a friend gave him a copy of an appeal to freemen Graham
had sent to Clap for approval in August of 1759. The previous
June the Wallingford case had closed with the censure of Dana
and the ordaining council. Already in the May session the Assembly was discussing the issue. Questions were in the air which only
the legislature could settle. Was the new society to receive recognition or would it have to go on paying to the old? How were the
church properties to be divided? Graham wanted the freemen to
nominate candidates for the Upper House who would be favorable
to the New Lights and suggested a public discussion of the issues.[63]
Gale now had proof positive that Clap's party was playing politics
and promptly published Graham's anonymous article.

Graham frankly instructed voters to choose not according to
some abstract standard of fitness but on the basis of sympathy
for the New Lights. In view of the candor displayed in previous
pamphlets, Graham's criticism of Old Light leaders came as no
shock. That degree of openness had become customary, but Graham
must have horrified the older generation when he told the freemen
to drop any candidate who displeased them, no matter how honored
or serviceable he had been. If any you have previously chosen,
Graham said to the freemen, prove to be "designing" men, "it is
in your power to drop them, and change them every year, till you
find men firmly attached to both your civil and religious interest."

---

[61] *Connecticut Gazette,* May 1, 1756; Aug. 7, 1756; Conn. Arch., Ecclesiastical Affairs, XI, 176.

[62] *Calm and full Vindication,* 25.

[63] Gale, *A Few Breif Remarks,* 4, 6-7.

The freemen's powers over their representatives, he went on, applied not only to the Lower House (where the New Lights were already in control) but to the fathers of society in the Upper House (where Old Lights predominated). Without asking for any formal revisions in the constitution, Graham proposed a revolution in the meaning of elections. The freemen were to choose not those eminent men whom God had obviously prepared to rule and placed at the head of society, but men, "firmly attached to both your civil and religious interests." Government was still to do the will of God, but as it was interpreted by the people; it was to be the servant of the populace, not its master. Graham argued that this rotation in office should not offend anyone, for the charter provided for just such treatment of officials. Annual elections were wisely included as having "the greatest tendency" to make rulers "tender of all your rights and privileges." [64]

Graham had no choice but to admit his authorship of this radical piece. As he brazenly commented, however, it was not his intention to turn out the majority of the Assembly from office, for the majority already supported the Wallingford minority. Indeed, the New Lights had their way to a great extent in 1759 and 1760. Their toleration campaign bore fruit in the recognition of Separate churches at Canterbury, White Haven, and Plainfield. The Assembly also made the Wallingford New Lights into a distinct society and freed it from any obligation to pay taxes to Dana's church. The following May the Lower House tried to make the minority the first society in Wallingford and to confirm the right of the consociation to intervene. This measure was vetoed, however, every member of the Upper House but one voting against it.[65] The New Lights had cause to rejoice, for their domination of the Lower House and probably of public opinion generally was certain. But they now knew that they must concentrate their energies on removing from the Upper House the prominent Old Lights whom popular veneration kept in office. Not until then could they be confident that orthodoxy would rule in Connecticut.

Even in 1760 it was clear that New Lights would one day over-

[64] Gale, *A Few Breif Remarks*, 8-10.
[65] Graham, *A Few Remarks; Conn. Recs.*, XI, 415-417, 323-326, 344, 461-462; *Letter to a Friend*, 16-17.

throw this last Old Light bastion, for secular discontent as well as
religious piety strengthened them. In 1757 Thomas Darling, an Old
Light pamphleteer, warned his readers that they must carefully
distinguish the two types of New Lights: "those honest people
who went off from our Communion from religious principles only,"
and "those that espouse the separating Party, not from Principle
and Conscience, but from political Views," and are best termed
"political *New-lights*." [66]

Among these New Lights, Gale discerned ambitious officeseek-
ers. His first pamphlet had been offensive not only to men who acted
under "a Pretence of Concern for the Church and Orthodoxy,"
but also to those "greedy of Promotion and Advancement in
Power." [67] Aspiring individuals joined the New Lights to insinuate
themselves into the government for the sake of the prestige attached to public office and for financial benefits. After Parliament
forbade the colony to issue loans, Connecticut met the desire for
currency by issuing bills of credit dispersed through purchases by
public officials. The wars with the French after 1750 raised the rate
of expenditure and put vast sums at the disposal of the commissioners in charge of provisioning Connecticut's troops. From 1755
to 1762 the colony spent upwards of £400,000, and its officials
were in a strategic position to line their own pockets or to bestow
plush contracts on their friends. Public men are strongly tempted,
Roger Wolcott wrote, to "look on the public treasury as a source
to feed and enrich themselves." [68] Those on the outside were
quick to suspect the men in power, but often they were equally quick
to exploit the possibilities of office when it was opened to them.

Such a base motive did not necessarily lie beneath all the political
conversions, for many men simply wanted the status office afforded.
Jared Ingersoll, a prominent Old Light attorney in New Haven,
playfully teased the aspiring politicians who switched parties when
it appeared that the New Lights were in the ascendancy. In a piece
entitled "Epitaph on Isaac Steady Esq," he satirized Isaac Dickerman, until 1754 a deacon in the Old Light First Church in New

[66] Darling, 50n.
[67] *Reply*, x.
[68] B. Trumbull, *Connecticut*, II, 386; Wolcott, *Memoir*, 327; cf. Gale,
Present State, 16-18.

Haven. Clap's overt opposition to the Reverend Mr. Noyes apparently persuaded Dickerman to change his membership to the White Haven Church, a New Light society formed during the Great Awakening. Isaac Steady was a virtuous man, Ingersoll commented, "yet was troubled with an Itch for Worldly Promotion." He courted both parties and in the end pleased none, to Ingersoll's amusement, failing in a bid for election to the Lower House in 1754.[69]

Ingersoll airily derided Dickerman in 1754 when the change of allegiance brought defeat. As New Light popularity grew, however, a transfer of loyalty held more promise for politicians, and the number so tempted ceased to be amusing. Roger Sherman, for example, conveniently changed his party affiliation to further his political ambitions. In 1751, when Sherman lived in New Milford, where fees as a colony surveyor supplemented the income from his store, he was a champion of Old Light principles. He defended the Saybrook Platform to prevent the organization of a New Light church in the town and wrote a tract against the acceptance of depreciated currency from neighboring colonies. In 1755 the government rewarded his loyalty by appointing him a justice of the peace for Litchfield County,[70] but a few years later he was in the other camp. As he expanded his business, opened a store in New Haven, and soon moved his household there, he sensed the drift of politics in town and shifted his loyalties. He joined the New Light church in White Haven instead of the Old Light First Church, and in 1759, even before he was well established, he ran unsuccessfully as a deputy from New Haven with the support of Clap and his friends. Shortly afterwards Clap made Sherman an officer of Yale, and in 1766 he was elected an assistant on a New Light ticket.[71] Whatever Sherman's motives for reversing his position, it facilitated his advancement. Watching his rise, and that of others like him, ambitious men of all types were tempted to follow his course.

Gale intimated in his 1755 pamphlet that entire factions as well

[69] Jared Ingersoll, "Selection," 228-229.
[70] Boardman, *Roger Sherman*, 38, 58, 56-57.
[71] Boardman, 60, 72, 73, 95; C. Whittelsey to E. Stiles, Sept. 25, 1759, E. Stiles, *Extracts*, 582.

as individuals were prone to ally themselves with the New Lights to promote special interests. In that year perhaps little more than a common opposition to Old Lights linked the groups that later merged. But Gale's comments provide clues to the economic and social bases of the two parties at a time when they were speaking of themselves primarily in terms of religious and political principles.

Gale put in the opposing camp the advocates of paper money, the tumbling values of which had been the excuse, he said, "for a great deal of Unrighteousness, and corrupted, and debauched the Morals of the People." He was particularly concerned about the currency of New Hampshire and Rhode Island bills, which had been deprived of legal tender status in 1752 but still circulated freely, draining silver out of the colony. His dislike of paper, of course, made him the enemy of eastern merchants who had been the first advocates of banks and later dealt in the inflated moneys of other colonies.[72]

Gale was particularly hostile toward the east, where there were no restraints on alien currencies, but he revealed an antipathy for traders in all sections. He believed that the government tax policies should favor farmers, or at least shift some of the burden onto commerce. Existing methods mulcted "the Farmer and Industrious" part of the colony. More taxes should be placed on "hurtful" things which "destroy our Health, drein our country of our Cash and best Produce" in return for commodities which at best "afford an empty show." He also suspected the merchants of a scheme to draw in silver to the government so that they might more easily get their hands on it to pay their debts abroad.[73] Gale's comments indicated that he and the Old Lights were tied to the large landholders and conservative merchants, the two groups which most disliked paper money, while the New Lights attracted enterprising merchants and small traders.

Judging from the attitudes of the parties toward the Susquehannah Company, New Lights also represented the interests of small farmers. In the early 1750's various groups in the colony had petitioned for a grant in northern Pennsylvania, which Connecticut claimed under the sea-to-sea clause in its patent. The Susquehannah

[72] *Present State*, 3, 2, 16-18.
[73] *Present State*, 20, 16-18.

Company, formed in 1753, amalgamated these petitioners, who purchased a deed from some Indians, sold stock to finance the venture, and asked the Assembly for help in removing Pennsylvania's objections. A few Old Lights who had invested in the Company withdrew when they realized how formidable the opposition in Pennsylvania was; they feared that a disturbance might jeopardize the always precarious charter.[74] By 1760 the Susquehannah claims, a potential boon to small farmers, were identified solely as a New Light cause.

The Old Lights gave sound political reasons for their opposition, but the Susquehannah men suspected that unstated economic interests carried greater weight. Migration from the colony lowered the value of land in Connecticut, especially wilderness land that was in direct competition with tracts opening up elsewhere. One man reported that prices in his town fell by nearly half when lots went on sale in Vermont and New Hampshire. When in 1763 it was rumored that 700 persons were ready to leave for Susquehannah, along with the flood of farmers already moving north—an estimated 30,000 between 1760 and 1774—large landholders had cause to worry. Migration on this scale lowered land values even in established towns and made labor scarce.[75] The New Light supporters of the Susquehannah Company suspected that these considerations motivated Old Light resistance. In 1774, when the controversy had become more vicious than earlier, Roger Sherman bluntly declared that the "gentlemen, who love to monopolize wealth and power, think it best for lands to be in a few hands and that the common people should be their tenants." But the people of the colony, knowing "the value of freedom and of enjoying fee-simple estates," would rather "give up the lands acquired for them by their ancestors" and move to Pennsylvania.[76]

Though denying any villainous intent, Old Lights openly expressed their preference that the population stay in Connecticut.

[74] *Susquehannah Company*, I, "Introduction" and pp. 1-26; B. Trumbull, *Connecticut*, II, 403-406; Morgan and Morgan, *Stamp Act Crisis*, 228.

[75] E. Stiles, *Extracts*, 50, 189; Steiner, *Guilford*, 146-147; Bailey, *Influences*, 229. In 1768 one Old Light was afraid that opening lands in the Great Lakes region would prevent manufacturing in Connecticut (John Devotion to E. Stiles, Feb. 8, 1768, E. Stiles, *Extracts*, 472).

[76] Quoted in Gipson, *Ingersoll*, 325-326.

A satire on the insatiable desire for new lands published in the *Connecticut Courant* ridiculed the "great propensity of late, to wander from home, upon the most romantic expeditions; and to plant new colonies before our own is half peopled, or one quarter cultivated." [77] Jared Eliot's famous *Essays on Field Husbandry* were as much a discourse on how to be content with small acreage as a venture into scientific agriculture. There was no call to feel "that we live too thick," if better techniques of husbandry were understood. In the Roman Empire men subsisted on four or five acres. Why then should Connecticut men leave the colony "for the sake of more room to the prejudice of the Places from whence they Remove, and oftentimes to their own hurt too!" [78]

Whatever the social division, geographically the New Lights and Old Lights were sectional factions, the former controlling the east and the latter the west. Clap in New Haven and Bellamy in Litchfield County led strong western New Light contingents, but after 1755 "eastern men" became a synonym for New Light. All the secular interests Gale identified with the New Lights arose in the east. Paper money advocates, traders dealing in Rhode Island and New Hampshire currency, even the preponderance of new merchants, all were there. [79] The headquarters of the Susquehannah Company were in Windham and Lebanon, and most stockholders lived in the surrounding eastern towns. Moreover, the Awakening had made its deepest impression in the east, creating there a host of radical Separates as well as more moderate devotees of experimental religion.

The sectional focus of Gale's New Light enemies, both secular and religious, was not simply a coincidence. Economic and religious radicalism had appeared in the same area for good reasons. Ultimately all were the result of rapid expansion in the eastern section after 1690, when immigration from Massachusetts, added to natural growth, swelled the population. The heightened demand for new land opened the door to speculation and the political tur-

[77] May 20, 1765; cf. Zeichner, *Connecticut's Years of Controversy*, 295.
[78] Eliot, *Essays*, 30, 49. The same theme was renewed later by Timothy Dwight (*Greenfield Hill*, 127).
[79] Zeichner, chaps. ii, iii. The colony reported that New London was Connecticut's major port (*Conn. Recs.*, XI, 630).

moil surrounding James Fitch. The settlement of new towns increased commercial opportunities and spawned the multitude of new traders who called for currency issues and dealt in Rhode Island and New Hampshire paper money. The population boom in the east filled the wilderness lands more quickly than in the west and compelled men there to look far afield for new farms. As early as 1735 residents were petitioning the Assembly for grants in unoccupied lands wherever the colony had a claim. Susquehannah Company stock sold rapidly in the east, not only to speculators but to ordinary farmers who were hard pressed to provide for their families.[80] In the midst of this expansion, worldly ambitions flourished and resistance to social authority mounted, and these were the two main causes of susceptibility to religious conversion. Here the Awakening made its largest impact. All the forms of radicalism were the outgrowth of the expansive spirit which touched everyone in the east.

The New Light party formed in the religious revivals thus automatically absorbed secular causes. Gale perceived the overlapping of forces and in 1766 was working on a manuscript describing the genealogy of "the several Factions wh. have subsisted in this Colony, originating with the N London Society—thence metamorphisd into the Faction for paper Emissions on Loan, thence into N Light, into the Susquehanna and Delaware Factions—into Orthodoxy," and finally (he added to bring the progeny up to date) "now into Stamp Duty." "The Actors," he said were the same throughout, "each Change drawing in some New Members." [81]

The New Lights in 1760 were, then, a powerful but heterogenous amalgamation. There were three distinguishable branches, sharing interests but differently balanced. The New Divinity branch contained the heirs of Jonathan Edwards and was characterized by piety and certain theological concepts formulated to protect pristine Calvinism. Bellamy was their spiritual leader and Litchfield County the center of their power. The Orthodoxy branch, by contrast, was

[80] Larned, *Windham*, I, 556-557; *Susquehannah Company*, I, 25, 26. For a comparison of the reaction in eastern and western towns, Caulkins, *Norwich*, 504; Steiner, 146-147.

[81] To Jared Igersoll, Jan. 13, 1765 (error for 1766), Jared Ingersoll, "Selection," 373.

not noted for its fervency and took little interest in the theological virtuosity of the New Divinity men. Under Clap's leadership, this branch sought mainly to stamp out heresy, concentrating its energies on Yale and New Haven County. The eastern branch, which contained the radicals and many moderates, was fervent, inclined to stress toleration, and merged economic interests with religious zeal. Significantly, no single ecclesiastical figure stood out in that area, which may explain its passive role in the twenty years before 1760 despite the large number of New Lights there. The leadership of this branch was shared by distinguished laymen who represented the dominant political and economic interests of the section.

In each phase of the Party's growth changing combinations of these interests accounted for the varying tone of New Light agitation. During the 1740's Bellamy's group and eastern New Lights stood together in favor of experimental religion and in opposition to civil intervention in religion, in the 1750's Clap and Bellamy joined hands to lead their groups in the war on heresy, and in the 1760's the secular interests of the east came to the fore. Fortunately for the party, the paramount concerns of each were not mutually exclusive, so that on most issues the dominant groups could count on support from the recessive branch. By working together, even while the tenor of the party was modulating, the New Lights became the major political force in the colony. In 1763 William Johnson marveled that the New Lights who in his memory "were a small party, merely a religious one," had "acquired such an influence as to be nearly the ruling part of the government owing to their superior attention to civil affairs and close union among themselves in politics." [82]

Drawing their support from these sources, the New Lights were the single most formidable political force in the colony. Yet, as Johnson observed, they were but "nearly" the ruling part. On most occasions they had strength in the Lower House but were unable to overcome the opposition of the eminent Old Lights who ruled in the Upper House and controlled the governorship. In 1763 the New Lights proved again what they had demonstrated in 1759 in connection with the Wallingford case: they could command a

[82] To J. Beach, Jan. 4, 1763, Samuel Johnson, *Samuel Johnson,* III, 266.

majority among the deputies but not in the Upper House. In that year Clap was challenged more seriously than ever when a group of distinguished individuals submitted a list of charges and called for an investigation. They said Clap was unable to keep order in the College and was moving to ever more severe and unjust measures. William Johnson and Jared Ingersoll, the colony's most skilled lawyers, made the case against Clap in the public hearings. Nevertheless, when the President had made his reply, the Assembly cleared him. The New Lights rallying to his support carried the day over the objections of the Upper House.[83]

On the other hand, the year before, the Susquehannah Company suffered a setback when Governor Fitch officially announced that the government disapproved of the scheme. The Company nonetheless proceeded to send settlers to Pennsylvania, but the Governor's proclamation had unfortunately been made just when the case was being examined in London and official support was needed. The next year the Board of Trade forbade Company settlers to enter their lands, and even the intrepid Susquehannah leaders dared not disregard that order. They learned their lesson, however: they would never enjoy clear sailing until the governor and Council as well as the Lower House gave Connecticut's claim full backing.[84]

There was a seeming contradiction in the ability of the New Lights to control the Lower House but not the Upper. Both were popularly elected, and if the New Lights could win enough votes to take one, why not the other? Only Connecticut's habitual deference to its eminent men prevented their controlling the Upper House. The colonists could not bring themselves to remove the exalted figures whose distinguished names headed the list of nominations.[85] The fathers of society exercised their influence, even though their policies clashed with the prevailing popular will. Only some deeply stirring conflict could persuade the voters to evict their Old Light rulers.

Restless New Lights had not long to wait, for intervention from abroad soon provided the very issue they needed. Old Lights knew

---

[83] Conn. Arch., College and Schools, II, 74; Tucker, 222-231.

[84] *Connecticut Gazette,* June 19, 1762; *New London Summary,* July 2, 1762; Zeichner, 32-33.

[85] Welling, "Connecticut Federalism," 306-307.

the Stamp Act of 1765 would be unpopular, but they miscalculated how much fury it would arouse. After strenuously combating its passage, they acquiesced reluctantly and made plans to execute the law. Jared Ingersoll, the colony agent who had represented Connecticut's interests when the Act was considered, agreed to administer it, genuinely believing that enforcement by a native would mitigate the severity of the tax. To his dismay, upon returning to Connecticut in August 1765, commission in hand, he found himself at the center of a storm. Protest meetings throughout the colony, especially among eastern New Lights, castigated him as the instrument of British tyranny. Riding to Hartford that fall to attend a special session of the legislature called to discuss the Stamp Act, he was intercepted by a mob from the east which refused to release him until he promised to abandon his commission. Following him into the capital, they compelled him publicly to announce his capitulation. Then he resigned.

The Act required the governor to take an oath faithfully to collect the tax, and Governor Fitch was ready to comply in November 1765. The Old Light members of the Upper House stood with him and agreed to administer the oath, but the New Lights were of another mind. When the day came, they withdrew from the council chambers, thus declaring their hostility to the Stamp Act and revealing openly a split at the highest level of government. This dramatic gesture after weeks of agitation turned the tide. The New Lights in the following spring met in Hartford to nominate a slate of candidates which excluded Governor Fitch and the councillors who had sworn him to enforce the Stamp Act. Moderates at the council refused to countenance such a "pernicious precedent, unknown to and unpracticed by the virtuous Founders and supporters of the Colony," but they could not prevent the eastern radicals from obtaining the convention's approval of acceptable candidates for governor and deputy governor.[86] When the votes were counted in May 1766, Fitch and the supporting councilors had lost. Former Deputy Governor Pitkin was chosen Governor, and the eastern New Light, Jonathan Trumbull, was in the colony's second post. The New Light triumph was complete.[87]

[86] Quoted in Gipson, 220.
[87] The Stamp Act story is told in detail in Zeichner, 44-77.

British oppression drew to the New Light camp marginal voters and even some acknowledged Old Lights. Paradoxically the Anglicans, who boasted of their uncompromising loyalty to the mother country, voted with the New Lights in return for the election of William Samuel Johnson, one of their number, to the Upper House. Yet without a doubt the New Lights were chiefly responsible for the innovation; their leaders engineered the whole campaign and their voters were the bulk of those who elected Pitkin.[88]

They won because they fought the Stamp Act more fiercely than the Old Lights, forcing the conservatives to appear negligent of Connecticut's liberties. But why the New Lights were more adamant in their opposition is difficult to explain. They were not distinguished for their dislike of the Stamp Act before its passage. Indeed, when the Assembly was drawing up reasons against passage in 1764, they called upon Ingersoll, an Old Light, to help and then commissioned him to carry their case to England. Privately and publicly Ingersoll industriously sought to block the act.[89] Nor was Benjamin Gale a friend of the Stamp Act. And Chauncey Whittelsey asked with some heat in April 1765 after its passage, "Pray tell me, what are all our boasted Charter priviledges, if we are thus liable to have any proportion of our Interest taken from us, whether we will or no, and without our Consent or Voice." [90] Fitch understandably felt misused in the election of 1766. In a pamphlet explaining his course, he reminded the freemen that he was as hostile to the Stamp Act as the radicals.[91]

Doubtless the New Light agitation was due partly to their previous grudges, and the Stamp Act contention provided the long-awaited opportunity to oust men they detested. Loaded into the New Lights' anti-Act rhetoric was a bitterness built up over many years.[92] Fitch and Ingersoll both had actively opposed the Susquehannah Company, the Upper House had stood in the way

[88] E. Stiles, *Extracts,* 63-64.

[89] Ingersoll to Thomas Whately, July 8, 1764, Jared Ingersoll, "Selection," 299; Morgan and Morgan, 230-232.

[90] Groce, "Gale," 706; Whittelsey to E. Stiles, April 16, 1765, E. Stiles, *Extracts,* 587.

[91] Fitch, *Some Reasons.*

[92] This is the interpretation of Zeichner, 71, and Morgan and Morgan, chap. xiii.

of full Assembly approval of the New Light church at Wallingford, and Stamp Act supporters had been Clap's chief assailants.

But to attribute the New Light agitation in 1765 and 1766 wholly
to their past feud with the Old Lights is to misjudge the sincerity
and fervor of the radicals. Their campaign for liberty was more
than a front for domestic political machination, for their pamphlets
and newspaper articles leave no doubt that the New Lights were
genuinely outraged. This act of arbitrary power, as both parties
judged it, triggered a more violent reaction in New Lights than in
Old.

The difference lay not in the facts of the objective situation, but
in the mentality of the two parties. The Old Light world was still
organized around traditional concepts of the social order. Its members derived personal security from the belief that authority, de-
scending from above through the agencies of government, could
keep the peace. Their positions in society, their religious values,
and their sense of control and order were sustained by this structure of authority. While able to tolerate limited conflicts, overthrow of the whole threatened them deeply. As one New Light
commented, the popular tumults most shocked those "accustomed
to venerate and obey lawful authority, and who delight in peace
and order." [93] The Old Lights themselves expressed this very fear
when they inveighed against the Stamp Act meetings as "a scandal
to government, tending to the breach of the peace and stirring up
SEDITION, the dreadful effects of which we already begin to
see." [94] In his official proclamation against the riots Fitch expressed
his concern that they tended to "the endangering all Order and Government." [95] One worried Old Light looking toward the end asked
in a newspaper article "Whether there is any safety for Men of
Property when once the inclosure of the Laws is broke down?" [96]
Rather than reach such an extremity, the Old Lights preferred to
support the Crown, whence all authority stemmed. "So long as
the Alternatives are *Submission* or *Civil War*," Ezra Stiles confessed, "I shall not hesitate to chuse and declare for the *first*, till

[93] *Connecticut Gazette*, Oct. 11, 1765.
[94] *Connecticut Gazette*, Sept. 13, 1765.
[95] *Connecticut Gazette*, Sept. 27, 1765.
[96] *Connecticut Gazette*, Sept. 13, 1765.

the consequences of the latter are less far less tremendous than the Effects of Oppression." [97] Operating in this personal and social context, Fitch placed more weight upon his obligation to "yield Obedience to the Requirements of the King and Parliament," than to defend Connecticut's liberty at all costs.[98]

The New Lights were not heedless of the worth of good order. They carefully pointed out that during the burning of a giant figure in New Haven, accused of being the foe of English freedom, "no unlawful Disorder happened." [99] But they held authority and government in less awe than Old Lights. New Lights had been accustomed to contending with the rulers of society ever since the Great Awakening, and their defiance of eminent men in government had become almost habitual. Hence for them a clash with King and Parliament was neither an innovation nor a shock. More important, the consequences were less drastic for the New Lights' sense of personal well-being. Their world was not organized around external law and authority as was that of the Old Lights, for most of them had escaped the power of the social order in the Awakening and immediately put their trust in God. The lives of the converted rested on a personal experience with the divine; for them the risk of overthrowing the external order was not so terrifying. The lawless mob worried Roger Sherman, whose conversion had been political and not religious, and he foresaw, as the Old Lights did, insuppressible "disorders and confusions." [100] But most secular New Lights apparently borrowed confidence from their religious compatriots and freely attacked the King, the very source of social order. While Old Lights checked their animosity against British tyranny in apprehension of utter confusion, the New Lights freely vented their anger.

In the long view, this willingness of the New Lights to resist is the greatest significance of their rise. Puritans had always held that governmental power was limited and that God sanctioned resistance when liberty was usurped. But before the Awakening no one of importance had dared assert that the civil authorities had

[97] Quoted in Zeichner, 67; cf. p. 271.
[98] Fitch, *Some Reasons*, 6-7.
[99] *Connecticut Gazette*, Sept. 13, 1765; cf. Gipson, 220.
[100] Boardman, 91-92.

actually overstepped their bounds. The importance of protecting
the social order always outweighed dissatisfaction with any policy,
and in the end factions had submitted or at least bowed before
the preponderance of popular and official disapproval. New Lights
had not been so timid. Beginning with their opposition to the
itineracy law, they had boldly accused government of trespassing
on the rights of the people, and in the Stamp Act agitation they
strenuously objected to "passive obedience" as positively wicked
in the face of British tyranny.[101] "When the fundamental rights of
community are invaded," one New Light preacher declared, "it
is so far from duty tamely to give them up, that, I conceive, duty
to God and religion, to themselves, to the community, and to
unborn posterity, require such to assert and defend their rights,
by all lawful, most prudent, and effectual means, in their power." [102]
That sort of pronouncement, long accepted in principle, now became revolutionary doctrine because the New Lights asserted that
those fundamental rights had actually been invaded.

In view of the makeup of the Puritan personality, the courage to
contend openly with the fathers of society had to have a religious
source. Only when faith in the divinity of earthly law and authority
had been weakened, could a party wholeheartedly seek the down-
fall of its rulers. After the civil government's hostility to the revival disillusioned the New Lights, conscience urged on rather than
limited political activity. The New Lights consequently had the
power to transform the character of politics. In the New Light train,
secular factions took heart and attempted to shape a government
policy favorable to their interests. To prevent New Light victories,
Old Lights themselves resorted to unprecedented methods for mar-
shaling public opinion. It became increasingly obvious after the
Awakening that candor was to be the norm of political expression
and that, because the civil authorities were now recognized as
imperfect instruments of the divine will, men would try to regulate
the government to suit their own purposes.

[101] Stephen Johnson, *Some Observations*, 21; B. Trumbull, *Letter*, 7;
Connecticut Gazette, Aug. 9, 1765.
[102] Stephen Johnson, *Some Observations*, 27; cf. *Connecticut Gazette*,
Sept. 13, 1765.

XVI

A New Social Order

&§ Measured against seventeenth-century standards, Puritan social institutions had deteriorated sadly by 1765. The social order
no longer restrained unruly human passions, and the rulers of Connecticut were unable to fulfill their commission from God to keep
peace and order. The old ambiguity about economic ambition,
which had formerly discomfited only a small section of the community, now troubled virtually the whole population. Men of all
classes who were eagerly seeking wealth clashed with the institutions
designed to keep order. The town, the churches, and the civil government felt the pressures of a generation bent on expanding its
worldly inheritance through land or trade and increasingly impa-
tient with the limitations rulers imposed.

The conflict between ambition and traditional authority found
a release in the Great Awakening. Guilty men surrendered to God,
admitted their culpability, and called upon Him to save them
by His grace. But the God to whom they surrendered was not
He whose authority invested social institutions. Newborn men relied
wholly on the God they had discovered in a personal experience.
Far from instilling submission to the old authority, the revival
planted the conviction that God's power was given to individuals,
clearing the way for men to resist in good conscience when the
occasion arose.

The subsequent political agitation shocked even rulers sympathetic to the revival. New and Old Lights alike were appalled "to
observe a levelling and seditious Spirit prevailing, and an Impatience
of all Rule and Restraint." [1] One preacher observed that all too
often men *"despised Dominion"* and freely *"speak evil of Dignities*

[1] Todd, *Civil Rulers*, 75.

and revile the Rulers of God's People." [2] The first reaction was
to attribute this contentious spirit to a "want of virtuous Principles." [3] Murmurers and complainers walked *"after their own
Lusts."* [4] But those epithets could not describe Benjamin Gale, an
educated and eminent Old Light, or Thomas Clap, rector of Yale,
or the friends of both among the ministers who indulged in the
same form of vituperation. The new condition in politics was
permanent rather than temporary.

The guardians of social order ran into equal difficulty in condemning the election of party men to represent special interests.
Conservatives were appalled that a civil officer should fail in an
election because his policies displeased the voters; they found it
dreadful that "a Magistrate of known Ability and approved Faithfulness is to be laid aside, merely because he cannot be brought
to consent to such Measures as he esteemes prejudicial to his
Country, tho' they happen to be popular." [5] The assumption had
always been that "Gentlemen of approved Capacity and Fidelity"
were to remain in office, however unpopular their actions, so long
as their character was unimpeached.

Popular fickleness could only be attributed to "the artful Applications of designing Men." [6] To block the schemes of the few
depraved individuals who formed such factions, the Assembly in
1756 passed an act to prevent bribery and corruption in elections.[7]
Rulers were admonished to "scorn the Suffrages of those that
would set you up, not for the public Good, but only to Serve a
Turn." [8] Keep a steady course, they were told, even "if thro the
Weakness of honest Men, or the Wickedness of others," they fell
from office. Such a fall would be a "noble Sacrifice, 'tis a Death
worth dying, a Death more honourable than a Life preserv'd by
a servile Temper, and mean Compliance." [9]

[2] N. Eells, *Wise Ruler,* 20; cf. Dickinson, *Sermon,* 52.

[3] Lord, *Religion and Government,* 14.

[4] Todd, *Civil Rulers,* 75; cf. S. Hall, *Legislatures,* 31.

[5] Hobart, *Civil Government,* 51; cf. Fish, *Christ Jesus,* 45.

[6] Lockwood, *Worth and Excellence,* 18n; *Connecticut Gazette,* Jan. 3,
1756; cf. Hobart, *Civil Government,* 37; Devotion, *Civil Ruler,* 28-29; *Connecticut Gazette,* Dec. 18, 1756.

[7] *Conn. Recs.,* X, 496; W. Williams, "Rough Sketch," 1.

[8] Fish, 46.

[9] Devotion, *Civil Ruler,* 28-29.

These assurances made sense so long as electioneering was confined to men of small moment and to a few centers of discontent
like New London.[10] But the strictures against "designing men" did
not apply when Thomas Clap, whose status as President of Yale
lent respectability to forthright campaigning for candidates, was
caught red-handed conniving at an election upset. Some reluctance
remained in 1766, when the New Lights wanted to drop Fitch
and the Old Light councillors, but not enough to stop the leaders
from preparing a slate of acceptable candidates and vigorously
campaigning for them. By then the politically ambitious freely
disregarded the admonitions to stand firm against factional arrangements. Disgusted by the pliability of candidates, an Old Light
deplored the disposition to "Cringe, Twist and Turn Twenty ways
to get into any post the Colony had to give"; yet experience seemed
to prove that compliance with popular wishes was to become a
fixed attribute of politicians.[11]

New Lights were as unhappy as Old about the increasing dependence on popular favor. The distress transcended party lines,
because the degree of democracy introduced in the 1750's contradicted the fundamental convictions about political society that
everyone had once accepted. All American Puritans doubted that
the people could rule themselves, because their wills were corrupt.
Democracy set the world on its ears by making the freemen "as
Sovereign as Nebuchadnezzar, King of Babylon" when they were
actually incapable of governing themselves individually, much less
society as a whole. The common people, it was believed, were
prone to think that "nothing is of general Benefit but what favours
their party-Interest; In consequence of which their Strength and
Zeal is put forth in promoting, not the real good of the Public,
but of their own Party." [12] A "factious, ungovernable Disposition
in the People does as effectually destroy the Foundations of public
Happiness, as Tyranny in the Rulers." [13]

According to the traditional view, public peace required rulers

[10] For the New London agitation in 1740, Caulkins, *New London,* 385;
Conn. Arch., Civil Officers, II, 399.
[11] Joseph Chew to Jared Ingersoll, June 8, 1763, quoted in Gipson,
Ingersoll, 318.
[12] Fish, 13-14.
[13] Hobart, *Civil Government,* 13

to hold to their course against all the buffettings of popular dislike. It was to be expected that "such Measures as are necessary, or highly conducive to the Public Good, shall be very unpopular." [14] "So different are the private Interests of Men," rulers were reminded, "so various and headstrong their Passions and Lusts, that good Laws and a strict Execution of them, will probably bring upon you the Odium of many." [15] Unflinching authority was the bulwark against these "Passions and Lusts," and hence despair ensued when the people presumed to elect whom they would to office and demanded compliance with popular will. What could the future hold but chaos, the end of peace and liberty, when "the Influence of Rulers is hereby Obstructed,—their Authority weakened, and their Hearts discouraged?" In 1760 a preacher warned the colony of "a *Selfish, dividing, party-Spirit;* that strives to make its way thro' the Land: threatning like a Bear, to rend us in Pieces." [16]

To reinforce the failing strength of the rulers, election preachers of both political factions stressed the familiar formula for civil obedience: God instituted governments among men to keep the peace; the authority of rulers was derived from God; therefore, men were conscience-bound to submit. To resist "in the Administration of that Power GOD hath committed to them" was "as it were to wage War against GOD himself." [17] Furthermore, men defeated their own best interests in doing so, for the rule of law protected them in their liberties. Without government, "we should be in a state of Confusion." "There would be *no Peace* . . . our Lives and Properties, and all that is dear to us, would hang in Suspence, and depend upon the ungoverned Lusts of the Sons of Fraud, and Violence." [18]

[14] Hobart, *Civil Government,* 37.
[15] Devotion, *Civil Ruler,* 49.
[16] Fish, 17, 45.
[17] Todd, *Civil Rulers,* 3.
[18] Dickinson, *Sermon,* 7. The best single statement of the classic Puritan view of government was Jonathan Todd's 1749 election sermon, *Civil Rulers.* However, the same view was made explicit on countless other occasions. For example, Lord, 30; A. Woodbridge, *A Sermon,* 6, 44; Lockwood, *Worth and Excellence,* 21; Devotion, *Election Sermon,* 25; Dickinson, *Sermon,* 7-13; E. Eells, *Christ,* 16.

The invocation of divine authority and popular liberty, however, was inadequate in the middle of the eighteenth century, as the Old Lights themselves admitted. The Awakening controversies seriously undercut the civil authorities' claims to divine approval. Neither branch of the New Lights was very impressed by the assertion that the rulers were God's vice-regents. The radicals, an Old Light complained, "would *put down all Rule, and all Authority, and Power* among Men: Pleading in Defence of their licentious Doctrine, that CHRIST *hath made all his People Kings.*" The moderates who claimed far less for the reborn men, nonetheless after the itineracy laws "encouraged many to *despise Government, and to speak Evil of Dignities*" by representing "the Leaders and Rulers of this People, as *unconverted and Opposers* of the Work of God, and usurping an Authority that did not belong to them." [19]

At the same time the word "liberty" assumed new political usages. At the beginning of the century the love of liberty was used as an incentive for submission to authority, since only rigid enforcement of the law adequately guaranteed each man his rights. The argument was well grounded so long as a consensus about the definition of individual rights existed. Each man had his own little area of freedom, protected from invasion by common obedience to law and authority. But the argument broke down when the boundaries between the rights of the people and the power of the state were in dispute. Men then turned against their rulers because of real or imagined trespasses on their rights. "PERVERSE and disingenuous Spirits," one preacher noted, petulantly cursed the government "if all the public Affairs" were not "ordered and conducted, in a Manner that suits their Humours." Unreasonable men were "ready to imagine their Freedom and Liberties are worth Nothing at all; to murmur and complain; to call for Chains and Shackles . . . to censure and condemn the whole Legislative Body of the Colony." [20] Liberty then became the battle cry of the rebellious.

Stephen Johnson, one of the radical preachers who had sounded the alarm against British tyranny in 1765, brooded over the problem after repeal of the Stamp Act and concluded gloomily in 1770

[19] Todd, *Civil Rulers*, 2, 74n-75n.
[20] Lockwood, *Worth and Excellence*, 16; cf. Todd, *Civil Rulers*, 50.

that no automatic balancing could be expected between the power of government and the liberties of the people.[21] This widespread uncertainty about the precise limitations of liberty, which in various forms troubled Americans ever after, weakened the link to order. Liberty thenceforth could imply resistance to authority as well as submission, and the older formula for civil obedience lost much of its power.

The traditional conceptions of the social order were not wholly obsolete. They remained in the armory of election sermon preachers for many years, too thoroughly integrated into the colony's theology to be discarded. Yet the old ideas were ineffective. Civil authority was disparaged, faction reigned in politics, and the people called for still greater liberties. A new rationale for the social order was needed as a basis on which to appeal to the people for submission to authority and obedience to law.

The 1750's and 1760's were a period of experimentation in social theory because everyday experience confronted people with the problem. Submission or resistance, liberty versus authority, orderliness or confusion, these were crucial alternatives. Not surprisingly, the theories born in this era were projections of personal methods for dealing with life and without strict correspondence to party lines. Not all New Lights agreed on the structure of the new social order. Drawing on whatever material in their experience seemed viable, some accepted a social order based on self-interest, while others considered such views anathema. Important centers of feelings and thought can be identified, but few pronouncements on social theory were pure expressions of a single conception.

Among Anglicans there had always been an aversion to disorder. Samuel Johnson accounted for his conversion to Episcopacy by remembering how distasteful he had found the "great animosities" and "virulent separations" in Congregationalism at the beginning of the century. The same dislike of "divisions and separations" precipitated a flood of conversions after the Awakening. Among people intolerant of confusion, political turmoil was equally odious. Johnson had always thought the Connecticut charter far too democratic, and after the revival multiplied political disputes, he urged its repeal nearly as strenuously as he petitioned for an American

[21] Stephen Johnson, *Integrity and Piety*, 7-8.

Bishop. All the disadvantages Connecticut labored under, he wrote the Archbishop of Canterbury, "are owing to its constitution being a little more than a mere democracy." Democracy in church and state were related evils; the colony's troubles were due to "the prevalency of rigid enthusiastical conceited notions and practices in religion and republican mobbish principles and practices in policy, being most on a level and each thinking himself an able divine and statesman: hence perpetual feuds and factions in both." [22] The charter made all the officers dependent on the people and thus likely "to consider not so much what is law or equity as what may please their constituents." The only permanent remedy lay in "demolishing these pernicious charter governments, and reducing them all to one form, in immediate dependence on the King." [23] Another Anglican clergyman thought Connecticut's rulers would welcome the change: "What would they not give for a dignity depending not on the fickle will of a multitude, but on the steady reason and generosity of a King?" [24] Buttressed by the incontrovertible authority of Bishops strictly holding the people to religious and political duties, such a social order would curb the "headstrong mob." [25] After the Stamp Act crisis, Anglicans pointedly wrote home reporting the willingness of their communicants to pay the tax.[26]

Many conservatives appreciated the virtues of a world kept in order by the awesome authority of King and Bishops. The Anglican vision was, after all, simply an extension of traditional conceptions, relying somewhat more heavily on a royal than a divine investiture of power. In the crisis of 1765, the gentlemen revealed that at heart they depended on the King's support anyway and were not prepared to repudiate the Crown for the sake of liberty.

The opposition to the appointment of a Bishop and repeal of the charter, however, demonstrated that conservatives were unwill-

[22] Samuel Johnson, *Samuel Johnson*, I, 11-12, 28, 295-296; cf. p. 298.

[23] To Benjamin Franklin, [1765?], Samuel Johnson, *Samuel Johnson*, I, 349; to Archbishop Secker, Dec. 20, 1763, *ibid.*, III, 280.

[24] Peters, *Connecticut*, 376-377.

[25] Johnson to Dr. Bearcroft, April 14, 1751, Samuel Johnson, *Samuel Johnson*, I, 146-147.

[26] Beardsley, *Episcopacy in Connecticut*, 240-245; Edwin Hall, *Norwalk*, 126.

ing to rely wholly on the King. They were too heavily committed to the charter. In earlier days, when liberty and order had appeared more compatible, they had become accustomed to lauding charter liberties. Whatever second thoughts were entertained by 1760, no loyal Connecticut man could gracefully disclaim a century of rhetoric. More important, a royal charter might restore order, but it would not assure political power to the traditional ruling families. If Massachusetts' experience was any guide, some individuals would receive royal favor, but a good many others would be replaced by alien officials. For all its attractions, the Anglican concept of society won over only those willing to make substantial sacrifices to guarantee order.

Samuel Johnson probably numbered the New Divinity men among the enthusiasts he despised, yet their view of society also aimed to restore order. Bellamy as much as Johnson despaired of an era when "subjects despise the Deity and contemn all authority, are full of discontentment and murmuring, divided into angry parties, ready to take fire on every occasion." [27] Sensitized by their religious experience to the odiousness of sin, New Lights were zealous to crush immorality by stringent laws. A Separate pastor asked impatiently in 1750 "how comes it to pass, that reveling and banqueting, fiddling and dancing, wicked, prophane, and filthy Conversation is so much connived at, and no more suppressed by the Rulers of this Land?" [28] But, for all their impatience with the manifestations of sin, many New Lights recognized that no reinforcement of authority would stop the vices of the people. "It is easier, you are sensible," Bellamy said to the Assembly, after publication of a rebuke of prevalent sins, "to issue out such a proclamation than it is to act up to the true purport and spirit of it." [29] "One might as well expect to subdue the Shrubs on yonder Plain, only by nipping off the Buds in the Spring," another preacher declaimed, "as to heal a vicious People of their mortal Diseases, by working perpetually upon their immoral Practices *alone*." [30] Law could eliminate only the symptoms, not the inner heart of evil, whence all disorder sprang.

[27] *Works,* I, 586.
[28] Frothingham, *Articles,* 260; cf. Hobart, *Civil Government,* 39.
[29] *Works,* 593.   [30] Fish, 59; cf. Dickinson, *Sermon,* 22.

The New Lights, particularly the New Divinity men, taught that the new birth alone could heal society, just as it alone had healed individual souls. The idea was not new, for the contribution of religious morality to civil government had long been a cliché of the election sermons. Even the radical notion that the law could not reach a vast number of common disorders had been advanced as early as 1721, and the necessity taught of an inward reformation to prepare men "to Prosecute the Publick Good truly and faithfully." [31] But in the Awakening the weary old belief came to life again. Edwards reported that the freshening of the Spirit in Northampton induced people as nothing had before to forsake "drinking, tavern-haunting, profane speaking, and extravagance in apparel," along with a host of other venialities. "In vain were laws made to restrain them, and in vain was all the vigilance of magistrates and civil officers; but now they have almost everywhere dropped them as it were of themselves." [32] The large number of conversions made it seem quite likely that God's grace might subdue people as law and authority had not.

Some New Lights pointed the obvious moral that grace made good citizens while it made saints: "Tis plain, that a Spirit of *Self Love, Party Zeal* and *cruel Enmity,* which enslav'd the Mind, and spoil'd the Society of all her peace, is *cast* out by the Spirit of Christ." [33] But the New Divinity men also saw social harmony as flowing naturally and inevitably from the very nature of rebirth. Following Edwards, they believed that grace conformed the mind and nature to the moral image of God, reborn men being made "partakers of his holiness," and that the holiness of God "summarily consists in benevolence." [34]

In *The Nature of True Virtue* Edwards had defined this benevolence as total unselfishness, a disinterested love for being in general that united the individual to the whole. And, while God was far the greater part of being in general, the earth and its inhabitants were included as well. Grace acting on a nation created union among the disparate, captious atoms that were the reprobate. Re-

[31] Marsh, *Essay*, 8-19, 48, 52-53; cf. Cutler, *Firm Union*, 32.
[32] *Works*, 296-297.
[33] Fish, 29; cf. p. 59; Dickinson, *Sermon*, 21-22.
[34] Lee, *Sermon*, 10.

born men shared their love for God with each other, and the whole of gracious society fell into harmony.

Apart from the theological splendor of the vision, the practical results were eminently satisfying. One of the pleasing prospects, Jonathan Lee remarked in an election sermon, was "the happy tendency of vital piety, to heal the maladies and rectify the disorders of the church of Christ, in its present militant state." Another was "the blessed tendency of vital piety to happify the civil state." God's grace working in man "would either prevent all occasion of complaints, or compose the minds, and calm the tempers of murmuring complainers, and malecontents in the state." [35] "Malice and envy" disappear from the towns, Bellamy exclaimed; the governor "is loved, revered, and obeyed by all his people, who live under him as one united, happy family." "Meanwhile," he continued joyously, "peace and plenty, universal love and harmony, reign from town to town, through all the province, through all the kingdom, yea, through all the kingdoms of the earth, where righteousness thus prevails." [36]

While not denying the efficacy of grace, the hardheaded doubted that Bellamy had grounds for erecting a social order on the new birth in one town much less "through all the kingdoms of the earth." During the revival, when grace supposedly inundated the colony, society was more often riven than united. True grace might indeed join pious hearts in love and brotherhood, but it was too rare and too easily counterfeited to cement a society composed largely of unregenerates. Old Lights and many New Lights as well were dubious of Edwards' proposal to create even one church of true saints. An entire society of reborn men was out of the question. Such dreams seemed practical only for those New Lights who believed in the imminent return of Christ and the organization of a millenial society.

More worldly individuals, the rationalists of their generation, felt that it was useless and probably unnecessary to fight human nature and preferred to construct a society frankly founded on self interest. Even the radical New Light Gilbert Tennent conceded that God

[35] Lee, 13, 16, 17.
[36] *Works*, 584-585. For an extensive discussion of these ideas, Heimert, *Religion and the American Mind*.

had planted an instinct in all creatures "to see after the greater natural Good" and to deny the instinct was "contrary to common Sense, as well as Religion." [37] A later preacher bluntly declared that "the principle of self-love alone, will engage men to that obedience to good rulers, by which their own happiness may be promoted, and secured." [38] The notion was not foreign to the Puritan tradition. Gurdon Saltonstall long before had asserted that the obvious benefits of government plant "a willingness and Disposition in the most, to submit to those Powers that God in his Providence placeth over them." [39] The property qualification for voting rested on the conviction that society served the interests of property owners who could therefore be trusted with a voice in government. These older ideas were reinforced when Locke's contractual theory of government gained currency at mid-century. Elisha Williams felt no compunctions in arguing that "it must be for their own Sakes, the rendering their Condition better than it was in what is called a State of Nature . . . that Men would willingly put themselves out of that State. It is nothing but *their own Good* can be any rational Inducement to it." [40] Those who accepted Locke's theories explicitly or implicitly affirmed that men formed the civilized state in pursuit of naked self-interest.

This argument implied the right to revolt as well as the obligation to obey. If the people judged their liberties violated, they could resist authority. But the rationalists refused to abandon the argument because political rebels misused it. Since liberties were safe only under law and authority, "when a People therefore grow uneasy under Government, and endeavour to overthrow the foundations of it; they are like a Pond that being weary of Confinement, contends for Liberty with the Dam upon which it depends for it's very Existence." [41] Rationalists were convinced that government did benefit the people and that obedience would be forthcoming if only the truth were made plain. Their encomia of Connecticut's polity drove home the moral that the colony's blessings carried the obligation of loyalty. "No one Government under

[37] *The Danger*, 12-13.
[38] Salter, *Sermon*, 28.
[39] *Sermon*, 4-5.
[40] E. Williams, *Essential Rights*, 4-5; cf. Lord, 1-3.
[41] Dickinson, *Sermon*, 7.

Heaven enjoyes greater, or better Privileges than we do," one preacher proudly declared, "if we may have Wisdom to know and use them well." [42] Therefore the people "Choosing our Rulers from among ourselves," men "so much an Honour to their Station, and a Blessing to the People; concerned for the Cause of God, and the Public Good," were under peculiar obligations "to live quiet and peaceable Lives in all Godliness and Honesty, paying a just Deference" to their rulers.[43] This appeal to self-interest was an effort to confute those who confused liberty with license.

Most of these preachers thought of self-interest in traditional terms: protecting personal and property rights, punishing vice and encouraging virtue—in short, maintaining the peace and good order of society.[44] Some rationalists, however, propounded a distinctly new definition of self-interest. Instead of limiting themselves to seventeenth-century values, they recognized that economic expansion had generated vital new concerns having to do more with trade and agriculture than morality. If the state supported these interests, which had led to turmoil in the first place, people might very well sustain government. "Civil government was originally instituted to protect and defend men's lives and liberties," a pastor began conventionally enough in 1765 but then added, "and promote their temporal interests and advantages." [45] Along with the punishment of injustice and the safeguarding of religion, the preacher of 1768 admonished the good ruler to give his attention to "whatever is useful and beneficial to society." "Agriculture will be encouraged, till the wilderness become a fruitful field, and the desart blossom as the rose. Trade so nearly connected therewith, as the second source of wealth, will be protected and cherished, that his own community may have riches and plenty from other parts of the globe, as well as their own." [46] Another minister told the Assembly "to shew Compassion to the Common-People under all their Wants and Grievances; and be ready to afford all reasonable Encouragements to every thing found among them laudable and commend-

[42] Beckwith, *That People,* 57; cf. Welles, *Patriotism,* 29.

[43] Throop, *Religion,* 36-37; cf. White, *Civil Rulers,* 25.

[44] Hobart, *Civil Government,* 6-23; E. Whitman, *The Character,* 18-25; S. Hall, 11; Todd, *Civil Rulers,* 8-23; Hunn, *Welfare,* 9; Worthington, *Duty of Rulers,* 7-10.

[45] Dorr, *Duty,* 17.

[46] Salter, 24; cf. Jonathan Ingersoll, *Sermon,* 40; Devotion, *Civil Ruler,* 48.

able," an obvious plea in 1761 to support the Susquehannah Company.[47]

These appeals to self-interest offended many New Lights. The rationalists seemed to be enlarging the role of self-love in society to monstrous proportions. No objection could be made to enumerating the blessings of government as an incentive to obedience so long as government was acknowledged to rest on God's desire and authority; but the rationalists who made the satisfaction of human desires the main end of government seemed to think that self-interest, if enlightened, could be given a free rein and made the very foundation of civil society.

The New Divinity men regarded this indulgence of self-interest as a dangerous and un-Christian attempt to reconcile egotistical impulses with the good of the whole. Religious experiences committed them to a total subjection of the human will to God. The retention of prideful desires in any form was a devilish scheme to prevent the abasement that had to precede rebirth. Bellamy and later Hopkins elaborated the theme that the only true virtue was a wholly disinterested benevolence. Even Clap repudiated vehemently the principle, which he considered the hallmark of the Arminian heretics, that "the only End and Design of the Creation is the Happiness of the Creature." "For a Man to make the *sole, supreme,* or *ultimate End* of all Being and Action to be for *himself alone* or his *own* Happiness," Clap thundered, "is the most absolute Inversion of the *Order, Dignity* and *Perfection* of Beings: and one of the worst Principles that can be in human Nature." [48]

Clap found a limited place for the "Principles of *Self-Love* or a *Ballance of Self-Interest*" in social life. As human laws, they could "keep the World from many hurtful Disorders," [49] but ardent New Divinity men were not so tolerant. "Irregular and inordinate self-love, and private interest, have so much dominion in the heart," one commented, "that unless true benevolence, and public spirit prevent, there is eminent danger that private interest will be pursued, at the expence, or built on the ruins of the public weal." [50] Few were as adamant as the New Divinity men in eschewing every

[47] Jonathan Ingersoll, 21.
[48] Clap, *Brief History*, 19; *Essay on Moral Virtue*, 19-20, 23, 16.
[49] *Essay on Moral Virtue*, 16.
[50] Lee, 7.

form of self-love, but many like Clap felt that self-interest must
be mortified. "A narrow, contracted and selfish Spirit, is pernicious
to the *State*," was an oft-repeated sentiment.[51] If "particular Interest must be the Standard by which, to measure the public Good,"
a moderate commented, "this is Mischievous to Society," and returns men to the state of nature.[52]

These objections prevented the rationalists from subscribing as
fully to the theory of self-interest as some New Lights accused
them of doing. In 1765 confidence in the natural harmonies of the
universe were not well enough established to permit the belief
that unfettered self-interest could work for the good of the whole.
The rationalists always tempered their position by acknowledging
that the public good must take precedence. Fortunately, they argued, individual well-being was too fully interwoven with the good
of all the society, for the two to be separated. "If therefore a
principle of self-love, prompts us to seek our own particular
happiness, because it is ours," Noah Welles observed, "the same
principle must induce us to love our country and seek its welfare,
because our own is involved in it, and inseperably connected with
it. And thus even from self-love and a desire of happiness, we are
directed to seek the good of the public." Self-interest was not as
brutal and destructive as was commonly supposed. "Though patriotism has its origin in self-love, and is ever consistent with it;
yet it is widely different from, or rather directly opposite to the
principle that commonly goes under that name." [53] Thus understood, self-love mght very well cement the social order.

Of course, Welles could expect concurrence when in 1763 he
redefined public good or patriotism to include concrete everyday
economic interest. Whereas public good at the beginning of the
century had implied the denial of private interests for the sake of
more transcendent values, it now contained the promise also that
government would serve private interests. The civil authority was
to act as the public's agent and not merely as its disciplinarian.
The colony was on its way to becoming a commonwealth in the
sense the town had once been.

[51] Lockwood, *Religion,* 28.
[52] Lord, 48; cf. Fish, 51.
[53] Welles, 8-10.

All three of these proposals—the Anglican, the New Divinity, and the rationalist—retained to a large degree the spirit of the older conception of the social order. The purpose of all three was to keep peace and order in society and to restrain human wilfulness. The New Divinity men were among the most avid proponents of rigid sumptuary legislation. Before the General Assembly Bellamy asked that "the Lord be with you in your attempts to suppress vice and immorality. And let that man be severely punished that shall dare to resist you." [54] Behind their justification of self-interest the rationalists were just as eager that contention cease. After declaring that public spirit grew out of self-love, Welles went on to declare that "public-spirit will totally extirpate the malignant seeds of disaffection and disobedience to authority,—crush the spirit of sedition and rebellion, and cultivate and cherish the true principles of loyalty, submission and peace." [55] The Anglicans rested all their hopes on the power of law and authority to subdue the factious.

Yet even the Anglicans, the most authoritarian of the three, were compelled to make concessions to popular will. Comforting a new clergyman who was appalled at the perversity of his Connecticut parishioners, Samuel Johnson acknowledged that "the spirit of liberty beats high in their veins, beyond what Europe ever knew." He hoped, however, that the new pastor would "make as large a stretch of candor as possible to comport with it. For the truth is," Johnson admitted a little ashamedly, "we can do little or no good to people here unless we do all we can to keep them in a good humor." [56]

The New Divinity men were quite forthright in explaining that the social order they envisioned was to be voluntary. Divine grace, after all, subdued whatever was "contrary to the divine will" and the soul then stood ready to conform to good principles "in a free, voluntary manner." After rebirth men obeyed not through "slavish fears of penal evil," nor "the force of law, so much as divine love." In this spirit, "people are voluntary in doing well," and

[54] *Works,* I, 594.
[55] *Patriotism,* 19-20.
[56] To Matthew Graves, June 27, 1748, Samuel Johnson, *Samuel Johnson,* I, 133.

"coercive measures are needless." [57] A free society was superior to one based on law and authority both in point of order and in the joy of the people.

The rationalists were still more daring. They carefully hedged the concept of self-interest, urging that it must be rational and subservient to the public good. They did not foresee a complete release of either acquisitive or enthusiastic impulses, but their proposed social order did not await a religious revival. Freedom of impulse was not restricted to those who laid some claim to grace. The role given to self-interest could easily be used as a justification by those who wanted to give freer rein to their desires. Later generations may have misconstrued the initial purpose of the rationalists' social theory, but the posthumous judgment that their conceptions paved the way to larger liberty was essentially correct.

Mixing these varying measures of voluntarism with traditional conceptions of law and authority necessarily altered the relationship of ruler and subject. The familiar belief in the derivation of political authority from God was still repeated but with a new meaning. Emphasis shifted from the subject's obligation to obey to the ruler's obligation to serve. The first election sermon preacher with New Light sympathies made a radical break in 1748 when he observed that the Assembly had listened to "frequent Discourses" showing how the civil rulers were "cloathed with Authority from the great Governour of the World" and had often "heard the People put in mind to be subject to Principalities and Powers, to obey Magistrates." It was time to hear of the obligations the investiture of divine authority placed on the ruler.[58] A later preacher was impressed that, "notwithstanding the People are Subjected to the civil Ruler, by divine Appointment yet if we consider their mutual Relation, the mutual Duties of the Relation, do of Course, and necessarily Arise." This preacher emphasized the ruler's duties "toward the Subjects of his Care." " 'Tis with Respect to those," the minister emphasized, "that his Vigilance, Care, Pains, and Talents, are to be employ'd in General, to seek and promote their Good." [59] Belief in the divine source of civil authority made demands on

[57] Lee, 11, 20.
[58] N. Eells, *Wise Ruler,* 1-2.
[59] A. Woodbridge, 8-9.

rulers as well as on subjects. Like the concept of liberty, a commission from God was a two-edged sword.[60]

The new stress on the ruler's obligation carried the implication that civil authority should respond to public needs. The rulers now heard that they were to pass such laws "as the General State of the People calls for; and to make such Changes as experience and observation teaches is necessary, or the change in the Circumstances of a People require." [61] Not Olympian considerations of justice and order, but "experience and observation" were to guide legislators. Besides the customary knowledge of the moral condition of the people, rulers were instructed to learn about "the methods of best increasing the numbers and wealth of the subjects," how to make "their necessary burthens more easy and equal," and how to "encourage their trade, husbandry and manufactures." [62] The ruler was a helper as much as a disciplinarian.

In some minds the helping functions overshadowed all others. One preacher suggested that rulers' power derived almost wholly from the capacity to serve. "The most likely, and the only rational, and scriptural way of gaining and securing" confidence and obedience was "for the magistrate to . . . pursue the common good and happiness of the subject." [63] During the Stamp Act crisis a Connecticut newspaper quoted approvingly an article that first appeared in Boston which argued that respect for rulers depended on their "pursuing the true and common interests of the nation or people they govern." [64]

Implicit in all these pronouncements was dislike of magisterial aloofness. Men received high stations in life not to please their vanity but to serve. An election sermon preacher frankly told the magistrates that government "was not appointed, that some Men might enjoy Riches, Dignity, and Power above others, exclusive of the good of the Public . . . That some might *be clothed in Purple, and fine Linen, and fare sumptuously every Day; while others must be fed with the Crumbs that fall from the Table.* No;

[60] White; Jonathan Ingersoll.

[61] White, 12.

[62] Salter, 13; cf. Devotion, *Election Sermon,* 26; excerpt from the *Connecticut Gazette* in the *Connecticut Courant,* Sept. 9, 1765.

[63] Salter, 26-27.

[64] *Connecticut Courant,* Sept. 9, 1765.

Societies were not formed for the sake of Rulers, but Rulers were made for the sake of Societies." [65] Another minister despised the rulers who took "Occasion from their advanc'd Station, to nurse false Conceptions of themselves, to feed their Vanity, and think themselves more than mortal Gods." It was sad, he thought, when "they grow giddy and look down from their Elevation with Contempt upon the rest of Mankind, as Creatures made only for their Service, and to bear Burthens." [66] Such declarations, delivered publicly, revealed that awe for exalted positions was waning. People might still believe a ruler to be above them, but they did not want him out of reach.

How far the prerogatives of rulers had been curtailed was measured precisely in Jared Ingersoll's encounter with the eastern vigilantes in 1765. Ingersoll was one of the most promising of the younger gentlemen in the colony. At Yale, where he graduated in 1742, he was a prize scholar, and soon after completing his study of the law, he was acknowledged to have a brilliant future. His abilities and close association with the Old Light rulers of the colony won him the appointment as King's Attorney in 1751. In 1763 he was chosen along with William Samuel Johnson to prosecute the case against Clap in the General Assembly. In 1758 and again in 1764 the colony selected him to represent them in London. In 1765 the governor was his close friend. Both in his own and in the public mind, Ingersoll was one of the gentlemen, prepared to rule by birth, experience, and natural talents.[67]

The calumny directed at him for accepting the Stamp Act commission shocked but did not intimidate Ingersoll. It was hard, he admitted to an English friend, to be insulted by the mob, "yet I keep up my Spirits and preserve, I think, as good Degree of Philosophic Fortitude." After all, he was bred to the conviction that the people were usually mistaken and rulers must shape policy regardless of popular feeling. "Let them say what they please of me here or there, Truth shall be my Guide, and dictate all I say and do." [68]

[65] Dickinson, *Sermon,* 6.
[66] Devotion, *Election Sermon,* 38.
[67] Biographical information in Gipson.
[68] Jared Ingersoll, *Mr. Ingersoll's Letters,* 48, 8.

Confident of his personal superiority, Ingersoll did not flinch when he received the report in September that three parties of eastern men were on the road to intercept him as he journeyed to Hartford for the General Assembly. He calmly sent instructions to his household to prepare to defend his property, remembering what had happened to Oliver in Boston. Then he readied himself to set out alone, though at the last minute two friends insisted on accompanying him. When 500 mounted men carrying white staves met him just south of Wethersfield, he coolly assured them he had no intention of escaping. When they gathered around him in the town square, he began at once to address them, assuming command without even hearing their demands. After he was told point blank that he must resign, he brashly asked, "What if I wont resign?" One daring soul replied, *"Your Fate."* Angered by the presumption of this threat, Ingersoll boldly announced that he could die "and perhaps as well now as another Time." [69] The mob leaders well knew the strength of his character and, embarrassed by the effrontery of the crowd, led Ingersoll into a nearby tavern for further talk. There they repeatedly assured him that no damage would be done to his estate and that they would treat him as a gentleman. They "behaved with Moderation and Civility," Ingersoll reported, and seemed ready to negotiate rather than to deliver an ultimatum. Face to face with Ingersoll inside the tavern, the committee was no match for him. They accepted his compromise proposals, and only the obstinacy of the crowd in rejecting the agreements prevented his release. Groups of men bursting into the room from the larger party outside made peremptory demands for resignation, but the leaders were not so bold. They fell back on the greater resolution of the crowd to persuade Ingersoll, telling him violence impended despite all the committee could do if he would not relent. The size of the party sent to intercept Ingersoll—and he probably met only a third of the total group that set out—gave each individual member courage to stand up to the gentleman.

A wave of relief swept over the crowd when Ingersoll finally announced his resignation, for the strain of resisting so eminent a figure had been distinctly uncomfortable. A number of persons

[69] Jared Ingersoll, *Mr. Ingersoll's Letters,* 64; the entire episode is related on pp. 61-68.

rushed up to shake his hand and assure him of their friendship. Ingersoll was known to be close to the governor and was a prominent official as well. In opposing him, the party had taken on the whole of established civil authority, an encounter they could not well bear alone.

Yet *en masse* they had resisted him, and their will had prevailed. The threat of tyrannical imposition on their liberties had raised the ire of these common men. As one of the party put it, "they lookt upon this as the Cause of the People, and . . . did not intend to take Directions about it from any Body." [70] They compelled Ingersoll to give three cheers for liberty and property and to toss his hat in the air. Seemingly humbled as well as humiliated, Ingersoll repeated over and over in later letters that he had never intended to contradict the minds of the people. His capitulation in the face of tremulous but determined popular wilfulness foreshadowed the fate of his whole class.

The testy independence of these protestants was akin to a quality later manifested in Thoreau, a quality more characteristic of Yankees than Puritans. The eastern Connecticut men were not disdainful or unconscious of authority. Their painful sensitivity to tyranny was evidence of the grip rulers still held. But Yankees in 1765 found courage to oppose each threatening move from above. Puritan resistance characteristically turned inward and produced guilt; Yankee resistance more often turned outward and produced conflict. The New Lights, acknowledged champions of popular liberties after the Stamp Act crisis, inveighed against the old doctrines of "passive obedience and non-resistance to what is called the divine right of magistracy in general, or of kings in particular." Only "abject minds of subjects, lost to all vertue and honor," they said, would tamely yield. People who responded to authority with the promise, "all that thou has said, we will do, and will be obedient," one New Light observed, obeyed out of "a slavish dread, and brutal subjection," while inwardly secret suspicions destroyed all veneration and love.[71] The Yankee claimed more liberty for himself and allowed less power to authority, reacting violently and

[70] Jared Ingersoll, *Mr. Ingersoll's Letters,* 62.
[71] Salter, 25-26.

quickly to the least oppression. It took considerably less to bring on a war of rebellion in 1775 than in 1689.

By 1765 the Yankee spirit had replaced the Puritan in other ways. Besides a passionate independence, the familiar avarice and shrewdness also characterized the Connecticut temperament. The avid pursuit of gain, partly condemned in 1690, was largely acceptable in 1765. The rulers, having failed to contain ambition, accommodated it; land was provided for crowded farmers and money for nascent capitalists, and when the turmoil accompanying expansion showed no signs of subsiding, many thinkers found an honorable place for self-interest in the social order. Once his ambitions were given respectability, the Yankee was at liberty to employ his skill at sharp dealing without fear of recrimination. By 1765 the door was open for a release of the cupidity that was in time to bring him such notoriety.

He was not at perfect liberty of course. The other side of Yankee avarice was philanthropy. The ancestral injunction to serve the public good no longer restrained the conduct of business as the Puritans had intended, but it directed profits toward charitable ends. Yankee enterprisers never wholly lost sight of the larger society. A remnant of Puritan conscience demanded that some portion of their energy and treasure go toward the common good.

One recessive trait, a hidden yearning for union with God, reappeared in the eighteenth century and stayed with Yankees for more than a century. While the first Puritans had experienced this longing frequently, later generations lost it in their obsession with law and authority. The Awakening revived the mystic spirit, which the writings of David Brainerd and Jonathan Edwards captured for posterity insofar as words could. Not many Yankees could make themselves, like Edwards, "to lie low before God, as in the dust," that they might "be nothing, and that God might be ALL"; but they stopped to listen when they heard a prophet speak in that strain.[72] Emerson held his audiences in his generation, and the elder Henry James fascinated the most critical observer, his own son. William's acknowledged inability to find the central mechanism of the mystical encounter with God even after examin-

[72] J. Edwards, *Jonathan Edwards,* 64.

ing it microscopically was probably just what attracted so many Yankee readers to *The Varieties of Religious Experience*.

The mystic strain never became dominant. Many listened to Emerson, but few followed him. For the most part a pungent respect for tangible fact ruled Yankee thinking in religion as in business and science. The release of feeling in rare moments of holy exaltation was most often succeeded by a return to reasoned control. Only the popularity of an occasional oracle attested the continued presence of a New Light soul under the Old Light demeanor. The Yankee's religious character, like his attitudes toward authority and wealth, is best described as a polarity.

Each of these traits—a defensive independence, cupidity tempered by regard for the public good, and yearning for the divine underlying hardheaded rationalism—was securely embedded in the cultural genes of the generation alive in 1765. No sudden mutation had caused them to appear. Each in its way was the release of an impulse present but checked in 1690. But the Yankee, if far from wholly liberated, was a much freer man than his Puritan progenitors, for he could acknowledge to himself and to the world more of what he was. Fewer impulses hid below the surface in fear of punishment. His social institutions were less confining, more easily escaped, more responsive to individual wishes. In politics, religion, and the economy human energies enjoyed a wider field of play.

This release of energy transformed the quality of Connecticut life. In the century after the Revolution Yankee society produced a flowering of individualism, a magnificent display of economic and artistic virtuosity. Yankees also learned the sorrows of rootlessness —fear, guilt, and loneliness. The light and the dark both were fruits of the liberty wrested in the eighteenth century from the Puritan social order.

Appendixes
Bibliographical Note
List of Works Cited
Index

Towns and Parishes, 1680—1760

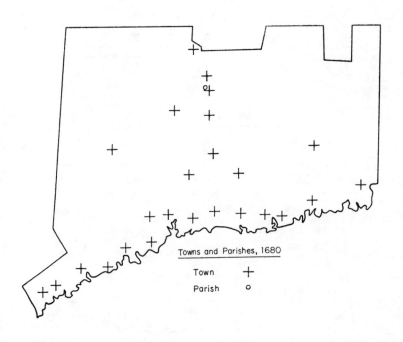

Towns and Parishes, 1680

Town   +

Parish   o

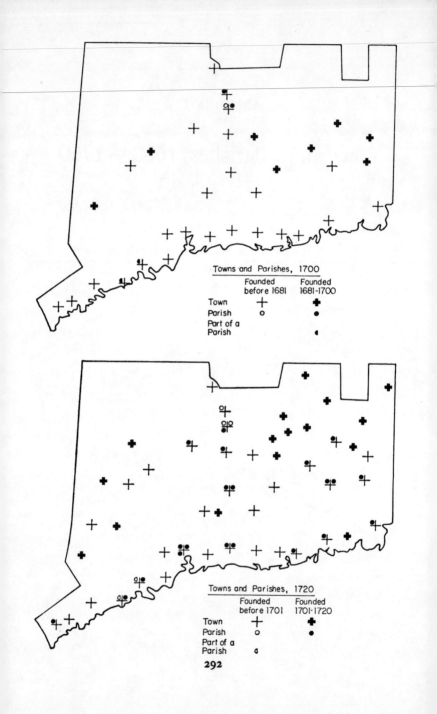

Towns and Parishes, 1700

	Founded before 1681	Founded 1681-1700
Town	+	✛
Parish	o	●
Part of a Parish		◖

Towns and Parishes, 1720

	Founded before 1701	Founded 1701-1720
Town	+	✛
Parish	o	●
Part of a Parish	◖	

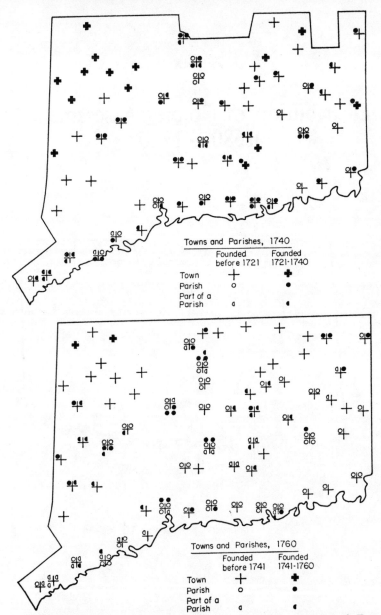

Towns and Parishes, 1740

	Founded before 1721	Founded 1721-1740
Town	+	✚
Parish	○	●
Part of a Parish	◖	◗

Towns and Parishes, 1760

	Founded before 1741	Founded 1741-1760
Town	+	✚
Parish	○	●
Part of a Parish	◖	◗

Source: Connecticut Historical Society, *List of Congregational Ecclesiastical Societies; Conn. Recs.* (For five charts above.)

293

Distribution of Colony Assessments
1680—1760

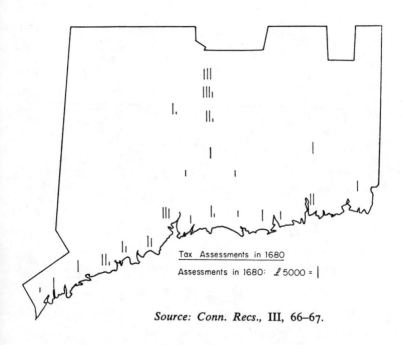

Tax Assessments in 1680

Assessments in 1680: £5000 = |

Source: Conn. Recs., III, 66–67.

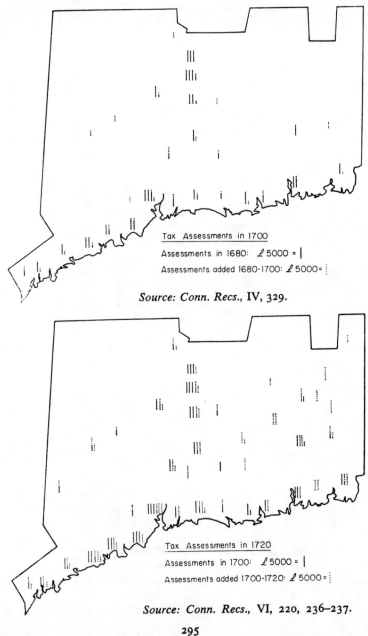

Tax Assessments in 1700

Assessments in 1680: £5000 = |

Assessments added 1680-1700: £5000 = ⁞

Source: Conn. Recs., **IV,** 329.

Tax Assessments in 1720

Assessments in 1700: £5000 = |

Assessments added 1700-1720: £5000 = ⁞

Source: Conn. Recs., **VI,** 220, 236–237.

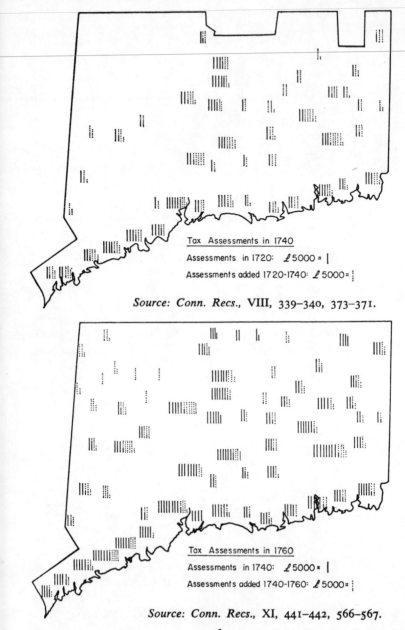

Tax Assessments in 1740

Assessments in 1720: £5000 = |

Assessments added 1720-1740: £5000 = ⦙

Source: Conn. Recs., VIII, 339–340, 373–371.

Tax Assessments in 1760

Assessments in 1740: £5000 = |

Assessments added 1740-1760: £5000 = ⦙

Source: Conn. Recs., XI, 441–442, 566–567.

Debt Cases in County Courts
1700—1730

Connecticut as a whole

Annual number of cases per
thousand of population

Annual value of debts sued for
per thousand of population[1]

County comparisons

Annual number of debt cases

Annual value of debts sued for[1]

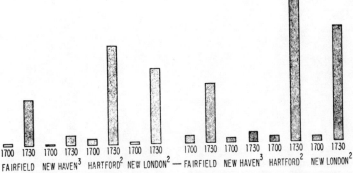

[1] Values in 1730 are adjusted for 225% inflation since 1700. (Bronson, "Currency," p. 52.)

[2] For comparative purposes, cases in Windham County (organized 1726) are divided between Hartford and New London in proportion to the area of Windham formerly in those counties.

[3] The number and value of cases in New Haven in 1730 are inexplicably low. Figures for the years before and after 1730 were in roughly the same range.

Bibliographical Note

Bibliographic information on Connecticut economic history can be found in Weaver, *Jonathan Trumbull,* and on the colony's political history after 1750, when political publications began to appear, in Zeichner, *Connecticut's Years of Controversy.* This note focuses on the materials useful for a social history of Connecticut in the first half of the eighteenth century.

PRIMARY SOURCES

Manuscripts

The richest depository of manuscripts is in the Connecticut State Library in Hartford. The petitions, resolutions, and other documents connected with the work of the General Assembly have been carefully preserved in bound volumes called Connecticut Archives. These are divided into groups, such as Ecclesiastical Affairs, Towns and Lands, and Trade and Maritime Affairs, and the documents are filed in roughly chronological order. Each series is minutely indexed by subject, place, and every individual name appearing in any of the documents.

The State Library also contains a hoard of local records. The extent and condition of these in the Library and throughout the state was surveyed in 1906 by Mead in "Public Archives of Connecticut." Since then many of the records previously held in the towns have been collected into the Library. All of the County Court records for the period to 1765 are there, and though not indexed, they contain a bounty for the patient researcher. All of the land records which are kept in the town—deeds, mortgages, and exchanges—have been microfilmed by the Church of Jesus Christ of Latter-day Saints and deposited in the Library. These records are fully indexed according to grantor and grantee. The Library now also has a large sampling of town meeting and proprietor records, though the bulk of these remain in the town clerks' offices. The Library is trying to collect early ecclesiastical records, both those of society meetings and of the pastors' records of discipline cases. Many churches that have been unwilling to deposit their records have lent them to the Library to be microfilmed. The Journals of the Upper and Lower Houses of the Assembly are extant for the years from 1708 to 1736 and 1738, respectively.

Information on individuals is available through the probate records, which now with a very few exceptions are all stored in the State Library. The archivists have also indexed all the genealogical information from town records in a master card catalogue and compiled other genealogical catalogues on church, Bible, and gravestone records. The State Library has a relatively small collection of personal account books.

A much larger collection is in the Connecticut Historical Society in Hartford conveniently catalogued chronologically. The Society also has the interesting "Narrative" of Roger Wolcott. The diaries and memoirs of Isaac Backus, who began his clerical career as a Separate in Norwich, are located in the Andover Newton Theological School Library in Newton Center, Massachusetts. The Nott "Life" is in Congregational House, Hartford, as are many of the records of county associations and consociations.

Printed Materials

At the forefront of the published official records are *The Public Records of the Colony of Connecticut. The Book of General Laws* for 1673 is also useful since it contains some statutes that do not appear in the public records. The official correspondence of Governors Talcott, Law, and Wolcott has been published by the Connecticut Historical Society, and much of Governor Fitz-John Winthrop's official correspondence is included in *The Winthrop Papers,* published by the Massachusetts Historical Society. The Winthrop papers are especially useful because they include personal letters, often more revealing than formal documents. Unfortunately, the correspondence of Governor Saltonstall is not collected, though various of his state papers are scattered through the Connecticut Archives, especially Civil Officers. Some town records have been published, such as *Hartford Town Votes,* and *Town Records of Derby. The Susquehannah Company Papers* help to clarify the situation of farmers in the 1750's.

A selection of printed papers and journals of individuals shed light on Connecticut history from various social perspectives. *The Wyllys Papers,* a collection of personal and official documents chiefly connected with George Wyllys, an early governor, and his descendants, help to recreate the life of an aristocratic colonial family in the seventeenth and early eighteenth centuries. A mid-eighteenth-century governor reminisced about his life in Wolcott, *Memoir.* The view from a less exalted station may be had in the *Diary* of Joshua Hempstead, a selectman and deputy from New London, and in the *Diary* of Manasseh Minor, a deacon in Stonington at the turn of the century. The vicissitudes of a conservative Hartford minister in the 1730's and 1740's are illustrated in Wadsworth, *Diary*. The revival mentality at its highest pitch finds expression in Brainerd, *Life,* and at a lower level in Hopkins, *Sketches.* The *Extracts* and the *Literary Diary* of Ezra Stiles are an important source for the opinions of a moderate Old Light and his friends after the Awakening. Views of a conservative lawyer are found in Jared Ingersoll, "A Selection from the Correspondence." Samuel Johnson's despair over Connecticut's decay and his campaign to strengthen episcopacy can be observed in the collection of his writings, *Samuel Johnson.* Long excerpts from the diary of a poor farm boy, Solomon Mack, who participated in the French and Indian Wars, accumulating and losing a number of small fortunes, are found in Bennett, "Mack."

The great bulk of the literature from the pens of Connecticut men before 1745 was sermons. Among the notable exceptions are the tracts written by Gershom Bulkeley, after the restoration of charter government in 1690, and the rebuttals of the colonial rulers. The most important of this group is Bulkeley's *Will and Doom,* one of the few publications in this period that offers a glimpse into the inner workings of Connecticut politics. The only other nonreligious publication was Roger Wolcott's *Poetical Meditations,* which appeared in 1725 with an illuminating introduction by John Bulkley. There are also interesting exchanges between Anglicans and Congregationalists, and a few tracts on the Baptists, Rogerenes, and Quakers got into print. The rest of the literature until 1740 is mainly election sermons, ordination and funeral sermons, and sermons delivered on noteworthy occasions like a fast, a catastrophe, or a parish controversy.

The Awakening widened the scope of the ministers' concerns and multiplied the occasions for publishing their sermons. More nonreligious works appeared after 1740 too. Jared Eliot began his *Essays on Field Husbandry* in 1748, and in 1755 Gale published his frankly political pamphlet, *The Present State of the Colony,* which elicited Clap's reply in kind and led to a series of skirmishes between the partisans of their parties. From the middle of the 1750's, newspapers become an important source for every aspect of history. A guide to their locations may be found in Zeichner, pp. 365-366.

Each researcher must plunge into the listings of eighteenth-century publications to find for himself what he wants. In J. H. Trumbull, *List of Books Printed in Connecticut, 1709-1800,* and Bates, *Supplementary List of Books Printed in Connecticut, 1709-1800,* there is a beginning. These two have the disadvantage of listing books by author rather than by date, but there is an index by years at the back of both. They also do not give a complete picture of the total output of Connecticut, for many ministers published in Boston and New York. These two aids, therefore, must be supplemented by Evans, *American Bibliography.* The problem here is to sift out the works of Connecticut men from the rest of the American imprints. Anyone bent on obtaining a comprehensive listing might go far toward compiling it by checking the names of the colony's clergy listed in Weis, *Colonial Clergy,* against Evans. Evans is useful for the researcher with a special interest because works are indexed by subject. The pamphlets on the Wallingford controversy, for example, are under Theology, Church History, Wallingford.

Anyone wishing to go beyond the microprints published by the American Antiquarian Society to the originals will find the largest collection of Connecticut sermons in the Connecticut Historical Society. Besides listing a given sermon under the author's name and residence, the catalog contains a chronological file of the sermons of a given type, such as funeral or ordination sermons.

Connecticut merchants were not as rabid or as frank as men from other colonies on the subject of currency, but the tracts in *Colonial Currency Reprints* help to reconstruct the general predicament of farmers and traders and the forces bearing on the land bank proposals.

Among the very few source books pertaining to Connecticut before 1765, Samuel Peters' *History of Connecticut* provides a few insights by a prejudiced Anglican writing near the Revolution. There is information on Connecticut in Douglass, *Summary,* and what the unknown author of *American Husbandry* says about New England is largely applicable to Connecticut.

Secondary Works

The best general history of Connecticut in the colonial period is Benjamin Trumbull, *Connecticut,* which focuses on ecclesiastical and military affairs. Since Trumbull was born in 1735 and was himself a New Light, his history gives a clue to partisan attitudes on many questions. Albert E. Van Dusen's *Connecticut* is the most recent complete history of the colony and state. Dunn, *Puritans and Yankees,* relates the involved struggle between Connecticut and her enemies in Massachusetts and England at the beginning of the eighteenth century. Morgan, *The Gentle Puritan,* and Tucker, *Puritan Protagonist,* penetrate political and ecclesiastical history as well as telling the story of Ezra Stiles and Thomas Clap. Heimert, *Religion and the American Mind,* while overemphasizing the political significance of New Divinity theology, is full of valuable insights. Zeichner covers political history after 1765, though he is weak on the influence of religious issues. Bailey, *Influences toward Radicalism,* has been made obsolete by Zeichner, but still contains material not treated elsewhere. N. P. Mead, *Connecticut as a Corporate Colony,* is the best summary of the formal structure of government.

Ecclesiastical affairs have been covered better than any other aspect of Connecticut's colonial history. Besides Benjamin Trumbull's detailed survey, there is M. Louise Greene, *The Development of Religious Liberty,* a work that covers far more than the church-state issue. Each of the dissenting groups has had a historian: Beardsley has written on Anglicanism in *Episcopal Church in Connecticut;* Isaac Backus on the Baptists in *History of New England;* Bolles and Williams on the Rogerenes in *Rogerenes;* and Goen on the Separates in *Revivalism and*

Separatism. The Awakening is described in Tracy, *The Great Awakening,* and in Gaustad, *The Great Awakening.* Byington discusses an episode that involved Connecticut men in "Breck Controversy." Various ecclesiastical topics are treated in an uneven collection of essays, *Contributions to Ecclesiastical History.* A rather sophisticated and interesting essay on theology and religion is G. L. Walker, *Some Aspects of the Religious Life of New England.* His *First Church in Hartford* is one of the best of the many histories of individual churches.

Economic history is less adequately treated. Weaver, *Jonathan Trumbull,* is an immensely valuable study of one merchant family. The great virtue of this work is that it describes commerce in the first half of the eighteenth century. Mercantile activity after 1750 is covered in Martin, *Merchants and Trade,* and Hooker, *Colonial Trade.* The details of currency issues and of loan policies are given in Bronson, "Historical Account." The history of the New London Society for Trade and Commerce is related in A. M. Davis, "A Connecticut Land Bank." Bidwell and Falconer, *History of American Agriculture,* contains much that is pertinent to Connecticut, as does Walcott, "Husbandry in Colonial New England," a study that concentrates on the seventeenth century. More specific for Connecticut, is Olson, *Agricultural Economy.* The sequence of settlement and some of the complications that arose in individual towns are described in Deming, *Settlement of Connecticut,* and *Settlement of Litchfield County.* Garvan, *Architecture and Town Planning,* explains in detail the origins and forms of settlement patterns in the Connecticut wilderness. Charles S. Grant, *Democracy in the Connecticut Frontier Town of Kent,* sheds a great deal of light on land speculation, absentee ownership, and town meeting democracy in one eighteenth-century town.

Town and county histories have been much maligned. Anyone going to them in the expectation of finding a connected story of development will be disappointed They will also frustrate the researcher looking for information on some special topic. Indexes are poor and some of the histories even lack a table of contents But a patient page-by-page study will reveal a vast collection of information that can be shaped to the reader's own categories of significance. The antiquarian temperament of the local historians compelled them to include sections on virtually everything that turned up in the ancient records, from the purchase of an organ for the meetinghouse to the names of those receiving lots in the periodic distributions of land. Among the many town histories of note, the ones most useful for this study were: Andrews, *River Towns* (a useful modern analysis); S. W. Adams and Stiles, *Wethersfield;* Beach, *Cheshire;* Bronson, *Waterbury;* Caulkins, *Norwich,* and *New London;* Cothren, *Woodbury;* C. Davis, *Wallingford;* Federal Writers' Project, *Milford* (not as helpful as the antiquarian studies); Fowler, *Durham;* Edwin Hall, *Norwalk;* Judd, *Hadley;* Labaree, *Milford* (concentrates on land distribution); Love, *Hartford;* Orcutt, *Stratford,* and

New Milford; Schenck, *Fairfield;* Steiner, *Guilford;* and H. R. Stiles, *Windsor.* Larned, *Windham,* is far and away the most useful county history, but Hurd, *New London County,* and J. H. Trumbull, *Hartford County,* have occasional bright spots. Crofut, *Guide to the History,* is a massive, unannotated bibliography to the secondary literature of local history.

The paucity of information on origins has discouraged biography, but a few books and a larger number of articles have appeared on various figures. Along with the works by Morgan and Tucker already mentioned, those that contributed most to this work were: Blake, "Saltonstall"; Boardman, *Roger Sherman;* Groce, "Benjamin Gale"; Dexter, "Thomas Clap"; Gipson, *Jared Ingersoll;* Hovey, *Isaac Backus;* J. Trumbull, *Jonathan Trumbull;* and Parsons, "Elisha Williams."

Anyone compiling a bibliography of Connecticut should be sure to consult the collection of pamphlets published as part of Connecticut's tercentenary celebration by the Tercentenary Commission of the State of Connecticut.

List of Works Cited

Activities of the Puritan Faction of the Church of England, 1625–33, edited and with an introduction by I. M. Calder (London, 1957).

Adams, Eliphalet, *A Discourse Shewing That so long as there is any Prospect of a Sinful People's yielding good Fruit hereafter, there is hope that they may be Spared . . . As it was Delivered at Hartford, May 10, 1733. The Day for the Election of the Governour, Deputy-Governour, and Assistants there* (New London, 1734).

————*The Gracious Presence of Christ with the Ministers of the Gospel, a ground of great Consolation to Them. As it was Represented in a Sermon Preach'd at Groton, On Occasion of the Ordination of the Reverend Mr. John Owen, Pastor of the First Society there* (New London, 1730).

————*A Sermon Preached at Windham, July 12, 1721. On a Day of Thanksgiving for the late remarkable Success of the Gospel Among Them* (New London, 1721).

————*The Work of Ministers, rightly to Divide the Word of Truth. A Sermon Preach'd at the Ordination of the Reverend Mr. William Gager, At Lebanon, May 27th, 1725* (New London, 1725).

Adams, Sherman W., and Henry R. Stiles, *The History of Ancient Wethersfield* (2 vols., New York, 1904).

Akagi, Roy Hidemichi, *The Town Proprietors of the New England Colonies: A Study of Their Development, Organization, Activities and Controversies, 1620–1770* (Philadelphia, 1924).

American Husbandry, ed. Harry J. Carman (New York, 1939).

Andrews, Charles M., *The Beginnings of Connecticut 1632–1662 (Publications of the Tercentenary Commission of the State of Connecticut* [no. 32], New Haven, 1934).

————*The Connecticut Intestacy Law (Publications of the Tercentenary Commission of the State of Connecticut* [no. 2], New Haven, 1933).

————*The River Towns of Connecticut (Johns Hopkins University Studies in Historical and Political Science,* 7th series, nos. 7–9, Baltimore, 1889).

Ashford, Connecticut, "Town Records 1728–1804" (MS, Connecticut State Library, Hartford).

Backus, Ebenezer, "Acct. book of Ebenezer Backus of Norwich, 1744–47" (MS, Connecticut Historical Society, Hartford).

———"Account Book of Ebenezer Backus of Norwich, 1748–50" (MS, Connecticut Historical Society, Hartford).

Backus, Elijah, Account Book of Elijah Backus of Norwich, Conn., 1749–87, marked "Ledger A" (MS, Connecticut State Library, Hartford).

Backus, Elijah, and Joseph Otis, "Elijah Backus and Joseph Otis Their Book, Lager A, 1761–72" (MS, Connecticut State Library, Hartford).

Backus, Isaac, "An Account of the Life of Isaac Backus" (MS, Backus Collection, Andover Newton Theological School, Newton Centre, Mass.).

———*All true Ministers of the Gospel, are called into that Work by the special Influences of the Holy Spirit . . . . Also Marks by which Christ's Ministers may be known from others, and Answers to sundry Objections* (Boston, 1754).

———*A Fish caught in his own Net. An Examination of Nine Sermons, from Matt. 16. 18. Published last Year, by Mr. Joseph Fish of Stonington* (Boston, 1768).

———*A History of New England with Particular Reference to the Denomination of Christians called Baptists*, 2nd ed. with notes by David Weston (2 vols., Newton, Mass., 1871).

———"Isaac Backus's Book—Being Some Account of my Life and of Gods dealings with me" (MS, Backus Collection, Andover Newton Theological School, Newton Centre, Mass).

Bacon, Leonard, *Thirteen Historical Discourses* ([New Haven], 1839).

Bailey, Edith Anna, *Influences Toward Radicalism in Connecticut, 1754–1775* (Smith College Studies in History, V, no. 4, Northampton, 1920).

Bailyn, Bernard, "The *Apologia* of Robert Keayne," *William and Mary Quarterly*, 3rd series, VII (1950), 568–587.

———*The New England Merchants in the Seventeenth Century* (Cambridge, Mass., 1955).

Bailyn, Bernard, and Lotte Bailyn, *Massachusetts Shipping 1697–1714, A Statistical Study* (Cambridge, Mass., 1959).

Baldwin, Alice M., *The New England Clergy and the American Revolution* (Durham, N.C., 1928).

Barnes, Viola F., *The Dominion of New England: A Study in British Colonial Policy* (New York, 1928).

Bartholomew, Andrew, *Some Remarks Upon the Claims and Doings of the Consociation Met at Wallingford, Relative to the Ordination of Mr. Dana. And also upon Some Things written in Defence of said Consociations* (New Haven, 1762).

Bates, Albert Carlos, *Supplementary List of Books Printed in Connecticut, 1709–1800* (n.p., 1938).

Beach, Joseph Perkins, *History of Cheshire, Connecticut from 1694 to 1840* (Cheshire, 1912).

Beardsley, E. Edwards, *The History of the Episcopal Church in Connecticut, From the Settlement of the Colony to the Death of Bishop Seabury*, 2nd ed. (2 vols., New York, 1869).

Beckwith, George, *Christ the Alone Pattern of True Christian Obedience. Two Sermons Preach'd at Lyme, North Society. On the Lord's-Day, Aug. 23d, 1741* (New London, 1742).

———*That People A safe, and happy People, who have God for, and among them. Shewed in a Sermon Preached before the General Assembly of the Colony of Connecticut, May 13th, 1756. Being the Day of the Anniversary Election there* (New London, 1756).

[Bellamy, Joseph], *A Letter to Scripturista; Containing, Some Remarks on His Answer to Paulinus's three Questions: Wherein, The Nature of a Test of Orthodoxy is exactly stated; the Church's Right to know and judge of the religious Principles of those, who are admitted to sealing Ordinances, and reject the Erronious, is asserted; and the Practice of our Churches in New-England, from their first Settlement in this Country, vindicated. And Also Three Questions More, Relative to the new Way of taking Persons into the Church, lately introduced at Wallingford by Mr. Dana stated* (New Haven, 1760).

———*The Works of Joseph Bellamy, First Pastor of the Church in Bethlehem, Conn. with a Memoir of his Life and Character* (2 vols., Boston, 1853).

Bennett, Archibald, "Solomon Mack and His Family," *The Improvement Era*, LVIII, no. 9 (Oct. 1955), to LIX, no. 5 (May 1956).

Benton, Josiah Henry, *Warning Out in New England, 1656–1817* (Boston, 1911).

The Bi-Centennial of the Congregational Society of Green's Farms 1711–1911 (n.p., n.d.).

Bidwell, P. W., and John I. Falconer, *History of Agriculture in the Northern United States, 1620–1860* (Washington, 1925).

Billings, William, *A Warning to God's Covenant People, Against Breaking the Covenant of God they are under* (New London, 1733).

Blake, S. Leroy, "Gurdon Saltonstall, Scholar, Preacher, Statesman," *Records and Papers of the New London County Historical Society*, I, pt. V (1894), 3–28.

———*The Separates or Strict Congregationalists of New England* (Boston, 1902).

Blakely, Quincy, *Farmington, One of the Mother Towns of Connecticut (Publications of the Tercentenary Commission of the State of Connecticut* [no. 38], New Haven, 1935).

Boardman, Roger Sherman, *Roger Sherman, Signer and Statesman* (Philadelphia, 1938).

Bolles, John R., and Anna B. Williams, *The Rogerenes, Some Hitherto*

Unpublished Annals Belonging to the Colonial Society of Connecticut (Boston, 1904).

Bozrah, Connecticut, "Ecclesiastical Society and Congregational Church (Formerly New Concord Society in Norwich), Records, 1737–1845" (3 vols., MS, Connecticut State Library, Hartford).

Bradford, William, *History of Plymouth Plantation 1620–1647,* ed. Worthington C. Ford (2 vols., Boston, 1912).

Brainerd, David, *The Life and Diary of David Brainerd,* ed. Jonathan Edwards (newly edited and with a biographical sketch of President Edwards by Philip E. Howard, Jr. [*Wycliffe Series of Christian Classics,* ed. Wilbur M. Smith, Chicago, 1949]).

Bridgeport, Connecticut, "United Congregational Church (Formerly Stratfield Society), Records 1695–" (4 vols., photostat, Connecticut State Library, Hartford, 1930).

Bronson, Henry, "A Historical Account of Connecticut Currency, Continental Money, and the Finances of the Revolution," *Papers of the New Haven Colony Historical Society,* I (1865), 171ff.

———*The History of Waterbury, Connecticut* (Waterbury, 1858).

Buckingham, Thomas, *Moses and Aaron. God's favour to His Chosen People, In Leading them by the Ministry of Civil and Ecclesiastical Rulers, Well Qualified for the Offices they are Called to Execute. Considered In a Discourse Had before the General Assembly of the Colony of Connecticut, on May 9th, 1728* (New London, 1729).

Bulkeley, Gershom, *Will and Doom, or The Miseries of Connecticut by and under an Usurped and Arbitrary Power, 1692,* with an introduction and notes by Charles J. Hoadly (*Collections of the Connecticut Historical Society,* III, Hartford, 1895, 69–269).

Bulkley, John, *An Impartial Account of a Late Debate at Lyme in the Colony of Connecticut, (On the Three following Heads, viz. I. The Subjects of Baptism. II. The Mode of Baptizing. And III. The Maintenance of the Ministers of the Gospel) . . . . Together, with a Disswasive not to Depart from the wholesome Truths, which People have been Instructed in* (New London, 1729).

———*The Necessity of Religion in Societies and Its Serviceableness to Promote the Due and Successful Exercise of Government in them Asserted and Shewed. A Sermon Preached before the General Assembly of the Colony of Connecticut at Hartford, May 14, 1713* (Boston, 1713).

Burnham, Jonathan, *A Small Tract of Arithmetick, For the Use of Farmers and Country-People* (New London, 1747).

Burnham, William, *God's Providence in Placing Men in their Respective Stations and Conditions Asserted and Shewed. A Sermon Preached before the General Assembly of the Colony of Connecticut, at Hartford, May 10, 1722* (New London, 1722).

Byington, E. H., "Rev. Robert Breck Controversy," *Papers and Pro-*

ceedings of the Connecticut Valley Historical Society, 1882–1903, II (1904), 1–19.

Caldwell, John, *An impartial Trial of the Spirit operating in this Part of the World; by comparing the Nature, Effects and Evidences of the present supposed Conversion with the Word of God. A Sermon Preached at New London-derry, October 14th. 1741* (Boston, 1742).

Campbell, Mildred, *The English Yeoman under Elizabeth and the Early Stuarts* (New Haven, 1942).

Cary, Wm. B., "Revival Experiences during the Great Awakening in 1741–44, in New London County," *New Englander*, XLII (Nov. 1883), 731–739.

Caulkins, Frances Manwaring, *History of New London, Connecticut. From the First Survey of the Coast in 1612, to 1852* (New London, 1852).

————*History of Norwich, Connecticut: From its Possession by the Indians, to the Year 1866* (Hartford, 1866).

A Caveat Against unreasonable and unscriptural Separations—in a Letter Sent from a Minister to some of his Brethren (Boston, 1748).

Chapin, Alonzo B., *Glastenbury For Two Hundred Years* (Hartford, 1853).

Chauncey, Nathaniel, *The Faithful Ruler Described and Excited: In a Sermon Preach'd before the General Assembly of the Colony of Connecticut at Hartford, May 9th, 1734* (New London, 1734).

The Christian History Containing Accounts of the Revival and Propagation of Religion in Great Britain and America, ed. Thomas Prince, Jr., nos. 1–104 (Boston, published weekly from March 5, 1743 to Feb. 23, 1745).

[Church, Benjamin], *Liberty and Property vindicated, and the St—pm–n burnt. A Discourse Ocasionally made, on burning the Effigy of the St—pm–n, in New-London, in the Colony of Connecticut. By a Friend to the Liberty of his Country* ([Hartford], 1765).

Clap, Thomas, *The Annals or History of Yale College, in New Haven, from the First Founding thereof, in the year 1700, to the year 1766* (New Haven, 1766).

[Clap, Thomas], *The Answer of the Friend in the West, to A Letter from a Gentleman in the East, entitled, The present State of the Colony of Connecticut considered* (New Haven, 1755).

Clap, Thomas, *A Brief History and Vindication of the Doctrines Received and Established in the Churches of New-England; with A Specimen of the New Scheme of Religion beginning to prevail* (New Haven, 1755).

————*An Essay on the Nature and Foundation of Moral Virtue and Obligation; Being a Short Introduction to the Study of Ethics; for the Use of the Students of Yale-College* (New Haven, 1765).

————*The Greatness and Difficulty of the Work of the Ministry. A*

Sermon Preached at the Ordination of the Reverend Mr. Ephraim Little, At Colchester, September 20, 1732 (Boston, 1732).

——A Letter from the Reverend Mr. Thomas Clap, Rector of Yale-College at New-Haven, To a Friend in Boston (Boston, 1745).

——The Religious Constitution of Colleges, especially of Yale-College in New Haven in the Colony of Connecticut (New London, 1754).

Colonial Currency Reprints 1682–1751, with an introduction and notes by Andrew McFarland Davis (4 vols., Boston, 1910–1911).

Colton, Benjamin, Two Sermons Deliver'd at Hartford, in the Colony of Connecticut. The first Sermon Treats of the Change of the Sabbath, from the Seventh, to the First Day of the Week . . . . The second Sermon Treats of Baptism (New London, 1735).

Connecticut Archives, Civil Officers (Bound MSS, Connecticut State Library, Hartford).

——College and Schools (Bound MSS, Connecticut State Library, Hartford).

——Crimes and Misdemeanours (Bound MSS, Connecticut State Library, Hartford).

——Ecclesiastical Affairs (Bound MSS, Connecticut State Library, Hartford).

——Finance and Currency (Bound MSS, Connecticut State Library, Hartford).

——Private Controversies (Bound MSS, Connecticut State Library, Hartford).

——Towns and Lands (Bound MSS, Connecticut State Library, Hartford).

——Trade and Maritime Affairs (Bound MSS, Connecticut State Library, Hartford).

——Travel Highways, Ferries, Bridges and Taverns (Bound MSS, Connecticut State Library, Hartford).

Connecticut, Colony of, The Book of the General Laws for the People within the Jurisdiction of Connecticut . . . Cambridge, 1673, reprint of the original edition with a prefatory note by George Brinley (Hartford, 1865).

——The Public Records of the Colony of Connecticut, 1636–1776, vols. 1–3 ed. J. H. Trumbull; vols. 4–15 ed. C. J. Hoadly (15 vols., Hartford, 1850–1890).

Connecticut, State of, The Public Statute Laws of the State of Connecticut, Book I (Hartford, 1808).

The Connecticut Courant (Hartford).

Connecticut Gazette (New Haven).

Contributions to the Ecclesiastical History of Connecticut; Prepared Under the Direction of the General Association to Commemorate the Completion of One Hundred and Fifty Years Since its First Annual Assembly (New Haven, 1861).

Cooke, Samuel, *Divine Sovereignty in the Salvation of Sinners, consider'd and improv'd. In a Sermon Preach'd before the Eastern Association of Fairfield County, on a publick Lecture in Danbury, July 29th. 1741* (Boston, 1741).

Cothren, William, *History of Ancient Woodbury, Connecticut from the First Indian Deed in 1659 to 1854* (Waterbury, 1854).

Crofut, Florence S. Marcy, *Guide to the History and the Historic Sites of Connecticut* (2 vols., New Haven, 1937).

Croswell, Andrew, *What is Christ to me, if he is not mine? Or, A Seasonable Defence of the Old Protestant Doctrine of Justifying Faith; With a particular Answer to Mr. Giles Firmin's eight Arguments to the contrary* (Boston, 1745).

Cutler, Timothy, *The Firm Union of a People Represented; and a Concern for it urged; upon All Orders and Degrees of Men: in a Sermon Preached before the General Assembly of the Colony of Connecticut, at Hartford, May 9, 1717* (New London, 1717).

[Darling, Thomas], *Some Remarks on Mr. President Clap's History and Vindication of the Doctrines, etc. of the New-England Churches* (New Haven, 1757).

Davis, Andrew McFarland, "A Connecticut Land Bank," *Publications of the Colonial Society of Massachusetts*, V *(Transactions,* 1897, 1898), 96–111; VI *(Transactions,* 1899, 1900), 6–11.

Davis, Charles H. S., *History of Wallingford, Conn. from its Settlement in 1670 to the Present Time* (Meriden, 1870).

Deming, Dorothy, *The Settlement of Litchfield County (Publications of the Tercentenary Commission of the State of Connecticut* [no. 7], New Haven, 1933).

———*The Settlement of the Connecticut Towns (Publications of the Tercentenary Commission of the State of Connecticut* [no. 6], New Haven, 1933).

Denison, Frederic, *Notes of The Baptists, and their Principles in Norwich, Conn., From the Settlement of the Town to 1850* (Norwich, 1857).

[Devotion, Ebenezer], *A Letter From a Gentleman in Connecticut To his Friend in London. In Answer to a Letter from a Gentleman in London to his Friend in America: Intitled, The Claim of the Colonies to an Exemption from Internal Taxes imposed by Authority of Parliament, examined* (New London, 1766).

Devotion, Ebenezer, *The civil Ruler, a dignify'd* [- - -] *the Lord, but a dying* [- - - -]. *A Sermon Preached before the General Assembly of the Colony of Connecticut, at Hartford, on the Day of the Anniversary Election, May 10th, 1753* (New London, 1753).

Dexter, Franklin Bowditch, *Biographical Sketches of the Graduates of Yale College with Annals of the College History* (6 vols., New York, 1885–1912).

———"Estimates of Population in the American Colonies," *American*

Antiquarian Society Proceedings, new series, V (1887–1888), 22–50.

————"The Removal of Yale College to New Haven in October, 1716," *Papers of the New Haven Colony Historical Society,* IX (1918), 70–89.

————"Thomas Clap and His Writings," *Papers of the New Haven Colony Historical Society,* V (1894), 247–274.

A Dialogue, or, Representation of Matters of Fact . . . . Occasioned by some Mismanagements which happen'd in respect of a Gentleman, whose Affairs lay under the Consideration of an Ecclesiastical Council ([New London], 1736).

[Dickinson, Moses], *An Answer to a Letter, From an aged Layman, to the Clergy of the Colony of Connecticut. In which the Rights of the consociated Churches are maintained; the consociation that appeared against the Ordination of Mr. Dana at Wallingford vindicated; and the Ministers like minded defended, against the Insinuations, and Reflections contained in that Letter. By an aged Minister* (New Haven, 1761).

Dickinson, Moses, *A Discourse Shewing that the Consideration, of God's Sovereignty, in working Grace in the Souls of Men, is so far from being a Discouragement to them in endeavoring to obtain it, that it is a most powerful Motive to quicken their Endeavours, Preached at Stratford, in the Colony of Connecticut* (Boston, 1742).

————*A Sermon Preached before the General Assembly of the Colony of Connecticut, at Hartford, On the Day of the Anniversary Election, May 8th, 1755* (New London, 1755).

Dorfman, Joseph, *The Economic Mind in American Civilization, 1606–1865* (New York, 1946).

Dorr, Edward, *A Discourse, Occasioned by the Much Lamented Death of the Honorable Daniel Edwards, Esqu; of Hartford; A Member of His Majesty's Council for the Colony of Connecticut; and One of the Assistant Judges of the Honorable, The Superior Court for the said Colony* (Hartford, 1765).

————*The Duty of Civil Rulers, to be nursing Fathers to the Church of Christ. A Sermon Preached before the General Assembly, of the Colony of Connecticut, At Hartford; on the day of the Anniversary Election; May ix[th], 1765* (Hartford, [1765]).

Douglass, William, *A Summary, Historical and Political, of the First Planting, Progressive Improvements, and Present State of the British Settlements in North-America* (2 vols., London, 1755).

Dunn, Richard S., *Puritans and Yankees: The Winthrop Dynasty of New England, 1630–1717* (Princeton, N.J., 1962).

Dwight, S. E., *The Life of President Edwards* (Jonathan Edwards, *The Works of President Edwards with a Memoir of His Life,* I, New York, 1830).

Dwight, Timothy, *Greenfield Hill: A Poem, in Seven Parts* (New York, 1794).

East Windsor, Connecticut, "First Ecclesiastical Society (Originally North or Fourth Society, Windsor), Records 1752–1933" (5 vols., photostat, Connecticut State Library, Hartford).

Edwards, Jonathan, *An Humble Inquiry Into The Rules of the Word of GOD, Concerning the Qualifications Requisite to a Compleat Standing and full Communion In the Visible Christian Church* (Boston, 1749).

————*Jonathan Edwards: Representative Selections,* with Introduction, Bibliography, and Notes by Clarence H. Faust and Thomas H. Johnson (Revised Edition, New York, 1962).

————*The Works of President Edwards in Four Volumes. A Reprint of the Worcester Edition,* 9th ed. (New York, 1856).

Edwards, Timothy, *All the Living must surely Die, and go to Judgment. A Sermon . . . Preach'd before the General Assembly of the Colony of Connecticut at Hartford, on the day of Election There, On May 11th 1732* (New London, 1732).

Eells, Edward, *Christ, the Foundation of the Salvation of Sinners, and of civil and ecclesiastical Government: illustrated in a Sermon, preached before the General Assembly of the Colony of Connecticut, on the Day of the Anniversary Election, May 14th, 1767* (Hartford, [1767]).

————*Some Serious Remarks upon the Rev'd Mr. Jonathan Todd's Faithful Narrative, of the Proceedings, of the First Society, and Church in Wallingford; relative to Mr. James Dana's Call and Settlement* (New Haven, 1759).

Eells, Nathanael, *The Evangelical Bishop. A Sermon Preached at Stonington, in Connecticut Colony, June 14th. 1733, At the Ordination of the Reverend Mr. Nathanael Eells* (New London, 1734).

————*The wise Ruler a loyal Subject. A Sermon Preached in the Audience of the General Assembly Of The Colony of Connecticut, On the Day of their Anniversary Election in Hartford, May 12th, 1748* (New London, 1748).

Eliot, Jared, *Essays Upon Field Husbandry in New England and Other Papers, 1748–1762,* ed. Harry J. Carman and Rexford G. Tugwell (New York, 1934).

————*Give Cesar his Due. Or, The Obligation That Subjects are under to their Civil Rulers, As was shew'd in a Sermon Preach'd before the General Assembly of the Colony of Connecticut at Hartford, May the 11th, 1738* (New London, 1738).

————*The Two Witnesses: or, Religion Supported by Reason and Divine Revelation, Being the Substance of a Lecture-Sermon, Preach'd at the North-Society in Lyme, October 29, 1735, Before the Association of the County of New-London; and Published at their Desire* (New London, 1736).

Ellsworth, John, "Account Book of John Ellsworth (1697–1784) East Windsor, Connecticut, 1720–55" (MS, Connecticut State Library, Hartford).

Estabrook, Samuel, *A Sermon Shewing that the Peace and Quietness Of a People Is a main part of the Work of Civil Rulers, and That it is the Duty of all to Pray For Them. Deliver'd at Hartford May the 8th, 1718. being the Day for the Election of the Honourable the Governour, Lieutenant Governour, and the Worshipful Assistants, for the Government of Connecticut* (New London, 1718).

Evans, Charles, *American Bibliography*, vol. 13 by Clifford K. Shipton and vol. 14 by Roger Pattrell Briston (14 vols., Chicago, 1903–1959).

Fairfield, Connecticut, "First Congregational Church, Records, 1694–1806" (MS, Connecticut State Library, Hartford).

———"Greenfield Hill or Northwest Society and Church, Records, 1668–1878" (3 vols., MS, Connecticut State Library, Hartford).

———"Town Records" (7 vols., MS, Connecticut State Library, Hartford).

Fairfield County, "Records of the County Court of Fairfield," collected and arranged by Henry T. Blake (MS, Connecticut State Library, Hartford).

Fairfield East Association, "A Book of Records for the Revd, the East Association in the County of Fairfield, 1734–1813" (MS, Congregational House, Hartford).

Fairfield East Consociation, "A Book of Records for the Venerable Eastern Consociation of the County of Fairfield, 1735/6–1813" (MS, Congregational House, Hartford).

Farrell, John Thomas, "The Administration of Justice in Connecticut About the Middle of the Eighteenth Century" (unpub. diss. Yale, 1937, photostat, Connecticut State Library, Hartford).

Federal Writers' Project of the WPA, *History of Milford, Connecticut, 1639–1939* (Milford, 1939).

First Congregational Church of Preston, Connecticut, 1698–1896 (n.p., 1900).

Fish, Joseph, *Christ Jesus the Physician, and his Blood the [- - - -] recommended for the Healing of a diseased People. In a Sermon Preach'd before the General Assembly of the Colony of Connecticut, at Hartford, on the Day of their Anniversary Election, May 8. 1760* (New London, 1760).

Fiske, Phineas, *The Good Subject's Wish or, the Desirableness of the Divine Presence with Civil Rulers, Opened and Applied in a Sermon Preached before the General Assembly of the Colony of Connecticut, at Hartford, May 12, 1726* (New London, 1726).

[Fitch, Thomas], *An Explanation of Say-Brook Platform, or, The Principles of the Consociated Churches in the Colony of Connecticut Collected from their Plan of Union. By One that heartily desires* the Order, Peace and Purity of those Churches (Hartford, 1765).

Fitch, Thomas, *Reasons why The British Colonies, in America, Should not be charged with Internal Taxes, by Authority of Parliament Humbly offered, For Consideration, In Behalf of the Colony of Connecticut* (New Haven, 1764).

————*Some Reasons that Influenced The Governor to take, and The Councillors to administer, The Oath, Required by the Act of Parliament; commonly called the Stamp-Act. Humbly submitted to the Consideration of the Publick* (Hartford, [1766]).

Fowler, William Chauncey, *History of Durham, Connecticut, from the First Grant of Land in 1662 to 1866* (Hartford, 1866).

Franklin, Connecticut, "Congregational Church (Formerly Norwich West Farms or Second Society), Miscellaneous Documents, 1730–83" (photostat, Connecticut State Library, Hartford).

Frothingham, Ebenezer, *The Articles of Faith and Practice, with the Covenant, That is confessed by the Separate Churches of Christ in general in this Land. Also a Discourse, Holding forth the great Privileges of the Church of Jesus Christ, and the same Privileges vindicated from the Sacred Scriptures; and some Points of Practice in the Church of Christ, that are in great Dispute between the Learned and Unlearned, fairly settled in a Line of Divine Truth* (Newport, 1750).

Gale, Benjamin, *A Calm and full Vindication of A Letter, wrote to a Member of the Lower House of Assembly: Shewing, That the Taxes imposed on the Students of Yale-College are stated higher than to defray the annual Expences of that School . . . Being a Full Answer To A Letter, wrote to a Member of the House of Representatives in Vindication of Yale-College; With Some Further Remarks on the Laws and Government of that Society* (New Haven, 1759).

————*A Few Breif [sic] Remarks on Mr. Graham's Answer; And On His Vindication of Mr. President Clap, Published in the Connecticut Gazette, of October last; And on A Letter to the President, of the 8th of August last, sign'd John Graham; And on a propos'd Address to the Freemen, Sign'd Philalethos, inclos'd in said Letter; Both which are said to be in the Hand-writing of the Rev'd Mr. John Graham* (New Haven, 1760).

[Gale, Benjamin], *A Letter to a Member of the Lower House of Assembly of the Colony of Connecticut: Shewing, That the Taxes of Yale-College, are stated higher than necessary to defray the annual Expences of that School; by which a very considerable Addition is made to the College Treasury annually. With some general Observations on the Laws and Government of that Society* (New Haven, 1759).

————*A. Z., pseud., The Present State of the Colony of Connecticut Considered. In a Letter from a Gentleman in the Eastern Part of* said Colony, to his Friend in the Western Part of the Same (n.p., 1755).

Gale, Benjamin, A Reply to a Pamphlet Entitled, The Answer of the Friend in the West, etc., with a Prefatory Address to the Freemen of His Majesty's English Colony of Connecticut (n.p., 1755).

Garvan, Anthony N. B., Architecture and Town Planning in Colonial Connecticut (New Haven, 1951).

Gaustad, Edwin Scott, The Great Awakening in New England (New York, 1957).

Gilman, Daniel Coit, A Historical Discourse, Delivered in Norwich, Connecticut, September 7, 1859, at the Bi-centennial Celebration of the Settlement of the Town, 2nd ed. (Boston, 1859).

Gipson, Lawrence Henry, Jared Ingersoll: A Study of American Loyalism in Relation to British Colonial Government (Yale Historical Publication Miscellany, VIII, New Haven, 1920).

Goen, C. C., Revivalism and Separatism in New England, 1740–1800: Strict Congregationalists and Separate Baptists in the Great Awakening (New Haven, 1962).

Goodwin, Joseph O., East Hartford: Its History and Traditions (Hartford, 1879).

Graham, John, An Answer to Mr. Gale's pamphlet; Entituled, A calm and full Vindication etc. Relating to Yale-College (New Haven, 1759).

———The Christian's Duty of Watchfulness against Error, and Establishment in the Truth: Opened and Urged, in a Lecture-Sermon, Preach'd at New-Milford on Wednesday August 23, 1732. (Occasioned by the Growth and Spreading of Quakerism in that Place.) (New London, 1733).

———A Few Remarks on the Remarker; Shewing, That Mr. Gale's Inferences from the Contents of a Letter, villainously intercepted and broke open, are entirely groundless and injurious (New Haven, 1760).

[Graham, John], A Letter to a Member of the House of Representatives Of The Colony of Connecticut, In Vindication of Yale-College against the false Aspersions, and scandalous Misrepresentations contain'd in a late anonymous Pamphlet, Intituled, a Letter of a Member of the Lower House, etc. with a more important Proposal to the honourable, the General Assembly, than that which is contained in the said Pamphlet. ([New London], 1759).

———Some Remarks upon a late Pamphlet Entitled, A Letter from a Minister of the Church of England, to his dissenting Parishioners . . . . Together with A brief Vindication Of the Presbyterians from those Reproaches therein cast upon them ([Boston], 1733).

———Some Remarks upon a Second Letter from the Church of England Minister to his Dissenting Parishioners (Boston, 1736).

Grant, Charles S., Democracy in the Connecticut Frontier Town of

Kent *(Columbia Studies in the Social Sciences* [no. 601], New York, 1961).

Grant, Ebenezer, and Roswell Grant, "Account Books of Ebenezer Grant (1706–1797) and Roswell Grant (1745/6–1834) of East Windsor, Connecticut, 1743–1783" (4 vols., MS, Connecticut State Library, Hartford).

Greene, M. Louise, *The Development of Religious Liberty in Connecticut* (Boston, 1905).

Groce, George C., Jr., "Benjamin Gale," *New England Quarterly*, X (1937), 697–716.

————"Eliphalet Dyer: Connecticut Revolutionist," in Richard B. Morris, ed., *The Era of the American Revolution, Studies Inscribed to Evarts Boutell Greene* (New York, 1939), 290–304.

————*William Samuel Johnson; A Maker of the Constitution* (New York, 1937).

Haffenden, Philip S., "The Crown and the Colonial Charters, 1675-1688," *William and Mary Quarterly*, 3rd series, XV (1958), 297–311, 452–466.

Hall, Edwin, *The Ancient Historical Records of Norwalk, Conn.; with a Plan of the Ancient Settlement, and of the Town in 1847* (Norwalk, 1847).

H[all], E[lihu], *The Present way of the Country in Maintaining the Gospel Ministry by a Publick Rate or Tax, is Lawful, Equitable and agreeable to the Gospel. As the same is Argued and Proved in Way of Dialogue Between John Queristicus and Thomas Casuisticus Near Neighbours in the Country* (New London, 1749).

Hall, Samuel, *The Legislatures Right, Charge and Duty in respect of Religion; Represented in a Sermon Preach'd before the General Assembly of the Colony of Connecticut, at Hartford, on the Day of Election, May 8th, 1746* (New London, 1746).

Hammond, Bray, *Banks and Politics in America, from the Revolution to the Civil War* (Princeton, 1957).

"Hanover Congregational Church, Sprague, Connecticut, Records 1761–1899" (6 vols., MS, Connecticut State Library, Hartford).

Hart, William, *A Discourse Concerning the Nature of Regeneration, and the Way Wherein it is Wrought* (New London, 1742).

————*A Few Remarks, upon the Ordination of the Rev'd Mr. James Dana, and the Doings of the Consociation, respecting the same: Being a Letter, to the Author of the Faithful Narrative, etc.* (New Haven, 1759).

————*The Holy Scriptures the Compleat and Only Rule of Religious Faith and Practice. Shewn in a Discourse, Which is now made public, with a view to its being of extensive Service* (New London, 1743).

[Hart, William], *A Letter, to Paulinus; Containing an Answer to His Three Questions, Lately Proposed to the Public, in the Connecti-*

cut *Gazette: Wherein the Claim of Right in the Church, to make and impose public Tests of Orthodoxy, is examined and refuted* (New Haven, [1760]).

Hart, William, *Remarks On a late Pamphlet, Wrote by Mr. Hobart, Entitled, The Principles of congregational Churches, relating to the Constitution and Authority of Ecclesiastical Councils; considered, and applied to the Case of the late Ordination at Wallingford. And a further Vindication Of the Council That acted in that Ordination* (New Haven, 1760).

Hartford County, "Records, Court of Common Pleas, vol. 5, February 1729/30–February 1730/31" (MS, Connecticut State Library, Hartford).

Hartford North Association, "The Register of the Rules and Resolves of the North Association of the County of Hartford, 1714" (MS, Congregational House, Hartford).

Hartford, Town of, "Register of Probate Records," vol. 6, 1697–1700. Actually contains the County Court records for 1697–1706 (microfilm, Connecticut State Library, Hartford).

Hartford Town Votes, Volume I, 1635–1716 (Collections of the Connecticut Historical Society, VI, Hartford, 1897).

Haskins, George Lee, *Law and Authority in Early Massachusetts: A Study in Tradition and Design* (New York, 1960).

Heimert, Alan Edward, *Religion and the American Mind: From the Great Awakening to the Revolution* (Cambridge, Mass., 1966).

Hempstead, Joshua, *Diary of Joshua Hempstead of New London, Connecticut Covering a Period of Forty-Seven Years from September, 1711, to November, 1758 (Collections of the New London Historical Society,* I, New London, 1901).

Hine, Orlo D., *Early Lebanon. An Historical Address Delivered in Lebanon, Conn., by Request On the National Centennial, July 4, 1876* (Hartford, 1880).

The History of the Town of Litchfield, Connecticut, 1720–1920, ed. Alain C. White (Litchfield, 1920).

Hobart, Noah, *An Attempt To illustrate and confirm the ecclesiastical Constitution of the Consociated Churches, in the Colony of Connecticut. Occasioned by a late "Explanation of the Saybrook Platform"* (New Haven, 1765).

————*Civil Government the Foundation* [- - - -] *Social Happiness. A Sermon Preached before the General Assembly of the Colony of Connecticut, at Hartford, on the Day of their Anniversary Election, May 10th, 1750* (New London, 1751).

[Hobart, Noah], *A Congratulatory Letter from a Gentleman in the West, to His Friend in the East: upon the Success of his Letter Entituled, the present State of the Colony of Connecticut considered* (New Haven, 1755).

Hobart, Noah, *The Principles of Congregational Churches, Relating to the Constitution and Authority of Ecclesiastical Councils, Considered, and applied to the Case of the late Ordination at Wallingford* (New Haven, 1759).

———*A Vindication of the Piece, Entitled, "The Principles of congregational Churches, relating to the Constitution and Authority of Ecclesiastical Councils, considered; and applied to the Case of the late Ordination at Wallingford." Occasioned by the Remarks Made thereon* (New Haven, 1761).

Holdsworth, Sir William, *A History of English Law* (13 vols., London, 1903–1952).

Hollister, G. H., *The History of Connecticut, from the First Settlement of the Colony to the Adoption of the Present Constitution* (2 vols., New Haven, 1955).

Hooker, Roland Mather, *The Colonial Trade of Connecticut* (Publications of the Tercentenary Commission of the State of Connecticut [no. 50], New Haven, 1936).

Hopkins, Samuel, *Sketches of the Life of the Late, Rev. Samuel Hopkins, D.D. Pastor of the first Congregational Church in Newport, Written by Himself; Interspersed with Marginal Notes Extracted from his Private Diary; To which is Added; A Dialogue by the Same Hand, on the Nature and Extent of True Christian Submission; Also, a Serious Address to Professing Christians: Closed by Dr. Hart's Sermon at his Funeral: with an Introduction to the Whole, by the Editor,* ed. Stephen West (Hartford, 1805).

Hosmer, Stephen, *A Peoples Living in Appearance, and Dying in Reality, Considered. A Sermon Preached before the General Assembly, of the Colony of Connecticut, at Hartford, May 12th, 1720* (New London, 1720).

Hovey, Alvah, *A Memoir of the Life and Times of the Rev. Isaac Backus, A.M.* (Boston, 1859).

Hunn, Nathanael, *The Welfare of a Government Considered. A Sermon Preach'd before the General Assembly of the Colony of Connecticut, at Hartford, on the Day of their Anniversary Election, May 14th, 1747* (New London, 1747).

Hunt, D., *History of Pomfret* (Hartford, 1841).

Huntington, E. B., *History of Stamford, Connecticut, from its Settlement in 1641, to the Present Time* (Stamford, 1868).

Hurd, D. Hamilton, *History of New London County* (Philadelphia, 1882).

Ingersoll, Jared, "Historical Account of Some Affairs Relating to the Church Especially in Connecticut" (MS, Library of Congress, Washington).

———*Mr. Ingersoll's Letters Relating to the Stamp-Act* (New Haven, 1766).

————"A Selection from the Correspondence and Miscellaneous Papers of Jared Ingersoll," ed. Franklin B. Dexter, *Papers of the New Haven Colony Historical Society,* IX (1918), 201–472.

Ingersoll, Jonathan, *A Sermon Preached before the General Assembly of the Colony of Connecticut, At Hartford, On the Day of the Anniversary Election, May 14th, 1761* (New London, 1761).

Johnson, E. A. J., *American Economic Thought in the Seventeenth Century* (New York, 1961).

Johnson, Edward, *Johnson's Wonder-Working Providence, 1628–1651,* ed. J. Franklin Jameson *(Original Narratives of Early American History,* New York, 1910).

Johnson, Emory R., T. W. Van Metre, G. G. Huebner, and D. S. Hanchett, *History of Domestic and Foreign Commerce of the United States* (2 vols., Washington, 1915).

[Johnson, Samuel], *A Letter from a Minister of the Church of England to his Dissenting Parishioners* (New York, 1733).

Johnson, Samuel, *Samuel Johnson, President of King's College His Career and Writings,* ed. Herbert and Carol Schneider (4 vols., New York, 1939).

[Johnson, Samuel], *A Second Letter From a Minister of the Church of England, To his Dissenting Parishioners, in Answer to Some Remarks made on the former, by one J. G.* (Boston, 1734).

Johnson, Stephen, *Integrity and Piety the best Principles of a good Administration of Government, Illustrated, in a Sermon, Preached before the General Assembly of the Colony of Connecticut, at Hartford, on the day of their Anniversary Election, May 10th, 1770* (New London, 1770).

————*Some Important Observations Occasioned by, and adapted to, the Publick Fast Ordered by Authority, December 18th, A.D. 1765. On Account of the peculiar Circumstances of the present Day* (Newport, 1766).

"Journal of the Lower House 1708–1738" (MS, Connecticut State Library, Hartford).

"Journals of the Upper House of the General Assembly of the Colony of Connecticut from May 1708 to October 1736" (MS, Connecticut State Library, Hartford).

Judd, Sylvester, *History of Hadley, Including the Early History of Hatfield, South Hadley, Amherst and Granby* (Springfield, Mass., 1905).

The Judgment of the Rector and Tutors of Yale-College, Concerning Two of the Students who were Expelled; Together with the Reasons of it (New London, 1745).

Labaree, Leonard W., "The Conservative Attitude Toward the Great Awakening," *William and Mary Quarterly,* 3rd series, I (1944), 331–352.

————*Milford, Connecticut The Early Development of a Town as*

Shown in Its Land Records (Publications of the Tercentenary Commission of the State of Connecticut [no. 13], New Haven, 1933).

Lane (William Griswold) Memorial Collection (Boxed MSS, Yale University, New Haven).

Larned, Ellen D., *Historic Gleanings in Windham County, Connecticut* (Providence, 1899).

———*History of Windham County, Connecticut* (2 vols., Worcester, Mass., 1874).

The Law Papers Correspondence and Documents During Jonathan Law's Governorship of the Colony of Connecticut 1741–1750, ed. Albert C. Bates (3 vols., *Collections of the Connecticut Historical Society,* XI, XIII, XV, Hartford, 1907–1914).

Lebanon, Town of, "Deeds 1685–1869" (32 vols., microfilm, Connecticut State Library, Hartford).

Lee, Jonathan, *A Sermon Delivered before the General Assembly of the Colony of Connecticut, at Hartford; on the Day of the Anniversary Election, May 8th, 1766* (New London, 1766).

A Letter From a Gentleman in Boston, to his Friend in Connecticut (Boston, 1744).

A Letter to a Friend, Occasioned by the unhappy Controversy at Wallingford. By a Layman and Platformist (New Haven, 1760).

A Letter to the Clergy of the Colony of Connecticut, from an Aged Layman of said Colony ([New York], 1760).

Lewis, Daniel, *The Good Minister. A Sermon Preach'd at Stonington, in the Colony of Connecticut, December 27th. 1732. When the Reverend Mr. Joseph Fish was Ordained Pastor of a Church there* (New London, 1733).

Lisbon, Connecticut, "Newent Congregational Church, Records, 1723–1932" (6 vols., MS, Connecticut State Library, Hartford).

"Litchfield County Association of Ministers 1752–1792" (MS copy, Congregational House, Hartford).

"Litchfield County Consociation 1752–1792," (MS copy, Congregational House, Hartford).

Lockwood, James, *Religion the highest Interest of a civil Community, and the surest Means of its Prosperity. A Sermon Preached before the General Assembly Of the Colony of Connecticut, at Hartford, on the Day of the Anniversary Election, May 9th, 1754* (New London, 1754).

———*The Worth and Excellence of Civil Freedom and Liberty illustrated, and a Public Spirit and the Love of our Country recommended. A Sermon Delivered before the General Assembly of the Colony of Connecticut, at Hartford, on the Day of the Anniversary Election. May 10th, 1759* (New London, 1759).

Lord, Benjamin, *Religion and Government subsisting together in Society, Necessary to their Compleat Happiness and Safety. A Ser-*

mon Delivered in the Audience of the General Assembly of the Colony of Connecticut, on their Anniversary Election at Hartford, May 9th, 1751 (New London, 1752).

Love, William DeLoss, *The Colonial History of Hartford, Gathered from the Original Records* (Hartford, 1914).

Manual of the First Congregational Church of Norwich, Conn. (Norwich, 1868).

Marsh, Jonathan, *An Essay, To Prove the Through Reformation of a Sinning People is not to be Expected; however Pious Rulers may be Spirited for the Work . . . . In a Sermon Preached Before the General Court of Election at Hartford in the Colony of Connecticut, on May 11th, 1721* (New London, 1721).

——*God's Fatherly Care of his Covenant Children; Shewed and Improved, in a Sermon Preached before the General Assembly of the Colony of Connecticut, on the Day of their Election at Hartford, May 13. 1736* (New London, 1737).

Martin, Margaret Elizabeth, *Merchants and Trade of the Connecticut River Valley, 1750–1820 (Smith College Studies in History, XXIV, Northampton, 1939).*

Mather, Azariah, *Good Rulers a Choice Blessing. A Sermon Preached before the Great and General Assembly of the Colony of Connecticut, at Hartford in New-England, May 13th 1725* (New London, 1725).

——*The Gospel-Minister Described, by the Important Duty of his Office, and Directed in the Faithful Discharge of it, in a Sermon Delivered at Newent in Norwich Dec. 10th. 1723 at the Ordination of the Reverend Daniel Kirtland There* (New London, 1725).

Mather, Cotton, *Agricola or, the Religious Husbandman: The Main Intentions of Religion, Served in the Business and Language of Husbandry* (Boston, 1727).

[Mather, Cotton], *A Brief Essay upon, a Town Happy, and Glorious: Recommending, Those things, by which a Town may come to Flourish with all Prosperity. A Discourse, wherein the State of All our Towns, is Considered: But the Peculiar Temptations and Occations of Some Towns among us, are more Particularly accommodated* (Boston, 1712).

Mather, Cotton, *A Christian at his Calling. Two brief Discourses. One Directing a Christian in his General Calling; Another Directing him in his Personal Calling* (Boston, 1701).

——*Durable Riches, Two Brief Discourses Occasioned by the Impoverishing Blast of Heaven; which the Undertakings of Men both by Sea and Land, have met withal* (Boston, 1695).

[Mather, Cotton], *A Letter to Ungospellized Plantations; Briefly Representing the Excellency and Necessity, of a Peoples Enjoying the Gospel of the Lord Jesus Christ among them* (Boston, 1702).

————*Ratio Discipline Fratrum Nov-Anglorum. A Faithful Account of the Discipline Professed and Practiced in the Churches of New England* (Boston, 1726).

Mather, Cotton, *A Very Needful Caution. A Brief Essay, to Discover the Sin that Slayed its Ten Thousands; and Represent the Character and Condition of the Covetous* (Boston, 1707).

Mather, Increase, *The Excellency of a Publick Spirit, Discoursed in a Sermon, Preached in the Audience of the General Assembly of the Province of the Massachusetts Bay in New England, May 27. 1702. Being the Day for Election of Counsellors in that Province* (Boston, 1702).

Mather, Moses, *The Visible Church, in Covenant with God: or, An Inquiry into the Constitution of the Visible Church of Christ. Wherein the Divine Right of Infant Baptism is defended; and, the Admission of Adults to compleat standing in the Visible Church, though destitute of a saving Faith, shown to be agreeable to the Revealed Will of God* (New York, 1759 [i.e., 1769]).

McDonald, Adrian F., *The History of Tobacco Production in Connecticut (Publications of the Tercentenary Commission of the State of Connecticut* [no. 52], New Haven, 1936).

Mead, Daniel M., *A History of the Town of Greenwich, Fairfield County, Conn., with Many Important Statistics* (New York, 1857).

Mead, Nelson P., *Connecticut as a Corporate Colony* (Lancaster, Pa., 1906).

————"Public Archives of Connecticut. County, Probate, and Local Records," *Annual Report of the American Historical Association for the Year 1906*, II, 53–127.

The Memorial History of Hartford County Connecticut 1633–1884, ed. James Hammond Trumbull (2 vols., Boston, 1886).

Meyer, Jacob C., *Church and State in Massachusetts, from 1740 to 1833: A Chapter in the History of the Development of Individual Freedom* (Cleveland, 1930).

Miller, Perry, *The New England Mind: From Colony to Province* (Cambridge, Mass., 1953).

Mills, Jedidiah, *A Vindication of Gospel-Truth, and Refutation of some Dangerous Errors, in Relation to that Important Question, Whether there be Promises of the Bestowment of special Grace, made in Scripture to the Unregenerate, on Condition of any Endeavours, Strivings, or Doings of theirs whatsoever? . . . Done in a Letter to the Rev. Dr. Samuel Johnson, Episcopal Missionary at Stratford* (Boston, 1747).

Minor, Manasseh, *The Diary of Manasseh Minor Stonington, Conn. 1696–1720*, ed. Frank Denison Miner and Hannah Miner (n.p., 1915).

Mitchell, Isabel S., *Roads and Road-Making in Colonial Connecticut* (*Publications of the Tercentenary Commission of the State of Connecticut* [no. 14], New Haven, 1933).

Mitchell, Mary Hewitt, *The Great Awakening and Other Revivals in the Religious Life of Connecticut* (*Publications of the Tercentenary Commission of the State of Connecticut* [no. 26], New Haven, 1934).

Morgan, Edmund S., *The Gentle Puritan: A Life of Ezra Stiles, 1727–1795* (New Haven, 1962).

Morgan, Edmund S. and Helen M. Morgan, *The Stamp Act Crisis: Prologue to Revolution* (Williamsburg, Virginia, 1953).

Morison, Samuel E., "A Generation of Expansion and Inflation in Massachusetts History, 1713–1741," *Publications of the Colonial Society of Massachusetts,* XIX (1916–1917), 271–272.

Moss, Joseph, *An Election Sermon, Preached before the General Assembly of the Colony of Connecticut, at Hartford, May the 12th. 1715. The Discourse sheweth, That Frequent Reading and Studying the Scriptures and the Civil Law of the Common Wealth, is Needful and Profitable for Rulers* (New London, 1715).

Nettels, Curtis P., *The Money Supply of the American Colonies before 1720* (*University of Wisconsin Studies in the Social Sciences and History* [no. 20], 1934).

New Haven Colony Historical Society, *Ancient Town Records,* ed. Franklin Bowditch Dexter (2 vols., New Haven, 1917, 1919).

New Haven County, "County Court Records," vol. 2, June 1699–March 1712/13; vol. 3, April 1713–January 1738/39 (MS, Connecticut State Library, Hartford).

New London County, "Records of Trials," vol. 7, June 1689–March 1703; vol. 17, November 1729–December 1733 (MS, Connecticut State Library, Hartford).

The New London Summary or the Weekly Advertiser (photostat, Connecticut State Library, Hartford).

Newman, A. H., *A History of the Baptist Churches in the United States* (*American Church History Series,* II, New York, 1894).

Norwich, Connecticut, "Fifth Congregational Church, Records of Baptisms, Marriages, Deaths and Church Admissions. . . . From 1739–1824," copied and indexed by Mrs. Jennie Gallup (typescript, Connecticut State Library, Hartford).

———"First Congregational Church, Records, 1699–1917" (7 vols., MS, Connecticut State Library, Hartford).

———"Norwich Town Book of Acts, Votes and Grants, December 6th, 1726, No. 3" (including votes from 1726 to 1764) (MS in yellow leather book included in red bound volume mislabeled "Norwich Town Votes, Etc., 1681–1727," Town Clerk's Office, Norwich).

————"Norwich Town Rate Granted December 1741. A Peny on the pound" (MS, Connecticut State Library, Hartford).

————"Proprietor Records, 1723–1838" (MS in yellow leather book included in a red bound volume mislabeled "Norwich Town Votes, Etc., 1681–1727," Town Clerk's Office, Norwich).

————"Second Congregational Church (Chelsea), Records, 1760–1918" (3 vols., photostat, Connecticut State Library, Hartford).

————Town Votes from ca. 1681 to ca. 1721 (MS mislabeled "Norwich Deeds, 1659–1712," in coverless book put in with "Old Records, Book No. 1," Town Clerk's Office, Norwich).

Nott, Samuel, "The Life of the Rev. Samuel Nott, D.D., Pastor of the Church of Christ in the First Society of Franklin, Connecticut" (typescript, Congregational House, Hartford).

Olson, Albert Laverne, *Agricultural Economy and the Population in Eighteenth-Century Connecticut* (*Publications of the Tercentenary Commission of the State of Connecticut* [no. 40], New Haven, 1935).

Orcutt, Samuel, *A History of the Old Town of Stratford and the City of Bridgeport Connecticut* (New Haven, 1886).

————*History of the Towns of New Milford and Bridgewater, Connecticut, 1703–1882* (Hartford, 1882).

Orcutt, Samuel, and Ambrose Beardsley, *The History of the Old Town of Derby, Connecticut, 1642–1880* (Springfield, Mass., 1880).

Osgood, Herbert L., *The American Colonies in the Seventeenth Century* (3 vols., New York, 1904–1907).

Paine, Solomon, *A Short View of the Differences Between the Church of Christ, and the established churches in the Colony of Conn.* (Newport, 1752).

Palfrey, John Gorham, *A Compendious History of New England from the Discovery by Europeans to the First General Congress of the Anglo-American Colonies* (4 vols., Boston, 1884).

Parsons, Francis, "Elisha Williams: Minister, Soldier, President of Yale," *Papers of the New Haven Colony Historical Society,* VII (1908), 188–217.

Parsons, Jonathan, *A Needful Caution in a Critical Day. Or, the Christian Urged to Strict Watchfulness, That the Contrary Part May have no Evil Thing to say of him. A Discourse deliver'd at Lyme, Feb. 4th, 1741,2* (New London, 1742).

————*Wisdom justified of her Children. A Sermon Preached (in Part) at the publick Lecture in Boston, on Thursday Sept. 16. 1742* (Boston, 1742).

Pemberton, Ebenezer, *The Duty of Committing Our Souls to Christ, Explained and Improved in a Sermon: The Substance of which was preach'd at Stratfield in the Colony of Connecticut, Sept. 13th. 1742* (Boston, 1743).

326 **WORKS CITED**

———*The Knowledge of Christ Recommended, in a Sermon Preach'd in the Public Hall at Yale College in New-Haven: April 19th, 1741* (New London, 1741).

———*A Sermon Preach'd in New-Ark, June 12. 1744, at the Ordination of Mr. David Brainerd, a Missionary among the Indians upon the Borders of the Provinces of New-York, New-Jersey, and Pennsylvania* (Boston, 1744).

[Peters, Samuel A.], *A General History of Connecticut from its First Settlement under George Fenwick, Esq. to its Latest Period of Amity with Great Britain . . . . by a Gentleman of the Province* (London, 1791).

Plainfield, Connecticut, "First Book of Town Meeting, 1699–1748" (MS, Connecticut State Library).

Records of the Congregational Church, Franklin, Conn., 1718–1860. And a Record of Deaths in Norwich Eighth Society, 1763, 1778, 1782, 1784–1802 (Hartford, 1938).

The Records of the General Association of the Colony of Connecticut. Begun June 20th, 1738. Ending June 19th, 1799 (Hartford, 1888).

Relyea, B. J., *Celebration in Green's Farms, the Historical Discourse Delivered at the Celebration of the One Hundred and Fiftieth Anniversary of the Formation of the Church in Green's Farms, Held Oct. 26, 1865* (New York, 1865)

Reynolds, Peter, *The Kingdom is the Lord's, or, God the Supreme Ruler and Governour of the World. A Sermon Preached before the General Assembly Of the Colony Of Connecticut, at Hartford, on the Day of the Anniversary Election, May 12th, 1757* (New London, 1757).

Robbins, Philemon, *A Plain Narrative of the Proceedings of the Reverend Association and Consociation of New-Haven County, against the Reverend Mr. Robbins of Branford, Since the Year 1741. And the Doings of his Church and People* (Boston, 1747).

Russel, William, *The Decay of Love to God in Churches, Offensive and Dangerous Shewed In a Sermon Preach'd before the General Assembly of the Colony of Connecticut, at Hartford, May 14, 1730* (New London, 1731).

Russell, Samuel, *Man's liableness to be deceiv'd about Religion Shewn and Caution'd against. Worldly Wisdom only seeming Wisdom. Religion true Wisdom, a Becoming Fools, in order to be Wise. A Sermon Preach'd at a Public Association-Lecture at West Haven, September 30th, 1741* (New London, 1742).

Salter, Richard, *A Sermon, Preached before the General Assembly Of the Colony of Connecticut, at Hartford On the Day of their Anniversary Election, May 12th, 1768* (New London, 1768).

Saltonstall, Gurdon, *A Sermon Preached before the General Assembly of the Colony of Connecticut, at Hartford in New England May 13, 1697* (Boston, 1697).

Schenck, Elizabeth Hubbell, *The History of Fairfield, Fairfield County, Connecticut* (2 vols., New York, 1905).

Scott, William Robert, *The Constitution and Finance of English, Scottish and Irish Joint-Stock Companies to 1720* (3 vols., New York, 1951).

Sewall, Joseph, *A Caveat against Covetousness in a Sermon at the Lecture in Boston, N. E. February 20. 1717/18* (Boston, 1718).

[Sherman, Roger], *A Caveat Against Injustice, or an Inquiry into the evil Consequences of a Fluctuating Medium of Exchange, Wherein is considered, whether the Bills of Credit on the Neighbouring Governments, are a legal Tender in Payments of Money, in the Colony of Connecticut* (New York, 1752).

Shipton, Clifford K., "The New England Clergy of the 'Glacial Age,' " *Publications of the Colonial Society of Massachusetts, XXXII* (1937), 24–54.

———*Sibley's Harvard Graduates* (13 vols., Cambridge and Boston, 1873–1965).

Sketches of Church Life in Colonial Connecticut, ed. Lucy Cushing Jarvis (New Haven, 1902).

Sly, John Fairfield, *Town Government in Massachusetts (1620–1930)* (Cambridge, Mass., 1930).

South Windsor, Connecticut, "First Congregational Church, Records, 1694–1838" (5 vols., MS, Connecticut State Library, Hartford).

Stark, Charles R., *Groton, Conn., 1705–1905* (Stonington, 1905).

Steiner, Bernard Christian, *A History of the Plantation of Menunkatuck and of the Original Town of Guilford, Connecticut, Comprising the Present Towns of Guilford and Madison, Written Largely from the Manuscripts of the Hon. Ralph Dunning Smyth* (Baltimore, 1897).

Stiles, Ezra, *Extracts from the Itineraries and Other Miscellanies of Ezra Stiles, D.D., LL.D. 1755–1794 with a Selection from his Correspondence*, ed. Franklin Bowditch Dexter (New Haven, 1916).

———*The Literary Diary of Ezra Stiles, D.D., LL.D. President of Yale College*, ed. Franklin Bowditch Dexter (3 vols., New York, 1901).

Stiles, Henry R., *The History and Genealogies of Ancient Windsor, Connecticut; including East Windsor, South Windsor, Bloomfield, Windsor Locks, and Ellington, 1635–1891* (2 vols., Hartford, 1892).

Stiles, Isaac, *A Prospect of the City of Jerusalem, in it's Spiritual Building, Beauty and Glory. Shewed in a Sermon Preach'd at Hartford in His Majesty's Colony of Connecticut, May 13th, 1742* (New London, 1742).

Stoddard, Solomon, *An Answer to Some Cases of Conscience Respecting the Country* (Boston, 1722).

——*The Defects of Preachers Reproved in a Sermon Preached at Northampton, May 19th. 1723* (New London, 1724).

——*Gods Frown in the Death of Usefull Men. Shewed in a Sermon Preached at the Funeral of the Honourable Col. John Pynchon Esq.* (Boston, 1703).

Stoughton, John, *A Corner Stone of Colonial Commerce* (Boston, 1911).

——*"Windsor Farmes." A Glimpse of an Old Parish together with the Deciphered Inscriptions from a Few Foundation Stones of a Much Abused Theology* (Hartford, 1883).

The Susquehannah Company Papers, ed. Julian P. Boyd (4 vols., Wilkes-Barre, Pa., 1930).

The Talcott Papers Correspondence and Documents (Chiefly Official) During Joseph Talcott's Governorship of the Colony of Connecticut 1724–41, ed. Mary Kingsbury Talcott (2 vols., *Collections of the Connecticut Historical Society,* IV, V, Hartford, 1892–1896).

Tawney, R. H., *Religion and the Rise of Capitalism: A Historical Study* (New York, 1926).

Tennent, Gilbert, *The Danger of an Unconverted Ministry, Considered in a Sermon on Mark VI. 34.* (Boston, 1742).

Thompson, Mack E., "The Ward-Hopkins Controversy and the American Revolution in Rhode Island: An Interpretation," *William and Mary Quarterly,* 3rd series, XVI (1959), 363–375.

Throop, Benjamin, *Religion and Loyalty, the Duty and Glory of a People: Illustrated in a Sermon. From 1 Peter 2. 17. Preached before the General Assembly of the Colony of Connecticut, at Hartford, On the Day of the Anniversary Election, May 11th, 1758* (New London, 1758).

——*A Thanksgiving Sermon, upon the Occasion, of the glorious News of the repeal of the Stamp Act; Preached in New-Concord, in Norwich, June 26, 1766* (New London, 1766).

Todd, Jonathan, *Civil Rulers the Ministers of God, for Good to Men. Or, the divine Original and Authority of Civil Government Asserted; and the Business and Duty of civil Rulers, and the Obligations on a People, to support their Authority and maintain their Character, shewed, in a Sermon preach'd before the General Assembly of the Colony of Connecticut, at Hartford, on the Day of Election, May 11th, 1749* (New London, 1749).

——*A Faithful Narrative, of the Proceedings, of the First Society and Church In Wallingford, in their Calling, and Settling the Rev. Mr. James Dana, in the Pastoral Office over them; and of the Doings of the several Councils relative thereto, with some Remarks interspersed . . .* (New Haven, 1759).

——*A Reply To the Reverend Mr. Eell's Serious Remarks, upon*

WORKS CITED 329

the faithful Narrative, etc. Wherein is made to appear, That as the most of the Facts mention'd in the Narrative are conceded to be justly related; so those few which the Remarker hath set in a different Light, are by him misrepresented (New Haven, 1760).

Town Records of Derby Connecticut 1655–1710, ed. Nancy O. Phillips (Derby, 1901).

Tracy, Joseph, *The Great Awakening. A History of the Revival of Religion in the Time of Edwards and Whitefield, Tappan and Dennet* (Boston, 1842).

Trumbull, Benjamin, *A Complete History of Connecticut, Civil and Ecclesiastical, from the Emigration of its First Planters, from England, in the Year 1630, to the Year 1764; and to the Close of the Indian Wars* (2 vols., New London, 1898).

————*Extracts of Letters to Rev. Thomas Prince, containing Historical Notices of Sundry Towns* (Collections of the Connecticut Historical Society, III, Hartford, 1895, 271–320).

————*A Letter to an Honourable Gentleman of the Council-Board for the Colony of Connecticut, Shewing That Yale-College is a very great Emolument, and of High Importance to the State; Consequently, That it is the Interest and Duty of the Commonwealth to afford it publick Countenance and Support: And Wherein such Objections are considered and obviated as would probably be made against the Tenor of such Reasoning* (New Haven, 1766).

Trumbull, James Hammond, *List of Books Printed in Connecticut, 1709–1800* (n.p., 1904).

————"The Sons of Liberty in 1755," *New Englander,* XXXV (1876), 299–313.

Trumbull, Jonathan, *Jonathan Trumbull, Governor of Connecticut, 1769–1784* (Boston, 1919).

The Trumbull Papers (Collections of the Massachusetts Historical Society, 5th series, IX, Boston, 1885).

Tucker, Louis L., *Puritan Protagonist: President Thomas Clap of Yale College* (Chapel Hill, N.C., 1962).

Van Dusen, Albert E., *Connecticut* (New York, 1961).

Wadsworth, Daniel, *Diary of Rev. Daniel Wadsworth, 1737–1747,* ed. George Leon Walker (Hartford, 1894).

Walcott, Robert R., "Husbandry in Colonial New England," *New England Quarterly,* IX (1936), 218–252.

Walker, George Leon, *History of the First Church in Hartford, 1633–1883* (Hartford, 1884).

————*Some Aspects of the Religious Life of New England* (Boston, 1897).

Walker, Williston, *The Creeds and Platforms of Congregationalism* (New York, 1893).

The Wallingford Case Stated; or, the Main Point in Question, Relating to the Wallingford Controversy; Collected from a Recital, and concise View, of Uncontroverted Facts (New Haven, 1761).

Weaver, Glen, "Industry in an Agrarian Economy, Early Eighteenth Century Connecticut," *Connecticut Historical Society Bulletin,* XIX (1954), 82–92.

———*Jonathan Trumbull Connecticut's Merchant Magistrate (1710–1785)* (Hartford, 1956).

Webb, Sidney, and Beatrice Webb, *The Manor and the Borough (English Local Government from the Revolution to the Municipal Corporations Act,* II, III, London, 1908).

Weber, Max, *The Protestant Ethic and the Spirit of Capitalism,* tr. Talcott Parsons (New York, 1952).

Weeden, William B., *Economic and Social History of New England, 1620–1789* (2 vols., Boston, 1890).

Weinbaum, Martin, *British Borough Charters, 1307–1660* (Cambridge, Eng., 1943).

Weis, Frederick Lewis, *The Colonial Clergy and the Colonial Churches of New England* (Lancaster, Mass., 1936).

Welles, Noah, *Patriotism Described and Recommended, in a Sermon Preached before the General Assembly of the Colony of Connecticut, At Hartford, on the Day of the Anniversary Election, May 10th, 1764* (New London, 1764).

Welling, James Clark, "Connecticut Federalism or Aristocratic Politics in a Social Democracy," *Addresses, Lectures and Other Papers,* (Cambridge, 1903, 266–311).

[Wetmore, James], *A Letter from a Minister of the Church of England to his Dissenting Parishioners, Shewing the Necessity of Unity and Peace and the dangerous Consequences of separating from the established Episcopal Church* (New York, [1730]).

Wheelock, Eleazar, *The Preaching of Christ, an Expression of God's Great Love to Sinners, and therefore a sweet Savour to him, though a Savour of Death unto Death to them. Illustrated in a Sermon Preach'd at North-Haven, December 25th 1760, at the Ordination of the Reverend Mr. Benjamin Trumble, to the Pastoral Office there* (Boston, 1761).

White, Stephen, *Civil Rulers Gods by Office, and the Duties of such Considered and Enforced. A Sermon Preached before the General Assembly Of the Colony of Connecticut, at Hartford, on the Day of their Anniversary Election, May the 12th, 1763* (New London, 1763).

Whitman, Elnathan, *The Character and Qualifications of good Rulers, and the Happiness of their Administration, Represented in a Sermon Preach'd before the General Assembly of the Colony of Connecticut, at Hartford, on the Day of their Anniversary Election, May 9th, 1745* (New London, 1745).

Whitman, Samuel, *Practical Godliness the Way to Prosperity. A Sermon Preached before the General Assembly of the Colony of Connecticut, at Hartford in New England, May 13, 1714* (New London, 1714).

Whittelsey, Chauncey, *A Sermon preach'd at New-Haven on the Sabbath preceeding the Publick Commencement, Sept. 9th, Anno Dom. 1744. Wherein is considered the true Notion of a Faithful Improvement of our Talents, and the Wisdom of being Early and in Earnest therein* (New London, 1744).

Whittelsey, Samuel, *A Publick Spirit Described and Recommended. In a Sermon Preach'd before the General Assembly of the Colony of Connecticut, at Hartford, May 13th, 1731* (New London, 1731).

—————*A Sermon Preach'd at the Ordination of Mr. Samuel Whittelsey, jun. at Milford, December 9. A.D. 1737. To which is added the charge given him by his Uncle the Reverend Mr. Nathanael Chauncey* (Boston, 1739).

Willard, Samuel, *The High Esteem which God hath of the Death of his Saints. As it was Delivered in a Sermon Preached October 7. 1683. Occasioned by the Death of the Worshipful John Hull Esq: Who Deceased October 1, 1683* (Boston, 1683).

Williams, Eleazar, *An Essay to Prove, That when God once enters upon a Controversie, with His Professing People; He will Manage and Issue it . . . . In a Sermon Preached before the General Court of Election at Hartford in the Colony of Connecticut, May 9th. 1723* (New London, 1723).

Williams, Eliphalet, *A Sermon, Preached in the Audience of the General Assembly of the Colony of Connecticut, At Hartford, on the day of the Anniversary Election, May 11th, 1769* (Hartford, [1769]).

[Williams, Elisha], *The essential Rights and Liberties of Protestants, A seasonable Plea for the Liberty of Conscience, and the Right of private Judgment, in Matters of Religion, Without any Controul from human Authority. Being a Letter, from a Gentleman in the Massachusetts-Bay to his Friend in Connecticut. Wherein Some Thoughts on the Origin, End and Extent of the Civil Power, with brief Considerations on several late Laws in Connecticut, are humbly offered, By a Lover of Truth and Liberty* (Boston, 1744).

Williams Papers (boxed MS, Yale University, New Haven).

Williams, Solomon, *Christ, the King and Witness of Truth, and the Nature Excellency, and Extent of His Kingdom, as founded in Truth, and only promoted by it* (Boston, 1744).

—————*The Comfort and Blessedness of Being at Home in God, or, Dwelling with Him: And the constant Safety and Protection they shall have, who make God their Abode. Shewed in a Sermon Preached to the First Society in Lebanon* (New London, 1742).

———*A Firm and Immoveable Courage to Obey God, and An Inflexible Observation of the Laws of Religion, the Highest Wisdom and certain Happiness of Rulers. Shewed in a Sermon Preach'd before the General Assembly of the Colony of Connecticut, at Hartford on the Day of Election, May 14th, 1741* (New London, 1741).

———*The More Excellent Way. Or, The Ordinary Renewing, and Sanctifying Graces of the Holy Spirit, More Excellent than all Extraordinary Gifts that can be Coveted or Obtained by Men. Shewed in a Sermon Preached at Goshen in Lebanon, December 21st, 1741* (New London, 1742).

———*The Sad Tendency of Divisions and Contentions in Churches, to Bring on their Ruin and Desolation. As it was shewed in a Sermon, Delivered at the West-Farms, in Norwich, on a Day of Fasting, Feb. 28, 1750* (Newport, [1751]).

———*The True State of the Question Concerning the Qualifications Necessary to lawful Communion in the Christian Sacraments. Being an Answer to the Reverend Mr. Jonathan Edwards his Book Intitled, An humble Inquiry into the Rules of the Word of God, concerning the Qualifications Requisite to a compleat Standing and full Communion in the Visible Christian Church* (Boston, 1751).

———*A Vindication of the Gospel-Doctrine of Justifying Faith. Being An Answer to the Revd Mr. Andrew Croswell's Book, intitled, "What is Christ to Men, if He is not Mine? Or A Seasonable Defence of the old Protestant Doctrine of Justifying Faith."* (Boston, 1746).

Williams, William, "Rough Sketch of the Proceedings of the Lower House of Assembly Met att Hartford 12th May 1757 the First of which I had the honor of being a Member" (MS, Connecticut Historical Society, Hartford).

"Windham Association Book," vol. I [1723–1813] (MS, Congregational House, Hartford).

Windham Consociation, *The Result of a Council of the Consociated Churches of the County of Windham: Relating to the Principles and Practices of the several Bodies of People in said County, who have separated from the Communion of the Churches in this Land, and set up an uninstituted Worship among themselves* (Boston, 1747).

Windham County, "Records," vol. 1, Trials, June 1726–February 1732 (MS, Connecticut State Library, Hartford).

Windham Ministers, *A Letter from the Associated Ministers of the County of Windham, to the People in the several Societies in said County* (Boston, 1745).

Windsor, Connecticut, "First Congregational Church Records, 1636–1932" (13 vols., MS, Connecticut State Library, Hartford).

————"Register of Proprietor Records, 1650–1724" (microfilm, Connecticut State Library, Hartford).

————"Town Book, 2nd Book," on spine "No. 2, 1683–1704" (MS, Connecticut State Library, Hartford).

Windsor, Town of, "Proprietor Acts 1724–1787" (MS, Connecticut State Library, Hartford).

Winslow, Ola Elizabeth, *Jonathan Edwards 1703–1758* (New York, 1940).

————*Meetinghouse Hill, 1630–1783* (New York, 1952).

The Winthrop Papers (Collections of the Massachusetts Historical Society, pt. III: 5th series, I; pt. IV: 5th series, III; pt. V: 6th series, III; pt. VI: 6th series, V, Boston, 1871–1892).

The Wolcott Papers Correspondence and Documents During Roger Wolcott's Governorship of the Colony of Connecticut 1750–1752 with Some of Earlier Date, ed. Albert C. Bates *(Collections of the Connecticut Historical Society,* XVI, Hartford, 1916).

Wolcott, Roger, *A Letter to the Reverend Mr. Noah Hobart* (Boston, 1761).

————*A Memoir for the History of Connecticut, 1759 (Collections of the Connecticut Historical Society,* III, Hartford, 1895, 321–336).

————"A Narrative of the Troubles in the Second Church in Windsor from the Year 1735 to the year 1741 with the Reasons why the Brethren of that Church Adhere to the Order of Church Government Assented to by the Church of New England A: Dom: 1648 And Refuse to Submit to the order of Discipline Agreed upon at Saybrook 1708. Published at the Desire of Severall of the Brethrin and others" (MS, Connecticut Historical Society, Hartford).

————*Poetical Meditations, Being the Improvement of some Vacant Hours,* with a "Preface" by the Reverend Mr. Bulkley of Colchester (New London, 1725).

Woodbridge, Ashael, *A Sermon Delivered before the General Assembly of the Colony of Connecticut, on the Anniversary Election at Hartford, May 14th, 1752* (New London, 1753).

Woodbridge, Samuel, *Obedience to the Divine Law, Urged on all Orders of Men, and the Advantage of it shew'd, in a Sermon Preach'd before the General Assembly of the Colony of Connecticut, at Hartford, May 14, 1724* (New London, 1724).

Woodward, John, *Civil Rulers are God's Ministers, for the Peoples Good. A Sermon Preached before the General Assembly of the Colony of Connecticut, at Hartford in New-England, May 8th. 1712* (Boston, 1712).

A Word of Advice, to such as are settling new Plantations (Boston, 1739).

Worthington, William, *The Duty of Rulers and Teachers in Unitedly Leading God's People, U[r]ged and Explained; in a Sermon Preached before the General Assembly of the Colony of Connec-*

ticut, at Hartford on their Anniversary Election, May the 10th, 1744 (New London, 1744).

The Wyllys Papers Correspondence and Documents Chiefly of Descendants of Gov. George Wyllys of Connecticut 1590–1796 (Collections of the Connecticut Historical Society, XXI, Hartford, 1924).

Zeichner, Oscar, Connecticut's Years of Controversy 1750–1776 (Williamsburg, 1949).

Index